BERKSHIRE

828

THOMAS.EDWARD B.1878

D1423171

A language
not to be betrayed

A language not to be betrayed

Selected prose of
Edward Thomas

BERKSHIRE COUNTY LIBRARY

Selected and with introduction
by EDNA LONGLEY

Carcanet Press in association
with Mid-Northumberland Arts Group

First published in Great Britain in 1981
by Carcanet New Press
330 Corn Exchange Buildings, Manchester M4 3BG
in association with Mid-Northumberland Arts Group
Wansbeck Square, Ashington

SBN 085635 3361 ✓
(C) 1981 Selection and Introduction, Edna Longley

All rights reserved
The Publishers acknowledge the financial assistance
of the Arts Council

Printed in Great Britain
by Billings, Guildford and Worcester

CONTENTS

ACKNOWLEDGMENTS

The editor and publisher would like to thank the following for permission to reprint copyright material:

Faber & Faber Ltd for extracts from *The Childhood of Edward Thomas*; Oxford University Press for extracts from *Letters from Edward Thomas to Gordon Bottomley*, ed. R. George Thomas (1968); *The Collected Poems of Edward Thomas*, ed. R. George Thomas (1978); and *A Literary Pilgrim in England* (Oxford Paperback, 1980).

Thanks are also due to the Library of University College, Cardiff.

I should use, as the trees and birds did,
A language not to be betrayed . . . .
Edward Thomas
'I Never Saw that Land Before'

BIOGRAPHICAL NOTE

EDWARD THOMAS: b. 1878 in London of 'mainly Welsh' parents. Boyhood spent in London. 1894: meets critic and writer James Ashcroft Noble, who encourages his literary ambitions. 1897: *The Woodland Life* published. 1899: marries Helen Noble. 1900: second-class history degree from Oxford; looks for work as a literary journalist. 1901: occasional reviewing for *Daily Chronicle*; moves to Rose Acre Cottage, near Maidstone. 1902: *Horae Solitariae* published; takes over from Lionel Johnson as regular reviewer for *Daily Chronicle*; starts to make reputation as critic, of contemporary poetry in particular. 1903-4: in addition to reviews, working on first commissioned books (*The Poems of John Dyer, Oxford, Beautiful Wales*); moves to Elses Farm, The Weald, near Sevenoaks. *Rose Acre Papers* published. 1905: meets and helps W.H. Davies. 1906-16: lives near Steep in Hampshire (moving house twice); continues to review and write books, including *The Heart of England, Richard Jefferies, The South Country, Algernon Charles Swinburne, George Borrow, The Icknield Way, Walter Pater, In Pursuit of Spring*. 1911: suffers a severe nervous breakdown. 1913: meets Robert Frost; begins *The Childhood of Edward Thomas*. 1914: 'year of friendship' with Frost; reviews Frost's *North of Boston*; begins to write poetry (December). 1915: enlists in the Artists' Rifles (July). 1916: based at Hare Hall Camp, Romford, as map-reading instructor; trains as officer cadet with the Royal Artillery (September); volunteers for service overseas (December); Selwyn & Blount accept collection of his poems. 1917: killed by the blast of a shell at the Battle of Arras (9 April); *Poems* published posthumously. (*Last Poems* published in 1918.)

Introduction

1

The reputation of Edward Thomas (1878-1917) rests on the poetry he wrote between December 1914 and his death in the Battle of Arras. Before Thomas's metamorphosis into a poet, however, prose was both his art and his trade. Driven by financial need to extraordinary productivity, he turned out books about the countryside, critical studies, essays, folk tales, introductions, and well over a million words of reviewing. Although during these years Thomas caricatured himself as 'a doomed hack' (p.256), the relevance of his prose 'doom' to his poetic destiny has been increasingly recognized.

This is the first selection from Thomas's prose to give pride of place to his criticism. Such an emphasis in fact defies Thomas's own caveat, in a review of *Jeffrey's Literary Criticism*: 'The disinterment of criticism is a rare and an unsavoury task.'[1] But although the savour of all Thomas's earlier writing has been enhanced with hindsight by his poetry, the imaginative prose, which contains the embryos of virtually all his poems, has been partially superseded by the ensuing live births. His criticism, on the other hand, unusual in being before the poetic event, survives as its best interpreter. It is not a matter of imposing on Thomas's poetry a superstructure which its very fibre seems to rebuff, but of indicating the substructure that exists. At the same time, Thomas's prose cannot finally be segregated into rigid categories, since it testifies to the interaction of all his interests. (Even the desperation that sometimes pads out a review with a description of Nature, or a Nature book from his reviews, does not result in the incongruity one might expect.) The self-criticism which accompanied his slow artistic development—he called *The Heart of England*, for instance, 'Borrow & Jefferies sans testicles & guts'[2]—is inseparable from the faculties he brought to bear on the work of others. More

i

broadly, Thomas disliked 'this stupid and wasteful contrast' between literature and life[3]. His criticism resorts naturally to natural imagery:

> We know the beauty of a sentence that sweeps without impediment in one gracious curve to its full stop, and the beauty, too, of a complex sentence in which the stops are as valuable as the division of a stanza of verse into lines, or as the hedges and littered crags and out-cropping rock by which the eye travels up a mountain to the clouds.[4]

(Thomas's poem, 'The Lofty Sky', was to exploit mimetically the second type of sentence.) Conversely, he announces in *Beautiful Wales*: 'Nothing is to be compared with the pleasure of seeing the stars thus in the east, when most eyes are watching the west, except perhaps to read a fresh modern poet, straight from the press, before any one has praised it, and to know that it is good.'[5] It is perhaps because Thomas kept open the frontiers between his imagination and his critical intelligence, that 'my silly little deformed unpromising bantling of originality'[6] stayed alive.

2

Edward Thomas's fully-fledged works of criticism are: *Richard Jefferies* (1909), *Feminine Influence on the Poets* (1910), *Maurice Maeterlinck* (1911), *Algernon Charles Swinburne* (1912), *George Borrow* (1912), *Lafcadio Hearn* (1912), *Walter Pater* (1913), *Keats* (1916), and *A Literary Pilgrim in England* (1917). The bias of these titles tilts representatively towards two traditions: the rural and the Romantic. William Cooke stresses the dates of publication (eight books completed from 1908 to 1913), in demonstrating how Thomas is the 'Critic As Artist'[7]. But while Thomas's critical activity expanded as he moved into his thirties, and he explored certain central issues in a more sustained fashion, Thomas the critic had already been around for some time—even though 'only reviewing' (p.9). During the first decade of the century the *Daily Chronicle* (thanks to H.W. Nevinson) was his most regular source of income. He also contributed extensively to the *Morning Post*, from October 1906 (when Hilaire Belloc became literary editor) to January 1911, besides being employed by such periodicals as *The Academy*, *The World*, *The Speaker* (later *The Nation*), *The Saturday Review*, Harold Monro's *Poetry and Drama*, and especially *The Bookman*. He often reviewed the same book for different journals, yet sold neither himself nor his editors short in that the various pieces generally complement rather than repeat each other. Incessant deadlines, Thomas's own punctiliousness and perfectionism, the additional

weight of book commissions, bred or intensified the depression and
self-doubt recorded in *Letters to Gordon Bottomley*:

> You don't know what it means to make £5 or £6 a week by
> reviewing. This week for example, I read review books all day on
> Monday & Tuesday, interrupted only by my little lots of house-
> work, lessons to Merfyn & meals. Then until tonight I have been
> reading & writing all day with the same interruptions. . . . And now
> I am so tired that I was amazed that I could merely enjoy some sea
> tales by John Masefield—also for review—an hour ago. My opinion
> therefore is worth nothing (except money). I greatly fear I cannot
> keep up to even my old standard. Original writing I dream about,
> but never get so far as to get out paper & pen for it. . . . The year has
> passed; the Spring has done without me; I have not had one good
> hour of standing still & forgetting time. But I make over £200 a
> year, or can expect to.[8]

Yet Thomas *did* keep up to his 'old standard', and was not always woe-
fully conscious 'of the futility of reviewing,—of my insolence in
Reviewing any book'[9]. Indeed he took the trouble to preserve
approximately two-thirds of his reviews in six massive scrapbooks,
now lodged in the library of University College, Cardiff. Professor
R. George Thomas computes the statistics of the scrapbooks as 'a
minimum of 1,122 reviews—just over a million words about 1,200
books'[10]. Thomas's output peaked in the years 1906 to 1912 when 'he
was contributing 100 signed (or full-length) reviews annually to
[newspapers and periodicals], besides at least fifty shorter notices to
weeklies and, after 1907, a monthly article or two-column unsigned
review to *The Bookman*'.[11]

  The chief planks of Thomas's reviewing platform were contemporary poetry, and prose 'announcements of our affection for the
country' (p.162). But at a time when reprints had become 'so
numerous, various, conspicuous and cheap',[12] and the Eng.Lit.'
industry was getting off the ground, he also discussed editions, letters,
biographies, and criticism covering a spectrum which no reviewer
today would contemplate: Chaucer, Lyly, Burton, Cowley, Pepys,
Traherne, Sterne, Crabbe, Blake, Whitman, Baudelaire, Wilde (to
name but a very few). He rarely touched fiction (an underlining of the
trend of his own writing towards symbol rather than narrative), but in
every other sphere qualified himself to relate the individual talent to
tradition. John Freeman notices 'the complete unostentatious
intimacy with English poetry which was conspicuous in Edward
Thomas's lightest critical work'[13]. Thomas would have been profoundly steeped in literature if he had never written a single review.
But his different assignments guaranteed constant scrutiny of the new

in the light of the old and vice versa—an early twentieth-century habit in which he anticipated T.S. Eliot:

> Poetry is a natural growth, having more than a superficial relation to roses and trees and hills. However airy and graceful it may be in foliage and flower, it has roots deep in a substantial past. It springs apparently from an occupation of the land, from long, busy, and quiet tracts of time, wherein a man or a nation may find its own soul. To have a future, it must have had a past.[14]

Thomas's poem 'Lob' recapitulates English tradition in the spirit of that observation. However, like his other poems, it hands out no reading-list, apart from a few evocations and echoes:

> This is tall Tom that bore
> The logs in, and with Shakespeare in the hall
> Once talked, when icicles hung by the wall.

At least as well-read as Eliot (and in European literature too), he uses the Shakespeare quotation to affirm the priority of life over literature. One can apply to Thomas's poetry his comment on John Davidson's *Triumph of Mammon*, both as it stands, and if 'reading' replaces 'philosophy': 'We ought to guess the philosophy from the poetry no more than we guess the athlete's meals from the length of his leap' (p.78). Thomas's reviews are evidence of the enormous literary meal he digested.

3

'Reviewing: An Unskilled Labour', Thomas's retrospect of the tread-mill, implies his own skills: 'the reviewer must seriously consider whether words like "striking and unique", "alive", "decadent", or "readable", coming from his pen, will, without abundant proof and illustration, have any weight outside his family circle' (p.3). Even at his weariest, Thomas disdains the vague puff, blast, or dustjacket cliché, in favour of 'abundant proof and illustration'. This selection should prove the practical nature of his criticism: its self-effacing attention to the text, and fulfilment of the obligation to quote and analyse (not so common at the period). His critical books gave him room to develop these powers, from the sensing of the last line of 'To Autumn' ('something light, thin, cold, and vanishing, especially by comparison with the mellowness and slowness of the other verses, with all their long "oo" and "ou" and "aw" and "z" sounds' (p.31)) to the exhaustive dissection of the styles of Swinburne and Pater. What has been called a Keatsian 'negative capability' in Thomas's poetry is pre-

figured by the empathy of his criticism, his flair for inhaling the atmosphere of an author, for sealing an insight with an image: D.H.
Lawrence's early poems as 'the tiny but solid beings of which novels
are the shadows artificially made gigantic' (p.105); in *Personae,* Ezra
Pound's 'abruptness as of a swift beetle that suddenly strikes your
cheek and falls stunned with its own force' (p.117).

Thomas's wit, too, keeps him on target: Whitman's 'inhuman excess
of humanity'[15]; in Laurence Binyon's *Auguries* 'the tranquillity overpowers the remembered emotion'[16]; 'we should not be surprised, if
[Chesterton's] portrait were not over-familiar, to hear that he was four
feet high and wore a sea-green butterfly bow and in his buttonhole the
faded rose of the tired hedonists'[17]. But, in contradiction of W.H.
Auden's dictum: 'One cannot review a bad book without showing
off'[18], the humour functions as humane-killer to scores of minor
versifiers: 'Many of [Lloyd Mifflin's] sonnets are so long that we can
scarce believe our eyes which see only fourteen lines'[19]. He merely
accords Ella Wheeler Wilcox a spoof eulogy[20], while reserving his big
guns for the big gunners, like Chesterton, or Rudyard Kipling:

> It is the combination of strength and tenderness that makes Mr
> Kipling's work remarkable. Or would these virtues of his be more
> accurately named brutality and sentimentality? It depends on the
> point of view; and the point of view depends on whether the style of
> these three hundred pages appears to you vigorous, manly speech,
> or the ranting and whining of an unpleasantly accented unpleasant
> voice.[21]

Inflation and pretentiousness provoked the giant-killer, whether in
the long battery of Pater, or in the shooting-down of Lascelles Abercrombie's *Emblems of Love*: 'It is all glittering, crashing, hurry-
ing abundance, endless multiplication, disorder, and sputtering
violence'[22]. Serious writers he always treats with patient seriousness.
Thomas's concern over the years for the progress of T. Sturge Moore,
W.H. Davies, Walter de la Mare and W.H. Hudson amounts to an
exemplary exercise of critical responsibility: 'enthusiasm is one's first
duty to a distinguished contemporary'[23]. This duty, which exacts
further self-effacement, he undoubtedly performs for W.B. Yeats:
'the critic ... can but offer his own shrill or drowsy chirp in place of
the author's full choir, and hope that the small may suggest the great'
(p.80). Critics and reviewers finally justify their existence in so far as
'they open a track for the appreciation of the little known, and send the
new into the current of thought in their own day' (p.7).

Thomas's inclination towards 'impressionism' (p.8), 'the power to
receive suggestions, to be stimulated' (p.80), coupled with the occu-
pational prickliness of the unskilled labourer, made him resistant to

authority, theory, and the advance of Academe. This was the period
during which the man of letters, the belles-lettrist, was giving way to
the scholar and the infant University English department. Thomas
disliked the tendency of each faction. On the one hand, he can be
amused by the arch-belles-lettrist, Edmund Gosse: 'Sometimes . . .
one feels that it is not necessary for Mr Gosse, though he reads everything, to write about everything'[24]. On the other, W.P. Ker's *Essays on
Mediaeval Literature* 'might wisely be exhibited after meetings of
literary men as, after the banquets of the Egyptians, a wooden image of
a dead body was exhibited, for a reminder of death.'[25] Walter W.
Greg's *Pastoral Poetry and Pastoral Drama*, a double-barrelled assault
on all that Thomas held dear, is

> a splendid, overhanging, rude and crumbling cliff of facts, fas-
> cinating, unscaleable . . . it is a monumental pledge of labour, and
> probably of the strange passion of love also. But what a passion! In
> order to explain 'Come live with me and be my love' he must needs
> erect vast woods and craggy mountains of crabbed fact, and send
> our tortured spirits to wander there, and coming back, enjoy the
> lyric as before.[26]

Milton Memorial Lectures, including contributions by Edward
Dowden and George Saintsbury, is 'a cause for regretting that something like taste is not more widely distributed in academic circles'[27].
Thomas did respect the scholarly zeal that had generated so many
'appeals to the public on behalf of William Blake'[28], the rediscovery of
Thomas Traherne, even the reprint assembly-belt. He admired E. de
Sélincourt's edition of *The Poems of John Keats*, with the reservation
that 'the notes and other apparatus should be printed apart from the
text, since the present arrangement, though the usual one, reminds us
of a dining-room which is a kitchen and scullery as well'[29]. Indis-
criminate edition-making and resurrection (still underway) he de-
plored, finding a collection of Prior 'one of the proofs that English
courage and endurance are not extinct . . . for when our heroes have
reached their peak in Darien they must see clearly that beneath them is
a dirty duck-pond'[30]. However, he did not entirely approve Ezra
Pound's cure for 'learned dullness': 'His aim at being better than
dryasdust by allowing his personality free play is . . . not so successful
as it is laudable' (p.123).

Thomas also sounded an early warning against the more purely
critical version of 'the academic objection to life'[31], which already fore-
boded the shape of things to come later in the century. In the work of
critics like Paul Elmer More, W.C. Brownell and Irving Babbitt he
discerned the limitations of 'a body of educated opinion such as would
tell heavily in a debating society' (p.5): '[Mr Babbitt] cannot endure

"indeterminate enthusiasms and vapid emotionalism". In fact, he has plenty of acid for attack; only we doubt whether he would look so well had he less hostile criticism to do . . .'[32]. Nevertheless, he praises J.W. Mackail's *The Springs of Helicon* as 'a farewell to the old school' and possibly 'a welcome to the new': 'He has discovered for himself the tremendous truth that there comes a time when actually you cannot go on talking about the poets, with a spice of history, a spice of generalization, a few quotations from them and from earlier critics, a graceful simile, a peroration, and then a condemning silence.'[33] A.C. Bradley emerges as Thomas's favourite academic critic, for being 'tremblingly in sympathy' with the time, and because: 'He would make the worst of debaters. He is only troubled about what is true' (p.13). The ancestral voice, however, is Coleridge. *Biographia Literaria*

> contains . . . the most profound literary criticism which has so far been written in English. Matthew Arnold is a journalist, Pater a dilettante, by comparison . . . . And chiefly on two matters is Coleridge to be heard, on poetic diction and on imagination. His scattered pages on poetic diction . . . are all that can at present form the basis of any true criticism of Poetry. . . .[34]

It was usually the pressing need for a true criticism of poetry that tempted Thomas himself into the realm of theory. (He eagerly followed some renewed attempts to pin down English prosody.) The contemporary critic who most often stimulated such a reaction was Arthur Symons ('the first of our literary critics')[35], caught up, like Thomas himself, in the creative currents of the day. Thomas may have marginally identified with Symons's 'docile, chameleon mind, always so valuable to a critic', including its handicaps: 'He is apparently too much entangled in the words of other writers ever to get quite free'[36]. Nevertheless, he bestows his ultimate accolade on a reprint of *The Symbolist Movement in Literature*: '[Mr Symons] approaches books as an artist approaches life' (p.14). *The Symbolist Movement* influenced the poetic generations of Yeats and Eliot. Born between these generations, Thomas suspected the lingering 'literary aesthete' in Symons (p.19), as well as arguing against the symbolist theory which lived on to affect the practice of Eliot and Pound. He sets out his fullest objections to symbolism in *Maurice Maeterlinck* (p.49ff.), but his reviews of Symons's two books on the Romantic Movement similarly dispute notions of 'pure' or purified poetry (p.6ff.).

Thomas's respectful quarrels with Symons do in fact demarcate a generation gap, not only in terms of the decline of aestheticism, but of a different response to the 'tradition'. Defending the long poem, the poem with 'rifts', Thomas declares himself an unreconstructed Elizabethans-and-Romantics man, and one to whom the complete achieve-

ment of the Romantics matters, not just the 'ore' extracted by
aesthetes or symbolists. These underlying allegiances might seem to
align Thomas predictably with the Georgians, but his critical and
artistic assimilation of Romanticism goes considerably deeper than
theirs—as John Burrow shows in his essay 'Keats and Edward
Thomas'[37]. He wrote curiously little about Wordsworth, whether
because he took him profoundly for granted (his fragmentary verse
juvenilia are mostly 'after the *manner* of Wordsworth'[38]), or because
the review books went elsewhere, but his many considerations of Blake
and Shelley suggest a stake in their unfinished spiritual business:

> An intelligent man who has once read a large part of Blake with
> patience can never again settle down with just the same dusty
> creases in his mind as before. He drenches the mind with eternity.
> We become, not necessarily wiser or kinder, or more just, but cer-
> tainly more like citizens of the universe and less men of the world or
> gentlemen after reading him.[39]

However, from Thomas's early appraisal of Tennyson: 'his sweetness
was apt to resemble wedding-cake' (p.34) to his eventual demolition of
Swinburne, he attacked the decorations of decadent Romanticism.
Two of Thomas's reviews in 1914 of Robert Frost's *North of Boston*
mention Wordsworth, and the delighted discovery of Frost con-
summated his critical recognition of the need to go back 'through the
paraphernalia of poetry into poetry again' (p.128), perhaps to the
primal moment of the *Lyrical Ballads*.

The 'Metaphysical' poets, in contrast, engaged him more selec-
tively. *Feminine Influence on the Poets* gives Donne his due as a love
poet ('One of the rare qualities of this poetry is that the woman is
apparently the man's equal'[40]), but Thomas never entirely retracts his
1902 judgment that Donne the philosopher 'as a rule chloroformed the
poet'[41]. He also finds the visionary qualities of Crashaw, despite his
'incomplete use of his intelligence'[42], or of Traherne's prose, more
truly congenial than Herbert's temperate zone: 'George Herbert loved
holy things with a calm sense of possession, as of wedded love, and
rising only at intervals to ecstasy'[43]. But if the Metaphysicals can be too
metaphysical for Thomas, the eighteenth century is much too 'social'.
His gut Romanticism surfaces in his invariable reference to a dinner-
table whenever Pope and his contemporaries are in question: 'The
dinner-table is no longer recognized as a knoll of Helicon ... We have,
in truth, long been a little weary of a literature which dealt with
nothing that was not discussed at the best houses.'[44] Though wishing
poetry to revive its connection with life, Thomas is basically at one
with Symons and the nineties in the 'revolt against exteriority, against
rhetoric' (p.15), and against conscious attempts (like that of John
Davidson) to reflect in poetry the external 'spirit of the age'.

4

Thomas unwaveringly believed that the new century required a new poetry, even if not one which would directly express its 'spirit'. His 'pure love of praising the new poetry'[45] has the character of a crusade, as he swims against the tide of reprints and rubbish, of critical and public indifference. With an almost mystical conviction, he divines 'the poet of the next age'—perhaps subconsciously sensing that the 'path farther into the unknown', charted by minor poets, leads towards some 'unseen moving goal' of his own (p.65). He prophesies in 1901:

> the lyric will prosper, at least so long as individualism makes way in literature. Increasing complexity of thought and emotion will find no such outlet as the myriad-minded lyric, with its intricacies of form as numerous and as exquisite as those of a birch-tree in the wind. (p.62)

The review also signals a related long-term preoccupation: 'the best lyrics seem to be the poet's natural speech'. Thomas's original blue-print, tracing the contours of a refined or redefined Romanticism, is filled in by subsequent explorations of 'individualism', 'the importance of personality in style'[46], the distinction between 'writing about oneself' and 'self-expression'[47], and by a further guideline in a review of Saintsbury's *The Later Nineteenth Century* (1907):

> Observation is more and more minutely used, and its success or failure depends upon the weight and variety of emotional value that can be attached to it; and more and more this emotion is indicated by the poet, not left to the reader to divine.[48]

Even though Yeats did not as yet satisfy all these demands, he was undoubtedly Thomas's first hero of the modern revolution. The 1901 review includes a heartfelt 'above all there is Mr Yeats', and Yeats remains 'above all' for his enviable mythology, 'natural magic' (p.84), and 'subtlety of feeling for which there is no parallel in another age' (p.86). A.N. Jeffares considers that Thomas (in the *Daily Chronicle*) 'probably took the largest view' of Yeats's 1908 *Collected Works* (p.85)[49]. J.M. Synge, in *The Playboy of the Western World*, also points the way: 'By nature or by art, we must achieve a speech something like this which corresponds with the thought almost onomata-poetically, or fail' (p.144). Thomas's notable interest in the Anglo-Irish Literary Revival, and in 'Irish rhythm' as 'a cause of renewal of youth in modern verse'[50], may be connected with his Welsh horizons. The national qualities of Irish poetry certainly chimed with his desire to substitute a more inward, local, cultural, and mythic sense of England for 'the word Imperialism' (p.198): 'They sing of Ireland herself with an intimate reality often missing from English patriotic poetry, where Britannia is a frigid personification.'[51] He drew the line, however, at trendy 'lovers of the Celt' (p.58), and especially at 'Fiona Macleod's' (William Sharp) 'recipe by which Celtic studies might be cooked *ad infinitum*'[52].

Thomas was the first to admit that contemporary poetry—or rather verse—could be its own worst enemy: 'An imbecile with ten pounds in his pocket can easily add one to the number of the volumes from which the lover of poetry has to choose' (p.66). His wit just about survives the tedium: 'we are not worthy to deal with the work of a man who has heard the nightingale in Autumn'[53]; 'It had become, thanks to Canon Rawnsley's industry, almost impossible to read a new sonnet without a slight measure of contempt.'[54] Thomas's reviews evoke an Edwardian underworld of no-hopers in the Muse's 'lottery'[55]: those tireless sonneteers Rawnsley and Mifflin, people who think up titles like *Garnered Beauty, The Pipes of Pan, A Faëry Flute, Carmina Ephemora, or Trivial Numbers, Ballads of the Briny, Bungalow Ballads* ('Mr Randell is a regimental schoolmaster in India, and knows what he is writing about'), *Ballads in Blue* (by a policeman)[56], *Songs of a Parish Priest, Echoes of an Every-Day Life*. ' "Sybilline Leaves", by "Musaeus", we mention only for the naïveté of the title and the pseudonym . . .'[57]. At a somewhat higher level, Thomas can be polite on occasion to the poetic right wing of Kipling, William Watson and Henry Newbolt, hearty inheritors of the 'exteriority' and 'rhetoric' abandoned by the aesthetes. More typical, however, are his back-handed compliments to Watson's *Sable and Purple*: his style 'has often made us think of Mr Watson as a poet who has long been dead and embalmed in some series of "British Poets", so little of mortality or modernity is there about him'[58]; and *The Muse in Exile*: 'Mr Watson shows that he still has the power to clothe in leonine numbers what another man would put into a letter or a newspaper paragraph.'[59] All Newbolt's verse 'might be described as an elaborate corollary to "Rule Britannia".'[60] When Alfred Noyes tries an Elizabethan epic: 'Time after time we are aware of Mr Noyes applauding Drake and his sailors as if he were at a cricket match.'[61]

Before Frost disclosed the true 'goal', Thomas devoted much critical energy to advancing the claims of four poets in particular: Charles M. Doughty, T. Sturge Moore, W.H. Davies and Walter de la Mare. The first two favourites look like rare instances of his being 'deceived by superficial resemblances' (p.3), but at least as regards Doughty, Thomas's enthusiasm had its roots in his own obsessions. Chiefly known, then as now, for the prose-work *Travels in Arabia Deserta* (1888), Doughty switched to epic poetry in his monumental *The Dawn in Britain* (1906-7): 'twenty-four books, or about 30,000 lines of blank verse' (p.75). He then updated his patriotic Muse in *The Cliffs* (1909) and *The Clouds* (1912), both 'written under the very solemn belief that Britain is to be successfully invaded by Germany'.[62] If less enamoured of Doughty's imperial vein, and always defensive about his archaism and 'eccentricity of construction' (p.77), Thomas overcame initial doubts ('I do hesitate about him & feel that he may turn out a Southey after all'[63]), to affirm: 'Doughty is great. I see his men & women whenever I see noble beeches, as in Savernake Forest, or tumuli or old encampments, or the line of the Downs like the backs of a train of elephants, or a few firs on a hilltop.'[64] This suggests how Doughty inspired a 'worthy sense of the rich great age of this home of my race' (p.76), which entered into Thomas's imagining of England. His literary relation to Doughty strangely parallels Yeats's attraction to the nineteenth-century Irish epics of Sir Samuel Ferguson; the older poet in each case establishing a crude mythological framework for the younger to refine. Thomas compresses Doughty's 'Dawn' into mysterious vistas like that of 'The Combe': 'The Combe was ever dark, ancient and dark./Its mouth is stopped with bramble, thorn, and briar. . . .'

Sturge Moore, Davies and de la Mare belong to that loose grouping of poets which Edward Marsh's anthologies eventually packaged and marketed as 'Georgian'. One of Thomas's reviews of *Georgian Poetry, 1911-12* betrays some irritation at Marsh's act of retrospective serendipity: 'Not a few of these had developed their qualities under Victoria and Edward' (p.112). But another soft-pedals this sarcasm, and generously salutes the anthology for promoting what Thomas himself had promoted for more than a decade: 'modern poetry' and 'the spirit of poetry' (p.113). He had previously, too, got the (slight) measure of lesser Georgians like Wilfrid Wilson Gibson and Lascelles Abercrombie. (His letters to another minor member of the group, Gordon Bottomley, incorporate an important critical dialogue.) He liked Gibson's 'later work, but temperately'[65]; while enthusiasm for Abercrombie's *Interludes and Poems*[66] waned to the disappointment with *Emblems of Love*, and scarcely waxed over *Deborah*, Abercrombie's first (and characteristically Georgian) effort at dramatic verse: 'The play is as readable as any of his poems. But it hardly marks an advance on them. It shows the same mingling of metaphysic with savage sensuousness. Some day Mr Abercrombie may decide between the two, or, better still, may truly combine them'.[67] Thomas's more genuine optimism for Sturge Moore runs through a series of detailed reviews that span ten years. He still calls him in 1914 'one of the most substantial, sincere, and original of living poets'[68], though an early difficulty with 'sluggish rhythms'[69] persists: 'His words are often like a slow, dogged tracing of the beautiful curves of an original under the tracing paper.'[70] If Thomas's analyses of Sturge Moore labour to release a constipated talent, with Davies and de la Mare he largely relaxes and enjoys. The extracts on pages 88-105 illustrate his grateful receptivity to Davies's 'freshness and simplicity' and de la Mare's 'magic'. Thomas's more strongly rooted talent was to draw on similar soil to these slender but authentic shoots of growth.

Thomas's understanding of Davies's technical flaws as a naïve poet ('his poems either sing themselves through like an old air or they break up and fall' (p.90)), and careful delimiting of de la Mare's terrain, show that he still held something in reserve. Frost's *North of Boston* brought it out into the open: 'This is one of the most revolutionary books of modern times, but one of the quietest and least aggressive. It speaks, and it is poetry' (p.125). In a sense Frost was an earned Messiah; Thomas had been looking steadily in the right direction, as for the stars in *Beautiful Wales,* and thus what he earned was ultimately a higher vocation than 'to be among the interpreters, the evangelists' (p.7). (Sending his first poems to Frost, he volunteered: 'I will put it down now that you are the only begetter right enough'[71], but later felt: 'since the first take off they haven't been Frosty very much'[72]). Already before the advent of Frost, Thomas's alertness to D.H. Lawrence revealed a growing appetite for stronger than Georgian meat: 'he does not write smoothly, sweetly and with dignity; nor does he choose subjects, such as blackbirds at sunset, which ask to be so treated' (p.106). Modernist meat, however, proved too strong. Thomas's volte face over Ezra Pound[73] can be seen either as a timid retreat from the future, or as a drawing-up of aesthetic battlelines still visible today (not only with respect to Pound's reputation). Even his first excited review of *Personae* put its finger on central problems: 'He is so possessed by his own strong conceptions, that he not only cannot think of wrapping them up in a conventional form, but he must ever show his disdain for it a little' (p.117). Reviewing Frost five years later, Thomas evidently perceived his approach as sign-posting a middle way between dead traditionalism and frenetic Modernism: 'The metre avoids not only the old-fashioned pomp and sweetness, but the later fashion also of discord and fuss' (p.126). Again, Pound's literariness was perhaps never likely to enslave a writer painfully weaning himself from the same vice.

Ezra Pound thought Thomas 'a mild fellow with no vinegar in his veins'[74]—possibly wishful thinking. If Thomas's fairness dilutes his acid, other preservatives ensure his continuing relevance to the debate about twentieth-century poetry. One reviewer of a posthumous reprint of *The Tenth Muse* (an abridgement of *Feminine Influence*) apparently shared Pound's opinion, finding 'in no small portion of Thomas's critical work . . . a certain illusory, tenuous, indefinite, intangible quality . . . a lack of individuality, a dislike of committing himself. . . . First and last, Thomas was a non-combatant of letters.'[75] Thomas's father replied fiercely: 'Just as little was he non-combatant in literature as in war.'[76] The reviews in fact display a unity of mind that renders its final poetic concentration unsurprising. The *Critical Heritage* volumes on Pound and Yeats contain several items by Edward Thomas; he features in the recent *Casebook* on Hardy's poems. It is time that his contribution to his own critical heritage was fully recognized. Thomas's sensitivity to his literary age affords one of its clearest mirrors, but his praise of Symons's *Symbolist Movement* can be redirected: 'the reader has to know them well in order to understand how much of [Mr Thomas] there is in these essays in discipleship, to see the study and the craft behind what might appear to be only supreme self abasement' (p.15).

5

Thomas's reminiscence, 'How I Began', articulates his long creative dilemma, which was not to be resolved for nearly two more years: 'A continual negotiation was going on between thought, speech and writing, thought having as a rule the worst of it. Speech was humble and creeping, but wanted too many fine shades and could never come to a satisfactory end. Writing was lordly and regardless' (p.254). An earlier self-portrait proclaims him 'a martyr to the arrangement of words', and confesses: 'Pen in hand he was a different man.'[77]

> The railway bank is clothed in winter weeds of dead grass and spoiled flowers; keeping hardly a sign of its favours past, of milk-white campion, meek blue harebell, and gold-lipped toadflax mouths apout. But the greensward is one broad fair flower that drinks this rich sun, potable gold, by a myriad lips.[78]

> The golden foliage is taking flight by leaf in the wood, the *cwm*; the rose is dropping hollowed petals reluctantly one by one in the room.[79]

These sentences, from essays printed in 1896 and 1898, faintly anticipate the 'rich scene' of 'October' (1915), with its 'mushrooms small, milk-white' only briefly adjectival before the bare 'Harebell and scabious and tormentil'. Thomas's prose contains many such semi-petrified prototypes ('October' alone has a substantial genealogy), but he could only chip away gradually at their encrustations. The relatively unadorned 'Diary' notes attached to *The Woodland Life* (1897) are less representative of Thomas's early style than *Horae Soli-*

tariae (1902) and *Rose Acre Papers* (1904), essays whose manner a reviewer summed up as: 'most delicately penned, surely with a gold nib upon vellum, in condescending recognition of Nature's beauty.'[80] Thomas's critical prose quickly shed youthful flourishes. His creative work following in slow motion, he was able to recognize Nature's beauty in a more robust, if still rather lush, fashion by the period of *The South Country* (1909); this giving way in turn to the 'leanness' of *The Childhood of Edward Thomas* (begun in 1913): 'I feel the shape of the sentences & alter continually with some unseen end in view.'[81] However, as Arthur Ransome points out in painting Thomas for 'The Bookman' Gallery: 'The author of *The Woodland Life* might have turned out a naturalist. The author of *Horae Solitariae* could only have been Edward Thomas.'[82] Ransome also comments: 'He was influenced by Pater and Richard Jefferies; by Pater in his precision of speech, by Jefferies in his accuracy of observation.' Although we think less highly than did Ransome of both *Horae Solitariae* and Pater, this contemporary sense of the confluence of Pater and Jefferies is interesting. Jefferies may have ultimately won hands down in any contention for Thomas's soul, but his passing obeisance to Pater certainly suggests an ambition beyond that of, say, W.H. Hudson.

Walter Pater and *Algernon Charles Swinburne*, particularly the former, mark the culmination of Thomas's critical quarrel with himself as artist. Pater's aestheticism has its origins in the fact that:

> For the last hundred years ideas and the material of ideas have come to the reading classes mainly through books and bookish conversation. Their ideas are in advance of their experience, their vocabulary in advance of their ideas, and their eyelids 'are a little weary'. (p.150)

Thomas always understood the irony of his critical position—as a carrier of the 'bookish' virus he strove to eradicate. In 1904, reviewing the Pateresque Vernon Lee, he admits: 'We have the misfortune to be literary, in the bad sense, ourselves'[83]; and *The Heart of England* (1906) can diagnose its own sickness:

> I always carry out into the fields a vast baggage of prejudices from books and strong characters whom I have met. My going forth, although simple enough to the eye, is truly as pompous as that of a rajah who goes through the jungle on a tall and richly encrusted elephant, with a great retinue, and much ceremony and noise. As he frightens bird and beast, and tramples on herb and grass, so I scatter from my path many things which are lying in wait for a discoverer. There is no elephant more heavy-footed and no rifle more shattering than the egoism of an imitative brain.[84]

Thomas's anatomy of Pater's 'exquisite unnaturalness' (p.161) lays bare, at least in theory, the remedy for his own less extreme case: 'to make words of such a spirit, and arrange them in such a manner, that they will do all that a speaker can do by innumerable gestures and their innumerable shades, by tone and pitch of voice, by speed, by pauses, by all that he is and all that he will become' (p.159). Frost completed the therapy by demonstrating in practice 'absolute fidelity to the postures which the voice assumes in the most expressive intimate speech'[85]. In May 1914 Thomas told Frost: 'you really should start doing a book on speech & literature, or you will find me mistaking your ideas for mine & doing it myself. You can't prevent me from making use of them: I do so daily & want to begin over again with them & wring all the necks of my rhetoric—the geese. However, my "Pater" would show you I had got on to the scent already.'[86]

In fact, before *Pater*, Thomas's reviews had sniffed the scent more and more keenly: 'the best lyrics seem to be the poet's natural speech'; Yeats's proof 'that the speech of poetry can be that of life' (p.82); Synge's 'onomatopoeia'; the contrasting rejections of Wildean 'wallpaper' (p.146) and of Francis Thompson's 'remoteness . . . from spoken English' (p.47). In *Pater*, as in *Swinburne* and *Lafcadio Hearn*, Thomas multiplies the images of linguistic death: 'marble', 'sterilized words in a vacuum', 'bricks', 'tin soldiers'. There is of course a moral as well as a technical dimension to his attack; a defence of 'living and social words' (p.159), necessary agents of that perfect accommodation between 'word' and 'thing' which constantly haunts him. If Pater's style is language at its most static and sculptural, Swinburne's suffers from excessive fluidity, 'the condition of music': 'in *Atalanta* rhythm was paramount, in rule sole and undivided' (p.42). Thomas's ideal 'natural expressive rhythm' (p.153), words 'Fixed and free / In a rhyme'[87], exists somewhere between these poles.

The development of Thomas's own style, as well as of his ideas about style, resembles that of Yeats—slow, in his own way, to cast off 'a coat/Covered with embroideries'[88]. Like Yeats, Thomas participated in the battle of early twentieth-century literature to exorcise the later nineteenth century. It sometimes seems as if what he was doing, in his theory and practice, was dismantling an ornate outdated literary edifice, brick by Pateresque brick, until it no longer blocked the way forward. Pound and Eliot were eventually to come along with their bulldozers, but bulldozers can inflict a lot of incidental damage. It was also more crucial for Thomas, and for English poetry, that he should locate some of the obscured essentials of his native tradition. Two poems, 'The Chalk Pit' and 'Sedge-Warblers', parallel Yeats's 'A Coat' in encapsulating the criticism that enabled their creation. One voice in 'The Chalk Pit' is that of an 'aesthetic spectator' like Pater

(p. 151), viewing the scene through a vocabulary of art: 'amphi-theatre', 'tragical', 'the end of a play'. The more persuasive second voice 'should prefer the truth/Or nothing'. 'Sedge-Warblers' begins by decoratively fantasizing about:

> Another beauty, divine and feminine,
> Child to the sun, a nymph whose soul unstained
> Could love all day, and never hate or tire,
> A lover of mortal or immortal kin.

But 'rid of this dream, ere I had drained/Its poison' (perhaps also a summation of Thomas's career), the speaker 'only looked into the water,/Clearer than any goddess or man's daughter. . . .' Yet the two voices in each poem both belong to Edward Thomas; the second silencing the first without denying it.

6

All the time, however, Thomas's most effective antidotes to aesthetic 'poison' were the countryside and country books. Such was his physical and spiritual intimacy with Nature, with the 'South Country', that he might from the start have 'looked into the water' and written. But there remained the problem of expression, of allying ver-bally 'the clearness of the physical' 'to the penetration of the spiritual vision' (p.174): 'There is no form that suits me, & I doubt if I can make a new form.'[89] The 'imitative brain' interfered again to complicate Thomas's relation to his inevitable subject-matter, since he possessed a knowledge of 'The Rural Tradition'[90] as comprehensive as his know-ledge of English poetry. Whereas his struggles with Paterism, and other preciosities of contemporary prose, amounted chiefly to a question of style, his consciousness of Gilbert White, George Borrow, William Cobbett and Richard Jefferies raised the issue of finding a new attitude to their material. Here Thomas's critical instincts played a more constructive part. His reading of country books from White to Hudson, as reflected and explored in his writings, constitutes an in-tensive effort to realize the point at which the rural prose tradition reaches *him*. He looks back from the perspective of 'the modern sad passion for Nature'[91] to the more innocent world of *The Natural History of Selborne*, with its pioneering 'minute and even loving enquiry into the life and personality of animals in their native surroundings' (p.165). Some paradise has been lost by the time of the 'pure inward Borrow'[92] of *Lavengro*. Jefferies, in arising 'out of the earth'[93], heals the split: 'The distance between Nature and other writers, even Wordsworth, is very great; they have, as it were, a burning-glass that puts fetters on the sun. In Jefferies there is no distance from Nature.'[94] Yet Jefferies' 'style expanded to aid ... larger purposes, thus being able in turn to depict nature from the points of view of the countryman, of the sensuous painter, of the poet of humanity' (p. 181). Thomas seems to see Jefferies as encompassing and culminating the entire course of rural literature: as epitomizing, perhaps, a progress from the soil to the soul. He repeatedly calls the Jefferies of *The Story of My Heart* a 'poet', and one might draw the inference that Jefferies had brought the prose tradition to a pitch where it demanded reunion with the poetic. (Thomas proclaims in other contexts a condominium of poetry and prose.)

Thomas's poetry, in effecting this reunion, obliquely recapitulates its prose inheritance. Jefferies is of course as much its 'begetter' as Frost, but in addition to White's observation (enriched by Keats's 'fidelity to the observation or feeling of the hour'[95]), we find a 'Borrowed' poem like 'The Gypsy', or the influence of George Bourne's (Sturt) Bettesworth on the speech of Thomas's old countrymen.[96] 'Lob' distils the spirit Thomas relished in the *Compleat Angler*: 'English fields, English people, English poetry, all together' (p. 230). 'Haymaking', which differently fulfils a long ambition to create 'a graven image' of a peculiarly English 'spirit'[97], acknowledges its legacy from a poet, a prose-writer, and two painters, as Thomas makes the scene archetypal or 'immortal'. The poem frames a whole landscape tradition:

> All was old,
> This morning time, with a great age untold,
> Older than Clare and Cobbett, Morland and Crome,
> Than, at the field's far edge, the farmer's home,
> A white house crouched at the foot of a great tree.

There is, however, a stylistic inheritance as well, in that these earthy prose-writers do not generally resort to 'sterilized words'. They helped to put Thomas on the track of 'speech & literature'. Bettesworth, in combination with memories of 'Dad' Uzzell (p.250), is an original fount. Reading Gilbert White: 'We are always pleasantly conscious of the man in his style, which strikes us as the lines and motions of a person's face strike us for good or for bad' (p.165). The bridging figure of Cobbett importantly adds a body to that face: 'The movement of his prose is a bodily thing. His sentences do not precisely suggest the swing of an arm or a leg, but they have something in common with it. His style is perhaps the nearest to speech that has really survived' (p. 168).

But if the past offered Thomas a finally clarifying vista, the present—despite Hudson, Bourne, and a few others—appeared hopelessly congested: 'It will soon have become impossible to see Nature for the books that are written about her.'[98] Thomas seems to have reviewed most of them. (A sample review of two duds and one modestly successful specimen is given on pages 186-188.) He endured: *Peeps into Nature's Ways*; *A Journey to Nature*; *The Quest of the Simple Life*; Canon Rawnsley again, with *A Rambler's Note-Book at the English Lakes* ('Many writers would hesitate to say anything poetical about the River Duddon or the daffodils of the lakes')[99]; *The Tree Book*, by Mary Rowles Jarvis, from which he quotes these 'lyric raptures':

> nature lovers should fling the making of dollars and dinners to the four winds, send duty to the right-about, and, with stout raiment and a pocket luncheon as a concession to the 'frailtyness o' natur'', go lightsomely off for a ten-miles tramp into the wonder-world.[100]

He was hit by an avalanche of guide books, animal books, bird books, plant books, garden books, 'books in which a writer who has found a pretty spot in the country ventures to take the public into her confidence'[101], newer-fangled accounts of motor-touring ('the restless body gadding about comfortably in search of an undesired rest'[102]), and quantities of that 'terribly easy concoction: some watery observation and a nip of sentiment in a glass of customary style'[103]. His two incubuses as a reviewer also collaborated to produce 'several thousand volumes annually of verse up to the neck in the country'[104] (p.185). Thomas was thus made acutely aware of the early twentieth-century 'society for organizing a return to Nature' (p.201) as both a literal and a literary phenomenon (one worthy of investigation today when it shows signs of revival). E. Herrick, in *Verse Pictures* (of Nature), might be regarded 'not as an individual, but as one voice of the collective consciousness, and of that part of it which is sensitive, literate, and given to reverie'[105].

Thomas was aware, too, of yet another irony in his situation: that fashion had overtaken his passion, that he had been farcically 'forestalled', as on the road to Spring (p.202). 'Sensitive, literate, and given to reverie' is a wry joke against himself. How could he communicate his own vision: 'We have reached, perhaps, the edge of a great mystery' (p.162), while being trampled underfoot in a grotesque Gadarene rush? 'Some Country Books' once more suggests his search for a 'clear motive' and 'sense of arrangement' (p.163), that would take him beyond the proliferating knowledge of country life. His reviews, like *Richard Jefferies*, frequently discriminate between the specialized viewpoint of the botanist, the ornithologist, the topographer, the archaeologist, the anthropologist of rural society, and a higher intention which includes and transcends them all. Similarly, 'The Unknown Bird' ponders the unclassifiable origin of his inspiration:

> I told
> The naturalists; but neither had they heard
> Anything like the notes that did so haunt me. . . .

To find a way of echoing these notes, Thomas subjected the landscapes of his prose to every kind of artistic pummelling ('The Chalk
Pit' and 'Sedge-Warblers' also parody this kind of imposition):
making them symbolic, meditating on them, mythologizing them,
often murdering them. In his more essentially descriptive passages the
drive towards an integrated vision shows itself in the comprehensive
range of sense-impressions, the minutely established contexts of
weather and season. Thomas's rebuking of Lafcadio Hearn's 'blind
attention to isolated detail' (p.148) implies the need for detail to
function within an organic imaginative cosmos.

The extracts from Thomas's rural books in this selection have been
chosen to illustrate the 'philosophy' of Nature and the countryside
which was to inform his poetry. These extracts speak for themselves,
but perhaps amount broadly to an empirical re-negotiation of the
Romantic relation between man and Nature, in which the respective
roles of subjectivity and objectivity are more finely distinguished and
adjusted, and to which Thomas's historical sense of landscape adds a
new dimension: 'of these many folds in our nature the face of the earth
reminds us' (p.212). Thomas's ultimately unifying idea is that of being
an 'inhabitant' or 'citizen of the Earth' (p.37). Like his Mr Stodham,
he was agnostically fond of misquoting Wordsworth to the effect that
the 'earth' ('world' in Wordsworth) is 'where we have our happiness or
not at all'[106]. His ideal Nature-study anticipates current environ-
mental notions in 'showing us . . . our position, responsibilities and
debts among the other inhabitants of the earth' (p.204), just as his ideal
history of the parish and unpatronizing attention to folk-culture
open up paths towards an understanding of the human species which
have been much trodden since.

A countryside belongs to a country: the ironically hedged (and pre-
war) 'Mr Stodham speaks for England' (p. 219) probes the 'bonds
distinguishing [any nation] from the rest of the world without isolating
it'. These bonds have nothing to do with Imperial *esprit de corps*
(Thomas's attitude is close to E.M. Forster's in *The Longest Journey*
and *Howards End*), but define an introverted national identity whose
soul derives from the character of the people, from landscape and
literature. The First World War may have helped to release Thomas's
poetry by urgently activating this consciousness of England. At the
beginning of the war, from 29 August to 10 September 1914, he did the
fieldwork for three essays commissioned by the *English Review*:
'Tipperary', 'It's a Long, Long Way' and 'England' (p.222ff.). These

essays, together with 'This England' (p.268ff.), suggest a completion whereby England at last solidifies as a crucial link in the chain that runs from the self to the parish to the larger earth: 'a system of vast circumferences circling round the minute neighbouring points of home' (p.231). There is almost a new chain of being in Thomas's crystallizing images which thus connect the macrocosm to the microcosm, 'heaven' to 'home': the South Country too is 'infinite' yet 'small', 'as when a mountain with tracts of sky and cloud and the full moon glass themselves in a pond, a little pond' (p.210).

7

The question remains as to whether or not Edward Thomas's prose writings compose a chronicle of wasted time. I believe that Thomas failed to be a poet of 1900, because the literary time was as much out of joint as he was: that he became inevitably a poet of 1914. The validity and value of the prose lies in its movement, on a wide diversity of fronts, towards the 'sureness' of 'thought' and 'word' that Frost admired.[107] Thomas's poetry, in language 'light as dreams,/Tough as oak', distils a literary as well as a personal past. It crowns his endeavours to reconcile 'speech & literature', a high sophistication with folk-song, the concreteness of the rural prose tradition with a poetic imagination, word with thing, *The Natural History of Selborne* with *The Story of My Heart*.

The achievement of that last reconciliation is probably the most crucial to the character of the poetry, where, in F.R. Leavis's well-known words, 'the outward scene is accessory to an inner theatre.'[108] With reference to the personal writing in Thomas's prose, Professor R. George Thomas observes: 'His poems are an extension and refinement of the same intense desire to interpret his spiritual autobiography.'[109] The last section of this selection contains some examples of his prose 'interpretations'. Still farther back, in the nineties, Thomas portrayed himself as a maudit *fin de siecle* figure, of whom features linger in Morgan Rhys's 'fantastic belief that the corpse is life's handiwork and its utmost end' (p.259) and Morgan Traheron's 'luxurious self-contempt' (p.261). The latter story is based on an actual suicide 'Attempt' of Thomas's; and, like the extracts from *The Icknield Way* (p.265ff.), at least shows the gap closing between Thomas's fictional selves and his searingly direct confessions to Bottomley and Eleanor Farjeon: 'the central evil is self-consciousness carried as far beyond selfishness as selfishness is beyond self denial, . . . and now amounting to a disease and all I have got to fight it with is the knowledge that in truth I am not the isolated selfconsidering brain which I have come to seem.'[110] *The Childhood of Edward Thomas* may have unblocked his past to clear the way for the poetry's blend of analysis and therapy. In any case, the stylized and inadequate 'Other' masks Thomas wears in his prose—in order to see or find himself, to 'reopen the connection between the brain and the rest'[111]—evolve into the flexible self-dramatization of the poems. The prose underlines, however, the coincidence between Thomas's extremely individual predicament and wider issues of the vulnerable isolation of twentieth-century man within a relative universe. His self-projection as 'Aurelius, the Superfluous Man' (p.264) exchanges the aesthete maudit for a more modern version of alienation. In an 'age of doubt and balancing and testing—of distrusting the old and not very confidently expecting the new,'[112] Thomas's quest for an earthly 'home' is representative: the South Country takes in 'those modern people who belong nowhere' (p.209). The war perhaps again focused this darker aspect of his consciousness. In the complex lyrical drama of 'Rain' (1916), which realizes Thomas's 1901 prophecy, the downpour of *The Icknield Way* fulfils its potential as a symbol of personal, social and universal dissolution—a chain of unbeing:

> But here I pray that none whom once I loved
> Is dying tonight or lying still awake
> Solitary, listening to the rain,
> Either in pain or thus in sympathy
> Helpless among the living and the dead,
> Like a cold water among broken reeds,
> Myriads of broken reeds all still and stiff. . . .

ABBREVIATIONS

A   *The Academy*

B   *The Bookman*

DC   *Daily Chronicle*

DN   *Daily News*

ER   *The English Review*

L   *Literature*

MP   *Morning Post*

NS   *The New Statesman*

NW   *The New Weekly*

PD   *Poetry and Drama*

WS   *The Week's Survey*

The bracketed numbers in the Introduction refer to pages in this
edition. The Notes to the Introduction and to the text are at the end of
the volume.

1   Critics and Reviewers

REVIEWING : AN UNSKILLED LABOUR

THERE SEEM TO be four principal kinds of reviews—the interesting and good; the interesting, but bad; the uninteresting, but good; the uninteresting and bad. Most are of the last kind. They are reading matter, usually grammatical, which probably bears some relation to something passing in the writer's mind, but keeps it secret. Nothing is revealed by them about the book in hand, except the author's name and presumed sex, and whether it is in prose or verse; nothing about the reviewer's feeling, except that he likes or does not like, or is indifferent to the book—which is not a matter of much importance unless the reviewer has somehow built up a system, or a past, to which his remarks instantly refer the reader. The bad, uninteresting review consists of second-hand words and paralysed, inelectric phrases; and the better these are strung together the worse it is, because it means that the wretched man, woman, or child, is deceiving himself, making a virtue of his necessity, his hurry, his obtuseness, his ignorance. Such work is terribly uninteresting to anyone without a superhuman interest in whatever is inhuman. Some-times it may be read in a comatose condition by readers with a respect for all printed matter, and in a sort of enthusiasm by relatives of the reviewer. But the only thing to be said for it is that it produces money, which produces food and clothing for aged parents, fair wives, inno-cent children. Against it must be set the fact that it is waste of time and energy, like sending clean things to a laundry—that it is nothing, masquerading as something—that the longer it exists the more respectable it is thought by those who do not care, by the majority. Most reviews are of this kind. That is to say that people of all sorts write them. Therefore, probably, it is very easy to fall into the habit, and very hard to see that you have done so. You read a book once or twice, or half read it; various thoughts are awakened as you proceed,

1

about the author, his subjects, his vocabulary, the influences he has felt, and, in addition to these, at the end you have some sort of general impression. When you come to write, you do not inquire into the history of your thoughts, or try to relate them; your object is to write without delay something continuous, and since some of the thoughts protrude too much for continuity you sacrifice them. The result is a piece of prose which only a man possessing a profound knowledge of you can accurately follow. What can anybody else do with your roundabout phrases, brought to birth by the union of unconsidered thoughts with memories of other reviews?

The more a man tries who was not born to write—unless he has an aim clearly before him—the worse he writes. Most reviewers have no aim clearly before them, except of covering space and putting the name of the book at the top. At best they want to get in a striking phrase, relevant or not. God help them. It is not a man's, certainly not a reviewer's, task, to better them, or persuade them that they could be bettered. Nor is it necessary here to attempt to throw light upon bad writing. I mention this class only because I believe that they hope to be interesting. They are distant, perhaps unconscious, disciples of Wilde's *Critic as Artist*. They are expressing themselves apropos of the book sent them for review: if they succeed, it is in this world a thing to be thankful for. The so-called review relating to one detail in the book, and then branching off to something which the reviewer has at heart, is justified if well done. Good writing is always justified. But this bad, interesting review is not of importance here. Both kinds are bad, because they are not reviews.

What, then, is a review? A review gives an account of an unknown book—its substance, aim and achievement; or it discusses a known book, or some point in it or connected with it, in a manner assuming some knowledge of it on the reader's part. To this second class belong most of the better reviews. Any good writer can write good reviews of this kind. But good reviews of the other kind are seen scarcely ever; for it by no means follows that if a good writer tries to produce them he will succeed. Few try, and perhaps the good writer tries least of all. He has established a scale of values, a system, a metaphysic, for which he is known among the scattered school of followers which at the same time he has created. For the most part he trusts to a few shorthand phrases, indicating to the intelligent that he likes a thing or not, and, to some extent, how and why. This, of course, is valuable in proportion to the merits of the critic. According as he has a wide or peculiar knowledge of men, and things, and words, and holds a vigorous and not stereo-typed view which has survived or sprung out of this knowledge, so must he be valued. At present he is not likely to reach very far. He will be read chiefly by literary people. The rest of the world, learned and unlearned, will go on discovering what suits them, unconsciously applying standards based on experience. Too seldom will the critic take trouble over writers who have, as it were, got out of hand— become popular; his temptation is thereupon to seek the faults which have led, in his opinion, to the popularity.

But the most difficult, and at the same time most practicable and useful review, is the one which gives some information about unknown books. To do this fairly with continuous prose books is not easy: with verse it is apparently so difficult that nobody attempts it. Reviewers are either too anxious to give a display of their own talent, or they prefer important-looking abstractions and generalities without reflecting on how far these will have any considerable meaning for the reader who has not made the reviewers his study. They are handicapped further by the fact that the tools of their trade are not really on the market at all. Practically no book is of any immediate use to them. To be able to employ Matthew Arnold's touchstones, except pedantically, is really the last test of culture: the man who applies them is usually, and roughly speaking, an ass. It is no common gift to be able to feel the greatness of great lines through and through, even after hearing that they are so from persons you have placed in authority. To feel what new lines have in common with them is what no man has done, so far as I know, while all sorts of men have shown that they can be deceived by superficial resemblances. No doubt the more a man truly knows of older literature, the better will be his judgment of the new. But mere scholarship, or the fact of having read, 'twixt waking and sleeping, only what was approved in older literature, is no qualification: true knowledge should put a man on his guard against imitations and superficial resemblances. The worst of it is that the critic is usually looking out for what is good or bad, along certain lines; whereas it is rather his business to find, like a plain man, 'something to read'—as intense a pleasure as possible in reading—not something that would, he imagines, be perfect to a different imagined being, though unreadable to himself. No man is a final judge of what he cannot enjoy, whether eggs, caviare, or castor oil, however brilliant he may be at telling us that what he cannot enjoy is bad. But by taking pains he can give an account of it.

A review giving an account of a book of verse is an object not too easy for any proud or accomplished man; nor need any heroic degree of impersonality be sought after. Only the reviewer must seriously consider whether words like 'striking and unique', 'alive', 'decadent' or 'readable', coming from his pen, will, without abundant proof and illustration, have any weight outside his family circle; whether it is any use informing us that the right book sometimes gets into the hands of the wrong reviewer, and that he fears this is now the case; whether he or anyone else gains by quoting verses and saying that they show a sense of melody, with a comment that this is the most essential of a poet's gifts, and the aside that though Whitman thought metre of no importance his best lines happened to be metrical. So long as bad reviewers are not condemned to a pension and the loss of their fingers and, if necessary, their toes, so long these things will be done. Honesty is a difficult virtue. The reviewer must be airing scraps of knowledge, trying to create an impression among inferiors, pretending to admire things which he does not like—which he would not read if he were not compelled—often for no better reason than that he could not do as well himself. Sometimes I have wished that there were more office boys turned on to reviewing. Better the honest opinion of a smart, pitiless, and unhistorically minded Cockney than all this rambling, hedging and ditching, half and half. As if office boys were more likely than anybody else to be honest and direct! They would be striving to conceal their identity, writing like the ordinary reviewer. But if only reviewers could aim at honesty! They need not return boring books to the editor; they must live; let them try to understand why they are bored and tell us, confessing also plainly what they most dislike, what they come nearest to liking, and so on. Everyone is declaring belief, or at least disbelief, in modern poetry; no one admits that he does not like poetry or only likes Tennyson. Yet nearly all reviews of verse are either loosely complimentary or have a bantering tone as if the bards were tiny little odd unreal creatures who earn no wages and have no human feelings. When a new book by an accepted verse writer appears, the reviewer's task is to compass some variation of the ordinary compliments. As to the unaccepted, it is Heads I praise, Tails I laugh. More often it is Heads, because those are the publisher's orders. No matter: mere praise is better than mere laughter, and the letter of praise does not exclude the spirit of criticism.

The reviewer lacks not excuse. In most cases he has no idea whom he is addressing, if anyone. He is writing in an indifferent vacuum. He does not care; his editor does not care; so far as he knows, nobody cares, provided he is not libellous, obscene, or very ungrammatical. Is he to address the author? Is he to address readers who know the book reviewed, or readers who do not? Is he to hold forth simply to his equals who happen not to write for a living? These questions will come up and ought to be answered. A careful answer might help to turn reviewing from unskilled into skilled labour. No one wants to interfere with good writers; I am speaking of the average reviewer. His unsupported opinion is mostly worthless. I believe it would be a useful and pleasant change if he were to cease expressing opinions and take to giving as plain and full an account of the book in hand, as time, space, and his own ability permit. The skill required would be of an order which no man need be ashamed to display, and few could achieve without labour. Gradually, efficient chroniclers would be, not born, but made. They might become as efficient as the best of the newspaper staff is held to be; they might form a standard which plain, hurried men could reach by moderate efforts, and would not fall short of without disgrace. The pioneers would perhaps have a hard time in getting rid of all those degraded loose phrases caused by uncertainty, or ignorance, or imitation, all the words like the advertiser's 'unequalled' and 'absolutely pure'. Even the egoistic reviewer, even the egoistic reviewer with a following, might learn from this method. In any case he would not be superseded, while personality and a corresponding metaphysic and literary power are respected, and he would be served by a rank and file of decent workers, instead of being surrounded and confused by a rabble of ridiculous and unlovely muddlers.

PD, II, 5, March 1914

Mr Brownell is a clever man. He deals with Thackeray, Carlyle, George Eliot, Matthew Arnold, Ruskin, and George Meredith; and, although more has been written about these men and women than they have written themselves, the new critic is not dull. He rarely says anything poor; more rarely does he say anything poorly. He has read his authors thoughtfully. In fact, every page proves that he is a very intelligent reader, one not to be duped; in short, such a one as the indifferent, affected, or over-subtle writer must loathe and fear. He baits Carlyle and praises him. Not one of these authors escapes his praise and blame. And yet we are not sure that he is anything more than a very intelligent reader. When he says of Mr Meredith that 'his analytic impulse is altogether out of proportion to his architectonic capacity', and that he is 'too much absorbed in phenomena to think of himself contributing anything to their recombination in accordance with his own vision or volition—at most occupied with attributions and exposition', we feel that such criticism might well be applied to Mr Brownell himself. We never meet his 'vision or volition' in all these pages. We have only a body of educated opinion such as would tell heavily in a debating society. We are left to wonder why he is interested in literature, except in so far as it gives him an opportunity of showing the world that he is, as we say, a clever man. He has learned hardly anything from Arnold, though his discussion of Arnold shows him at his best. Of Arnold's criticism, he says:

It is eminently the antithesis of impressionist criticism. It has behind it what may fairly pass for a body of doctrine, though a body of doctrine as far as possible removed from system and pedantry. It is wholly unfettered by academic conventions, such as, citing

Addison, he calls 'the sort of thing that held our fathers spellbound in admiration'. But it is still more removed from the irresponsible exercise of the nervous system, however attuned to taste and sensitised by culture. Certain definite *ideas*, held with elastic firmness but not developed into any set of Procrustean principles, formed his credo, and his criticism consisted in the application of these as a test and measure of quality and worth. Their simplicity and their searchingness made their application fundamental, whether or no in every case it was either sound in emphasis or sufficient.

Arnold was not always thoroughly well-informed; he was certainly not free from the faulty criticism of which Mr Brownell speaks above; but the passage is on the whole very just. Call it a system, or a doctrine, or a mature and intellectualized personality, Arnold had that possession which makes criticism art and literature. He treated literature, and life as he found it there, just as the true artist treats actual life. The result is—and it would have been more emphatically so if Arnold had not only been more careful of what he wrote, but had written more, in the sphere of criticism—that he built a kind of philosophy out of books, reinforced, of course, by his experience in life. That, Mr Brownell does not achieve. For, in spite of his cunning analysis, it is evident that he is often led by books into a train of thought which he would otherwise never have pursued, and once pursued he leaves it alone. Thus, each book means an independent and unrelated flash of thought in his mind. Every book that Arnold seriously considered left an essential addition to his house of thought. Mr Brownell merely adds to his museum. Even so, it does not follow that Mr Brownell has no gift of criticism. There is another mode of making literature out of criticism. It is the mode of Ruskin and Pater. It is more eclectic than Arnold's, and less intellectual. It consists in seizing an idea in the book or picture under criticism and making far more of it than the author intended. These critics pretend to explain their authors; but Ruskin, in criticism of Dante or Homer, and Pater, in criticism of Rossetti or Du Bellay, simply borrow or steal a thought and speculate with it, until it produces 100 per cent. Still less can Mr Brownell do this; at least he never attempts it. And, in our opinion, no other mode of making literature out of 'criticism' so called, remains. Other 'criticism' is really a branch of polemics, and he certainly makes no polemics. He is, in fact, as we have said, a very intelligent reader. He explains his authors, their method, their style, their personality, their philosophy; he meets and makes objections; and all this he does with quite unusual brilliance. But such intelligence, though it adorn the lecture room, the breakfast table and the railway train, would become rather an evil than a good, if it should spread and cause, as in Mr Brownell's case, an increase in the tonnage of the British Museum.

From review of *Victorian Prose Masters* by W. C. Brownell,
DC, 9 May 1902

... A very prominent opinion of our critic's is that 'the common, the average, the sane', etc., is what is valuable in literature. He is all for straightforwardness, for preference of subject to style (whatever that may be), and is unwilling to see that a man may be quite straight-forwardly and inevitably 'affected', just as he himself is as 'personal' as possible when he appears to us so 'impersonal'. Again, 'one can go back,' he says, 'to *The Vicar of Wakefield*; but can he read a second time *The Woman in White*?' And altogether he is surprisingly imper-sonal in 'the re-reading of books.' Only 'the normal, the sane, the simple,' he repeats, 'have the gift of long life'; as if *Pantagruel* or *Religio Medici* or *Hamlet* were normal and sane and simple. And we begin to suspect that Mr Burrough's admiration of these things is bred of phlegm, when he says, 'Each of us has about all the happiness he has the capacity for.'

Mr Burroughs would perhaps agree that in every age there will be at least three types of critics: those who are occupied in relating books to life; those who are occupied in relating books to books, and striving for a standard; and finally, the secluded lovers of books, who move among them just as 'men of the world' move among men. They are the gifted readers. The supreme felicity of their criticism will probably be a quotation. All will justify themselves in so far as they 'make litera-ture', and especially in so far as they open a track for the appreciation of the little known, and send the new into the current of thought in their own day. They will, in a measure, help genius to its own in good time. Mr Burroughs is particularly aware of the difficulty of doing this. He is irritably anxious to discover a nostrum by which we shall learn who will last. Will Emerson? Will Mr Meredith? But to us it seems that the Critic should find rather what the times are in need of. If a writer shall serve or nobly please the men of his day he does his duty. If he shall not, but shall have to wait a century, he is unfor-tunate, and may be immortal; but the critic is not to be blamed for not being among the prophets. It is far more difficult to be among the interpreters, the evangelists. And as for seeing things as in themselves they really are, it is a dull occupation, even when successful. To suggest the case by analogy, what is a fine summer's day as in itself it really is? Is the Meteorological Office to decide? or the poet? or the farmer?

From review of *Literary Values and Other Papers* by John Burroughs,
DC, 14 July 1903

We were much taken with Mr More's first volume of Shelburne Essays. He used a plain philosophic style with careful ease and fair precision. He wrote on Thoreau, Hawthorne, Carlyle, Tolstoy, Mr Arthur Symons; and showed training, reading, and a grave interest in literature, which were remarkable in what we believed to be a first book. The essays in the second volume are of the same order. He writes of Lafcadio Hearn, Lamb, FitzGerald, Crabbe, Mr Meredith and Mr Kipling, Hawthorne again, and always with the same lofty reasonableness, yet with a monotonous severity and respectability that have in the end the same effect as a nasal unctuousness in the voice—that is, laughter. If the whitened statue of Cobden, which looks seriously upon the Hampstead trams, were to speak, even thus would he comment upon books and life, after so many days and nights of elevated and solitary immobility.

Mr More would not deny this; for in his title-page he has put some words from *The Republic* which insist that a man must not be considered in preference to the truth. Also, in his essay on Mr Meredith, he has pointed out with disgust, which is as near animation as dignity would allow, that Stevenson and Mr William Watson and others have expressed diverse views on the novelist, without giving 'a rational explanation of their opinions'; and has asked 'in amazement' whether this 'irresponsible impressionism' is to oust the judgment from criticism. Many other passages in Mr More's two volumes would lead us to attribute this attitude to a belief in Matthew Arnold and the dignity of criticism, as much as to a regard for the truth. Arguing in an abstract way, we should not care to urge that 'irresponsible impressionism' is to supersede reasonable judgments; but we think that reasonable judgments have caused more waste of paper and more of that tedium which is sapping the vitality of the old races, than all the irresponsible impressionism. Reasonable judgments are so often related to obesity of mind, to unconscious hypocrisy and a retarding respect for authority, whether conventional or not, that we are disposed to pass them over eagerly in search of the voice of a human being. We are weary of hearing a man saying, without a smile or even a vigorous frown, that 'Ibsen has violated the law of tragedy by descending to trivialities and by using prosaic language'; that *Macbeth* 'purges the passions'; that ours is a 'prosaic civilization'. . . .

It is a truism that a critic, as distinguished from a reviewer, should praise. The truth seems to us to be that he should be enthusiastic—should see a book, as a man who is not a critic sees a landscape or a character—should, in short, be inspired by it. Arnold was, in a measure, inspired in his 'Maurice de Guérin' which is good; but not in his 'Shelley', which is indifferent. Pater was inspired in his 'Aesthetic School', which is good; Stevenson was not, in his 'Thoreau', which is indifferent. But Mr More does not see that the pure intelligence can never exhaust a subject or produce a perfect impression, while the enthusiasm, of which we have spoken, means to us a power which, perhaps wilfully, but divinely too, makes one aspect of a thing entirely its own. The difference is as the difference between a man going about with a lantern in a dark wood, and a man sitting afar off and seeing it in the glimpses of the moon. In Mr More, this fatal ignorance of the true value of impressionism is everywhere illustrated. Would he, other- wise, have wished that Lamb could more often have 'laid aside his pose' and have found confidence 'to lose his wit in the tragic emotions that must have waked with him by day and slept with him at night'? We think not, and in his strange willingness to record in print his laboriously but incompletely considered antipathies, we see a grave fault. In criticism it is so grave as often to refuse admittance to any of the virtues or the graces. Anger is bad enough, but at least it is a passion; contempt is worse, but at least it may be allied to irony; but reasonable judgment is barren, like the critical exercises of school- boys and professors. For it is in reading such criticism that we see the grain of truth in the vulgar remark that many critics have less know- ledge than the men criticized.

It is, then, the duty of a critic to be open, passionately open, to impressions, to have a personality, just as it is his duty to detect the same openness, the same personality in writers of books. When Mr More not only fails very often to have the rich and joyous perceptions of an enthusiast, to have a personality, but fails also to detect the personality in his author, he seems to us condemned. He sees that Mr Meredith is extraordinary, and he merely complains. Our critic is thus one of the immense number of men who do not know what they like, or if they like a thing cannot like it heartily, and go about the world trying to be interested. He likes Hawthorne and Lafcadio Hearn; he can write of them like an educated man; but he has so wasted his abilities in pondering his dislikes that he is very nearly dull. The result is that he —a man of many remarkable and rare abilities—has become little more than a 'cultured' talker about books to persons who like a 'cultured' man. Such readers will find much to enjoy in his essays. They are full of educated, shrewd comment, gracefully expressed, on interesting subjects. In 'Lafcadio Hearn' he shows a knowledge of East and West so great, that we reflect sadly that, had it been a little less professorial, it might have pleased lovers of Hearn by other means than mere critical explanation, i.e., by original composition. Then his essays on 'Delphic and Greek Literature' and 'Nemesis, or the Divine Envy' are grave and learned enough to accuse us fairly of violating our own laws of good criticism, by refusing to see the full and peculiar value of Mr More's work. But then we are only reviewing.

From review of *Shelburne Essays: Second Series* by Paul Elmer More, *A*, 19 August 1905

One of the most obvious results of every new body of poetry which has come into the modern world has been a new body of criticism. The business of the critic has largely been to praise, to justify, and to explain; incidentally, he has usually condemned the poetry that has been superseded. Thus the romantic poetry of the nineteenth century produced a romantic school of criticism. Survivors of the old school meantime did not hesitate to condemn Wordsworth and Keats very much as Dr Johnson would have done. We have therefore naturally become cautious in our loyalty to the school of our own time, and this caution is perhaps responsible for our preference of 'appreciation' to 'Criticism':

> Critics, said Matthew Arnold, give themselves great labour to draw out what in the abstract constitutes the characters of a high quality of poetry. It is much better simply to have recourse to concrete examples; to take specimens of poetry of the high, of the very highest quality, and to say: The characters of a high quality of poetry are what is expressed *there*. They are far better recognised by being felt as the verse of the master, than by being perused in the prose of the critic. Nevertheless if we are urgently pressed to give some critical account of them, we may safely, perhaps, venture on laying down, not indeed how and why the characters arise, but where and in what they arise. They are in the matter and substance of the poetry, and they are in its manner and style. Both of these, the substance and matter on the one hand, the style and manner on the other, have a mark, an accent, of high beauty, worth, and power. But if we are asked to define this mark and accent in the abstract, our answer must be: No, for we should thereby be darkening the question, not clearing it.

Here, certainly, is a reason for caution, if a critic whose importance is proved as fully by his opponents as by his supporters, writing for a popular audience of vague taste, can found himself on nothing firmer than this in an essay on the 'study of poetry'. The passage has a certain fitness for our moods of more sensuous meditation, but we question whether a brown study of poetry is what the critic desired. Other modern critics have furnished some excellent writing, and helped many towards a subtler enjoyment of poetry; but they tend to regard it mainly from the point of view of the poet himself, and have established little save that poetry must be 'indefinably poetical'. When Arnold himself is forced to a definite statement he is apt to put us off with such as this: 'It is advisable to construct all verses so that by reading them naturally—that is, according to the sense and legitimate accent—the reader gets the right rhythm.'

Advisable! Mr Liddell's book is, in a sense, an enforcement of this idea to its utmost limit of expansion. That verse form is primarily 'a rhythmic arrangement of the successive parts of an idea' is the one of his conclusions upon which he most insists. It is natural, therefore, that Mr Liddell should start not very gently with a condemnation of the school of dilettante criticism and pleasing 'views'. He questions, too, the adequacy of our current notions of poetry.

> We are told, he says, characteristically, that 'poetry is a thing of God'; that it is 'the finer spirit of knowledge'; that it is 'something divine'; that it is 'the inner thought of things'; that it is 'the completest expression of humanity'; that it is 'the language of ideality'; that it is 'the expression of the inner motions of the soul'. These are but a few of the vague and meaningless forms of literary expression that so-called definitions of poetry take.

He destroys these phrases one by one somewhat in the manner of a logic lecturer; and yet we are allowed to feel at last that Wordsworth's noble phrase, 'The breath and finer spirit of knowledge', is not meaningless and has even gained in intention from Mr Liddell's fine elucidation of the difficult ways and strange by which poetry acts. . . .

Le mécanisme de la pensée, to use Joubert's phrase, is his theme, especially as it is exhibited in English poetry. By an examination of some passages from the Psalms and Beowulf, he shows that the primary and essential element of all poetry is an aesthetic arrangement of 'the moments of thought', which is his technical term for a phrase—e.g., this line is divided into three thought moments: 'O night! / do I not see my love / fluttering out among the breakers? / . . .

Alliteration, rhyme, etc., is but 'added adornment', let the young poet as well as the student remember, 'to an aesthetically-proportioned structure'; though we would substitute 'emphasis' for 'adornment'. . . .

. . . English poetry is, in Mr Liddell's words, 'a rhythm not of sound but of ideas', where we think that the opposition between sound and ideas is false. Poetry is thus, as it were, absolutely onomatopoeic, or has under command onomatopoeia, and all correlated mysteries of language; and nowhere is this more brilliantly shown than in Mr Liddell's chapters on the general principles of stress and on rhythm waves. There lies the main value of his book. On the other hand, he fails to reveal a quality in verse which has not been, or in future may not be, achieved in prose. Perfect prose has always a music of ideas, and its stresses are, or should be, as subtle and constant as in verse. The millennial prose may unfold a rhythm, and possibly even a rhyme, of grander music than Dante's or Homer's, availing itself, nevertheless, of all their mighty inventions. Meantime, *le mécanisme de la pensée* is here finely set forth. The student will no longer be content with saying that the subject of a great poem is 'worthy of poetry', and that the verses are in the 'grand style'. He will gain just such an understanding of poetry as is implied in the utterance of a Coquelin or a Kean. He will have, so to speak, a *dramatic* knowledge of verse. Something of the kind he has had before, we admit. . . .

From review of *An Introduction to the Scientific Study of English Poetry* by Mark H. Liddell, *WS*, 20 September 1902

Mr Liddell tells us himself that he has proved that his system is practicable. We have no hesitation in saying that his book is more likely to interest and serve the student of English poetry than any we have seen before. If it were necessary to have a standard of poetry, we should say that there is an excellent one between these covers. It is not a new system of prosody, though it makes the old one ridiculous. It affords no basis for a classification of metres; it leaves blank verse, as before, an infinitely varied line usually of ten syllables. Its strongest quality is that it states the grounds for the appreciation of verse which have been used by the best critics of every age; it states them subtly and amply for the first time, and in such a way as not to offend those who are far from wishing to study poetry as they study economics.

From another review of *An Introduction*, *DC*, 18 September 1902

Dr A.C. Bradley's *Shakespearean Tragedy* was one of the newest and most weighty books that have come from an Oxford professorial Chair for a generation. His *Oxford Lectures on Poetry*, now for the first time collected, were also delivered from the Chair of Poetry at Oxford, and they are of the same quality, of good substance closely woven. They will gain few readers from among the indolent. For though they have grace, they are utterly without graces. There is a true intellectual passion in them, but no charm. Their structure is often admirable, but it is never displayed by artifice. A paradoxical critic might safely go so far as to say that Dr Bradley cannot write, so unattractive are his sentences, so inelegant and struggling his phrases. All the more remarkable then is the power which he gradually gains over us. It is a power somewhat unusual in these days. We live in a time of special pleaders, of preachers; we expect personality before everything from a writer, or it would be truer to say that we expect the trappings of personality, eccentricities of vocabulary, construction, gesture, and are easily put off with them; we demand that a man should always take a side, should express himself very positively even to the point of extravagance, and should never hint at doubt. Now Dr Bradley has not taken sides. He would make the worst of debaters. He is only troubled about what is true. Nor is he bent on making converts, least of all to a belief in his own infallibility. He is not afraid to show perplexity or to formulate a half-truth as such. When, for example, he writes of the sublime he says that he 'proposes to make some remarks on this quality, and even to attempt some sort of answer to the question what sublimity is'; and when he speaks of beauty he is neither pedantic enough to assume that everybody knows what he means, nor journalistic enough to give a brilliant definition straight away. He laboriously hews out a path through his subject, turning neither to the right nor to the left when to do so would be merely to show his agility. In the end he has given us no memorable phrases, but he has given us the very deep and unusual pleasure of watching his thought facing its subject honestly, and of accompanying him through the whole process in a manner so intimate that the reader might be excused who believed that it was he himself who had come to these conclusions and that Dr Bradley had been looking on . . . .

. . . He does not take a well-worn point of view and colour it afresh, nor does he picturesquely amplify a single point to display his rhetorical power, nor does he treat us to a hotch-potch of various opinions and biographical extracts. In the lecture on Wordsworth he redeems that poet from the charge of narrowness and mere Puritanism, and gets decidedly nearer to a clear statement of the peculiar 'visionary' power his mind than anyone else has done. Keats, again, he proves from the letters to have been something very different from the aesthete who once fought a butcher boy of the ordinary legend, to have been a man of just such various qualities of mind as we usually expect from a great poet. In the essay on Shelley's view of poetry as shown in his prose and poetry he expresses in a concise form his opinion on a very important matter, the relation of poetry to ideas:

> The specific way of imagination is not to clothe in imagery consciously held ideas; it is to produce half-consciously a matter from which, when produced, the reader may if he chooses extract ideas. Poetry (I must exaggerate to be clear), psychologically considered, is not the *expression* of ideas or of a view of life; it is their discovery or creation, or rather both discovery and creation in one. The interpretation contained in *Hamlet* and *King Lear* was not brought ready-made to the old stories. What was brought to them was the huge substance of Shakespeare's imagination, in which all his experience and thought was latent; and this, dwelling and working on the stories with nothing but a dramatic purpose, and kindling

into heat and motion, gradually discovered or created in them a meaning and a mass of truth about life which was brought to birth by the process of composition, but never preceded it in the shape of ideas, and probably never, even after it, took that shape to the poet's mind.

This too short passage further illustrates the quality of Dr Bradley's mind. It is suggestive, not creative. He is feeling, and helping us to feel, a way to a truer attitude towards poetry, and doubtless his ideas are destined to find fuller and more notable expression, but for the honesty and freshness of his contribution we cannot be too grateful. Here and in the brilliant lecture on the long poem in Wordsworth's age he seems by his patient method to have opened channels by which truths of first-rate significance can now more easily flow into the mind of our time, with which indeed he is more tremblingly in sympathy than any other writer, not a poet, whom we can call to mind.

From review of *Oxford Lectures on Poetry* by A. C. Bradley,
MP, 10 June 1909

Mr Arthur Symons has three uncommon qualifications as a critic. He is a scholar; he is an eager adventurer, ever looking out for new beauty; he has a 'wise passiveness' in dealing with books, by which he becomes penetrated with their secrets, allowing them one by one to colour, as so many new windows to his soul, the light that comes to him. And, on the whole, none of his books shows all these qualities quite so well as his *Symbolist Movement in Literature*, i.e., in French literature. Few, if any, Englishmen could have done it at all. For these eight men—Gérard de Nerval, Villiers de l'Isle Adam, Rimbaud, Verlaine, Laforgue, Mallarmé, Huysmans, and M. Maeterlinck—all of them writing in French, have a certain detachment from the life of the householder which, even in the artist, we are in the habit of resenting when it goes beyond an inexpensive personal oddity or two. Matthew Arnold's 'What a Set!' is at the top of the notepaper of nearly all our critics. But Mr Symons, as well as being an exact and sober man, has all the sympathy which Walt Whitman desired to have. He approaches books as an artist approaches life, and he interprets and so criticizes. It is necessary to understand at least so much in case we should accuse him of lacking a sense of proportion when he deals with these men, all of them, except Verlaine and M. Maeterlinck, not of the first or of the second order. Perhaps for the purpose of reaching an English audience, or more likely from a hatred of schoolmasterly comparisons, he avoids showing the Symbolist writers in their relation to their predecessors and contemporaries. Some day he will do this and make it clear that they are not so exceptional or so new as they appear in his pages, or, rather, that their finest achievements, as distinct from the theories of Mallarmé, for example, are neither in a backwater nor at a fountain head. He never wearies us by taking a standard line from Dante or Shakespeare and comparing Verlaine or Mallarmé with it. He is dogmatic only when he seems to accept Poe's quibble that not merely is 'the age of epics past, but that no long poem was ever written, the finest long poem in the world being but a series of short poems linked together by prose'.

His business is to prove that these writers live, not that this or that is their probable haunt upon Parnassus. This he does admirably, beginning with this large claim for the movement as a whole:

> In this revolt against exteriority, against rhetoric, against a natura-
> listic tradition; in this endeavour to disengage the ultimate essence,
> the soul, of whatever exists and can be realized by the conscious-
> ness; in this dutiful waiting upon every symbol by which the soul of
> things can be made visible, literature, bowed down by so many
> burdens, may at last attain liberty and its authentic speech. In
> attaining this liberty it accepts a heavier burden, for in speaking to
> us so intimately, so solemnly, as only religion had hitherto spoken
> to us, it becomes itself a kind of religion, with all the duties and
> responsibilities of the sacred ritual.

He puts this more clearly and satisfactorily in the essay on Gérard de Nerval when he says that he had divined that poetry should be 'not a hymn to beauty, nor the description of beauty, nor beauty's mirror, but beauty itself; the colour, fragrance, and form of the imagined flower as it blossoms again out of the page'. In essay after essay he reveals these men as they have not, except to the few, revealed them-selves, in the same way as an artist reveals a landscape which has been for centuries but so many acres and cubic feet of land, air, water, and vegetation. The 'Mallarmé', the 'Verlaine' and the 'Maeterlinck as Mystic' are especially fine portraits, and not only because the first two were known to him personally. They speak through him, and the reader has to know them well in order to understand how much of Mr Symons there is in these essays in discipleship, to see the study and the craft behind what might appear to be only supreme self-abase-ment. . . .

From review of *The Symbolist Movement in Literature* by Arthur Symons, *MP*, 14 May 1908

It is a peculiarity of [Mr Symons] that he thinks the poetry of the Romantic Movement not only a new kind but actually more poetical. He says in his introduction that—

> Poetry at the beginning of the nineteenth century wastes surprisingly little of its substance, and one main reason of this is that it realises, as its main concern, what to most of the poets of the past had been, though their existence depended upon it, but lightly regarded—that imaginative atmosphere which is the very breath of poetry, and adds strangeness to beauty.

'Lightly regarded', he says, as if an eye which came to regard it consciously and seriously were likely to have more of it. And the final words of this introduction are:

> It was realised that the end of poetry was to be poetry; and that no story-telling or virtue or learning, or any fine purpose, could make amends for the lack of that one necessity. Thus it may be affirmed that in studying this period we are able to study whatever is essential in English poetry; that is, whatever is essential in poetry.

Yet in the whole book it is hard to learn what poetry is except that it must have a poetical substance—which prose also may have—and that it must have regularly recurring rhythms which distinguish it from prose. What makes the book so good is not this definition, but Mr Symons's own taste, which he is not articulate enough to explain, but which he applies in a very nearly faultless manner to half a dozen great poets and a score of lesser ones. His pages are often subtle and brilliant. Lurking behind them and giving its unique quality to the book is this unexpressed personality and taste which, we feel, is far finer than anything he can say. If only he could have expressed it! He is in possession of a secret which would be more valuable than all the criticism even Coleridge has left to us, if it could be published. It cannot be.

Even so its mundane and visible workings in this book are fascinating enough, so much so that it was only at the end that we really perceived that though many fine things had been said about poetry and about individual poetry, the secret remains hid. It is a tantalizing thought, and we wonder if Mr Symons also is aware of it. Was he aware of it when he said that Blake was 'the only poet who is a poet in essence'? For if so would he not have stopped short at Blake, have burnt the preceding pages on Wolcot, Hannah More and the rest, and have concentrated his attention upon Blake until the 'poet in essence' stood revealed? Or, again, when he came to Coleridge and discovered that 'Kubla Khan' may be used as a touchstone, that 'it will determine the poetic value of any lyric poem which you place beside it', did he entirely know what he was saying? Was it not as much as to say that anyone who—like himself—knew why 'Kubla Khan' was pure poetry, could recognise the same qualities in other poems, and therefore had no need of 'Kubla Khan' or any other poem as a touchstone? For it is certain that many men and women whom that poem has enchanted have made hundreds of mistakes in judging lyric poems, needless to say, by living poets, but also by the dead. If pure poetry is so unmistakable a thing, if it is independent of its age, as Mr Symons believes, if it can be tested by touchstones, there is no need of error any more, and we could wish that he might be persuaded to come down among us and award the palm without the dust to the living.

From review of The Romantic Movement in English Poetry
by Arthur Symons, DC, 7 October 1909

Mr Arthur Symons has for a long time been one of the most interesting of writers, not merely for his fastidious accomplishment, but for his long-continued development and promise. He had reached one kind of perfection a good many years ago in *The Symbolist Movement* and in *London Nights,* and another kind again in the more recent poems of 'The Fool of the World' and the prose of his introduction to John Clare's poetry. He has grown more austere, more himself, or at any rate less conspicuously of a certain school. And now *The Romantic Movement in English Literature* is seldom recognizable as his, except that no other critic of poetry has so fine a taste to serve so considerable a scholarship. The introduction to Clare's poetry stood alone among Mr Symons's writings when it appeared, but by far the greater part of this new book is of the same class, as closely knit and as pure of mannerism. The book is not the variation upon a well-known air, which is usually offered as criticism of the Romantic Movement of the Nineteenth Century. The movement is not treated as a movement at all. Each writer is taken separately, and for the most part Mr Symons leaves it to his readers to flounder in generalizations if they will, for he gives them few. He takes it for granted that genius is always above its age, and that every genius is essentially independent of every other. His object has been to face each of the poets—good and bad, an extraordinary multitude of them, in fact everyone who was born before and died after 1800—to face them afresh and define their qualities as they appear by contact with their sensitive critic's mind. . . .

And yet we have been struck almost as much by the doubtful philosophy which Mr Symons holds, if he does not always obey, as by the brilliance of what he does with or in spite of it. We are of opinion that this philosophy is not only doubtful but radically wrong and likely to mislead. It first appears in the Introduction, where Mr Symons tells us that 'No one has ever written more lucidly or more tenderly than Chaucer, more nobly or more musically than Spenser; but to Chaucer poetry was exclusively the telling of a story, and to Spenser it was partly picture-making and partly allegory.' And, again, while he admits that there is not so much poetry to be found anywhere in the world as in the Elizabethan; 'it is more often than not in scattered splendours and fragments severally alive'. It is in the nineteenth century that he finds poetry more pure and simple than in any earlier age. Poetry then he thinks 'wastes surprisingly little of its substance' because 'it realizes as its main concern what to most poets of the past had been, though their existence depended upon it, but lightly regarded—that imaginative atmosphere which is the very breath of poetry and adds strangeness to beauty'. It is not only poetry of a new kind but is more thoroughly poetry: 'it was realised that the end of poetry was to be poetry'. This looks very much like a revival and extension of Poe's opinion that there could be no such thing as a long poem. And so we find him criticizing a poem like 'Tintern Abbey' and telling us that 'we have to unravel the splendours and if we can forget the rest'. Apparently his advice to poets in general would have been Keats's advice to Shelley—to 'load every rift with ore', as if poetry were a precious substance to be procured at great cost, or by a great adventure like pearls or ivory. In one place he actually says: 'Opium might have helped to make Southey a poet', as if a man might procure poetry at the cost of ruining his stomach and moral fibre. The same heresy lurks in what he says of Keats: 'Passion was not less a disease to him than the disease of which he died, or than the art of writing verse.' Now, we should have been prepared to grant Mr Symons, for the time being, some of these extraordinary assumptions if he had not written his essay on Keats. That poet, in whom there is no personal utterance but only 'an enchantment which seems to have invented itself', so that 'we think of him as of a flattering mirror, in which the face of beauty becomes more beautiful; not as of the creator of beauty'—that poet is the most perfect example so far of the writer who has taken his own or Mr Symons's advice. And nevertheless, in finding 'numberless faults' in Keats, he has to admit that 'however closely we may look, and however many faults we may find, we shall end, as we began, by realising that they do not matter'. It is a fatal admission. It is one which can easily be so extended as to prove that the critic was on a wrong track, had accepted an imperfectly tested preference of his own, when he found only 'scattered splendours and fragments severally alive' in the Elizabethans, when he believed that he thought some of 'Tintern Abbey' unnecessary, when he allowed himself to except from certain poems a stanza, and even from certain stanzas a line which was not ore. The fact seems to be that in this critic's composition the literary aesthete is too predominant still, as at one time it was supreme. Several instances might be given to show that fortunately this too exclusive philosophy has not been perfectly followed in practice, but it has fettered him nevertheless. For it is an attempt to exalt a personal habit into a law. It is his habit to look for that loading of every rift with ore, and undoubtedly it has been valuable to him and is interesting to us. But it is not his whole nature, which is far too subtle for that. His whole nature has guided him to a very notable reconsideration of the romantic movement: it was by an error that he came to attribute so much more importance to that one side of it as to think it a judge instead of a witness. He has lighted upon many truths. But the truth he cannot extricate. He cannot show us what lies in his own mind behind such statements as that Blake is 'the only poet who is a poet in essence'. Wordsworth 'the supreme master of poetical style', Shelley one who cannot write unpoetically, Keats one to whom 'the thing itself and the emotion were indistinguishable'.

From review of *The Romantic Movement in English Literature* by Arthur Symons, *MP*, 20 January 1910

2 Earlier Poetry

WILLIAM BLAKE

IT IS IMPROBABLE, think Mr Maclagan and Mr Russell, that Blake will ever be a popular poet. It may be true; it is certainly a truism. But why should he be? Shakespeare is not popular: that is to say, the multitude does not sincerely admire his true excellences: nor is Milton. Tennyson's poetry is not exactly popular; it is the 'May Queen' that is popular. We are inclined to think, moreover, that the only poet who was ever popular is Longfellow, and even that exception depends upon the admission that he was a poet.

But of all poets Blake is the least likely to gain popularity. For it is part of his distinction that he speaks a language that few can understand. He had the supreme imagination which is the most reverend quality of great poetry, but which most effectually sets poets against the world; they see the world, as it were, from among the stars, while those who see it from the elevation of five or six feet, see it distorted and not as it really is. And Blake had this quality almost alone. In his youth, he had a gift of simple and fair speech; but he lost it. Although he could always catch the heavenly harmony of thoughts, he could seldom mount them on a fitting chariot of rhythm and rhyme. His fine passages were the direct gift of the Muse, and are followed by lines of other origin.

He wrote before his time, not because he was an innovator, but because he had glimpses of what the dead are supposed to see. Nothing he touched but he raised to its highest power. The microscope is a toy compared with his vision. He made human the stars and the seasons, and he made starry the flower and the grass. When he says, in this book, 'I write in South Molton Street what I both see and hear', the street seems to be something more than its builder knew. He saw the world as a commonwealth of angels and men and beasts and herbs; and in it horrible discords that we scarcely hear seemed to strike the stars. . . .

He wrote as a seraph and for seraphim. Men are not fit for this world.

Beautiful as it is and full of a glory which even the ignorant knows to be divine, it is full also of things which are, in his words: 'Shadowy to those who dwell not in them, mere possibilities,/But to those who enter into them they seem the only substances.'

It may be that 'this vegetable Universe' is but the faint shadow of his 'Real and Eternal World', but we that are shadows cling to the super-stition that we are not, and have but prejudiced and fearful ears for his prophecies. We recommend the book to those who can delight to lose themselves in a *selva oscura* and be content to guess at what hides therein. None save the impudently sane can affect not to be deeply moved by it. Nor are the trees thereof without fruits and flowers of beautiful colour and taste. Only, we admit that until Mr Russell and Mr Maclagan publish their explanation, and perhaps an explanation of that, there will be much 'believing where we cannot prove'. About matters of the spirit, men are all engaged in colloquies with them-selves. Some of them are overheard, and they are great poets. It is Blake's misfortune that he is not often overheard in *Jerusalem*.

From review of *The Prophetic Books of William Blake: Jerusalem*, ed. E.R.D. Maclagan and A.G.B. Russell, *DC*, 11 January 1904

ROBERT BURNS

IT IS ONE of the chief glories of Burns that he wrote love poems which every age, and not only his own, must recognize as equally true at once to the spirit of life and to the spirit of poetry. With his songs upon our lips Chloe seems a paper girl, and even Stella but a woman looking out of a picture, an old picture, on a wall. Except Shakes-peare's and Donne's there is hardly a woman of the lyric poets to be compared with Burns', who will stand the sunlight and the breath of life like his. . . .

In Burns, as in the earlier lyrists of Scotland, and more perfectly, love and a natural rusticity are in complete and most happy accord. The women have an outdoor grace: 'Blythest bird upon the bush / Had ne'er a lighter heart than she.'

They are like the rose of June; they are as fresh as a May morning, as sweet as evening among the new hay, and as blithe and artless as lambs. Only women like these, and men like their lovers from the fields and the hills, could express themselves in words and rhythms so light and so fresh as these, for example:

> Near me, near me,
> Laddie, lie near me!
> Long hae I lain my lane—
> Laddie, lie near me!

It is as near to the music as nonsense could be, and yet it is perfect sense. No other poet praises youth equally well for the cheerful and active sides of its characteristic virtues. Spirit and body are one in it— so sweet and free is the body and so well satisfied is the spirit to inhabit it. If they are sometimes sorrowful, either they will die quickly of sorrow or they will forget. Few poems are more unlike than these to the literature of 'emotion remembered in tranquillity'. They seem almost always to be the immediate fruit of a definite and particular occasion. They are not solitary poetry like 'I cannot give what men call love', which never was to be spoken except to the unpeopled air. They suggest instantly two persons, the lover, the beloved, one of them speaking or singing in a voice which does not know ennui or melancholy, or more than one feeling at any one moment; and the lover and the beloved are young and of good stature, with bright eyes, ruddy skins, and feet that can run and dance. They are a superb expression, with a few variations, of what a man of simple and hearty nature, full of blood, feels at the sight of a woman worthy to awaken his desire. But lover of individual women as Burns was, his poems do not individualize: they call up images only of woman, of youth and of desire.

Feminine Influence on the Poets, 285-94

LOVE POETRY

LOVE opens the door, but it does not know what is within, whether it be treasure, nothingness or devils; and of the unimagined things beyond the door love poetry is the revelation. The love poetry seems so often to have little to do with love is because we forget that there are matters in the presence of which any man and Shakespeare are equally impotent and silent. Many love poems were never shown to their begetters, many would not have moved them nor were in a sense meant for them at all. The love poem is not for the beloved, for it is not worthy, as it is the least thing that is given to her, and none knows this better than she unless it be the lover. It is written in solitude, is spent in silence and the night like a sigh with an unknown object. It may open with desire of woman, but it ends with unexpected consolation or with another desire not of woman. Love poetry, like all other lyric poetry, is in a sense unintentionally overheard, and only by accident and in part understood, since it is written not for any one, far less for the public, but for the understanding spirit that is in the air round about or in the sky or somewhere.

It is not only the present or past lover of one particular woman that can read and penetrate and enjoy love poems, and this fact alone might show how vain it is to regard them as addressed merely to those whose names they may bear. When do the words of love poems come into the mind or on to the lips? It is upon a hundred different occasions having nothing in common save that beauty is there or is desired. The sight of a fine landscape, recovery from sickness, rain in spring, music of bird or instrument or human voice, may at any time evoke as the utterance of our hearts the words long ago addressed to a woman who never saw them, and is now dead. And as these things revive poems in the mind of a reader, so certainly they have given birth to some of those poems in the minds of poets; and the figure of a woman is introduced unwittingly as a symbol of they know not what, perhaps only of desire; or if there is no woman mentioned, it will as often as not bring one into the thoughts and so prove, if need were, that hers was the original incantation. We treat them as parts written for ourselves to act, in the spirit, as they were written by the poet, in the spirit. *Feminine Influence*, 76-7

[Women's] chief influence in love has been exerted by the stimulation of desire—desire to possess not only them but other known and unknown things deemed necessary to that perfection of beauty and happiness which love proposes. It is a desire of impossible things which the poet alternately assuages and rouses again by poetry. He may attempt to sate it by violence in pleasure, in action, in wandering; but though he can make it impotent he cannot sate it: or he may turn his attempt inward upon himself. In either case he comes late or soon to poetry. There may seem to be infidelity in the act of writing, with its inevitable detachment from the very object of praise or complaint. If there were no night, no need of rest or food, no limit to the strength of the body or the vigour of the spirit, no obstacles of distance, custom, necessity and chance, not to speak of the woman's possible inability to love in return, it would be reasonable to speak of infidelity. There could be no love poetry in Paradise. It is made by unsatisfied desire, and that is made by our mortality and the conditions of life, which are essentially unalterable.   91-2

PERCY BYSSHE SHELLEY

JUST AS OAKS and roses do not abound entirely to make a botanist's holiday, but partly for birds to nest in, for schoolboys to climb in, and for young men and maidens to make garlands of; so Shelley's poetry is by no means entirely designed to provide amusement and advancement for critics, grammarians, lexicographers, professors of poetry, reviewers, collectors, spiders, etc. Keats may be a greater poet. Wordsworth and Byron may be more effectual. Matthew Arnold has said as much, and there are many who believe in the efficacy of repeating it, although it is not clear whether the critic condemned Shelley for any better reason than that he did not wear side-whiskers; but, as the satirist says, only so long as poets are under the direction of the Muses do they speak the truth.

Shelley is an immortal sentiment. Men may forget to repeat his verses; they can never be as if Shelley had never been. He is present wherever youth and love and rapture are. He is a part of all high-spirited and pure audacity of the intellect and imagination, of all clean-handed rebellion, of all infinite endeavour and hope. The remembered splendour of his face is more to us than the Houses of Parliament; the story of his life is mightier to move us than the eloquence of Bright or the energy of Faraday; one strophe of the 'Ode to Naples' is more nourishing than Mr Carnegie's gold.

How many times has Shelley (and the violets of Devon or the olives of Italy) been the half of a great passion? To how many does he not seem, during a great and lovely tract of life, to have been the half of spring and summer days, of autumn when it lays one finger on the land and the bryony leaf is suddenly burnt purple in the hedge; of night and dawn and noon; of youth enjoying these things? To such it comes as the final defeat, when Shelley is left dusty on the shelf; and the defection of a poet from the tribe of Shelley is the great apostasy of the nineteenth century. . . .

And even if we grant that it is true, and sometimes true it is, that Shelley fades, as the love of watching all the dawn will fade and give way to a liking for—let us name no names—and sunsets seen from a drawing-room; yet youth remains, if youths must pass, and it is surely much to be said for a poet that, at the moment when youth is most exultant, his poetry is thumbed night and day; that a page of his book is opened at random, as Virgil used to be opened, for a word big with fate; that his words come to the lips, seeming as suitable to light and darkness as Cassiopeia's crown, or as the sun when it works exquisitely in precious cloud and radiance on the hills. . . .

From review of *The Poetical Works of Percy Bysshe Shelley*, ed. Thomas Hutchinson, *DC*, 29 August 1905

JOHN CLARE

IT IS HARD to imagine a combination with more possibilities for wretchedness than that of poet and agricultural labourer. I mean a poet of any known breed. Of course, it is easy to invent a poet suddenly making poetry of all that dignity and beauty in the labourer's life which we are so ready to believe in. But such a one has not yet appeared. It is doubtful if he ever will, or if we ought to complain of the lack, since what we want to see in some perhaps impossible peasant poetry has always been an element in great poetry. If we knew their pedigrees, we should find more than one peasant among the ancestors of the poets. In fact, every man, poet or not, is a more or less harmonious combination of the peasant and the adventurer.

In no man have these two parts been more curiously combined than in John Clare, a real poet, however small, and actually an agricultural labourer out and out. He was far from being the kind of peasant poet who would be invented in an armchair. Mortal man could hardly be milder, more timid and drifting, than Clare. He heard voices from the grave, not of rustic wisdom and endurance, but

> Murmuring o'er one's weary woe,
> Such as once 'twas theirs to know,
> They whisper to such slaves as me
> A buried tale of misery. . . .

He looked back to childhood, asking: 'When shall I see such rest again?'
Contact with the town—'In crowded streets flowers never grew,/But many there hath died away.'—sharpened his nerves for natural beauty. The poet consumed the labourer in him, or left only the dregs of one, while the conditions of the labourer's life were as a millstone about his neck as poet. . . .

Unlike Burns, he had practically no help from the poetry and music of his class. He was a peasant writing poetry, yet cannot be called a peasant poet, because he had behind him no tradition of peasant litera- ture, but had to do what he could with the current forms of polite literature. The mastering of these forms absorbed much of his energy, so that for so singular a man he added little of his own, and the result was only thinly tinged with his personality, hardly at all with the general characteristics of his class. . . .

But it was in his power to do for his native district something like what Jefferies did for his. He possessed a similar fresh, sweet spirituality to that of Jefferies, a similar grasp and love of detail. Some of his plain descriptions anticipate and at least equal the nature article of to-day. His was a pedestrian Muse:

> who sits her down
> Upon the molehill's little lap,
> Who feels no fear to stain her gown,
> And pauses by the hedgerow gap.

And he often wrote long formless pieces full of place-names and of field-lore charmingly expressed, songs uttering his love and his pathetic joy in retrospection, poems mingling the two elements. A thousand things which the ordinary country child, 'tracking wild searches through the meadow grass', has to forget in order to live, Clare observed and noted—as, for example, how in July's drought 'E'en the dew is parched up/From the teasel's jointed cup.' In putting down some of these things with a lowly fidelity, he often achieves a more rustic truth than other poets, as in 'And rambling bramble-berries, pulpy and sweet,/Arching their prickly trails/Half o'er the narrow lane.' Sometimes he attains almost to magic, as in

> For when the world first saw the sun,
>   These little flowers beheld him, too;
> And when his love for earth begun,
>   They were the first his smiles to woo.
> There little lambtoe bunches springs
>   In red-tinged and begolden dye,
> For ever, and like China kings
>   They come, but never seem to die.

He was something more and less than a peasant become articulate. For example, he had an unexpected love, not only of the wild, but of the waste places, the 'commons left free in the rude rags of Nature', 'the old molehills of glad neglected pastures'. Though he did call the henbane 'stinking', he half loved it for the places, like Cowper's Green, where he found it, with bramble, thistle, nettle, hemlock,

> And full many a nameless weed,
> Neglected, left to run to seed,
> Seen but with disgust by those
> Who judge a blossom by the nose.
> Wildness is my suiting scene,
> So I seek thee, Cowper Green.

To enumerate the flowers was a pleasure to him, and he did so in a manner which preserves them still dewy, or with summer dust, perhaps, on 'an antique mullein's flannel-leaves'. Can he ever have cultivated his garden? If he did, and then wrote: 'Hawkweed and groundsel's fanning downs/Unruffled keep their seeded crowns', he must have been a kind of saint; and, indeed, he had such a love for wild things as some saints have had, which he shows in the verses:

> I left the little birds
> And sweet lowing of the herds,
> And couldn't find out words,
>   Do you see,
> To say to them good-bye,
> Where the yellowcups do lie;
> So heaving a deep sigh
>   Took to sea.

When he lamented leaving his old home, he did not mention the building itself, but the neighbouring heath,

> its yellow furze,
> Molehills and rabbit tracks that lead
> Through beesom, ling, and teasel burrs . . .

the trees, the lanes, the stiles, the brook, the flowers, the shepherd's-purse that grew in the old as well as the new garden: 'The very crow/Croaked music in my native fields.'

One of his Asylum Poems, first printed by Mr Arthur Symons, is full of place-names that were music to him, and become so to us: 'Langley Bush', 'Eastwell's boiling spring', 'old Lee Close oak', 'old Cross-berry Way', 'pleasant Swordy Well' again, 'Round Oak', 'Sneap Green', 'Puddock's Nook', 'Hilly Snow'—as he mourns:

> And Crossberry Way and old Round Oak's narrow lane
> With its hollow trees like pulpits I shall never see again.
> Enclosure like a Buonaparte let not a thing remain,
> It levelled every bush and tree and levelled every hill
> And hung the moles for traitors, though the brook is running still
> It runs a naked stream cold and chill.

But he had the farm life also by heart, and, along with blackbird and robin and magpie, drew the dog chasing the cat, the cows tossing the molehills in their play, the shepherd's dog daunted by the rolled-up hedgehog, the maids singing ballads at milking or hanging out linen around the elder-skirted croft, while

> The gladden'd swine bolt from the sty,
>   And round the yard in freedom run,
> Or stretching in their slumbers lie
>   Beside the cottage in the sun.
> The young horse whinnies to his mate,
>   And, sickening from the thresher's door,
> Rubs at the straw-yard's banded gate,
>   Longing for freedom on the moor.

No man ever came so near to putting the life of the farm, as it is lived, not as it is seen over a five-barred gate, into poetry. He gives no broad impressions—he saw the kite, but not the kite's landscape—yet his details accumulate in the end, so that a loving reader, and no one reads him but loves him, can grasp them, and see the lowlands of Northamptonshire as they were when the kite still soared over them.

A Literary Pilgrim in England, 229-35

Love, Nature and Liberty are three, but indivisible on the pages of many poets, of young poets who sit like Lamartine upon an island like a poet's dream in a fair sea, and foster the double dream of those who are worthy to dream great things: Love and Liberty. To that island they have gone to look upon sky and sea, to let the spirit evaporate in the sun, to feel and to record the ferment of youthful impressions, sentiments, and ideas which some day will make poetry. . . .

Perhaps the most unanswerable testimony of all is to be found in the poetry which John Clare wrote during his twenty years' imprisonment in a madhouse. He had already in earlier days called his Muse a wild enchantress, and had wooed her on a bed of thyme, and had seen solitude as a woman with wild ringlets lying unbound over her lily shoulders. He had already written a poem on the 'Death of Beauty':

> Now thou art gone, the fairy rose is fled,
> That erst gay Fancy's garden did adorn.
> Thine was the dew on which her folly fed,
> The sun by which she glittered in the morn. . . .

But he was to get far beyond this statement that with the death of the woman died Nature's beauty. These latest and finest poems leave personifications far behind. His native trees and fields, and the women he loved after they had died or vanished, haunted him in his prison. His mind seemed to shed all its mere intelligence and all its conventionality in the use of words. He was left free as a spirit in his ghastly solitude. Then to him his Mary became a part of the spring, a part inexplicably absent. He had talked to the flowers when a child, and when a man they had 'told the names of early love' : now that he was alone, they decked 'the bier of spring'. But if one of the Marys came into his mind it was in as complete a harmony with Nature as one of Wordsworth's women, yet with little or nothing of his thin spiritual quality. The woman of 'The Invitation' is real:

> Come with thy maiden eye, lay silks and satins by;
> Come in thy russet or grey cotton gown;
> Come to the meads, dear, where flags, sedge, and reeds appear,
> Rustling to soft winds and bowing low down.

If she is a spirit, she is a spirit of the English earth, not of the transparent air. . . . Perhaps the maddest and most perfect of the asylum poems, 'Love lives beyond the tomb', is remarkable for nothing so much as for its eloquent but inexplicable expression of this harmony of nature and love. It must therefore be quoted in full:

Love lives beyond the tomb,
And earth which fades like dew!
I love the fond,
The faithful and the true.

Love lives in sleep:
'Tis happiness of healthy dreams:
Eve's dews may weep,
But love delightful seems.

'Tis seen in flowers,
And in the morning's pearly dew;
In earth's green hours,
And in the heaven's eternal blue.

'Tis heard in spring,
When light and sunbeams, warm and kind,
On angel's wing
Bring love and music to the mind.

And where's the voice,
So young, so beautiful, and sweet
As Nature's choice,
Where spring and lovers meet?

Love lives beyond the tomb,
And earth, which fades like dew!
I love the fond,
The faithful and the true.

This and perhaps all of his best poems show Clare as one of those who
have in them the natural spirit of poetry in its purity, so pure that
perhaps he can never express it quite whole and perfect. They are
songs of innocence, praising a world not realized, or, it is more
reasonable to say, a world which most old and oldish people agree to
regard as something different. For such a writer the usual obstacles
and limits are temporary or do not exist at all, and as with children the
dividing line between the real and the unreal either shifts or has not
yet been made. No man or woman is a poet who does not frequently, to
the end of life, ignore these obstacles and limits, which are not just and
absolute but represent the golden mean or average, and have less
reality than the equator. Few, except idiots, can escape them altogether, since they are produced by weariness and compromise, which
are produced by time and without effort. Some great men escape while
seeming to accept them, but there is hardly a pleasure in the world
equal to that of seeing one who is not a child and has yet escaped them
so happily as Clare. He reminds us that words are alive, and not only

alive but still half-wild and imperfectly domesticated. They are quiet and gentle in their ways, but are like cats—to whom night overthrows our civilization and servitude—who seem to love us but will starve in the house which we have left, and thought to have emptied of all worth. Words never consent to correspond exactly to any object unless, like scientific terms, they are first killed. Hence the curious life of words in the hands of those who love all life so well that they do not kill even the slender words but let them play on; and such are poets. The magic of words is due to their living freely among things, and no man knows how they came together in just that order when a beautiful thing is made like 'Full fathom five'. And so it is that children often make phrases that are poetry, though they still more often produce it in their acts and half-suggested thoughts; and that grown men with dictionaries are as murderous of words as entomologists of butterflies.

Here, I think, in 'Love lives beyond the tomb', in this unprejudiced singing voice that knows not what it sings, is some reason for us to believe that poets are not merely writing figuratively when they say, 'My love is like a red, red rose', that they are to be taken more literally than they commonly are, that they do not invent or 'make things up' as grown people do when they condescend to a child's game. What they say is not chosen to represent what they feel or think, but is itself the very substance of what had before lain dark and unapparent, is itself all that survives of feeling and thought, and cannot be expanded or reduced without dulling or falsification. If this is not so, and if we do not believe it to be so, then poetry is of no greater importance than wallpaper, or a wayside drink to one who is not thirsty. But if it is so, then we are on the way to understand why poetry is mighty; for if what poets say is true and not feigning, then of how little account are our ordinary assumptions, our feigned interests, our playful and our serious pastimes spread out between birth and death. Poetry is and must always be apparently revolutionary if active, anarchic if passive. It is the utterance of the human spirit when it is in touch with a world to which the affairs of 'this world' are parochial. Hence the strangeness and thrill and painful delight of poetry at all times, and the deep response to it of youth and of love; and because love is wild, strange, and full of astonishment, is one reason why poetry deals so much in love, and why all poetry is in a sense love poetry.

Feminine Influence on the Poets, 80-7

JOHN KEATS

The Odes

'TO AUTUMN', also [like the 'Ode to Psyche'], it would be perverse to class with 'Isabella' mainly on account of the customary sadness of Autumn, the use of 'soft-dying', 'wailful', 'mourn' and 'dies' in the last verse, and in the last line, 'And gathering swallows twitter in the skies', something light, thin, cold, and vanishing, especially by comparison with the mellowness and slowness of the other verses, with all their long 'oo' and 'ou' and 'aw' and 'z' sounds, as in the line, 'Thou watchest the last oozings hours by hours.'

The 'Ode on Melancholy' is one of the central poems of this period, admitting, as it does so fully, and celebrating, the relationship between melancholy and certain still pleasures. Nowhere is the connoisseurship of the quiet, withdrawn spectator so extremely and remorselessly put. The 'rich anger' of the mistress is to be a precious, delicious object; her 'peerless eyes' are to be devoured as roses. Richer juice could not be extracted from poison-flowers. Miss Mary Suddard, one of his best critics, says that 'Keats, like Jaques, spent his whole life chewing the cud of sweet and bitter fancy, and, still more, of sweet and bitter sensation'; and the poem, taken literally, seems to say that the bitter with the sweet is worth while—is the necessary woof of life—and makes for the fullness of the banquet, which is so gorgeous that death seems its solemn closing music, and it is 'rich to die'. In short, he flatters life and the bitterness of it, and men that have to drink it. Since the Greeks called the Furies the Blessed Ones there has been no choicer flattery of life. Like the other odes, but above them, this one on Melancholy touches the summit of expression for what Miss Suddard called the 'ruminant' nature.

'To a Nightingale' is in the same tone, except that it has an outdoor setting, and is tinged with action, and comes to an end with a slow restoration of every-day light and with a question. Nor does it pretend to content. There is a pain in the numbness, a desire of escape from the 'embalmed darkness', an impatience of any end to the banquet saving death. Yet the variety in the richness of the poem is made by that very pain, desire, and impatience. To complain of the opening, 'My heart aches, and a drowsy numbness pains/My sense, as though of hemlock I had drunk', is useless. For England does not send poets into exile with crowns; our civilization is by no means assured what is good and what is evil, and whether the evil is to be rejected, since, after all, men are lower than the angels. Only a very bold man, outside a pulpit, would pronounce that such poetry infects life and literature. What is most excellent in its kind establishes that kind. You cannot prove that this poem hastens the decay of those who incline towards such things in life and in literature; still less, that to take it away is to arrest their falling. Many that admire it have no such inclination, and will suffer from a vision of these things at best no more than men in the old days suffered by thinking of Paradise. Instead of corrupting them it will deepen their taste of life, and perhaps also their understanding. They will enjoy it; their enjoyment of very different things, like Pindar's or Shelley's poetry, will be increased. But I am not attempting to answer the man who should say that after boiling the ode 'To a Nightingale' he found only peevishness at the bottom of it. I do think, however, that melancholy (in spite of the ode) is too disparaging a name for this mood, and that we have been deceived into suspecting evil of the poem because it is beautiful and attributes divinity to what we think a weakness. None today would complain if the thought had remained in this lyrical form:

> Welcome joy, and welcome sorrow,
>   Lethe's weed and Hermes' feather!
> Come today, and come tomorrow;
>   I do love you both together;

we should begin to talk earnestly of the gospel of pain.

I shall not set about a demonstration from the beginning that the ode truly is one of the things that are most excellent. I will, however, mention one indication of its excellence. It and the ode 'On a Grecian Urn' are of a texture so consummate and consistent that the simple line, 'The grass, the thicket, and the fruit-tree wild,' in one of them, and an equally simple line in the other, 'With forest branches, and the trodden weed,' both gain from their environment an astonishing beauty, profound and touching.

The ode 'On a Grecian Urn' is preferred, by some people and some moods, to 'The Nightingale' and the rest, because it is the most universal and intellectual, the calmest as well as the stillest, of all. Its personality is submerged, and the more intense for that. The poet flatters the figures on the urn because they are dead and fixed in attitudes of desire, so that they will never suffer like living men, 'a heart high-sorrowful and cloy'd,/A burning forehead, and a parching tongue,' and forasmuch as they have the intensity of beauty which can 'tease us out of thought' into their own marble blessedness. The poem has two doubtful blemishes, the suggestion of a pun in 'O Attic shape! Fair attitude!' and the odd break in the last line but one which compels us to attribute 'Beauty is Truth, Truth Beauty,' to the Urn, and '—that is all/Ye know on earth, and all ye need to know,' to the poet. But this last may be an accidental typographical error, and these things rarely, as a matter of fact, modify in the least degree the impression left. The poem also is free from all but the lightest touch of the morbidity of 'Melancholy' and 'The Nightingale', if indeed 'a burning forehead and a parching tongue' and 'for ever panting' are felt as morbid—I incline to think they are universal as the rest, as the whole is.

Thus in the odes the poet made for himself a form in which the essence of all his thought, feeling, and observation, could be stored without overflowing or disorder; of its sources in his daily life there was no more shown than made his poems quick instead of dead. Their perfection is like that of a few of Milton's and Spenser's poems. They are among the unquestionable mortal achievements.

Keats, 53-7

ALFRED TENNYSON

SIR ALFRED LYALL has overcome many of the difficulties of his task. He has inwoven, with perhaps too little narrative, a biography of Tennyson's poetic life. Above all, he has given us, as he is well able to do, a vivid impression of what the poet was to his own time. And though he has wisely not taken the opportunity, somewhat illegitimate in a book of this kind, of refining his own general and scattered judgments and giving us what he may regard as Tennyson's special quality and particular achievement, yet here and elsewhere there is shrewd material for one of those estimates which are the natural outcome of lively interest in a poet's work. Such an interest may suggest that among English poets one division can be made without violence. On the one hand are those whom we may call the men of action in fields of thought and imagination, men puzzled to some purpose by the riddles of their own day, men whose loftiest moods are warmed or troubled by the strife of their contemporaries. Thus, not to go farther back, Shelley confessed to a passion for reforming the world, and Crabbe did nothing else. On the other hand, there is a long line of poets who, even if, like Sidney, they are in the sphere of action a great part of their own age, yet write like recluses, and might belong to any age. Sidney, Carew, Gray and Keats are of this family. They are the poets' poets. Of these Tennyson is not the least. Nearly all his immediate predecessors had been at some time conspicuously moved by the great tremors of their day. Tennyson's age, as Sir Alfred Lyall says, was one 'of practical liberalism, of strong intellectual fermentation stimulated by the growing power of the Press; of energetic agitation for political, economical, and legislative reforms'—in short, an age that would not easily and directly impress a poet's mind. In accordance with this temper he was 'one of the few great English poets who have fallen in readily with the ways and manners of a cultured class and their social surroundings, who did not in their youth either hold themselves apart from the ordinary life of school or college, or live recklessly or rebel against social conventions'. The length and calm undulation of his own life was in remarkable harmony with the years in which he lived. He was never much in love with any wandering that meant a long remove from his high-backed chair. It was, therefore, not to be expected that he should be in a very obvious way influenced by 'the spirit of the age'. Here, then, was an opportunity for the artistic temperament to develop within its own world, 'in a green shade'.

And to us Tennyson's poems seem to be the history of a sensibility and an intellectual balance in unrivalled combination. He contracted tricks; his sweetness was apt to resemble wedding-cake; and his weakest performances almost justify the opinion that he was the greatest minor poet that ever lived. Nevertheless, he shows at his best a felicitous choice of subject and an execution that remind us of Raphael. We may almost say of him—such is his voluptuous avoidance of excess—'His strength is as the strength of ten,/Because his heart is pure.' From his eighteenth year, when the *Poems by Two Brothers* were published, to 1842, his thirty-fourth year, when the *Morte d'Arthur* appeared, his life met the utmost needs of his exquisite poetic frame. He was devoted to the beautiful in art, Nature, books and human life. The nature of his devotion is to be read in 'The Lady of Shalott', 'A Dream of Fair Women' and 'The Palace of Art'. These poems and their companions, as we think, place him high among the lotus-givers of life, among those who make 'a flowery band to bind us to the earth'. As we read the verses,

> There she weaves by night and day
> A magic web with colours gay.
> She has heard a whisper say,
> A curse is on her if she stay
>   To look down on Camelot.
> She knows not what the curse may be,
> And so she weaveth steadily,
> And little other care hath she,
>   The Lady of Shalott.
>
> And moving through a mirror clear
> That hangs before her all the year,
> Shadows of the world appear.
> There she sees the highway near
>   Winding down to Camelot:
> There the river eddy whirls,
> And there the surly village-churls,
> And the red cloaks of market-girls,
>   Pass onward from Shalott.

. . . we are sometimes disposed to think of the poet writing with 'little other care'. The curse that threatened him was of the same kind. Whenever he turned to contemporary life, except in his own person, the mirror received a crack, his power decreased. For he never saw life dramatically. When he thinks, he is a much-read child. Luckily, in his golden age, he never thinks. Sir Alfred Lyall has much to say about the moral of, for example, 'The Palace of Art'. But could anything be sadder than that a man should spin those perfect verses in order to point the same moral as a hundred pulpits? As it seems to us, a far subtler moral may be drawn from the capacity of a most delicate soul for a diversity of sensuous enjoyments that yet does not fail in strength or in sympathy with everyday life. Tennyson has done more to assert the true nobleness—we had almost said saintliness—of the perfect artist than all the apologists. Sir Alfred Lyall insists, more and more as we reach and pass *The Princess* and *In Memoriam*, upon the importance of Tennyson's attitude towards life. That he was always occupied as a man with the questions of his day is true, but at his finest period he seems to have felt that his powers were out of place in the world which attracted Browning. From no poet do we so often quote for the sake of beauty. From no poet is the thought—except his later thought, and that from the pulpit—so rarely quoted. His command of pathos, for the same reason, is usually slight; and his finest passage (in *Morte d'Arthur*) comes straight from Malory. If Coleridge discovered, in Shelley's phrase, a kind of 'thought in sense', Tennyson amplified it and revealed its fullest possibilities. He was a sybarite in sensuous meditation and meditative emotion. He never wrote a successful poem on a subject (vulgarly speaking) of any importance. What we value is the quality of his voice, just as in a great singer. . . .

We have alluded to his 'thought in sense'. Nowhere is that more opulent than in his treatment of nature. Sir Alfred Lyall lays stress on his 'painting' nature, as distinct from Wordsworth's method of describing nature by her effects. At his best he certainly proves nature a sentient and passionate thing. A cadence, an epithet, a grouping, in nearly all his descriptions, seems to give the landscape a brain and heart that fluctuate with his own. But here again he is the recluse. His nature has not 'that universal spirit of the world' which Bacon felt in April. His is an entirely personal impression, far different from Wordsworth's, which made of nature a neighbour commonwealth to our own. We are interested in the one man 'Who paced for ever in a glimmering land, / Lit with a low large moon.' When he begins to think, nature is 'red in tooth and claw'; and we become interested only in seeing Darwin done into verse. Parts of *In Memoriam* are melancholy attempts, followed by innumerable others, to show the world that he kept up with the thought of his time.

From review of *Tennyson* by Sir Alfred Lyall, *DC*, 7 October 1902

GEORGE MEREDITH

AS MR G.M. TREVELYAN says: 'The characters in [Meredith's] novels put on their full grandeur only when they stand in direct contact with Nature: Vernon Whitford in his sleep under the wild white [double] cherry-tree; Diana by the mountain pool above the Italian lake; Beauchamp at sea or under the Alps at dawn; Ottilia at sea or in the thunderstorm; Emilia by Wilming Weir or in the moonlit fir-tree glade; Carinthia Jane when she goes out to "call the morning" in her mountain home; Lucy by the plunging weir, amid the bilberries, long grass, and meadowsweet.' But in his poetry you have in its concentrated hieroglyphics the religion of which the novels exhibit some of the characteristics as found in the laity. Then you have walking—

> A pride of legs in motion kept
>   Our spirits to their task meanwhile,
> And what was deepest dreaming slept

—and the incidents of walking, as a pleasure, as a joy, as a medicine. For the Tramps themselves, and for all other Sunday or weekday walkers who delight in one another's company, and talk as they walk, he wrote the 'Stave of Roving Tim':

> You live in rows of snug abodes,
>   With gold, maybe, for counting:
> And mine's the beck of the rainy roads
>   Against the sun a-mounting.

And the joy of the limbs, the senses, and the brain, during country walks—in certain isolated days—are expressed by Meredith once and for all, with a kind of braced hedonistic Puritanism. But though he loved what he saw and heard and touched, his poetry was never purely sensuous, and it became less and less so. Like Shelley, he felt the moral qualities of Nature. It has been said of Shelley's lark, 'Bird thou never wert'; and of Meredith's, that it is a real lark. But this is a mistake. Meredith was more of a naturalist, and he belonged to a generation of amateur naturalists, but he gets at least as far away from the bird as Shelley does, if he starts closer. Tastes differ, but to me what is descriptive in the poem reminds me too much of the bird. I can always hear a lark, and no man can do more than interest me by an imaged inventory of what it says. The opening passage of 'The Lark Ascending' shows observation, admiration, and delight, and they are well served by fancy; the result is an encumbrance of words and a dispersed impression, half sensuous, half intellectual. That it was done with the eye on the object is obvious, but not to the point, except that it is thus distinguished from other poems relating to larks. What gives it a great claim is that it was done, and that very clearly, by a man in whom, as in no other, says Mr Justin McCarthy, the physical and mental forces were absolute rivals and equals. The same is true of a great portion of Meredith's poetry, and I shall not dispute whether it can be fully enjoyed by those possessing neither the same powers nor the same balance between them. Nature to him was not merely a cause of sensuous pleasure, nor, on the other hand, an inhuman enchantress; neither was she both together. When he spoke of Earth, he meant more than most mean who speak of God. He meant that power which in the open air, in poetry, in the company of noble men and women, prompted, strengthened, and could fulfil, the desire of a man to make himself, not a transitory member of a parochial species, but a citizen of the Earth. . . .

He is always lean and hard, an athlete among poets. Sometimes he is overtrained, too fine. He got away from the Earth and the things of the Earth to intellectual analogues of them, outran the measure (wrote, for example, a kind of shorthand instead of poetry), allowed his love to exceed too far 'a simple love of the things/That glide in grasses and rubble of woody wreck', forsook 'the great heaths' bordering the Portsmouth Road—he always lived near the Portsmouth Road—and took to regions of the mind where blows a keener and more desolating wind than ever blew from the thirty-two points. But at best his poetry is good walking country in good walking weather. His nightingales are 'real nightingales', very distantly related to Philomela. There are no fumes in his brain, and thence in his poetry. His country is English— not so English as Tennyson's; it is too Meredithian for that—his planet is indubitably the Earth, of which he was one of the most loyal and distinguished inhabitants.

A Literary Pilgrim in England, 49-52

WILLIAM MORRIS

CHAUCER is the only one of our great poets belonging to the middle ages, and consequently the only one whose life and work can remind us that there was a day when the poet was only incidentally, and as it were without knowing it, an artist. He was in no essential separated from the society in which he moved. He did many things in London, at Windsor and abroad, and his writing was one of them and harmonious with them. He reveals himself far less obviously and deliberately than other poets because the poet, like the man, was social and not isolated. His work was naturally and happily himself: it was not an individual but a corporate view of life, and represents his age more than it does Chaucer. He did not assert himself because he was not so cut off from his audience that he was bound to do so. In the changed world of the

Reformation no writer shows this social quality except the maker of street ballads. Even Shakespeare is solitary and exceptional. The man himself stands apart from his age in a kind of inevitable exile: Chaucer, on the other hand, is his age and can merge his identity in it with safety. As for lyric poets, they appear but sudden sharp voices as of birds flying over in a dark night: only elaborate historical work can in part destroy this illusion. And as time advances more and more of the poets are in a like isolation. It has become an exaggerated truism that poets may mean far more to posterity than to their own age. They are unnoticed spectators standing on the outside or at the edge of the life which they record. Milton was consciously out of place in his age and out of sympathy with it. The poets of the Augustan age, through their politics, seem to be exceptional; but they are more professional than ever, and moreover they have not weathered the passing of time as well as others. What a difference, again, between Chaucer and Cowper! Chaucer with so little appearance of being exceptional save in the intensity of his powers, writing about neighbours for neighbours; Cowper buried away with a few friendly women and ministers, addressing the world as out of a hermitage, interesting largely as a curiosity, even to himself 'a stricken deer'.

This increase of solitude has continued. Shelley began by talking with a kind of gaiety about writing for a dozen people, and ended with a feeling, something like paralysis, due to the total lack of communion with an audience. Nor has the spurious publicity of gossip in our own times done anything to alter the conditions of authorship. The break-up of religion, the disorganization of society, the multiplication of readers, have isolated artists more and more. Hence an infinite variety, a tendency to insist upon individuality for its own sake, so that there are men of singular ability who only appeal to a handful, a hundred, a few hundreds, whom they may or may never reach.

But from time to time men have arisen who have broken away by dint of extraordinary personality from the solitude of professional author-ship, and have gained half their power by calling attention to them-selves and their work at the same time, instead of remaining like needles in their own haystacks. Byron in poetry and Borrow in prose are supreme examples. Everything about their lives is eagerly devoured and discussed, and their work gains by additions from their lives: it is impossible yet to look at their work simply as art, as we can look at Wordsworth's or Keats's.

William Morris was a man of such personality that his failure to become one of these men like Byron and Borrow is somewhat astonishing. He appears to have failed just because of the diversity which was his power. . . .

Whatever he did he did well, and in many things he was an originator and more than a good performer. But for a modern artist he dissipated his forces too much. No one work of his can be taken alone and fairly be held to represent his powers. His work shows him as a firm rather than as one man, as 'Morris & Co.', even though it was all essentially William Morris. So many qualities were related and united in the man which appear separate and weak in the poet and craftsman. Valuing as he did above all things 'consciousness of manly life', and thinking the arts a part of this, he was perhaps incapable of the artificial pampered concentration of a man like Tennyson. Modern conditions preyed upon him overmuch for this. In his lecture on 'Art and its Producers' he betrays a feeling that troubling about arts and crafts might seem 'petty and unheroic' to those who have been brought face to face with 'the reckless hideousness and squalor of a great manufacturing district'. He cared for both, for the arts and crafts and for the 'shabby hell' of the city and he did not think or find the two cares incompatible, but rather insisted that they were one, though he found one crowded life, busy, never hurried, and of no unusual length, too small for his purpose. A similar apparent division of passion is to be seen in 'The Message of the March Wind', where the lover on an eve when his mistress is given to him and to gladness asks:

> Shall we be glad always? Come closer and hearken:
> Three fields further on, as they told me down there,
> When the young moon has set, if the March sky should darken,
> We might see from the hill-top the great city's glare.

But here the division is healed in a beautiful union between love of one woman and of the world, and the lover ends:

> But lo, the old inn, and the lights, and the fire,
>   And the fiddler's old tune and the shuffling of feet;
> Soon for us shall be quiet and rest and desire,
>   And to-morrow's uprising to deeds shall be sweet.

This union makes the poem one of the finest single poems of Morris and of his age.

From review of *The Collected Works of William Morris*,
B, February 1911

ALGERNON CHARLES SWINBURNE

Atalanta in Calydon

[THE] STORY IS obliterated by the form of a Greek drama, by abundant lyrics put into the mouth of a Greek chorus, by Greek idioms and cast of speech, and by an exuberance and individuality of language which could not always transmit instantaneously a definite meaning. But the obscurity is not one of incompetence, the imperfectly intelligible speech is not an imperfection: at least it persuades and insinuates itself so into the mind that perhaps not many pause at the end of the first sentence, part of the Chief Huntsman's address to Artemis:

> Maiden, and mistress of the months and stars
> Now folded in the flowerless fields of heaven,
> Goddess whom all gods love with threefold heart,
> Being treble in thy divided deity,
> A light for dead men and dark hours afoot
> Swift on the hills as morning, and a hand
> To all things fierce and fleet that roar and range
> Mortal, with gentler shafts than snow or sleep;
> Hear now and help and lift no violent hand
> But favourable and fair as thine eyes beam
> Hidden and shown in heaven; for I all night
> Amid the king's hounds and the hunting men
> Have wrought and worshipped toward thee; nor shall man
> See goodlier hounds or deadlier edge of spears;
> But for the end, that lies unreached at yet
> Between the hands and on the knees of the Gods.

The effect must always be partly that of a translation even to those who are familiar with Greek religion; the words have a shade of the quality inseparable from a translation, whether it is or is not creative, for it is to be found in the Authorized Version of the Bible; the reader is a little confused and yet not unduly, when he hears of Artemis as a light 'for dead men and dark hours', of the fair-faced sun that kills 'the stars and dews and dreams and desolations of the night', for it is not English thus to collect four things of four different classes, each requiring a distinct change in the meaning of the verb which governs them all. Perhaps the reader at first accepts 'hidden and shown', and even the alternative pairs, 'roar and range', 'snow or sleep', 'favourable and fair' etc., as part of the foreignness. It does not decrease. It is not absent from:

> When the hounds of spring are on winter's traces,
>   The mother of months in meadow or plain
> Fills the shadows and windy places
>   With lisp of leaves and ripple of rain;
> And the brown bright nightingale amorous
>   Is half assuaged for Itylus,
> For the Thracian ships and the foreign faces,
>   The tongueless vigil and all the pain.

Only, here it is apparent that 'the shadows and windy places' may be due to rhyme; at least it seems a false limiting or defining of the action of the lisp of leaves and ripple of rain, as later on 'peril of shallow and firth' is a distinction with insufficient definiteness of difference. But the metre is powerful enough to overcome this difficulty, or to keep it from rising; it makes us feel that we may go astray if we ask why the nightingale is called 'bright' as well as 'brown'. Later on it may be suspected that 'bright' is due partly to Swinburne's need of alliteration, partly to his love of the 'i' sound and of brightness. Anyone inclined to show and expect a stiff exactingness will be shocked at finding 'summer' and not 'spring', 'autumn', or 'winter'—'remembrance' without 'forgetfulness' and so on—in the famous lyric:

> Before the beginning of years
>   There came to the making of man
> Time, with a gift of tears;
>   Grief with a glass that ran;
> Pleasure, with pain for leaven;
>   Summer, with flowers that fell;
> Remembrance fallen from heaven,
> And madness risen from hell.

This, however, has that appearance of precision which Swinburne always affected, which is nothing but an appearance. Nor would he have claimed that it was anything more. He was filling his verse with solemn images acceptable to that part of the human brain which is not occupied with the music of the words and the reverberation of earlier images. It may be that Time received the 'gift of tears' instead of the 'glass that ran' solely for the sake of alliteration. It would doubtless be better if it were not so, but nothing can be perfect from every point of view, and this deceitful deference to the pure intellect I speak of chiefly to show what Swinburne's use of the sounds and implications of words can overcome. Reverberation of sound and meaning as in Milton's: 'Chariot and charioteer lay overturned:' and Coleridge's icicles: 'Quietly shining to the shining moon:' are a great part of *Atalanta*. Scores of times words and sounds are repeated as in:

> Saw with strange eyes and with strange lips rejoiced,
> Seeing these mine own slain of mine own, and me
> Made miserable above all miseries made:

'Breath' calls for the rhyme of 'death', and 'light' for 'night', with more transparent purpose than in other writing; 'all' demands to be repeated with a persistency that is not to be denied.

Some of the repetitions may indicate simply the poet's infatuation with certain words, but that infatuation would not be without significance. The use of the verb and the substantive 'dream' six times in eighteen lines spoken by Althaea, and the constant use of 'divide' and 'division' (not to speak of 'sever' and 'sunder'), and above all of 'fire' and 'light', 'bright' and 'shine'—these are not accidents. 'Fire' and 'light', 'bright' and 'shine', with 'desire' and 'high' and 'sky', and other words which their vowel sound and Swinburne's usage make cognate, were to become master words in his poetry. It can almost be said that he never writes one of those words without repeating it or matching it with one of the others. Whether it be through the influence of these words or something in the 'i' sound that his nature found expressive, I cannot say, but in many of the poems in all his books it is predominant, so that when he praises a thing he must call it bright: the wind is bright, the sea is bright: and for him the characteristic quality of the human face is its light.   *Algernon Charles Swinburne*, 13-17

The play cannot be abridged or divided without complete destruction. There are few separable phrases or passages in it that are not far more beautiful in their places, because the key to them is only to be found in the play, not in the human breast. The whole should be read, or heard, at a sitting, for the first time at least. Pause, to let in the light of every day, and it may seem as it did to Browning, 'a fuzz of words'. It is very nicely balanced above folly. It is one-sided and makes but a single appeal. It can suffer by the intrusion of the world, the sound of men talking or nightingales singing. For it does not appeal to us as men knowing aught of men or nightingales: experience can add nothing to it, or take away anything; and today it cannot be seriously blamed for a chorus which, as Tennyson said, abused the deity in the style of the Hebrew prophets. The words in it have no rich inheritance from old usage of speech or poetry, even when they are poetic or archaic or Biblical. They have little variety of tone, being for the most part majestically mournful, and never suddenly changing tone. Variety is given chiefly by the metre, and the differences of that are almost numberless. The blank verse changes and does everything save speak. As to the lyric verse it is of many forms, and each is so clear cut and so masterful to words without show of tyranny that a man might suppose any words would do as well and would maintain the same joy of metre. Hardly do we notice in the sweetness of it an un-English phrase like 'imminence of wings' or 'the innumerable lily', after the opening: 'O that I now, I too were/By deep wells and water-floods. . . .' Again and again it tempts us to recall the opinion that the words are everything, and say that they are nothing; certainly it matters little what exactly is meant by 'bodies of things to be in the houses of death and of birth'. It is sufficient that the words never impede the music, and often colour it with something noble, or delicate, or pathetic, that the 'rhythm', as

Burne-Jones said, 'goes on with such a rush that it is enough to carry the world away.' Swinburne could make even a line of monosyllables swift and leaping by using in the unaccented places negligible words, like 'and', 'of', and 'the', which are almost silent. Tennyson wrote to the poet telling him that he envied him his wonderful rhythmical invention. Tennyson's own had always been carefully experimental and subordinate; in *Atalanta* rhythm was paramount, in rule sole and undivided.   21-3

Poems and Ballads

Love of sound and especially of rhyme persuaded [Swinburne] to a somewhat lighter use of words than is common among great poets. Space would be wasted by examples of words produced apparently by submission to rhyme, not mastery over it. The one line in 'Hesperia': 'Shrill shrieks in our faces the blind bland air that was mute as a maiden', is enough to illustrate the poet's carelessness of the fact that alliteration is not a virtue in itself.

Since the adjective is most ready when words are wanted he used a great number, yet without equally great variety. He kept as it were a harem of words, to which he was constant and absolutely faithful. Some he favoured more than others, but he neglected none. He used them more often out of compliment than of necessity. Compare his 'bright fine lips' with the passages quoted by Ruskin from Shakespeare, Shelley, Suckling, and Leigh Hunt. They do not belong to the same school of language as 'Here hung those lips', or Suckling's

> Her lips were red, and one was thin
> Compared with that was next her chin.
> (Some bee had stung it newly.)

'Bright' and 'fine' could doubtless be applied to lips with perfect aptness, but they are not applied so here. They are complimentary and not descriptive. Swinburne admired brightness, and he called a woman's lips 'bright' and in the next stanza but one a blackbird 'bright'. I do not know what 'fine' means, but I suspect that it is not much more definite than the vulgar 'fine' and his own 'splendid'. A group of his epithets, as in 'the lost white feverish limbs' of the drowned Sappho, has sometimes the effect of a single epithet by a master like Keats. Many epithets express the poet's opinions of things as much as their qualities, as in 'marvellous chambers', 'strange weathers', 'keen thin fish', 'mystic and sombre Dolores', 'strong broken spirit of a wave', 'hard glad weather', 'purple blood of pain', 'feverish weather', 'shameful scornful lips', 'splendid supple thighs', 'sad colour of strong marigolds', 'clean great time of goodly fight', 'fair pure sword', 'like a snake's love lithe and fierce', 'heavenly hair', 'heavenly hands', 'mute melancholy lust of heaven', 'fine drouth', 'fierce reluctance of disastrous stars', 'tideless dolorous midland sea', 'fresh fetlocks', 'fervent oars' or the fourteen epithets applied to Dolores. The epithets in the last stanza of 'A Ballad of Death' are all appropriate to the intention of the poet — 'rusted', 'rain-rotten', 'waste', 'late unhappy' — and in keeping with the ideas of fading, sighing, groaning, bowing down, evening and death—but are for the most part but indifferently fitted for their respective places, and could perhaps safely be transposed in half a dozen ways without affecting the sense, though I shall not prove it. That transposition would change and probably spoil the total effect there is no denying.

But Swinburne has almost no magic felicity of words. He can astonish and melt but seldom thrill, and when he does it is not by any felicity of as it were God-given inevitable words. He has to depend on sound and an atmosphere of words which is now and then concentrated and crystallized into an intensity of effect which is almost magical, perhaps never quite magical. This atmosphere comes from a vocabulary very rich in words connected with objects and sensations and emotions of pleasure and beauty, but used, as I have said, somewhat lightly and even in appearance indiscriminately. No poet could be poorer in brief electric phrases, pictorial or emotional. The first line of 'Hesperia' — 'Out of the golden remote wild west where the sea without shore is', is an example of Swinburne's way of accumulating words which altogether can suggest rather than infallibly express his meaning. 'Golden', 'remote', 'wild', 'west', 'sea', and 'without shore' all have already some emotional values, of which the line gives no more than the sum, the rhythm and grammatical connection saving the words from death and inexpressiveness. In the whole opening passage of this poem there is the same accumulation, aided by the vague, as in 'region of stories' and 'capes of the past oversea'.

Perhaps the greatest of his triumphs is in keeping up a stately solemn play of words not unrelated to the object suggested by his title and commencement but more closely related to rhymes, and yet in the end giving a compact and powerful impression. The play of words often on the very marge of nonsense has acted as an incantation, partly by pure force of cadence and kiss of rhymes, partly by the accumulative force of words in the right key though otherwise lightly used. Hardly one verse means anything in particular, hardly one line means anything at all, but nothing is done inconsistent with the opening, nothing which the rashest critic would venture to call unavailing in the complete effect. Single words are used in some poems, verses in others, as contributive rather than essential; their growth is by simple addition rather than evolution.   94-8

Later Poems

Altogether, hardly any of our poets have written more short poems, save those like Herrick, who wrote many of only a few lines apiece. This multitude includes Latin, French, and border dialect poems, narratives, descriptions, odes, poems of reflection and of passion and of both, and some translations. But the great variety of forms and subjects is no obstacle to one fairly clear but accidental division. On the one hand lie perhaps the only poems which have a distinguishable subject, those confessedly connected with a particular person, place, or event: these include the political poems, the poems relating to men, whether friends or great men, living and dead; and with these go the translations. On the other hand lie those poems which essentially exist in Swinburne's books or in the memories of his lovers and nowhere else, and have no important connection with anything outside—poems which at their best could not be paraphrased or abridged or represented by anything but themselves, which could hardly be thought of as better or worse than they are or in any way different.

The second class is superior to the first, because as a rule either Swinburne abated his style for the sake of things known to the world, or he made an unsuccessful attempt to envelop them in it. The best example of this failure is the poem entitled 'A Channel Passage', which is a travel sketch in verse, and never does more than remind us that the actual scene was one of uncommon magnificence. The poet calls the steamer a 'steam-souled ship' and the same translation of reality into poetry—to put it in a crude intelligible way—is the essence and the fatal fault of the poem. Whenever art allows a comparison with Nature, wherever Nature intrudes in her own purity and majesty, art fails. Uniformity of illusion is a condition of success. In 'A Channel Passage' there is hardly any illusion: it is a man being poetical on a steamer, which is no less and no more absurd than being poetical in an omnibus; but being poetical is not poetry. 'Stern and prow plunged under, alternate: a glimpse, a recoil, a breath, / As she sprang as the life in a god made man would spring at the throat of death. . . .' is a versification and rhetorical treatment of notes, whether in a pocket-book or not. The prose description of the same scene in *Essays and Studies* is brief and suggestive and humane. The poem is an inhuman perversion of language and metre.

'The Lake of Gaube' in the same volume is also founded upon an actual, perhaps a single, experience, with an entirely different result. The experience has been digested; the illusion is complete, and no comparison with the lake itself possible except as a late afterthought to those who know it; the same world, Swinburne's world, is with us from the first words, 'The sun is lord and god', until the last. Swinburne's style touches actual detail only at its peril. When he speaks of 'one sweet glad hawthorn', a 'dyke's trenched edge', 'the steep sweet bank', and 'the dense bright oval wall of box inwound', he can seldom avert the fatal comparison. It gives occasion for the just and cruel smile at the poet 'turning beautiful things into poetry', as the world says. There are poets who can speak of 'when the northering road faced westward' and 'as the dawn leapt in at my casement', but Swinburne cannot. After them the various metrical forms of 'Loch Torridon', and the excited words, can do no more than show us a composition in an intermediate stage, between a memory and a poem. Lines like these:

> But never a roof for shelter
> And never a sign for guide
> Rose doubtful or visible. . . .

can be translated into prose, and have possibly been translated out of it—not into poetry.   150-3

Rhyme certainly acted upon Swinburne as a pill to purge ordinary responsibilities. He became sensible to many of the values of words, ancient and modern, ordinary and figurative, etymological and melodic. Thus he played with the literal meaning of Gautier's Christian name, Théophile: 'Dear to God', he said, and went on to speak of the God that gives men 'spirit of song'. Thus he played with the name of Cape Wrath: 'But north of the headland whose name is Wrath, by the wrath or the ruth of the sea. . . .' Another form of play is noticeable in: 'Enmeshed intolerably in the intolerant net', and still more in:

> And in the soul within the sense began
> The manlike passion of a godlike man,
> And in the sense within the soul again
> Thoughts that made men of gods and gods of men.

This may turn out to be very nearly nonsense; but certainly it fills a place harmoniously in 'Thalassius', a poem which is not nonsense. The line before it is an example of another kind of play with words. Instead of saying 'the nightingale' he says 'the singing bird whose song calls night by name'; a thing 'eight hundred years old' is one 'that has seen decline eight hundred waxing and waning years'. Speaking of himself and others who read Tennyson in their teens, he says that it was 'ere time in the rounding rhyme of choral seasons had hailed us men,' which is more than mere periphrasis. The next line but one contains an example of a kind of play which surprises us by making perfect sense: 'Life more bright than the breathless light of soundless moon in a songless glen.' Its perfect sense is, I think, not more important than its pattern, which is of a kind that seems instantly to forbid examination save by the ear. . . .

It is important to notice that verse permits the poet to use 'the hands of thy kingdom' and a thousand other aids to length and opacity. Thus in 'Ex Voto' he thinks of his 'last hour'—he personifies it vaguely— and how she will kiss him.

> The cold last kiss and fold
> Close round my limbs her cold
> Soft shade as raiment rolled
> And leave them lying.

It bears analysis, but, except to lovers of the rhymes and this stanza form, must seem long-winded. Rhyme and the stanza excuse him when he pictures England not only with: 'The sea-coast round her like a mantle', but with: 'The sea-cloud like a crown.' This would be a grave weakness in a poet who encouraged reading closely with eye and ear. In the next stanza of the same poem, 'The Commonweal', the rhyme 'deathless' leads him to speak of 'the breathless bright watch-word of the sea'. This is extraordinarily near nonsense, almost a bull's-eye. He is speaking of Englishmen bearing 'in heart' this watchword, 'breathless' means perhaps silent or inner, and 'bright' is compli-mentary: but it is a near thing.   158-62

Such a lover of words and music could only spend his full powers on poems which essentially exist in his books or in the memories of his lovers, and nowhere else, having no important connection with any-thing outside. Sometimes, as in the 'Elegy on Sir Richard Burton', he triumphed with a distinguishable subject; but his best work is where he makes no overt appeal to our interest or sympathy, though the richer we are in the love of life and of words the greater will be our pleasure. The same is true of all poets, but not in this degree. For it may be said of most poets that they love men and Nature more than words; of Swinburne that he loved them equally. Other poets tend towards a grace and glory of words as of human speech perfected and made divine, Swinburne towards a musical jargon that includes human snatches, but is not and never could be speech.   171

FRANCIS THOMPSON

BECAUSE FRANCIS THOMPSON'S style was about as remote as it could be from spoken English of today it is assumed—it may be true, but it is only an assumption—that he did conscious violence to words. Some even go so far as to accuse him of insincerity; that also may be true, but the only source of evidence for the accusation is in the grave.

And on the face of it Thompson's work bears the stamp of an absolute sincerity. Only sincerity could have produced such a large consistency of character in spite of lesser inconsistencies. Insincerity would have been more artful, would not have permitted the poet not only to speak of 'The mighty Spirit unknown/That swingeth the slow earth before the embannered Throne, . . .' but also in at least two other places to show his means of approach to that magnificent image; and to speak at least twice of the Earth as dancing like David before the Ark. No, in Thompson artificiality of style was due to his extraordinary love of his medium. Language, in fact, appears to have been more than a medium to him. It was a realm of experience of equal beauty and strangeness to the other realms in which he travelled. The same, it will be said, is true of all artists in words, only they are wiser than to say of earth:

> Who scarfed her with the morning? and who set
> Upon her brow the day-fall's carcanet?
>   Who queened her front with the enrondured moon?
>   Who dug night's jewels from their vaulty mine
>   To dower her, past an Eastern wizard's dreams,
>   When hovering on him through his haschish-swoon,
>   All the rained gems of the old Tartarian line
> Shiver in lustrous throbbings of tinged flame?
>   Whereof a moiety in the Paolis' seams
>   Statelily builded their Venetian name. . . .

But it is truer of Thompson than of most others because he never seems to have got on terms, as it were, of married familiarity with words, so that they remain in his verse as a permanent memorial of this nympholepsy. No doubt in conversation he used a vocabulary not unlike other people's. But in the written word the artist has to make up for all those advantages of tone and look and gesture and other unspoken speech, of which he is deprived, in solitude. There are as many ways as there are artists of doing this. Rhythm, of course, and especially recurring rhythm, which hardly exists in conversation and is never noticed, along with a choice vocabulary and an uncolloquial use of metaphor and simile, are the most obvious means. There is no great joy of rhythm in Thompson. Metaphor is his supreme method. And here again it is surely understood that we are not speaking of a perfectly conscious method. Conscious effort of intellect through endless time will not produce 'Absent thee from felicity awhile'. And so Thompson's style also could not have been achieved by merely taking thought. It is the implicit heresy in Pater's criticism—exemplified to the point of absurdity in his own style—that the *mot propre* can be reached by thought, and 'the infinite capacity for taking pains'. We defy anyone to write verse like the dedication to Coventry Patmore by malice aforethought:

> Lo, my book thinks to look Time's leaguer down,
> Under the banner of your spread renown!
> Or if these levies of impuissant rhyme
> Fall to the overthrow of assaulting Time,
> Yet this one page shall fend oblivious shame,
> Armed with your crested and prevailing Name.

There, at the beginning of his *New Poems,* is his one article of faith. The word is the thing and the thing is the word. The only indictment of it must come from the schoolmaster who has set his boys to paraphrase these verses and has been content with the result. Of course it must be granted that there are places where words have advanced from their position of equality with things to one of superiority, because Thompson thought words greatly beautiful; and that for most of us this is a faulty balance of power. For example, in 'The After Woman' the lines:

> Unbanner your bright looks,—advance,
> Girl, their gilded puissance,
> I' the mystic vaward and draw on
> After the lovely gonfalon
> Us to out-folly the excess
> Of your sweet foolhardiness . . .

seem to suggest that Thompson could not see the girl through the words, which is a very different state of things from what he describes in the lines:

> How should I gauge what beauty is her dole,
> Who cannot see her countenance for her soul,
> As birds see not the casement for the sky?

No doubt, too, the phrase 'disease of language' will be used by scientists if they ever trouble to read 'The Hound of Heaven' and especially the passage:

> Across the margent of the world I fled,
>   And troubled the gold gateway of the stars,
>   Smiting for shelter on their clangèd bars . . .

where the metaphor of a gateway appears to have lured him into the actual vision of a solid gate that resounds to the touch.

But the important fact is that even so did a human spirit feel and see in his way through life. Every one of his poems has this in common with great art that it lifts objects and ideas out of the dullness and weariness of blank acceptance in which we chiefly dwell into just that sumptuous visibility which they had for him. His forty-seven years, of life were devoted to the seeing and making seen of the beauty of the body and spirit of things. In his work they are one. His words are 'the gold, the incenses, and myrrhs' with which he decks them for their praise. If we are not mistaken, rich and heavy as is the dress, it is after all only an image that it clothes, and through the image we are helped to see, behind no veil at all, the unconcealable spirit. In a narrower sense the words are the garment of his personality, and no one can say that this does not emerge from the book before us very gorgeously in its deep sorrow and deeper joy.

From review of *Selected Poems of Francis Thompson*,
MP, 12 November 1908

MAURICE MAETERLINCK

First Poems: 'Serres Chaudes'

WHEN MAETERLINCK was a young man of twenty-four he met Villiers de l'Isle Adam and other symbolists in Paris. He became a symbolist himself. His early poems, some of them published during that visit to Paris and collected afterwards with others in 'Serres Chaudes', are symbolist or they are nothing; his early plays were accepted as symbolist. It is not obvious what is here meant by symbolism, but it is not merely the use of symbols. 'It is all,' writes Mr Symons, 'an attempt to spiritualize literature, to evade the old bondage of rhetoric, the old bondage of exteriority. Description is banished that beautiful things may be evoked, magically. . . .' Writing of the sonnets of Gerard de Nerval (1808-55) he says that here, 'for the first time in French, words are used as the ingredients of an evocation, as themselves not merely colour and sound, but symbol'. Probably it is meant that they are used solely as an evocation, and deliberately so. One of the examples, 'El Desdichado', has something like the magic of the not quite intelligible song of Taliesin, beginning:

> Primary chief bard am I to Elphin,
> And my original country is the region of the summer stars; . . .
> I was with my Lord in the highest sphere,
> On the fall of Lucifer into the depth of hell;
> I have borne a banner before Alexander . . .

for it ends: 'Am I Eros or Phoebus? . . . Lusignan or Biron? My brow is still flushed from the queen's kiss; I have been dreaming in the grotto of the syren . . . and twice have I victoriously crossed Acheron playing on the lyre of Orpheus, sometimes in the tone of a saint's sighing and at

other times of a fairy's cry.' It is hardly necessary to say that the words
do not take us farther or deeper than certain phrases of older poets and
even prose-writers, like: 'And battles long ago;' or 'Merry it was in
Silver Wood;' or 'Visit'st the bottom of the monstrous world;' or, 'The
famous nations of the dead'; or, 'Apame, the King's concubine, the
daughter of the admirable Bartacus, sitting at the right hand of the
King, and taking the crown from the King's head, and setting it upon
her own head'; or, 'And the world shall be turned into the old silence
seven days.' We know that the words of poets and of others who can
handle words often mean much more than the same mean in another
place or at another time. We are almost certain that their words have
often come to mean something different from what was consciously
present in their minds when they wrote, and often more vast. Maeterlinck knew this, and expressed it in 1890, in a criticism now printed in
Gerard Harry's *Maurice Maeterlinck*, 'Is it not,' he asks, 'by examining
what he has not consciously intended that we penetrate the essence of a
poet? The poet premeditates this, premeditates that, but woe to him if
he does not attain something else beside!' But the symbolists, having
come late into this world, are more self-conscious than men before
them, and it appears to be their task to produce consciously the strange
echoing and branching effects of magic which came to earlier men
straight from the gods. Mr F. Y. Eccles puts it in this way in the brilliant Introduction to his *Century of French Poets*:

> Of the many tendencies imputed to symbolism this is the most
> characteristic—out of an acuter perception of what all poets have
> always known, that words are insufficient if their power is bounded
> by their meaning, emerged an audacious doctrine which branded
> their representative function as inferior, and sought to shift the
> poetical interest from what they signify to what they may suggest.
> In the Parnassian system description was paramount, and feeling
> sprang from it immediately: the emotion which symbolism pursues
> bears no constant relation to the objects represented or the ideas
> expressed; rather it aims at the recovery of vanished moods by
> curious incantations, by the magical use of verbal atmosphere. To
> fashion a true likeness of the material world it holds a vain and
> illusory undertaking: it values sights, sounds, scents, and savours
> for their secret affinities with states of the soul. . . .

It is a little unkind to words to suppose that they can be bounded by
their meaning, but apparently the symbolist must insist that his words
are not only not so bounded, but have a further significance which is
quite precise; otherwise there were no difference between the old and
the new. It is a dangerous difference. For a poem of the old kind has a
simple fundamental meaning which every sane reader can agree upon;

above and beyond this each one builds as he can or must. In the new there is no basis of this kind; a poem means nothing unless its whole meaning has been grasped. Take, for an example of the old, a seventh-century Chinese poem from Mr Cranmer-Byng's *Lute of Jade*. It is called 'Tears in the Spring':

> Clad in blue silk and bright embroidery,
> At the first call of spring the fair young bride,
> On whom as yet Sorrow has laid no scar,
> Climbs the Kingfisher's Tower. Suddenly
> She sees the bloom of willows far and wide,
> And grieves for him she lent to fame and war.

This is explicit enough and amazingly condensed; but, even so, the many elements in it combine, and then fall away and leave something more than the sum of them all, and that something over gives the poem its great beauty, which we may call symbolical if we like, but not symbolist. A symbolist might have used the same scene, but probably with this difference, that he would have drawn no conclusions from it; he would have left it to make its own effect. In the same way a symbolist poet might have seen the Highland reaper as a symbol, but would not have interpreted the symbol like Wordsworth. But, look at 'Ennui' from Maeterlinck's 'Serres Chaudes':

> The careless peacocks, the white peacocks, have fled; the white peacocks have fled from the ennui of waking. I see the white peacocks, the peacocks of today, the peacocks in rows during my sleep, the careless peacocks, the peacocks of today, arriving lazily at the sunless lake. I hear the white peacocks, the peacocks of ennui, awaiting lazily the sunless days.

This is a dangerous poem for those who think that symbolist poems must be judged by new standards. There is no meaning upon which all of them would agree. The first wish of the tolerant reader seeking for profound and designed significance must be for a dictionary to explain 'peacocks', especially 'white peacocks'. He will be all the more disturbed by his lack of comprehension, because probably he would like to think of white peacocks; but this the words will not allow. The birds have to be examined like an heraldic device. The most he can do is to think—perhaps upon a suggestion from a remembered picture—of a large grey house with white peacocks on the empty terraces, and over all a Sunday desolation of ennui and silence. Nor is this poem the most difficult—not to understand, but to meet in such a way that understanding is possible. For the poem seems to contain interpretation as well as a symbol; so does 'Fauves Lasses', with its 'yellow dogs of my sins', 'squint-eyed hyenas of my hates', 'flocks of temptations'.

'Chasses Lasses' is a poem written in cypher, and containing a glossary of its own terms:

> My soul is sick today; my soul is sick with absence; my soul has the sickness of silence; and my eyes light it with tedium.
>
> I catch sight of hunts at a standstill, under the blue lashes of my memories; and the hidden hounds of my desires follow the outworn scents.
>
> I see the packs of my dreams threading the warm forests, and the yellow arrows of regret seeking the white deer of lies.
>
> Ah, God! my breathless longings, the warm longings of my eyes, have clouded with breaths too blue the moon which fills my soul.

If this method is characteristic of the 'decadence' and modern France, it is not new. Is it not upon the same model as the song which Musidorus, in Sidney's *Arcadia*, sang to Pamela, 'to show what kind of a shepherd he was'. This is the song:

> My sheep are thoughts, which I both guide and serve;
>   Their pasture is fair hills of fruitless love:
> On barren sweets they feed, and feeding starve:
>   I wail their lot, but will not other prove.
> My sheep-hook is wan hope, which all upholds:
>   My weeds, desire, cut out in endless folds:
>   What wool my sheep shall bear, while thus they live.
> Dry as it is, you must the judgment give.

Then Pamela turns to Mopsa and says: 'Take heed to yourself, for your shepherd can speak well. . . .' This passed in Sidney's time for the language of emotion, as that of 'Chasses Lasses' does in our own. Both appear to be purely fanciful writing according to a fashion, and more cannot be said of them than that the exposure of the symbols has given the lines a naïve decorative value.

It is harder to speak of the poems which are not thus translated for us by the one man who has their secret, Maeterlinck himself. It would be simple to accept them all together as a not obscure symbol of something familiar—youth; or to take the words of them as bounded by their customary meaning, the words that recur, most of them, many times—sadness, weariness, ennui, melancholy, pallor, feebleness, immobility. These are truly *mots propres*, the right words not sought but inevitable and significant, like Shelley's 'wingèd' or Ruskin's 'entirely'. The poems seem to represent a weariness, a melancholy, an unrest that belong to the writer only when he writes. These feelings, when they are profound, are not so eager to be quickly told. The pallor and melancholy are parts of the writer's refinement, and are unconsciously chosen, partly, perhaps, out of respect for the pictures by

Burne-Jones on his walls, and partly as an easy method of distinguishing himself from a vile world not in the least melancholy and pale, or desiring to be so. If there is anything here to be called sorrow it is no more passionate than wall-paper, and is not due to loss of faith, fortune, wife, health, leg, teeth, or the like, but to this excessive refinement in protest against those whom he despises, and in imitation of the admired. In the absence of information it is impossible to be certain, but it seems likely that most of 'Serres Chaudes' is due to Paris and the literary life. The little of his still earlier work which I have seen has nothing of this character. 'The Massacre of the Innocents', a perfectly Flemish piece of objective realism, is as unlike as possible, and this may have been written before the visit to Paris, though, whether it was or not, its lucidity and entire lack of display of emotion make it a significant contrast with the languor and confusion of 'Serres Chaudes'.

When referring, years later, in 'The Buried Temple' to his early plays, Maeterlinck spoke of them as the work of 'some obscure poetical feeling' within him which believed in a hostile and encompassing fate, and he claimed that, with the sincerest poets, a distinction has often to be made 'between the instinctive feelings of their art and the thoughts of their real life'. What else is this than what Keats wrote in the dedication of *Endymion* when he was at the same age as the Maeterlinck of 'Serres Chaudes'? 'The imagination of a boy is healthy, and the mature imagination of a man is healthy; but there is a space of life between, in which the soul is in a ferment. . . .' In a young man of the middle class living an easy, sheltered existence, chiefly in our modern cities, as it is so natural and common to do, the brave fervour of youth is often girt up neither by experience in the past nor by a sufficient object in the present; it must spend itself, and it does so upon little things, borrowed things, which are presently seen for what they are, and share with the fervour the same neglect and even contempt. The poem called 'Serres Chaudes' expresses the sense of strangeness and vanity which comes to this state when life is at once too languid and too difficult because it is all cloistered within the brain:

O hothouse in the midst of the woods, with your doors for ever closed; and all the things under your dome, with their counterparts in my soul!

The thoughts of a hungry princess; the weariness of a sailor in the desert; a brass band playing under the windows of incurables.

Seek the warmest corners! Such, a woman fainting on a harvest day. Postillions are in the courtyard of the hospital; while in the distance passes an attendant, once an elk-stalker.

Look closely, by moonlight! How out of place is everything here!

Such, a mad woman before the justices; a man-of-war under full sail on a canal; night-birds perching on lilies; a noontide death-knell (there, under those bell-glasses!); a station for the sick in the open fields; the smell of ether during a day of sunshine.

Ah, God! God! when shall we have the rain and the snow and the wind in the hothouses?

Here, too, 'with their counterparts in my soul', if not a complete explanation, is a timid admission of the need of one. But the piece is hardly more than a catalogue of symbols that have no more literary value than words in a dictionary. It ignores the fact that no word, outside works of information, has any value beyond its surface value except what it receives from its neighbours and its position among them. Each man makes his own language in the main unconsciously and inexplicably, unless he is still at an age when he is an admiring but purely aesthetic collector of words; certain words—he knows not why—he will never use; and there are a hundred peculiarities in his rhythms and groupings to be discovered. In the mainly instinctive use of his language the words will all support one another, and, if the writing is good, the result of this support is that each word is living its intensest life. The first few words of a work of art teach us, though we do not know it at the time, exactly how much value we are to give to all the rest, whether they are to be words only, or images, or spirits. They admit us, or teach us that we cannot be admitted, to the author's world. Any writer whose words have this power may make a poem of anything—a story, a dream, a thought, a picture, an ejaculation, a conversation. Whatever be the subject, the poem must not depend for its main effect upon anything outside itself except the humanity of the reader. It may please for the moment by the aid of some irrelevant and transitory interest—political interest, for example; but, sooner or later, it will be left naked and solitary, and will so be judged, and if it does not create about itself a world of its own it is condemned to endure the death which is its element. These worlds of living poems may be of many different kinds. As a rule they are regions of the earth now for the first time separated from the rest and made independent; they may be lit by the sun of every one, or by another, or by the moon, or by a green lantern: whatever they are, they are stronger than this world, and their light more steadfast than sun or moon. Wordsworth writes a poem in the hope of making it give the same impression as a certain hawthorn-tree gives to him; Keats because he cannot dismiss from his mind the words, 'Dost thou not hear the sea?'; Burns because a girl pleases and evades him. Anything, however small, may make a poem; nothing, however great, is certain to. Concentration, intensity of mood, is the one necessary condition in the poet and in the poem.

By this concentration something is detached from the confused immensity of life and receives individuality, and this creativeness brings into my mind the inhuman solitariness of the world at the moment when Deucalion stooped to make the first men out of stones; and the waste of waters when the dove bore an olive-leaf into the ark out of the monotonous waste. But the early Maeterlinck turned no stones into men, nor found the crest of a tree piercing the dead sea. Nothing in 'Serres Chaudes' persuades us to see this creative high value in the words; they give no help to one another. It is as far from the writing of a sloven or a common man as from that of a master, but it says nothing save that it belongs to a school to which it has turned in the confusion of its unrest. Whatever its intention, it has not that quality of style which at once takes and retains possession of the reader.

To give such a poem significance it would be necessary to make a key to it, like St Melito's key to the Bible, where it is shown that in one place the word 'Camelus' stands for Christ, in another for love of this world; that 'Leo' means Christ, Mark the Evangelist, the Devil, Antichrist; that 'Unicornis' is Christ, but 'Unicornes' the proud. But the extreme example of such symbolism is found in a verse by Adam de St Victor, where the word 'dragon' is used three times in three different senses within two lines—Christ, the Devil and something like Antichrist. But this is not literature; as well might algebra be called literature. It is not deep enough. It was no symbolism of this kind that gave the words, 'I believe in the forgiveness of sins' inexorable significance to Luther as if the door of Paradise had been thrown wide open. William James, from whom this example is taken, gives other examples of persons for whom 'Philadelphia' and 'chalcedony' had 'a mighty fascination', and 'the words *woods* and *forests* would produce the most powerful emotion'.

> Most of us [says James] can remember the strangely moving power of passages in certain poems read when we were young; irrational doorways, as they were, through which the mystery of fact, the wilderness and the pang of life, stole into our hearts and thrilled them. The words have now perhaps become mere polished surfaces for us; but lyric poetry and music are alive and significant only in proportion as they fetch these vague vistas of a life continuous with our own, beckoning and inviting, yet ever eluding our pursuit. We are alive or dead to the eternal inner message of the arts according as we have kept or lost this mystical susceptibility.

A curious example of this value of a single word or phrase may be seen in George Herbert's poem, 'My Master', and in the treatise on 'The Song of Angels' by a fourteenth-century English mystic, Walter Hilton:

Some man setteth the thoughts of his heart only in the name of Jesu, and steadfastly holdeth it thereto, and in short time him thinketh that the name turneth him to great comfort and sweetness, and him thinketh that the name soundeth in his heart delectably, as it were a song; and the virtue of this liking is so mighty, that it draweth in all the wits of the soul thereto. Whoso may feel this sound and this sweetness verily in his heart, wete thou well that it is of God, and, so long as he is meek, he shall not be deceived. But this is not angel's song; but it is a song of the soul by virtue of the name and by touching of the good angel.

This is an example of the extreme and highest symbolism of words. Were it common in this degree there could be no more poetry, or it would be more accurate to say that there could be nothing else but poetry.

It is an old opinion that all visible things are symbols. Sallustius, the friend of Julian the Apostate, says Professor Gilbert Murray, held the world itself to be a great myth, and the myths to be all allegories. Paris, for example, being 'the soul living according to the senses', and therefore only able to see beauty, which is Aphrodite. For him the value of a thing lay 'not in itself, but in the spiritual meaning which it hides and reveals'. Heraclitus of Ephesus 'deliberately expressed himself in language which should not be understood by the vulgar and which bore a hidden meaning to his disciples', and he said that 'if Homer used no allegories he committed all impieties'—on which Professor Murray makes the illuminating comment that 'on this theory the words can be allowed to possess all their own beauty and magic, but an inner meaning is added quite different from what they bear on the surface'. Ruskin seems to have held a similar opinion to this of Heraclitus, for he sees a designed significance in the fact that Ophelia's name means 'serviceableness', and seriously writes: 'Hamlet is, I believe, connected in some way with "homely", the entire event of the tragedy turning on betrayal of home duty.' But had Shakespeare paused to secure effects of this kind, assuredly he could not have produced so many that are infinitely more powerful. The laws governing aesthetic and spiritual effects are innumerable; those which can be discovered are probably few in comparison, and if these are deliberately followed it is more than likely that many others will be fatally disobeyed. Maeterlinck, for example, had learnt a few when he wrote 'Feuillage du Coeur':

Under the blue crystal bell of my weary melancholy moods, my dim bygone griefs take gradually their motionless form:

Symbolic growths! Brooding water-lilies of pleasures, slow-growing palms of my desires, cold mosses, pliant bindweed:

Alone among them a lily, pale and weak in rigidity, marks its motionless ascent above the grief-laden foliage:
And in the glimmer which it radiates, gradually, moon-like, lifts its mystical white prayer to the blue crystal.

But is there anything here in addition which can awaken and gratify the profound receptivity of spirit most fit for communion with a poet? Mr W. B. Yeats, in his essay on 'The Symbolism of Poetry', rebukes those—the journalists—who, in his opinion, are certain 'that no one, who had a philosophy of his art, or a theory of how he should write, has ever made a work of art' and supports himself by the words of Goethe: 'A poet needs all philosophy, but he must keep it out of his work.' The qualification he half rejects, but when he comes to give examples of potent symbolism he finds them chiefly in writers like Burns, who did not know the word and would perhaps have been astonished and even amused by the theory itself. Even Mr Symons, loyal critic of the professed symbolists, has to say that 'Symbolism, as seen in the writers of our day, would have no value if it were not seen also, under one disguise or another, in every great imaginative writer.'

It must now be apparent that entirely conscious symbolism comes very near to being allegory, which of all things is abhorred by symbolists. Mr Yeats himself is a poet who is far more than a symbolist, yet it is possible to see in his work this danger skirted, and sometimes upon the wrong side. He confesses, in the notes to his *Wind among the Reeds,* that he 'has made the Seven Lights, the constellation of the Bear, lament for the theft of the Rose, and has made the Dragon, the constellation Draco, the guardian of the Rose, because these constellations move about the pole of the heavens, the ancient Tree of Life in many countries, and are often associated with the Tree of Life in mythology.' It was natural that he should have said, after quoting from Goethe, that to keep his philosophy out of his work is not always necessary for the poet; for, had he kept his own out of the notes to the *Wind among the Reeds,* the annotated poems must have fallen short of his reader. An example is 'Mongan laments the change that has come upon him and his beloved', beginning:

Do you not hear me calling, white deer with no horns?
I have been changed to a hound with one red ear;
I have been in the Path of Stones and the Wood of Thorns,
For somebody hid hatred and hope and desire and fear
Under my feet that they follow you night and day. . . .

'I got my hound and deer', runs his note, 'out of a last century Gaelic poem. . . . This hound and this deer seem plain images of the desire of man "which is for the woman" and "the desire of the woman which is for the desire of the man", and of all desires that are as these.' It may be that a day will come when the force of Mr Yeats's genius will have added to common culture the special knowledge through which alone the poem is intelligible. At present the language of it is dead or merely private, like that of Heraclitus, and the note, so far from helping the poem, attracts attention exclusively to itself. It is again a question of style. The poet's words refuse to make any impression corresponding to his intention; they speak to the brain alone, and can reveal only his interest in mythology. Similar notes to 'Serres Chaudes' must have been extraordinarily interesting; but if Maeterlinck does not write them it is doubtful whether any one else can or will.

Maurice Maeterlinck, 18-34

THE CELTIC TWILIGHT

BUT THERE IS another kind of human being—to use a comprehensive term—of which I stand in almost as much awe as of authors and those who know the famous things of Wales. I mean the lovers of the Celt. They do not, of course, confine their love—which in its extent and its tenuity reminds one of a very great personage indeed—to the Celt; but more perhaps than the Japanese or the Chinese or the Sandwich Islander the Celt has their hearts; and I know of one who not only learned to speak Welsh badly, but had the courage to rise at a public meeting and exhort the (Welsh-speaking) audience to learn their 'grand mother tongue'. Their aim and ideal is to go about the world in a state of self-satisfied dejection, interrupted, and perhaps sustained, by days when they consume strange mixed liquors to the tune of all the fine old Celtic songs which are fashionable. If you can discover a possible Celtic great-grandmother, you are at once among the chosen. I cannot avoid the opinion that to boast of the Celtic spirit is to confess you have it not. But, however that may be, and speaking as one who is afraid of definitions, I should be inclined to call these lovers of the Celt a class of 'decadents', not unrelated to Mallarmé, and aesthetes, not unrelated to Postlethwaite. They are sophisticated, neurotic—the fine flower of sounding cities—often producing exquisite verse and prose; preferring *crème de menthe* and *opal hush* to metheglin or stout, and Kensington to Eryri and Connemara; and perplexed in the extreme by the Demetian with his taste in wallpapers quite untrained. Probably it all came from Macpherson's words, 'They went forth to battle and they always fell'; just as much of their writing is to be traced to the vague, unobservant things in Ossian, or in the proud, anonymous Irishman who wrote *Fingal* in six cantos in 1813. The latter is excellent in this vein.

Let none then despise [he writes] the endeavour, however humble, now made, even by the aid of fiction, to throw light upon the former manners and customs of *one of the oldest and noblest nations of the earth*. That *once we were*, is all we have left to boast of; that *once we were*, we have record upon record. . . . We yet can show the stately pharos where waved the chieftain's banner, and the wide ruin where the palace stood—the palace once the pride of ages and the theme of song—once *Emuin a luin Aras Ullah*.

The reader feels that it is a baseness to exist. *Beautiful Wales*, 10-12

ERNEST DOWSON

ERNEST DOWSON'S collected poems, viz., 'Verses', 'Decorations' and 'The Pierrot of the Minute', are introduced by Mr Arthur Symons, their proper editor. The introduction is perfect; and the poems need it. In the nineties they would have needed no introduction, for Dowson belonged to a considerable caste of poets with a considerable caste of readers, beyond which he could hardly then have reached. But misfortune has overtaken them all; they are dead, or their incomes are regular, or they are restoring their hair, and the man who read Dowson's poems when they first appeared, and now at length opens them again, will certainly be reminded that the years are full and dying, and will repeat Dowson's verses on old age:

> When I am old,
>   And sadly steal apart,
> Into the dark and cold,
>   Friend of my heart!
> Remember, if you can,
> Not him who lingers, but that other man,
> Who loved and sang, and had a beating heart—
>   When I am old! . . .

[Moralists] will talk of the connection between excess and a feeble frame, and liver, delirium, and despair; and it is likely they will end with a lament and a question as to what Dowson might have done had he been moderate, in spite of the testimony of the thousands of moderate persons who black our boots and write our reviews; he might have become an Imperialist, a picturesque grandfather, a discoverer of something less nourishing than Grape Nuts.

Yet is it not clear that Dowson was simply the embodied groan of one brief stage of humanity's long probation on the wheel of Time? No elderly person, it is true, who had met him and known his life, would have lacked the courage to try to lure him into a nice, quiet office or a home for inebriates; but perhaps not so many would have refused to be silent when they heard the voice of the poet singing his 'Sapientia Lunae':

> The wisdom of the world said unto me:
> 'Go forth and run, the race is to the brave;
> Perchance some honour tarrieth for thee!'
> 'As tarrieth,' I said, 'for sure, the grave.'
> For I had pondered on a rune of roses,
> Which to her votaries the moon discloses. . . .

For, small and short and ill-managed as were his experiences, it was yet given to this man to find melodious and moving words for some of the oldest, deepest miseries of men; and it might be worth while for some wise man to question whether the life which enabled him to write as he did was not a great and worthy, at least a necessary, life. He who should say that Dowson made nothing new would be no lover of verse. To us he seems to have rediscovered regret and all the emotions which the inaccessible and irrecoverable arouse, since he expressed them with a beauty and simplicity which no contemporary equalled. Truly he seems to be discovering these things for the first time when he writes of this short life and how it rebukes long expectations; of April foreseeing, amidst her joys, 'The burden of the days that are to be'; of the lunatic whose dreams divine 'Lift his long, laughing reveries like enchaunted wine,/And make his melancholy germane to the stars;' of love dreaming of when love is dead; of pleasure sicklied over by passion; of melancholy, 'tired of everything that ever I desired'; of vain resolves: 'Yea! as it hath been, it shall ever be,/Most passionless, pure eyes!' Of dreams: 'Dream though has dreamt all this, when thou awake,/ Yet still be sorrowful, for a dream's sake.'

Of impenitence, if only he may hear again 'the viols in her voice'. The passion in his swaying, his tortured or his simple rhythms, and in his clear, pure, and simple diction is such that although hundreds have said the things he says, none but the great have said them in a way which can appeal nearly so much to men of his own day. Deep within the dark background of them all is the comic, terrible cry of the superfluous man. Those of his own day should make much of him, because his language, his images, his melody, his mood, are those of no other day. And perhaps, in a little while, of all their self-pity, self-love, self-hate, of that regret and hunger, for they know not what, which are their only emotions that touched the sublime, their misery that will be seen in its depth and decorativeness; of these perhaps nothing will be remembered, except as they are expressed, with the loudness of a sigh and the length only of a caress, in these poems by the most concentrated of them all, who already seems but an unbodied melancholy.

From review of *The Poems of Ernest Dowson*, with a Memoir by Arthur Symons, *DC*, 26 May 1905

3   Contemporary Poetry

EARLY LAST CENTURY it was boldly prophesied that dramatic poetry would supersede all other branches of the art. Lyric and epic were classed as outworn, barbarous forms, incapable of expounding the complexity of modern life. If the speculation arose from any known facts, it was from the culmination of the drama among the nations of Europe when they had attained a high degree of Imperial unity. Calderon, Shakespeare, Molière, Goethe and their circles might have been given in evidence. Negative proof lay in the absence of a significant Italian drama, for Italy had no unity. As in a sense a national force it might be admitted that literature did achieve its supreme felicity then; by no other artifice, we think, can such claims on behalf of the poetic drama be supported. The speculation was paradoxical in a bad sense, for it remains a paradox. At that very time the lyric was asserting a supremacy which it has never lost. The very dramas of the day were often lyrical, and had only lyrical good qualities. 'Prometheus Unbound' is actually called by Shelley 'a lyrical drama'. The noblest literary achievements were in the lyric. So puissant was it that its caress entrapped philosophy. Coleridge, Wordsworth, Shelley and their great contemporaries revealed its adaptability to every mode of thought and emotion. The names of those who followed them are on every lip, and in many hearts. Today at least the place of the lyric seems assured. There are Swinburne and Meredith, of a passing age; in the lyric drama, the drama which is essentially lyric, though not in form, there is Mr Phillips, and above all there is Mr Yeats. And its place in poetry is almost equalled by its place in homoeopathy. Thousands of the sad people in the streets write lyrics, following Goethe, no doubt, to get rid of their dreams, their debts, and the effect of reading other men's verse. To the careless reader, however, what is the amusement of these gentlemen may seem painful enough. But we venture to think that for this, and for still nobler reasons, the lyric will prosper, at least so long as individualism makes way in literature. Increasing complexity of thought and emotion will find no such outlet as the myriad-minded lyric, with its intricacies of form as numerous and as exquisite as those of a birch-tree in the wind. For instance, Mr E. M. Holden and Miss Buckton, among the writers before us, have used several dainty forms with more or less success, though we do not think that these forms appeal to aught but the outward eye or ear.

The lyric may claim other points of superiority. Contrasted with the drama in couplets or blank verse, how much more truthful it is. As an ejaculation, a volume of laughter or lament, the best lyrics seem to be the poet's natural speech. In one of his prefaces Wordsworth writes as if he thought that passion chastened the speech. Does it? Solemnity and force it gives; but the only excuse for Hamlet's dying words, as Shakespeare gives them, is that their solemnity probably equals in effect, though it does not resemble, the solemnity of a dying man. The lyric, on the contrary, lays no such claim as the drama to reality. Nobody supposes, for example, that Mr S. Weir Mitchell would think of saying in mixed company, as he does in his charming 'Ode on a Lycian Tomb', 'What gracious mimicry of grief is here?' He was impressed by the tomb, determined to write, and in order to impress possible readers, chose conventional means, rhythm, rhyme, and an unnatural language—with delightful effect. There is no deception. He says frankly: I am writing an Ode. The lyric then is self-expression, whether by necessity or by mere malice aforethought. Those that practise the art include men who have spent a laborious life in sounding their own stops, like Shelley or Sidney, and also the men (and women) who mistake the lowest form of vanity for the highest form of art. Everyone must have noticed, standing on the shore, when the sun or the moon is over the sea, how the highway of light on the water comes right to his feet, and how those on the right and on the left seem not to be sharing his pleasure, but to be in darkness. In some such way the former class views life. Their sense even of common things is so poignant that it must be unique; so Coleridge writes: 'Wait only till the hand of eve/Hath wholly closed yon western bars.'

So Miss Buckton, on seeing one little cloud:

> Sail long, blessèd cloud!
>   With thy burden tender,
> On, till thou art all dissolved
>   In the endless blue,
> And my spirit falls again,
> Through the heavens, silently
>   Born anew!

So, too, Mrs Wilson writes: 'Still half the fields return the sun,/Still laughs the running wheat.'

'Running wheat' is right. It shows something at least of the power that can give us truth 'with more than truth exprest', i.e., poetically. Others have seen wheat running under the wind; some have written it down; but we do not remember seeing it rightly put before.

The second is a larger class, including Aleister Crowley. They are in search of thoughts, which, never finding, they describe. Aleister Crowley, it seems to us, does not justify by any wit, or legitimate pathos, or music, his choice of subjects, difficult or unclean, which make him a sinister rival to the mutoscope. These few lines cannot suggest the unpleasant whole of his ode on 'Sin', but they are quite characteristic of his manner:

> Ye rivers, and ye elemental caves,
>   Above the fountains of the broken ice,
> Know ye what dragon lurks within your waves?
> Know ye the secret of the cockatrice?
>   The basilisk whose shapeless brood
>   Take blood and muck for food?

The author, too, has a strong stomach. In another place he twits the sea with being 'cave-rolling'. Most modern lyrists apparently think that in 'Nature' they have a subject ready-made. Nature is as productive of bad poetry as were Chloë and Delia long ago.

From review of new verse, *DC*, 27 August 1901

Minor poetry might profitably be used for other purposes than the making of spills, for which the choice paper on which it is printed is an apt material. Some persons keep a shelf for these books as *lapsus Naturae*, or collect them from a kindly belief that the proper study of mankind is men. But we would recommend a generous and serious study. For the minor poet himself the study of his peers would have the wholesome effect of exercising his mind upon those weaknesses which he never perceives in himself; he might even learn that his most valued peculiarities are shared by scores. For the ordinary uninspired person, on the other hand, such books hold out not only a hope of discovery, like digging for coal in Kent, together with a solemn amusement, but also a fertile land of reflection. To take only one point among many, minor poetry is, we believe, significant, because it is abundantly prophetic of the future of poetry. We do not deny that it is imitative, especially in manner; but we do assert that it is in a large degree original. The youthfulness, the exuberance which distinguishes nearly all minor poetry succeeds in masking the new thoughts which are almost equally characteristic. In the minor poet himself these thoughts are seldom matured. They lie in a sort of life-in-death until the touch of a mighty hand grants them their full development. For the great poet comes at the end of a period, the *résumé* of a score of mediocrities, as Wordsworth was. We make no pretence of being able to create imaginatively the poet of the next age from the material in the books before us. We seem, nevertheless, to see in the best of them the beginnings of a path farther into the unknown.

From review of new verse, DC, 27 December 1902

We have lately had the privilege of reading forty volumes of verse, all sent into the world during the unspeakable summer and autumn of the present year. With thirty of these we feel, for various reasons, unqualified to deal; for they come rather within the province of preventive medicine than our own. Setting aside those submerged three-quarters, good or bad, but to us indifferent, we have been astonished by the diverse excellences of the remainder. We find amongst them dignity, style, imagination, and humour, and serious pondering of life, such as would be sufficient to equip a poet of the first rank. They fill us with respect for the poetry of the twentieth century. In short, we know of no other age that has abounded in lesser writers of verse with so much individuality. We have to look back as far as Tottel's *Miscellany* or *England's Helicon* for an assembly of contemporaneous versifiers anything like this.

From review of new verse, DC, 26 November 1903

No one who possesses this book, and a few dozens more, including that which gives specimens of work by the women poets from Christina Rossetti to Katharine Tynan, can doubt that, at the lowest estimation, the poets of today—excluding Mr Swinburne and Mr Meredith—make up a body of poetry equal to the complete work of any of our poets, except the greatest; and far more than equal to that of Tennyson, for example. We believe also that their poetry, whatever its enduring merits, has in it elements deserving as wide a popularity as poetry can ever have among contemporaries. For our poets are seriously absorbed in the life, social, political, philosophic, and artistic, of our day, and they have abundant gifts of expression, of melody, of enthusiasm which ought to domesticate their work in our hearts.

But we recognize also that there are immense and, so far, insuperable difficulties in the way of any such popularity and of the influence which is their due. Reprints of old, well tested, or well guaranteed poetry abound and catch the attention of the most timid and unobservant; and not only poetry, but such prose as satisfies similar needs, as for example *Religio Medici* and *The Opium Eater*, which were probably never before so much bought. The prose of our own time is also rich in poetic qualities, and it finds its way into the confidence of the numerous half-educated people who are, we fancy, afraid of the form of verse and perhaps distrustful of poets as eccentrics, dreamers, etc., while, even among the educated, writers like Stevenson, Mr Conrad, and Mr W. H. Hudson must also turn aside some who would in another age have read more poetry. Foreign literatures and translations add still further defences which new poetry has to scale.

Then the multiplication of authors, and of writers in verse in particular, makes choice very difficult. An imbecile with ten pounds in his pocket can easily add one to the number of the volumes from which the lover of poetry has to choose. Finally, in a centrifugal age, in which principles and aims are numerous, vague, uncertain, confused, and in conflict, the lack of good criticism, or even of moderately good criticism that has any authority, defrauds many noble and beautiful voices of the ears which expect them. . . .

These poets are writing the autobiography and the criticism of our age as sincerely, as delicately, as their predecessors whom we all applaud. They sound notes which were never heard before, notes which, if our ears refuse to hear them, will never to the end of time bear quite their true meaning again. Their multitudinousness, their subtlety, their variety, their fineness, their enthusiasm and aspiration, their sadness, their introspection, their love of what is old and of what is very new, make clear large claims upon almost all of us. Even where curiosity, working inward and more inward, becomes sad and opaque for lack of the north-west wind of real publicity and criticism and applause, there is often a charm which expresses some of our own secret and never before expressed thoughts and emotions.

From review of *The Book of Living Poets,* ed. Walter Jerrold, and
*Poets and Poetry of the Nineteenth Century, Christina Rossetti to
Katharine Tynan,* ed. Alfred H. Miles, *DC,* 13 January 1908

THOMAS HARDY

IT WOULD BE interesting to learn how a great prose writer regards his verse. He will have a tenderness for it as for the fairer and perhaps the elder child; but in what frame of mind does he who can say so much in prose and denies himself no subject or mood in it, turn to verse? Is it an instinct for finality in form, a need of limitation and strict obedience to rule, or a desire to express but not to explain, or is it partly for the sake of the royalty of the robes and the great tradition? Mr Hardy is silent. That he cares much for the forms of verse is clear from the number which he uses, and there is one at least which he has made distinctively his own, that of the poem on 'One We Knew (M.H. 1772-1857)':

> She told us how they used to form for the
>   country dances—
> 'The Triumph', 'The New-rigged Ship'—
> To the light of the guttering wax in the
>   panelled manses,
> And in cots to the blink of a dip.

And yet, though he indulges in many varieties of rhyme and stanza form, it is hard to believe that it is for any sensuous quality. For they have almost none, and we wonder what subtle reason he had for using a lyric stanza like the following for a narrative full of conversation:

> We moved with pensive paces,
>   I and he,
> And bent our faded faces
>   Wistfully,
> For something troubled him and troubled me.

There are sonnets in the book, but so unlike sonnets in spirit that many will read them without observing that they have this form. Often it might be thought that he dresses 'his thoughts' in these 'noble and famous garments' in a mood of solemn mockery. That, whether its intention or not, is its effect. He laughs at the external beauty of verse by making it clothe a corpse, a withered old man, or a woman of faded youth. The utmost positive effect of the verse is to give brevity and solemnity. The poems do not materially differ from his stories except that they are shorter than anything he has done in prose, and that they gain a greater solemnity from their more uniform colouring, their greater simplicity and lack of explanations.

  Many of the poems are narrative. Even when called lyrical they suggest a chain of events. They are full of misunderstandings, forebodings, memories, endings, questionings. These the subjects, and they are the atmosphere of the book, from which there is no escape. Other poetry allows a great richness and diversity of interpretation; Mr Hardy's allows none. He will not give his readers a moment's liberty. He gives them not only actions and characters, but their results; not only their results, but what is to be thought of them. He may not give us these things in so many words, but, if not, he does so by unmistakable implication. We cannot think of any other poetry so tyrannous; and this in part makes us restive under the conventional form, which adds a grotesqueness by means of the necessary inversion and other poetic licence to the philosophic prose diction.

The work belongs to very different periods, but chiefly to an early one, about 1866, and to a late one, ending in the present year with a fine poem on George Meredith. There is little difference in character, and the following might belong to 1907, instead of to 1867. It is called '1967':

> In five-score summers! All new eyes,
> New minds, new modes, new fools, new wise;
> New woes to weep, new joys to prize;
> With nothing left of me and you
> In that live century's living view
> Beyond a pinch of dust or two;
> A century, which, if not sublime,
> Will show, I doubt not, at its prime,
> A scope above this blinkered time.
> —Yet what to me how far above?
> For I would only ask thereof
> That thy worm should be my worm, Love!

The one difference is that the later method is less fluent, more rich and dramatic, and the sonnets, for example, belong to the earlier period.

The obvious quality to point to in all the poems is the sense of the misery and fraudulence of life. The men and women have been happy and are not, and the happiness is now nothing; or they are or ought to be happy, but there is an inexplicable sigh; or they compare their own day unfavourably to an older. The poems abound in phrases such as: 'Before the birth of consciousness,/When all went well——', or

> Yet, Dear, though one may sigh,
>   Raking up leaves,
> New leaves will dance on high—
>   Earth never grieves!—
> Will not, when missed am I
>   Raking up leaves——

or

> But she will no more stand
>   In the sunshine there,
> With that wave of her white-gloved hand,
>   And that chestnut hair——

or 'O friend, nought happens twice thus, why,/I cannot tell!'

The book contains ninety-nine reasons for not living. Yet it is not a book of despair. It is a book of sincerity, 'sweet sincerity', and to a poem of that name there is a memorable conclusion. It is dated 1899:

> Yet, would men look at true things,
> And unilluded view things,
> And count to bear undue things,
> The real might mend the seeming,
> Facts better their foredeeming,
> And life its dis-esteeming.

He does not believe that life is worth living as these men and women lived, even if they did, and he gives us little chance of believing so. But he thinks it is to be altered. He has a poem on a christening, where a lovely child makes the congregation smile with pleasure—while the unmarried mother weeps on the gallery stair:

> 'I am the baby's mother;
>   This gem of the race
> The decent fain would smother,
>   And for my deep disgrace
> I am bidden to leave the place'.

Bitter as the poem is there is hope in it. For it demands, at least, if it does not foresee, a time when values and judgments will be truer than they are, when we of our day shall be held as callous as those who hung men for sheep-stealing. Mr Hardy looks at things as they are, and what is still more notable he does not adopt the genial consolation that they might be worse, that in spite of them many are happy, and that the unhappy live on and will not die. His worst tragedies are due as much to transient and alterable custom as to the nature of things. He sees this, and he makes us see it. The moan of his verse rouses an echo that is as brave as a trumpet.

Review of *Time's Laughingstocks and Other Poems*,
DC, 7 December 1909

Mr Thomas Hardy's new book, *Time's Laughingstocks*, consists of not far short of a hundred poems, of which the first score are specially grouped under that title. It is almost unnecessary to say that there is hardly one poem to which the title does not perfectly apply, though the other sub-titles are 'Love Lyrics', 'A Set of Country Songs' and 'Pieces Occasional and Various'. Perhaps the only exceptions are 'The Dark-eyed Gentleman', founded on a popular song—'And he came and he tied up my garter for me'; and a playful little piece on the blackbird in Wessex. In fact, these sub-divisions are quite arbitrary, since many of the lyrics are narrative, nearly all the narrative poems are in stanzas of lyrical quality, and love or the death of love is in all of them. The only other possible arrangement would be chronological, for a number of them are dated, the earliest belonging to nearly fifty years back, the latest to this year. We rejoice to see that the new are more than equal to the old in form, in substance, and in spirit. Many stanza forms are used; the rhymes are often elaborate; and assonance is sometimes used instead of rhyme.

This enduring ripeness and strength of Mr Hardy's is not so surprising as at first sight when we consider that in his verse, at least as much as in his prose, his work is mainly intellectual and its emotion chiefly dramatic, if we accept the general emotion which pervades it all. There is no ecstasy or glory or magic for him to lose, save what is in the things themselves as distinct from his treatment of them. His austere, condensed, and fateful manner has lost nothing. His felicity in detail may be witnessed by phrases such as 'blasts that besom the green' and 'leaden concaves round her eyes', and by such a verse as

> Dance; how a' would dance!
> If a fiddlestring did but sound
> She would fling out her coats, give a slanting glance,
> And go round and round.

In at least one—a poem describing the home-coming of a bride to her husband's unknown, desolate house—there is a changing burden which is full if not of magic yet of a deep and strong suggestion of something which the intellect alone cannot handle: 'Gruffly growled the wind on Toller downland broad and bare,/And lonesome was the house, and dark; and few came there.' The movement of that last line is characteristic. Another poem also of three perfect verses, 'The Voice of the Thorn', though precise and severe, creates the personality of a tree comparable with Wordsworth's thorn, but quite different in its lack of expressed emotion.

As a rule Mr Hardy's poems are the sum of their parts, and it would be easy to show what it is that produces their strong, calm effect. Seldom does anything creep in from Nature or the spirit of humanity to give his work a something not to be accounted for in what he actually says. His mood is that of 'Tess' and 'Two on a Tower', and the 'President of the Immortals' is the dominant figure, if not always personally introduced. There is something plaintive, almost naïve and rustic, in Mr Hardy's unvarying sadness—not mere despondency or melancholy or weakness, but the positive and hopeful quality of sadness; as there is something rustic in the question 'And what's the good of it' following ' "I have finished another year," said God.' There is, too, a religious quality, as of darkened lights and voices intoning. Sometimes the sadness might seem almost perverse, as in his poem of the pine-planters where, after the beautiful lines describing how the tree begins to sigh as soon as it stands upright, he interprets that sighing as

> Grieving that never [? ever]
>   Kind Fate decreed
> It could not ever
>   Remain a seed.

But that is only because it is more unmistakable here than usual that the sadness is definitely Mr Hardy's (or Marty South's) and not that of life itself. It is true that he wishes the poems to be regarded as 'dramatic monologues', yet the prevalent tone must be his, and so is the tone of many separate poems, such as that on a deathbed, which ends:

> We see by littles now the deft achievement
> Whereby she has escaped the wrongers all,
> In view of which our momentary bereavement
>   Outshapes but small.

He cannot escape from his own muffled cadences, which at their liveliest suggest old people dancing an old dance, his reluctances and pauses; or from his sombre intellectual vocabulary. He makes no concession to the fact that he is writing verse except by using the word 'swain' and by such construction as in 'And nevermore sighted was even/A print of his shoe.' He is not in the least afraid of colloquial prose as in 'I faltered: "Well . . . I did not think/You would test me quite so soon." ' He would abide with equanimity and certainty of ultimate approval any too nice questioning as to whether his verses are poetry. Whether his poems are a few lines or several pages long they are almost always stories, and it is to his repeated triumphs in representing a sequence of events and emotions and enduing them with a clear colouring and form that we should point if this question were raised.

Only poetry could produce with such economy and sureness the effects in 'A Tramp Woman's Tragedy', 'Sunday Morning Tragedy', 'The Rejected Member's Wife', 'On the Departure Platform', 'The Dawn after the Dance' and 'The Dead Quire'. These are too long and closely knit to quote, but we will give an example from one of the early poems which are least dramatic in character:

> The grey gaunt days dividing us in twain
> Seemed hopeless hills my strength must faint to climb,
> But they are gone; and now I would detain
> The few clock beats that part us; rein back Time
> And live in close expectance never closed

In change for far expectance closed at last,
So harshly has expectance been imposed
On my long need while the slow blank months passed.
And knowing that what is now about to be
Will all *have been* in O, so short a space!
I read beyond it my despondency
When more dividing months shall take its place,
Thereby denying to this hour of grace
A full-up measure of felicity.

Here the form is a sonnet, and if it is in a sense a 'moment's monument', the moment is full of years, and it is an implied narrative. This
one is particularly useful as showing probably the author's own personality, and the tendency which controls the poems in which there
are other actors. If this is so, two other poems may be quoted as
showing the far from negatively pessimistic conclusions at which he
has arrived—

Let me enjoy the earth no less
Because the all-enacting Might
That fashioned forth its loveliness
Had other aims than my delight. . . .

and

Yet, would men look at true things,
And unilluded view things,
And count to fear undue things,
The real might mend the seeming,
Facts better their foredeeming,
And Life its disesteeming.

These passages are a necessary key to the poems and to Mr Hardy's
work as a whole.

Another review of *Time's Laughingstocks, MP*, 9 December 1909

But there is a greater than Duck or Barnes still among us, a wide-
ranging poet, who is always a countryman of a somewhat lonely heart,
Mr Thomas Hardy. For I do notice something in his poetry which I
hope I may with respect call rustic, and, what is much the same thing,
old-fashioned. . . . He has written songs and narratives which prove
his descent from some ancient ballad-maker, perhaps the one who
wrote 'A pleasant ballad of the merry miller's wooing of the baker's
daughter of Manchester', or 'A new ballade, showing the cruel
robberies and lewd life of Philip Collins, *alias* Osburne, commonly

called Philip of the West, who was pressed to death at Newgate in London the third of December last past, 1597', to be sung to the tune of 'Pagginton's round'. Some of the lyric stanzas to which he fits a narrative originated probably in some such tune.

And how often is he delighted to represent a peasant's view, a peasant's contribution to the irony of things, a capital instance being the Belgian who killed Grouchy to save his farm, and so lost Napoleon the battle of Waterloo.

With this rusticity, if that be the right name for it, I cannot help connecting that most tyrannous obsession of the blindness of Fate, the carelessness of Nature, and the insignificance of Man, crawling in multitudes like caterpillars, twitched by the Immanent Will hither and thither. Over and over again, from the earliest poems up to *The Dynasts*, he amplifies those words which he puts into the mouth of God,

> My labours, logicless
> You may explain; not I:
> Sense-sealed I have wrought, without a guess
> That I evolved a Consciousness
> To ask for reasons why. . . .

Napoleon, in *The Dynasts*, asks the question, 'Why am I here?' and answers it, 'By laws imposed on me inexorably,/History makes use of me to weave her web.'

Twentieth-century superstition can no farther go than in that enormous poem, which is astonishing in many ways, not least in being readable. I call it superstition because truth, or a genuine attempt at truth, has been turned apparently by an isolated rustic imagination into an obsession so powerful that only a very great talent could have rescued anything uninjured from the weight of it. A hundred years ago, Mr Hardy would have seen 'real ghosts'. Today he has to invent them, and call his Spirits of the Years and of the Pities, Spirits Sinister and Ironic, Rumours and Recording Angels, who have the best seats at the human comedy, 'contrivances of the fancy merely'.

Even his use of irony verges on the superstitious. Artistically, at least in the shorter poems, it may be sound, and is certainly effective, as where the old man laments on learning that his wife is to be in the same wing of the workhouse, instead of setting him 'free of his forty years' chain'. But the frequent use and abuse of it change the reader's smile into a laugh at the perversity.

Mr Hardy must have discovered the blindness of Fate, the indifference of Nature, and the irony of Life, before he met them in books. They have been brooded over in solitude, until they afflict him as the wickedness of man afflicts a Puritan. The skull and crossbones, Death the scythed skeleton, and the symbolic hour-glass have been as real to him as to some of those carvers of tombstones in country church-yards, or to the painter of that window at St Edmund's in Salisbury who represented 'God the Father . . . in blue and red vests, like a little old man, the head, feet, and hands naked; in one place fixing a pair of compasses on the sun and moon.' If I were told that he had spent his days in a woodland hermitage, though I should not believe the story, I should suspect that it was founded on fact.

But the woodland, and the country in general, have given Mr Hardy some of his principal consolations. And one, at least, of these is almost superstitious. I mean the idea that 'the longlegs, the moth, and the dumbledore' know 'earth-secrets' that he knows not. In the 'Darkling Thrush' it is to be found in another stage, the bird's song in Winter impelling him to think that 'some blessed Hope' of which he was unaware was known to it. He compares town and country much as Meredith does. The country is paradise in the comparison; for he speaks of the Holiday Fund for City Children as temporarily 'changing their urban murk to paradise'. Country life, paradise or not, he handles with a combination of power and exactness beyond that of any poet who could be compared to him. . . .

From 'Three Wessex Poets', In Pursuit of Spring, 192-8

I prefer Mr Hardy's poems to his novels, and there the place-names offer many pleasures and provoke several kinds of curiosity. Some-times the place is given, it appears, out of pure fidelity to the fact. He writes no poetry that could suffer by names and dates. That some-thing happened 'At this point of time, at this point in space,' it pleases him to put on record, as when he signs 'Max Gate, 1899,' at the end of 'An August Midnight': [poem quoted].

Somehow the two stanzas of 'The Comet at Yalbury or Yell'ham' do as much as 'Two on a Tower' to 'set the emotional history of two infinitesimal lives against the stupendous background of the stellar universe':

> It bends far over Yell'ham Plain,
>   And we, from Yell'ham Height,
> Stand and regard its fiery train,
>   So soon to swim from sight.
>
> It will return long years hence, when
>   As now its strange swift shine
> Will fall on Yell'ham: but not then
>   On that sweet form of thine.

The rustic names, if anything, emphasize the littleness, yet save it from abstraction. Sometimes Mr Hardy gains the same effect of reality by withholding the name, conspicuously as in 'Her Dilemma' (in—— Church), tacitly as in 'At an Inn' and 'The Rejected Member's Wife' where everything is precise but names are omitted. The general effect of using local names with no significance for the stranger, and no special private value of sound or association for the poet, as in 'From Pummery-Tout to where the Gibbet is...', or 'Scene—A sad-coloured landscape, Waddonvale', or 'By Mellstock Lodge and Avenue', or 'Not far from Mellstock—so tradition saith—', or 'While High Stoy trees twanged to Bubb Down Hill,/And Bubb Down to High Stoy', the general effect is to aid reality by suggestions of gross and humble simplicity. It might become a trick or device, but in Mr Hardy it is not either, though it succeeds in different degrees. In a recurring line like the following, the name gives even a kind of magic reality, and perhaps magnifies the wind which has no name: 'Gruffly growled the wind on Toller downland broad and bare.' The least effect is to make sure of keeping the poem to earth by keeping it to Dorset, so that a storm strikes freshly on jaded ears by means of

> The drone of Thorncombe trees,
>   The Froom in flood upon the moor,
> The mud of Mellstock Leaze.

A Literary Pilgrim in England, 149-51

CHARLES M. DOUGHTY

THESE TWO VOLUMES contain the last eight books of Mr Doughty's epic. In twenty-four books, or about 30,000 lines of blank verse, with constant passion and infinite richness of workmanship, he has given us a strong, beautiful impression of the ascent of the British people out of prehistoric gloom, through a period of offensive foreign war under Brennus, and the years of vivid but disintegrated life before the Roman invasions, down to the defensive struggle under Caractacus, the introduction of Christianity by Joseph of Arimathaea, and the marriage of a Christian Britoness with a Roman knight.

He has not attempted to give a narrow and pedantic unity to the vast and numerous and scattered events which he sings, but I venture to think that the more the poem is read, the more of a passionate moral unity in the whole will be revealed. Such are his imagination, his learning, his patience, that even had he written in prose, or had his verse no positive merit, the narrative would have deserved the highest praise as an introduction to the study of Britain, its people, its visible beauty, its personality.

It has no competitors. To turn from Livy on Brennus, or Caesar on the state of this island, or Tacitus on Cartimandua, Queen of the Brigantes to Mr Doughty's poem is like turning from a list of deaths to 'Lycidas' and 'Adonais'. Even where his material is the same as that of those historians, his superiority is clear. Now, for the first time in written words, Brennus and Caractacus and Boadicea are made alive, beautiful, and strong. Their battles, their feasts, their wooings, their partings, their thoughts under the stars, their deaths, have a clearness and truth and passion which raise their creator to the same class as the famous epic poets—I do not say to their level, because I do not know; but that his effects and theirs are of the same order is certain.

Supposing that he had not done this, then his picture of early Britain, vast, wild, sunlit, coloured, perfumed, full of the songs of birds, with here and there a town and here and there the burial mounds of princes and unknown men—that picture would alone have made the poem deserve an undying name. It is a little matter, but I had no worthy sense of the rich great age of this home of my race until I found it here; it is not a little matter that (some day) children will grow up with the emotion of this book in their breasts, with such an harmonious view of early history and folklore and ancient monuments and the physical beauty of Britain as we can only grope after.

But the book is not only poetry in substance and spirit; it is poetry in form. That is to say, its verse makes it something different from the prose narrative which the same man might have written; different, of loftier beauty, monumental, tense beyond the reach of prose. Except Milton and Spenser, no English writer has wrought out a style as consistent, poetical, and perfectly his own as Mr Doughty's; and it has this, too, in common with theirs, that, when it fails, it becomes dull, but does not cease to be poetry. And it is simpler than theirs, with as little that can be accused of verbosity as that of Wordsworth, or the early William Morris, or Mr Yeats. It is very modern, for example, in its daring and just use of unimportant syllables, as at the beginning of a line, over and above the usual weight.

Enough has perhaps been said about Mr Doughty's vocabulary and the structure of his phrases in our notices of the first four volumes. The vocabulary is unusual, abounding in words or forms that have become obsolete, or even in those which were probably never in use; it is as eclectic as Milton's or Keats's; but with the aid of Mr Doughty's notes, the glossary, and a little patience, it is easily mastered, and is seen in the end to have a curious fitness and consistency, so that, if it sometimes puzzles, it never jars. The structure owes something to Latin and Greek, but everything, it must be observed, to a pursuit of what is logical and most brief. After an hour's reading it offers no difficulties, and in a short time the poetry may be read aloud with ease and joy, so as to disclose the admirable concentration, the melody, the accents that obey and serve the sense.

From review of *The Dawn in Britain*, V and VI, *DC*, 7 February 1907

For [his poem's] reception at the present day, Mr Doughty has made a further difficulty by using a vocabulary and constructions of his own. We meet such words as caterf (Lat. *caterva*), bavin, crome, pilch, yex. We meet such sentences as: 'Careless of warfare, which, erewhile, with Romans;/How may they only eat, seek dying Britons', or as this beautiful one: 'And hearken, a far-off bray, ah, heavy note,/If any feared to die, of Roman clarion!' It is true also that sentences like this (a speech of Caractacus at Rome) abound:

> Romans! whilst I viewed, from hence,
> Your palaces, your gilded temple roofs,
> I marvelled, ye could covet our poor cotes!

and that his style allows of a fine simplicity in touching a simple matter, as here:

> Grey deep, how wholesome, to a shipman's eye!
> And who is 'scaped, from ape-faced world, not joys
> Look forth, o'er thy vast wandering breast, abroad,
> From some lone cliff, and snuff up thy salt breath?
> Eternal flood! how thy waves' sullen sound,
> Doth seem, as mother's voice, to wakening child!

But when I add that his blank verse has a hundred surprises for those who have scamped their Shakespeare and Milton and know nothing of Mr Yeats or Mr Sturge Moore, it will be clear that Mr Doughty is not asking for a sixpenny edition within twelve months.

The result is that the reader's first hour with the poem is full of doubt and confusion and pain. Some have probably shut the book for ever after the first half hour. But we are quite sure that because *Endymion* and much of Browning and *The Ancient Mariner* and *Paradise Lost*, not to speak of the poems of Donne, do not now appear to be in a foreign tongue, they never did appear so? When the style of a book by a manifestly big man offends us it is worth while to ask some such question. Also, the present reviewer, a hurried man, with little scholarship, has found that in an hour or two the difficulty of the style disappeared, and its wonderful brevity, precision, consistency and power emerged without a cloud. Of course it does remain a subject for speculation: whether an entirely great man would hamper himself with a vocabulary and an eccentricity of construction so much outside the tradition of English poetry. And yet is it not idle speculation, since the result achieved by this style is prodigious?

From another review of the same, *B*, March 1907

JOHN DAVIDSON

LITERATURE AND PHILOSOPHY appear in his work, now as partners, philosophy a sleeping one, having talked itself to sleep; and again as civil enemies. These differences seem to be due to the fact that the philosophy is exclusively intellectual, the poetry essentially passionate. We ought to guess the philosophy from the poetry no more than we guess the athlete's meals from the length of his leap.

But Mr Davidson is at the beginning of a new age, or is convinced that he is. He appears to believe himself the first poet to confront this age and all its most characteristic activities quite honestly—like M. Maeterlinck in prose; and the knowledge or belief that this is so has disturbed him as much as might have been expected. It is very well for him to say that critics have been talking about his 'metaphysical and philosophical poetry', and to reply with:

> There can be no metaphysical or philosophical poetry; a poet may employ metaphysics and philosophy as he may employ history and science, but all poetry is poetical. It is not a new metaphysic, a new philosophy, or a new theology which I begin: Metaphysics, theology, and philosophy itself, in its esoteric sense, are to me fallacies, as each insists on a great world of matter and spirit. It is a new poetry I begin, a new cosmogony, a new habitation for the imagination of men.

A poet may be a metaphysician and a great one, but not at the same time, or if he is we should salute him as we should one who is poet and baker and composes with dough, currants and icing. It is extraordinary that Mr Davidson should know this, yet write things like *The Testament of a Prime Minister* and *The Triumph of Mammon*. Its effect upon his writing alone ought to have told him that he had gone wrong. He must know that there is no reason why he should use blank verse for this—in a bridal chamber conversation:

> To be a beast?—it is to be a star!
> Nothing is bestial, nothing mean or base;
> For all is Universe, an infinite
> Ethereal way and being of myriad-minded
> Matter: substance and soul, all matter, wanton
> As lightning, chaste as light, diverse as sin.

If this crude and furious pamphlet has any merit it is as an allegory. A dramatic allegory—from the author of Fleet Street Eclogues and 'A Runnable Stag'! We assume that Mr Davidson has hoped to do with his one mind what no one mind has done before—to face contemporary life and invent (out of excellent material) a new cosmogony better suited to its needs, brand-new and dirt-cheap. Hence his failure. You cannot make yourself into a giant by bolting two or even three oxen and a complement of potatoes.

From review of *The Triumph of Mammon*, *DC*, 30 April 1907

W. B. YEATS

THE CELTIC TWILIGHT has been doubled in size and charm by the addition of a score of slender chapters. The new portion is the issue of almost the same mood as the old, and like that slips through the fingers of criticism. We had rather criticize Plynlimmon or the Valley of the Dove than this book. For to us it seems just such a part of Nature's physiognomy as they. Nearly all the chapters are concerned with Irish legends of every date, recorded in Mr Yeats's well-known economical style with so little obvious egoism that the anthropologist might attribute them to some lucky pupil of Mr Tylor. The writer merely seems at first sight to have taken notes from Biddy Early or 'A woman that I know' and printed them; he says himself that he tells these things as accurately as he can, and with no theories to blur the history. But it is impossible to travel far in this 'region of stories' without coming under the spell of a cadence or mixing one's own thoughts in the crucible of Mr Yeats's dreams. After that, even if one is a mere Saxon, one has the honour of being kidnapped by the 'gentle people', the faery....

It is often the fate of a dreamer not to be able to give away his dreams. On reading this book, many a dreamer will envy Mr Yeats his good fortune in moving about a world where perfect dreams are as cheap as evening papers. He is indeed to be envied, like a man with a fine house. He has a fine house, but we are mainly concerned with the way he has furnished it. And everywhere there is evidence, not always on the surface, of his inspired skill. Often enough, when telling an old peasant's story, he finishes it with a touch that may not be his own, but which only an artist would seize. Paddy Fynn saw the banshee 'batting the river with his hands'. In the same way Dante saw Chiron parting his beard with an arrow. So again, one of the old women whom Mr Yeats can use so well describes the heroic faery women: 'Those with their hair up have short dresses, so that you can see their legs right up to the calf' like Burns's 'vision'. All these things Mr Yeats will write down with the precision of a telegram, and the sweetness of one who writes for the pleasure of writing, like a heaven-sent Stevenson without a patent reading-lamp....

From review of *The Celtic Twilight*, New edn., *DC*, 12 July 1902

The serious criticism of bad books I can understand; for it is explained by weakness, or poverty, or servility, or bad taste: but not the serious criticism of good books. The better a book is the more difficult and the more unnecessary is the criticism of it. For the one essential quality of a critic is the power to receive suggestions, to be stimulated, and in the end to advance a little way the influence of the book with which he deals. In the case of a small book, it is easy for the critic to use this power, if we may assume that he is content to deal only with what he admires. In the case of a fine book, or above all a fine contemporary book, it is most difficult and almost always immodest. For the critic, unless he be in possession of the matter in the same degree as his author, can but offer his own shrill or drowsy chirp in place of the author's full choir, and hope that the small may suggest the great. He brings a rose and says that in his author's garden all the flowers are lovelier. He points to a star and says, it is the least bright. He is, in short, an advocate in the surprising position of being undone by the very merits of his case.

Mr W. B. Yeats, in our generation at least, cannot be advocated. The compass and quality of his powers are probably high, certainly unique. No one, therefore, can advocate them without in some considerable degree diluting them. I console myself in the act of diluting them, only by the thought that were they in their fullness not too strong for our generation, he would be more widely esteemed than he is, and not the idol and perhaps the victim of a 'movement'.

In these two volumes he seems to be the victim of the Irish literary movement. Were he not, I think that he would hardly have chosen none but Irish subjects, and those slender ones all. The little prose plays, 'The Hour Glass', 'Cathleen' and 'The Pot of Broth', are perfect in construction; and they are excellent for their humour, their pathos, their symbolism, their gay and easy flow and conflict of dialogue, and their simple, idiomatic, and melodious prose. But not one of them, not even 'The Hour Glass' seems to me to have drawn upon all those qualities of Mr Yeats's mind, and especially the intellectual qualities, which I have from time to time recognized in his printed and spoken utterances. In 'On Baile's Strand', also, which is part prose, part verse, I think that he is so much occupied with the rich, heavy fabric of Irish heroic life, that he has lost some of the more inward beauties in the gleam of their raiment, a gleam which makes it almost worth while.

But he has done nothing finer than 'The King's Threshold'. The legend of the poet whom a king sent away from the high table at the request of jealous soldiers and priests; who refused to take a lower seat, in spite of the king's offer of all other honours and goods; who would not be persuaded by a lover, a princess, or a disciple, to forgo the right of poetry; who at last recovered his place, because his disciples would rather have been strangled than grant that the king was in the right, and so persuaded the king that poetry was more powerful than monarchy; the legend alone would make the fortune of the play. It draws out to their full blossoming Mr Yeats's imagination and command of myth. Above all, it has enabled his blank verse to come to its perfection. The blank verse is (to use a bad, intelligible word) the most realistic I have seen. No two lines are alike. There is not a convention anywhere, no mere smoothness or regularity of rhythm. Mood, sentiment, passion—everything that is character—is expressed in his infinitely varied measure. In his opening speech, the king addresses the poets as those who understand—

> Stringed instruments,
> And how to mingle words and notes together
> So artfully, that all the art is but speech
> Delighted with its own music. . . .

'Speech delighted with its own music' is the best definition of Mr Yeats's verse. He can do everything with it. He is incapable of using blank verse, as so many have done, as a mould with a few variations, into which anything can be poured. The thoughts and emotions of his characters may be seen to mould the verse. Here and there, of course, the blank verse comes near to prose, so various are the characters; at its best, and usually, it is simple, sincere speech that cannot be read sympathetically except as most harmonious verse, although it has a superficial appearance of being chopped prose.

In reading the play, I seem to find, with astonishment, that verse is the natural speech of men, as singing is of birds. . . .

From review of *Plays for an Irish Theatre*, vols. 2 and 3,
WS, 18 June 1904

This volume contains three plays in verse, *The Shadowy Waters*, *The King's Threshold* and *On Baile's Strand*, and the short poems which were published under the title: *In the Seven Woods*. It is a pleasant and cheap form in which to have the second period of this poet's work, though to be complete it should have included *The Wind Among the Reeds*. But not only does the book once more remind the public of the strange and the strong beauty of these poems, but, as might have been expected, it is interesting on account of the many changes in handling and detail to be found in the plays. No poet has troubled himself (and some of his readers) so much by revision as Mr Yeats.

It is not that he outgrows his work, but that he does not outgrow it, and that, since all art is only an approach to perfection, he never loses the patience needed to bring it a little nearer to his desire. And yet we cannot but wish, a little petulantly, that he had thrown all this energy of heart and head into new work.

The Shadowy Waters is almost a new play. For the 'galley' of the original scene has become 'an ancient ship' and, what is more, the sailors have been treated more grossly, so that we get a jumping-off place to the unknown like that, for example, in *Utopia*, and this is a real improvement. Thus the second speech of 'the other sailor' is no longer:

> How many moons have died from the full moon,
> When something that was bearded like a goat
> Walked on the waters, and bid Forgael seek
> His heart's desire where the world dwindles out.

It has become

> And I had thought to make
> A good round sum upon this cruise, and turn—
> For I am getting on in life—to something
> That has less ups and downs than robbery.

The character of Aibric is blunter, too, so as to contrast clearly with Forgael's in speeches like:

> I have good spirits enough.
> I've nothing to complain of but heartburn,
> And that is cured by a boiled liquorice root.

There is also a more gradual development of the union between Forgael and Dectoror and the failure of her attempt to rouse a meeting is more striking; so, too, is the excitement of the sailors over the treasure in the captive ship. The effect in the end is as if we saw the gods coming and going among real sailors on a salty ship and not among enchanted sailors on an enchanted ship. It is, we think, a gain.

The burden of all the changes is a comic realism going along with a translunary quality in that harmony which only Mr Yeats can achieve. The beauty of certain blank verse speeches cannot be overpraised, but it is also hard to pass by. We are now more than ever struck by the beauty of the ordinary speeches which, in their naturalness and real poetry, prove as much as Wordsworth's preface that the speech of poetry can be that of life. The blank verse of most modern plays is ridiculously antique and professional compared with that of Mr Yeats.

From review of *Poems, 1899-1905, DC,* 1 January 1907

Mr Yeats writes the most beautiful prose of our time. It is very likely not the greatest prose, but it provides greater pleasure for its readers than any other. There are writers more heavily adorned, more witty, more stately, more elaborate. Mr Yeats has got beyond adornment and stateliness into simple power. His style is serious, imaginative, flexible, and most sweet. It has not an astonishing word in it. We have, in fact, re-read many of the essays several times out of pure self-indulgence, to revel in this shadowy crystal element that is lovelier than anything coloured.

The book is so singular a pleading and a confession that little would be gained in discussing it except by a competent critic who had the whole of this page to use. Only to a few will it come as a surprise, though it is a slap in the face to those who persist in admiring his other work. The revision of *The Shadowy Waters* and of the stories of Red Hanrahan prepared us for it. In his first essay he is annoyed by a play that is 'full of sedentary refinement and the spirituality of cities'. In the next he is asking: 'How can I make my work mean something to vigorous and simple men, whose attention is not given to art but to a shop, or teaching in a National school, or dispensing medicine?'

Speaking of musicians, he says: 'We may even remind them that the housemaid does not respect the piano-tuner as she does the plumber.' He praises old wives' tales and ends by recalling that he once thought Tolstoy's *War and Peace* the greatest story he had ever read: 'And yet it has gone from me; even Launcelot, ever a shadow, is more visible in my memory than all its substance.' He likes *The Iliad, The Odyssey,* and 'the swift and natural observation of a man as he is shaped by life'. It is beautifully and truly said of two pictures: 'Neither painting could move us at all, if our thought did not rush out to the edges of our flesh, and it is so with all good art. Art bids us touch and taste and hear and see the world. . . .' And yet, again, when he has said that all symbolic art should rise out of a real belief, he points to a real weakness in modern poetry in that its matter 'has not entered into men's prayers nor lighted any through the sacred dark of religious contemplation'. The individual is everything in it: society has not been considered. But then society is not alive, it is a lump that exists. Reform society, not the artist.

Though Mr Yeats loves old wives' tales, he is at the head of the living men who lead us away from them. His style is the reverse of the old wives' tale. That says little and suggests much: into Mr Yeats's you must plunge deep and plunge again before getting all that is in it, but it suggests nothing. He is really not for the plumber. When he depicts heroic men, the equals of the Agamemnonian phalanx, there is a languor about them; he has wreathed poppies in their parsley crowns, and there is nothing of the dawn in their eyes. But, then, only a man in the forefront of this age could worry about what moves 'natural men'. He is so new that he must to his opposite and would take Sycorax for a beauty. He praises a girl playing a banjo—'her movements call up into the mind, so erect and natural she is, whatever is most beautiful in her daily life'—but the common people prefer the musician in evening dress at the shiny piano. Who are the common people, by the way? There are educated and there are half-educated people; but there is no peasantry, or anything like it. Perhaps it is different in Ireland. Mr Yeats can enjoy the pianist, too, can enjoy 'the merely scholarly and exceptional'. He is aware of all periods, and this book expresses with fascinating subtlety his doubt and pain as he ranges among them, saved from self-consciousness and death by his mysticism, by the rapt flight that has melted even into the heavenly blue. Our only fear is that these discoveries and hesitations may add yet another check to the productiveness of an artist like Mr Yeats.

Review of Discoveries, DC, 18 May 1908

Some, attracted by the opportunity of possessing all [Mr Yeats's] work and in so respectable a form will doubtless now read the whole or very large parts of it for the first time, and we should be very glad to know the effect of this singular work, so concentrated and so much of a piece, upon an intelligent mind chiefly familiar with the poetry of past generations. There can be no doubt that it will produce an effect without any parallel in the past. If this effect is strong and favourable it will most likely be due largely to the 'natural magic' of the poetry. 'Natural magic' is usually a very uncertain and fleeting quality. It seldom pervades a whole poem. The same poet may at different times be conspicuous for this possession or for his lack of the gift. But Mr Yeats has it always, at least in such poems as it could possibly enter. Often enough he has nothing else. He can plunge us, as few other poets writing in English can, into a world where all the values are changed and the parochialism of humanity is forgotten, or rather it is inconceivable that it should ever have existed. Such is that poem which ends:

> Come, heart, where hill is heaped upon hill:
> For there the mystical brotherhood
> Of sun and moon and hollow and wood
> And river and stream work out their will;
> And God stands winding His lonely horn,
> And time and the world are ever in flight;
> And love is less kind than the grey twilight,
> And hope is less dear than the dew of the morn.

... Mr Yeats's 'natural magic' is peculiarly his own because it is far less sensuous than any other man's. It is full of 'the essences of things' and not of the things themselves. In this way he is typical of the modern revolt against 'that picturesque and declamatory way of writing... which a time of scientific and political thought has brought into literature'. But had he been a less curious critic he had perhaps made fewer mistakes in his poetry. At his best his poetry is fine because its symbols are natural, ancient, instinctive, not invented, but his discovery that it was a survival of a religious attitude that made natural magic possible has apparently led him into the error of using old mythological terms as if in themselves they had some effect besides their quaintness— which they have not, we believe. But it is out of place to disparage a poet of this magnitude who is as yet so little known though universally heard of. Nor would we leave the impression that he is only a poet of Nature, though we believe that his nature is so deeply moved by the unseen and the old things that they are never entirely to be separated from any of his work.

From review of *The Collected Works of William Butler Yeats*, MP, 17
December 1908

Apparently, all of Mr Yeats's work in verse and prose, except his letters to the Press, has been included in these eight volumes, together with an excellent bibliography; but there is nothing ill-considered, nothing that does not deserve the handsome binding and clear print. The grey cloth and parchment and gold are impressive, and we regret only that here at length is a sort of knighthood conferred on a man who seemed far too busy in a hundred ways to have time for such things. Yet if he were to do nothing more, the body and spirit of his work are large enough to make a very notable achievement. Seeing his work altogether, as we now easily can, his position seems not only assured, but pre-eminent among the distinguished poets still in their prime.

We are particularly glad to see here the critical articles from *Samhain* and elsewhere, which a good many of Mr Yeats's readers must have missed. They are full of admirable doctrine and of judgment and practical sense. His prose is always beautiful, perhaps the most beautiful of our time, certainly the most enchanting. These articles as a whole make a body of critical ideas which it would be impossible to equal in England today.

... In making changes in his prose and verse, Mr Yeats is moved by two distinct motives. Sometimes, as in revising the stories of Red Hanrahan, he rubs out the too physical highly-coloured beauty of his prose; while, in revising *The Shadowy Waters*, he tries to bring his scenes a little nearer to life as the majority know it by touches of common speech or thought. But these changes, especially of the second class, make no serious difference to work already so profoundly impressed by the feeling and cadence characteristic of the poet. If we object to them, it is only because we regret that he should have given to ineffective labour time which might have otherwise been given to something new.

Those two ways of changing his work correspond to the two apparently distinct ideas which have almost from the beginning been curiously harmonized in his poems and in his criticism. On the one hand he longs for ideals of literature and life belonging to times before 'the newspapers, all kinds of second-rate books, the preoccupation of men with all kinds of practical changes', drove 'the living imagination out of the world'. He sees the vestiges of these ideals among the peasantry today, and he asks: 'Will not our next art be rather of the country, of the great open spaces, of the soul rejoicing in itself?' And yet he knows that he is of this age when 'he who does not strive to be a perfect craftsman achieves nothing'. He is little like the peasant when he says that 'those who care for the arts have few near friendships among those that do not'. Why, even so far back as Shakespeare he sees this separation of the artist from the common man, 'when solitary great men were gathering to themselves the fire that had once flowed hither and thither among all men'.

Mr Yeats works out for himself not a way to an older world, but a position that looks detached from any life that numbers of men together have ever known. In truth, he is gazing as much forward as backward when he writes that 'we must admit that invisible beings, far-wandering influences, shapes that may have floated from a hermit of the wilderness, brood over council chambers and studies and battle-fields', or again, that 'the arts are about to take upon their shoulders the burdens that have fallen from the shoulders of priests, and to lead us back upon our journey by filling our thoughts with the essences of things, and not with things'. Thus his own work combines the beautiful simplicity of language, the rich tales, and sometimes the ballad form of the people with a subtlety of feeling for which there is no parallel in another age. Through all of it runs that cry for the essences of things, for the spirit against the body. He seems to have got beyond our critical interest in old things, folk-lore, spiritualism, etc., as much as Wordsworth got beyond Percy. The heavy, voluptuous splendour of much of his work has yet a ghostliness as of the palace made magically of leaves. Even his heroes and beautiful women are aware of this, as when Naisi is calm 'with the calm of one who has passed beyond life', and are careless of 'heavy mortal hopes that toil and pass' and in love with music 'that but cries sleep, sleep, till joy and sorrow and hope and terror are gone'. He never leaves us, any more than Crashaw, content with the glory alone. It calls our attention to a spirit behind and beyond, heaping high lovely, invisible things only that it may show the greater beauty that can survive their crumbling into dust. In this way his glorious work, related at first sight only to the clouds that pass and the flowers under our feet, plays and must play a great part in the movement of this age towards a finer and deeper spirit, and will enrich literature by revealing new riches in life.

From another review of *The Collected Works*, *DC*, 5 March 1909

J. M. SYNGE

J. M. SYNGE gave what is probably its finest comedy to the modern stage, and though he wrote in prose, it was of that rich poetic texture which was so common in Elizabethan drama, and has been so rare ever since. It was, therefore, with some surprise that we learnt he had written verses that he wished to publish. But altogether they fill only twenty or thirty pages, or not that, for some of the pieces are translations from French and Italian poetry into prose. And as they are small and few, so they are spare in character; they are poetry of the most unquestionable kind, but poetry shrunk almost to its bones.

There is nothing here with the exuberance and charm that is found in some of the speeches of Pegeen and the Playboy himself. Synge did not express over again in verse what he had put in prose into the mouths of Nora Burke or the Douls, though 'Beg-Innish' is a song they might have sung, and 'Patch-Shaneen' a ballad they would easily have understood. The man himself, as Mr Yeats tells us, was 'a solitary, undemonstrative man, never asking pity, nor complaining, nor seeking sympathy but in this book's momentary cries'. Momentary cries they are indeed. They betray nothing, or the little they reveal makes us aware how much is left out. They beget admiration, love, and also awe as at the darkness that follows upon a flash. The constant quality is simplicity, and it is often saturnine, as in the two verses written 'after looking at one of A. E.'s pictures', and entitled 'The Passing of the Shee':

> Adieu, sweet Angus, Maeve, and Fand,
>   Ye plumed yet skinny Shee,
> That poets played with hand in hand
>   To learn their ecstasy.
> We'll stretch in Red Dan Sally's ditch,
>   And drink in Tubber fair,
> Or poach with Red Dan Philly's bitch
>   The badger and the hare.

And it can be quaint, as in:

> Thrush, linnet, stare, and wren,
>   Brown lark beside the sun,
> Take thought of kestrel, sparrow-hawk,
>   Birdlime, and roving gun.
>
> You great-great-grandchildren
>   Of birds I've listened to,
> I think I robbed your ancestors
>   When I was young as you.

It is individual chiefly by its very impersonality of manner.

  The pieces were written during a period of nearly twenty years— about one a year. They are the work of a man who knew his art, whether or not they are all he wrote. They are exact and lucid as Greek epigrams, and most of them seem to have been written without remembering any poetry. They overstate nothing, which is more than can be said of most very good verse. They are notes such as a man sitting alone might scratch on a window at an inn, or on the dust of a road, or in a letter that was never posted. They add, if that be possible, to our sense of the truth and sincerity of the plays. The translations into prose are chiefly from Petrarch, and the Irish-English is a pleasure to read, giving them a genuineness that a verse translation is unlikely to have. But the effort is a tour-de-force for which Petrarch was hardly the proper occasion. Villon, however, it suits perfectly, and 'An Old Woman's Lamentations' from that poet is—almost as good as some of the speeches of Mary and Martin Doul; we cannot say more.

Review of *Poems and Translations, DC,* 26 July 1909

W. H. DAVIES

MR WILLIAM DAVIES is a Monmouthshire man. He has been active and passionate. He has been poor and careless and hungry and in pain. 'I count us,' he says, in his 'Lodging House Fire' which is as simple as a caveman's drawing on bone, and yet of an atmosphere dense with old sorrow:

> I count us, thirty men,
>   Huddled from winter's blow,
> Helpless to move away
> From that fire's glow.

  He has travelled: he knows Wales, London, America, and Hell. These things and many more his poems tell us; and to see him is to see a man from whom unskilled labour in America, work in Atlantic cattle boats, and a dire London life, have not taken away the earnestness, the tenderness, or the accent, of a typical Monmouthshire man. I have often wondered idly how I should meet the apparition of a new poet—it was so easy to praise small or middling writers of verse—and now all that I can do is to help to lay down a cloak of journalists' words, over which he may walk a little more easily to his just fame.

His greatness rests upon a wide humanity, a fresh and unbiassed observation, and a noble use of the English tongue. His humanity is so wide that, though he writes much about himself, he is less egoistic than another man who writes of fair Rosamond or Medea. He can write commonplace and inaccurate English; but it is also natural to him to write, much as Wordsworth wrote, with the clearness, compactness, and felicity which make a man think with shame how unworthily, through natural stupidity or uncertainty, he manages his native tongue. In subtlety he abounds; and where else today shall we find simplicity like this?

> No man lives life so wise
>   But unto Time he throws
> Morsels to hunger for
>   At his life's close.

Where else shall we find the song as simple and passionate as here?

> Where wert thou, love, when from Twm Barlum turned
> The moon's face full the way of Alterreen,
> And from his wood's dark cage the nightingale
> Drave out clear notes across the open sheen. . . .

From review of *The Soul's Destroyer, and Other Poems,*
DC, 21 October 1905

It is now nearly two years since a book appeared with this title-page:

The Soul's Destroyer, and Other Poems.
By WILLIAM H. DAVIES.
Of the Author, Farmhouse, Marshalsea-road.

For some months no notice was taken of the book, which was published by the author without advertisement. Then it was discovered that he was an exceedingly poor man in a common lodging-house, and had but one leg. He was a nine days wonder. There had been a postman-poet, a policeman-poet; why not a one-legged tramp-poet? Photographs and interviews were plentiful. . . . [The] verses were extraordinary. The feeling for the country was profound, and equalled only by the observation. London appeared in them as it has certainly never appeared in any poetry except James Thomson's, and at his best

Mr Davies achieved a simplicity and directness which were beyond the author of *The City of Dreadful Night*. There were pathetic reminiscences of his early childhood in Monmouthshire, not merely pathetic, but beautiful and strong and clear, and some epigrammatic pictures of lodging-house characters. There were a few poems which might have belonged to Crashaw's age. There was no imitation. Altogether the book plainly revealed a surprising genius, which was acknowledged from very different points of view.

Mr Davies's second volume, *New Poems*, repays our confidence in his capacity for observation and expression. Some of the pieces relate to his London experience: the majority deal either with the country and his life in it or with subjects independent of time and place, such as music and his infancy. They include nothing, perhaps, as concentrated and shapely and powerful as his 'Lodging-house Fire', but the best of them are noble. 'The Likeness', though far from being his best, shows his simplicity and clearness and is short enough to quote:

> When I came forth this morn I saw
>   Quite twenty cloudlets in the air;
> And then I saw a flock of sheep,
>   Which told me how those clouds came there.
>
> That flock of sheep, on that green grass,
>   Well it might lie so still and proud!
> Its likeness had been drawn in heaven,
>   On a blue sky, in silvery cloud.
>
> I gazed me up, I gazed me down,
>   And swore, though good the likeness was,
> 'Twas a long way from justice done
>   To such white wool, such sparkling grass. . . .

And there is hardly a poem which is not a thing of entirely new beauty on account of its truth and imagination, and above all the impression it leaves of coming straight from the spirit of a strange, vivid, unlearned, experienced man. It is a pity that he admitted the long poem which fills his last fourteen pages. His long poems, though they contain good things, invariably fail. They lure him into indefiniteness, incoherence, inconsequence. Perhaps they demand purely intellectual gifts in which he is not rich, and they put a severe strain upon his constructive faculty, which is weak; his poems either sing themselves through like an old air or they break up and fall.

From review of *New Poems*, *MP*, 3 January 1907

The autobiography of a poet like Mr W. H. Davies was bound to be good. The ups and downs in his life which his poems suggested were likely to make an uncommon narrative, which his gift of beautiful honest writing, always neglecting what is not of first-rate importance to himself, would make a life without incident or variety or difficulty profoundly significant. Few, however, could have guessed that Mr Davies was a prose writer more closely related to Borrow and Defoe than any other of our time, by virtue of his strength and simplicity and nonchalant grasp of life.

That he is any page in the book will prove, whether it is a mere record of commonplace incidents on a road, or a picture as remarkable as this one of his grandfather who had towards the end of his life given up the ship he once owned and commanded:

In the dark winter evenings I would sit with my grandmother, my brother and sister, painting ships or reading before a large fire that was never allowed to burn below its highest bar. My grandfather, with his old habits, would pace slowly up and down the half-dark passage, shutting himself out in the cold. Every now and then he would open the front door to look at the stars or to inform himself from what latitude the wind blew. The wind never changed without his knowledge; for this wary mariner invariably surprised it in the act of doing so. Three or four times in the evening he would open the kitchen door to see that his family was comfortable, as though he had just made his way from the hurricane deck to inquire after the welfare of passengers in the cabin. When this was done, the old lady would sometimes say, rather peevishly, 'Francis, do sit down for a minute or two.' Then he would answer gruffly, but not unkindly— 'Avast there, Lydia', closing the door to begin again his steady pacing to and fro.

Mr Shaw, in his sprightly and generous introduction, naturally thinks the book worth reading by literary experts for its style alone. If the majority of writers were not incorrigibly stupid or bound to write for a living they would give up trying, after seeing the ease and sincerity and inevitableness of Mr Davies' English.

... The characters of his tramp companions are drawn kindly, humorously, and with obvious truth; no other writer on tramp life can be compared with him for sincerity, simplicity and style. His fellow lodgers in a London doss-house are made to live by such quick means that we recall the minor characters of *The Bible in Spain*. He was to have gone to the Klondyke, but missed his footing on a train that was to have given him a free ride, and so lost one leg. He then returned to England and learned a good deal about sixpenny lodging-houses and humanity. He has been birched for theft, he has begged without shame, he has consistently avoided work that does not come naturally and easily to him. The only work he likes is writing; he has a genius for it, and he does nothing else but walk and think, and indulge his love of Nature and men. He is, on the whole, a favourite of what used to be called Providence, and what Mr Shaw calls the Life Force. He survives; he enjoys; he does good work which no one else has done or could do. He has solved the most difficult questions without knowing it. So far he has earned nothing by his writings. His life thus proposes some very troublesome economic questions, as well as the unanswerable question, how it is that a man is able by sheer force of his inner nature to use words so as to create pictures, actions, characters, more vivid than life itself. But it is by no means astonishing that poetry like his should arise out of a life so quiet, full and simple.

From review of *The Autobiography of a Super-Tramp*,
DC, 23 April 1908

It was impossible for Mr W. H. Davies or any man living to improve upon the best work in *The Soul's Destroyer* and *New Poems*. But these *Nature Poems and Others* show that, without losing any of his incomparable freshness, he is becoming more critical. This is his finest book, because it is all, or very nearly all, excellent of its kind. Mr Davies is not a discoverer. There is no new order of beauty in any of his work. He has found no new fields, no new music. But he has found himself, and has been divinely gifted with a power of expression equal to that of any other man of our day. Divine gifts are perilous things, and we have always been a little anxious, before looking at new poems by this man, lest the gift should have been withdrawn. But it has not been withdrawn, and we now feel that Mr Davies is master of his fate, and will go on securely in his work.

The poems express a simple, hearty nature, loving joy and physical freedom, loving women, children, animals, the country, hating misery, tyranny, and the town. In English poetry so lucid and simple a nature has seldom appeared. The Scottish lyrists before Burns, could they have been transported to this age and dipped in the life of cities, would have sung thus. Blake and John Clare and Chalkhill sounded the same notes, and so did Herrick when he thought of flowers and of maids like flowers. But has any of these men written more perfectly than the author of this—not by any means his best, and of a Horatian lucidity that touches only half his nature, but still exquisite? It is 'The Muse':

> I have no ale,
>   No wine I want;

No ornaments,
   My meat is scant.

No maid is near,
   I have no wife;
But here's my pipe,
   And, on my life,

With it to smoke,
   And woo the Muse,
To be a king
   I would not choose.

But I crave all
   When she does fail—
Wife, ornaments,
   Meat, wine, and ale.

In the poems which follow, the simple lucid expression of beauty and joy is a thing to wonder at continually. Although there is nothing exalted in the subjects, nothing majestic in the thought, yet the air they breathe is of such astonishing purity that I could scarcely endure the stale sight of half the things that met my eyes in the street after reading the book. This man is so right that the dull, the ugly, the unnecessary things, the advertisements at the railway station, and so on, disgusted me as so many obstacles to the life which these verses seem to propose to us. Izaak Walton is not more sweet than this man, whom all things love:

The horse can tell,
   Straight from my lip;
My hand could not
   Hold any whip. . . .

The poems on a still-born child, on children coming out of school, on a child known long ago, on 'a merry hour': 'You heard the cuckoo first, 'twas he;/The second time—Ha, ha! 'twas Me', on love's birth, on the laughers, on a swallow that flew into the room, on Beauty's Danger, express old things as if they were but now just born. And how absolute the style is, from the mere brevity of this: 'Content, though sober, sleeps on stone,/But Care can't sleep with down and ale', up to

      Now we
Lived in a city dark, where Poverty,
More hard than rocks, and crueller than foam,
Keeps many a great Ulysses far from home.

And

> I had a sweet companion once,
>   And in the meadows we did roam;
> And in the one-star night returned
>   Together home.

And such an opening as: 'Now I can see what Helen was', which is worthy of Villon; and 'Ah, what is Beauty but vain show/If nothing in the heart is sweet.' But these things, though they prove his power, cannot hint at his abundance, at his hundred felicities in suggesting the visible world which he loves so well, at his hundred touches of child-like sincerity and truth that would make us love him without any other gifts. Here are no trappings whatever, neither robes of ceremony nor grave clothes, but the word that is the life.

From review of *Nature Poems and Others, DC,* 4 September 1908

Mr William H. Davies, author of *The Autobiography of a Supertramp*, is one of the few living poets of whom it could safely be said that his work would have been as readable three centuries ago, and will be, if it survives, three centuries hence. It varies down to doggerel, but when it counts at all it has the limpidity of Wordsworth. There is a truth and freshness in the writing that is a pledge of the author's absolute sincerity. . . .

Mr Davies's simplicity is natural, though it may owe something to his love of Wordsworth. It is also invariably consistent, and not to be mistaken for any other man's. And yet it is not quite so novel as it is natural. The book as a whole is novel, because it reveals a character of singular joyousness, tenderness, and uncorrupted frankness, and a love of animals and children and Nature and poor men, that are not to be found in the same combination elsewhere. Certain poems, too, like 'A Maiden and her Hair', could only have been written at the present day; but these are few. The one weakness of the book is that it makes no advance, no change for better or worse, from the past. It opens no new worlds, nor makes the attempt. Half the poems are fit for an anthology, and we could almost believe that they came from one. It is a nice question whether poems which would have been excellent a hundred years ago can thus late take the place which their beauty seems to claim. But it must not be supposed that they are echoes. They would be more fitly described as poems which Herrick, Wordsworth, and Blake left unwritten.

From another review of *Nature Poems, MP,* 31 December 1908

For those who already know his *Soul's Destroyer* and *Nature Poems* it is enough to say that in the new book [Mr Davies] repeats old successes. Once or twice, it is true, he uses old subjects again, and where he does not the poems have a familiar sound, because his style is so matured and its intensity so narrow, and his range of ideas so limited. It is full of the loveliness of trees and birds, women and children, of simple and strong passions, of the cruelty of London and fate, of the goodness of the sun, of ale, and of books. He uses such simple and familiar words and such well-known stanza forms that at times he is flat, while he still lacks the mere dexterity to eliminate weaknesses due to the difficulty of rhyme. Probably he will always lack it, just as he will always be more pleased than his readers with variations upon 'God made the country, but man made the town.' These weaknesses are not frequent or obtrusive. We even find them reassuring, because they make it more certain than ever that Mr Davies's good things come of just that inexplicable unconscious simplicity which used to be called inspiration and has never had a more sufficient name. It is therefore only to be expected that when a writer of this instinctive kind comes to the end of a period of composition he should fear that no other will succeed. This fear must have dictated the 'Farewell to Poesy'.

It is not easy to define this poetry which appears to owe nothing to any directly literary influence since Wordsworth. It is simple in vocabulary and rhythm and thought, and it is without conscious art; and yet the forms, the occasional conceits, and certain turns of expression make it clear that it owes much to the Elizabethan, Jacobean, and Caroline lyric as well as to Wordsworth and Blake. The spirit which subdues those influences and combines them to a perfectly original result is that of a man who knows modern civilization only through the hideousness of its towns. It could probably be asserted without injustice that the only subject which Mr Davies knows anything about is tramping. He has very little knowledge of facts, and what he knows he leaves out of his verse, and still less acquaintance with modern ideas. He loves animals, birds, and flowers, but he would probably have done so had he lived a thousand years ago. And withal he has no living equals except Mr Charles M. Doughty and Mr Yeats. He sees things entirely afresh. In writing poetry only one or two conventions beset him, and those either superficially or only at long intervals. He cannot judge himself, but writes in a kind of natural hypnotism in forms unconsciously suggested and tinged by Herrick or Blake. . . .

From review of *Farewell to Poesy, MP,* ? February 1910

Freshness and simplicity are such obvious qualities in Mr Davies that his others are in danger of being overlooked. In

> Gone are the days of canvas sails!
> No more great sailors tell their tales
> In country taverns, barter pearls
> For kisses from strange little girls.

and in the drinking song: 'Ye who have nothing to conceal,/Come, honest boys, and drink with me', the simplicity has an archaism, doubtless quite unconscious, which is part of its charm and is far removed from a really modern simplicity, like Walt Whitman's. There is one quality usually combined with his simplicity which is superficially unlike it and might even be opposed to it by some. I do not know what to call it; but it is actually akin to simplicity, if it be not simplicity itself playing truant; and I believe that only a simple man could have written the conclusion of the 'Milkmaid's Song'—he has asked her to marry him as she sang over her pail:

> She laughed in scorn, and tossed her head,
> And she had milked the crimson flood
> E'en to my heart's last drop of blood.

Only simplicity could be unaware of the barriers which common sense can see between this and itself. There are places where this faculty—or absence of control—strays so deep that, as in 'The Kingfisher', it leads almost to a new myth:

> It was the Rainbow gave thee birth,
>   And left thee all her lovely hues;
> And, as her mother's name was Tears,
>   So runs it in thy blood to choose
> For haunts the lonely pools and keep
> In company with trees that weep.

I enjoy this heartily, but am not sure if it is not rather fancy still working than poetry achieved. Closely allied to this quality is a charming artificiality probably due to a combination of nature and memory of books, as in

> My Love she is so fair
>   When in this angry way,
> That did she guess my thoughts,
>   She'd quarrel every day.

This artificiality is part of Mr Davies's simplicity. For it is of the essence of simplicity that it is without fear. The improbable, the unusual, the hackneyed, the grotesque, are not known to it by their names. Hence the wide, vague, indescribable beauty of

> The Sun that sank long since
> At Severn's Mouth, with that great sail of gold
> That covered all the west.

Hence the huge scale of this, which is so effective:

> Since June
> Has sent forth one white hair to draw the black
> Into that treason which dethrones my youth.

Hence, too, the slips of grammar and syntax in his work, the formality of words and phrases and apparently bookish fancies adopted and made real as Blake adopted ornament. These are trifles. They are the very low price which he has to pay for his freedom of the world visible and invisible, and the unique beauty of his poetry.

> From another review of *Farewell to Poesy*, B, May 1910

WALTER DE LA MARE

A FEW YEARS AGO Mr de la Mare published a little volume of poems called *Songs of Childhood*, and they proved that yet another writer had arisen who could use English as a living tongue.

Some of his poems were perfectly beautiful; all were unusually interesting, because there clearly was a man who wrote so much from his individual heart and brain that every verse was characteristic and his own, just as every nightingale's egg is olive, and not yellow or freckled or blotched.

Then followed the same author's *Henry Brocken*, a lovable, finely-conceived romance, that failed, in spite of its wonderful sense of beauty, because the world could not comfortably take so many deep gulps of fantasy one after the other. And now his new *Poems* confirm our hopes and set new ones up.

For here is the same sincerity, speaking, as sincerity always does, a strange new tongue, because it is unlike our muddy conventional speech; but here, too, is an opaqueness of thought that has come to trouble the almost transparent lyric stream of the first book. There is no 'Slim Sophia' and no 'Bunches of Grapes' among the new poems.

But though this new element is not always easy to enjoy immediately, the careful reader, for whom alone Mr de la Mare has written, will find himself soon with an additional sense of gratitude to the poet for so passionately putting his spiritual life into his work. There is more sadness here. The cry against passing time comes more than once. The personal note has become commoner. There are more moods.

Joy and intensity of life, whether joyful or not, are seen in this volume to be snatched with difficulty from among the flames and swords. Some of the poems are but as sweet lights and songs already threatened and surrounded by tempestuous winds and clouds. Others are frankly dejected, but without weakness, because they have the strange joy of sorrow that is simple and passionate.

And yet more than half of the poems come under none of these heads. There are some dedicated to indignation, even to hate, to regret, to laughter, to pure fantasy of imagination. In fact, they have so little of the sameness due to mannerism or self-imitation that I despair of suggesting the quality of the book by quotation on any possible scale. All are short, most of them less than twenty lines in length. The verse forms are much varied. All are dense with feeling or observation or thought; some, in fact, so dense that I wonder sometimes whether the poet has truly reached the ultimate form for his idea.

The writing is that of one who uses a phrase or a word never because it will seem to the careless reader to be musical or poetical, but always because only with its help can he tinge the paper with his soul; and if it has a fault, it is that it creeps along, at times, rather weary with the burden of thought added to thought. One technical fault he has, and that is a trick of printing 'heav'n' for 'heaven', and so on, though it is elsewhere clear that his ear does not habitually reject an extra syllable in his lines.

Briefly, in these poems are to be found the very accent and features of a living man whom the world does not yet know.

Review of *Poems, DC,* 9 November 1906

In 1902 appeared a book of one hundred and six small pages called *Songs of Childhood* with the name 'Walter Ramal' on the title-page. Two years later the short prose romance of *Henry Brocken* revealed that 'Walter Ramal' was W. J. de la Mare. *Poems* by Walter de la Mare followed in 1906, of about the same length as the first book. Since then a few poems and stories by him have been seen in two or three different journals and magazines; but these three are all his books. He has made no other appearance, nothing has been told of him, nothing said or done which might connect in the public mind the name of Walter de la Mare with this small body of poetry, as the names of men and their work are in the course of time connected so that the name comes to smell, as soon as heard, simply or subtly of the whole work and awakens a rich image of it. For nothing in his books except the beauty could encourage curiosity. The personal quality is intense and consistent, but it has no obvious egotism, no significant first person singular, no confession, defiance, lament, or hinted mystery. Mr de la Mare's work is, in fact, the perfection of personality, and, in an impersonal way, without deliberation or obtrusiveness. He remains an entirely hidden magician behind his work. Seldom does he show himself, the author, even as much as in the beginning of 'Miss Loo':

'When thin-strewn memory I look through,/I see most clearly poor Miss Loo.'

For the most part his poetry has been what nearly all would agree to call lyrical. The chief exceptions are the series of 'Characters from Shakespeare' in *Poems*, and even these are not unquestionable exceptions, because, though in blank verse and relating to well-known matters, they have an all but independent life. If it is of the essence of the lyric that it should have an independent life singing itself into the brain of the reader with no aid of past knowledge or present thought, but directly through the door of the individual spirit, then no question but Mr de la Mare's poems are the purest lyrics. Most are very short and rhymed, the majority are no longer than a sonnet, but in a great variety of metres and stanza forms. The seconds during which the eye drinks up these few words are not too short for a door to swing silently wide open upon a dim-spread and strange world. Neither is this power due to any violence, extravagance, or marked peculiarity of thought or of rhythm, or of vocabulary, nor to any extraordinary choice of subjects. The movement of his verse is always half-hidden under the thought of which it forms a part. It is at its best in the inward melody, the spiritual or apparently bodiless rhythms, so characteristic of this age, in the work of men like Messrs Bridges, Yeats, and Sturge Moore. Yet he can, and many times does much with customary and decided rhythm as in 'No sound over the deep, only the desolate foam,/White in the evening mist, of the last wave home.'

He has another poem called 'Reverie' in the stanza of 'La Belle Dame Sans Merci', used without innovation, in fact with greater rigidity; yet creates with ease a picture of perfect and singular loveliness of a young girl: 'It seems an inward melody/She paces to.'

Another remarkable and characteristic achievement in this poem is that it makes us feel the absolute fitness of the girl's name. She is introduced at once in the opening line: 'When slim Sophia mounts her horse . . .'

And yet from beginning to end we do not hesitate; for not only is the name fit, but the poem gives a subtly powerful new personality to the name even in spite of any obscure prejudice due, perhaps, to its Hanoverian associations. Neither here nor perhaps anywhere else does the poet rely on fine words or references to traditionally rich or beautiful things. Out of what a simple and unadorned element is the beauty of 'Lovelocks' made:

> I watched the Lady Caroline
> Bind up her dark and beauteous hair;
> Her face was rosy in the glass,
> And 'twixt the coils her hands would pass,
>   White in the candleshine.

> Her bottles on the table lay,
> Stoppered yet sweet of violet;
> Her image in the mirror stooped
> To view those locks as lightly looped
>   As cherry-boughs in May.

It is only in his poems of childhood—not always poems for children—that he uses conventions very noticeably.

It is no journey for Mr de la Mare to his goblins, elves, witches, pilgrims, and mariners. They are as much a part of his world as the sea, or almond-trees, or flowers: his hooting goblins and droning bees are equally alive and impressive. He is Lord of Tartary, though he has written a poem on what he would do supposing that he were:

> If I were Lord of Tartary,
>   Myself and me alone,
> My bed should be of ivory,
>   Of beaten gold my throne;
>
> And in my court should peacocks flaunt,
> And in my forests tigers haunt,
> And in my pools great fishes slant
>   Their fins athwart the sun. . . .

And this is too nearly humorous to contradict what has been said of the poet's habitual indifference to pomp or rather to the language of pomp. Nowhere is the triumph of his hushed magic more complete than in these poems of childhood.

> Review of *Songs of Childhood* and *Poems*, *ER*, December 1910

Reverie has never made a more magical book than Mr Walter de la Mare's third book of poems. For the most part, either they take the form of childish memories or their atmosphere is like that of overpowering memory. Never was child so tyrannous a father to the man. He does not recall things as Jefferies did the yellowhammer singing in the sun upon an ash branch in the field called Stewart's Mash, but always drowned, softened, reduced, and with a more or less distinctly sad sense of remoteness. Sometimes he announces the element of memory by beginning 'When thin-strewn memory I look through' or 'Once' or 'One Summer's Day', while in 'The Journey' voices 'seemed' to cry 'vaguely from the hiding place of memory'. The number of poems thus labelled is small, but coming together at the beginning they give an unmistakable keynote to the whole.

In one poem he relates how Martha used to tell the children stories beginning 'Once upon a time':

And her beauty far away
  Would fade, as her voice ran on,
Till hazel and summer sun
  And all were gone:—

All foredone and forgot;
  And like clouds in the height of the sky,
Our hearts stood still in the hush
  Of an age gone by.

Even so is the world often 'all foredone and forgot' in these poems, and
the poet's and the reader's hearts thus stand still—to see the three
cherry trees:

There were three cherry trees once,
Grew in a garden all shady;
And there, for delight of so gladsome a sight,
Walked a most beautiful lady,
Dreamed a most beautiful lady . . .

or the very old woman living alone, who once was young,

But age apace
  Comes at last to all;
And a lone house filled
  With the cricket's call;
And the scampering mouse
  In the hollow wall.

Once he goes far back—'hundreds of years away'—and sees a Guine-
vere, a Helen, and a Cleopatra, unlike those of any other poet. Once the
witch's eyes slant 'through the silence of the long past'. Once he uses
the device of an epitaph: 'Here lies a most beautiful lady,/Light of step
and heart was she.'
  The scene of one poem is a stone house, in a forest by a lake, named
only 'Alas'. At the moonlit door of another lone house a traveller
knocks:

But only a host of phantom listeners
  That dwelt in the lone house then,
Stood listening in the quiet of the moonlight
  To that voice from the world of men.

Or the scene is the palace of the King of Never-to-be or a graveyard, or
in 'the shades of Arabia'. Arabia is the name of one of Mr de la Mare's
provinces, and it is a proof of his mastery that he can use this name and
make it so perfectly his own while retaining all that the name means to
those who are neither travellers nor geographers. It would be valuable
and delightful to study the elements which contribute to the mystery

of these poems. There are palaces, cottages, orchards, graveyards, all having something of the partly conventional, partly fantastic quality of those things to a child of small experience: the graveyard in particular is such a perfect idea of a graveyard as a child might make out of a story or a poem, yet I do not know where to find a more vivid sense of the grave than in this first verse of 'The Bindweed':

> The bindweed roots pierce down
> Deeper than men do lie,
> Laid in their dark-shut graves
> Their slumbering kinsmen by.

Mr de la Mare's birds and flowers are most beautiful, but his book is not natural history. His 'Owl and Newt and Nightjar, Leveret, Bat and Mole', are of the sixteenth century. The Asphodel and Amaranth are among his flowers, as Lethe is among his rivers. Dreams come to him from 'gloomy Hades and the whispering shore'. His hawthorn 'hath a deathly smell'. His snow frightens the starlings with its pale glare. There are witches in his country who carry 'charms and spells and sorceries' in their packs. Cupid has once been met there, certainly alive. But the dead in that country are more than the living.

Without such a study, it is clear that Mr de la Mare's magic is very richly compounded of childish experience, of Nature and books, of queer, half-understood or misunderstood things, and of the oldest mysteries. For all the atmosphere is tinged with sadness; very beautiful things—'and clash of silver, beauty, bravery, pride'—are seen in a faintly malevolent haze of time or distance. That when the poet speaks in his own person his melancholy should be overt cannot surprise anyone who realizes how few of any man's hours can after all be given to reverie; how difficult or unlovely must appear the broken, scattered, or jangled things outside that province. He writes as an 'exile' who would certainly not write if he were not exiled, if he could always be at 'Alas' or the 'Dark Chateau', or upon those mountains whose 'untroubled snows' his ghost is thirsting for. He is one of the most welcome of the many exiles who have been among us.

Review of *The Listeners and Other Poems*, B, August 1912

The best of English ballads, songs and nursery rhymes, the best of Coleridge and Poe, have combined with something, not to be found anywhere else, to make Mr de la Mare's poetry the most featherweight original poetry of our time. It is poetry, and nothing but poetry. It is never only good verse. Some will complain that there is too much poetry in it, that it has no body to hold its spirit and to give variety of form to the unvarying pure essence.

But no one of the five volumes of his poetry—*Songs of Childhood, Poems, The Listeners, A Child's Day,* and this—gives less cause to complain. That they are so much alike is a proof of their sincerity. That they are all so different is a proof that the poet can avoid the seductions of his own delicious tunes. Even those who know all the four earlier volumes will meet with some surprises. They will not, I think, have any disappointments. They will find the same feeling as before for children, old people, houses, trees, and England, but they will find also much that they could not have foretold from that gamesome but visionary eye watching the modern and the timeless world:

> Behind the blinds I sit and watch
> The people passing—passing by;
> And not a single one can see
>   My tiny watching eye.
>
> They cannot see my little room,
> All yellowed with the shaded sun;
> They do not even know I'm here,
>   Nor'll guess when I am gone. . . .

The fact is that his book does away once and for all with the suspicion that peacock pie is a thing to be looked at. The fine feathers do make a fine bird in this case, but they also cover excellent meats. The poetry is good enough for those who take their peacock pie only once a year, and it is homely enough for 'human nature's daily food'.

From review of *Peacock Pie: A Book of Rhymes, DC,*
18 September 1913

How pleasant it would be only to review books when I like them—not when I think I see from afar off that they are good, but when I really like them. Yet I am not sure, because the muscles of happy praise become stiff and I shrink for the other man's sake and my own, from giving a display of ungainliness. I feel this very much after reading, *Peacock Pie.* I do not suppose that Jack Horner would have been harder hit than I am, if he had been asked to extend the words 'What a good boy am I', to a sonnet's length. I am continually putting in my thumb, pulling out a plum, and experiencing a sensation which cannot, I should say, be surpassed by consciousness of virtue.

The book is worthy of its name. That is to say, in the first place, it is a pie. It is something to be eaten. Furthermore it consists of pastry and of something else covered up by the crust. In the second place, that something else in the pie is discovered to be so much above the ordinary pigeon, steak and kidney, or veal and ham, that it must be called Peacock Pie. Most of it can be eaten with only one possible cause

of regret, namely, this undoubted fact, first delivered by Mr de la
Mare:

> It's a very odd thing—
>   As odd as can be—
> That whatever Miss T eats
> Turns into Miss T.

Not all can be eaten, or it would not be Peacock Pie. What cannot be,
what does not give precisely that feeling which, I suggest, is as pleasant
as consciousness of virtue, what represents the peacock's glorious
uneatable plumage, is none the worse for that. I mean the poems like
'Nobody Knows'.

> Often I've heard the Wind sigh
>   By the ivied orchard wall,
> Over the leaves in the dark night,
>   Breathe a sighing call,
> And faint away in the silence,
>   While I, in my bed,
> Wondered, 'twixt dreaming and waking,
>   What it said. . . .

It is now pretty well-known that Mr de la Mare is a master, is *the*
master, in this style. And in the new book he gives us a variety of choice
examples: I will quote one more:

> I heard a horseman
>   Ride over the hill;
> The moon shone clear,
>   The night was still;
> His helm was silver,
>   And pale was he;
> And the horse he rode
>   Was of ivory.

You cannot be said to eat these things, but to absorb them
chameleon-fashion. . . .
   . . . There is always at least a phantom of a peacock feather about your
helping, but nobody else can mingle so variously jollity with magic as
Mr de la Mare can. His first book, *Songs of Childhood*, contained a
poem—contains a poem—called 'Bunches of Grapes', differentiating
three children in three verses, of which the last is:

> 'Chariots of gold,' says Timothy;
> 'Silvery wings,' says Elaine;
> 'A bumpity ride in a wagon of hay
> For me,' says Jane.

Now, I cannot be more exact than if I say that Mr de la Mare's new book will satisfy Timothy, Elaine and Jane. Maybe Timothy will see a silveriness about his chariot horses; the wings may sometimes carry Elaine to a region so far off and magical as to be melancholy; Jane may have doubts whether her wagon be not winged; but personally, I am content to travel any part of England or no man's land with this poet, on chariot of gold, silvery wings, or wagon. *Songs of Childhood* was distinguished by its chariot, *The Listeners* by its wings: *Peacock Pie* triumphs upon all three.

From another review of *Peacock Pie*, B, September 1913

D. H. LAWRENCE

IF THE READERS OF *The White Peacock* and *The Trespasser* do not buy Mr Lawrence's poems, those who buy his poems will want to read his novels. For it is certain that the writer of these extraordinarily original close-packed poems has plenty of material for novels, and must have had good reason for adopting the form. More than half are the quintessences of novels. Not mere novels in little, not mere sketches or embryos of novels; but, as it were, the tiny but solid beings of which novels are the shadows artificially made gigantic.

Most of them are in uniform sets of stanzas, in some of which the rhyme is almost indifferent and unnoticeable, while in others it is made the more conspicuous by its apparent arbitrariness. But three or four of the poems, like the 'Snapdragon', which is in *Georgian Poetry* but not here, are remarkable because the metre changes three or four times, both in dialogue and in monologue. In either case, it is not easy to say at first how much of Mr Lawrence's power is due to these forms.

But it is obvious at once that the poems would be impossible in 'In Memoriam' stanzas, for example. Their metrical changes, like their broken or hesitating rhythms, are part of a personality that will sink nothing of itself in what is common. They have the effect which Whitman only got now and then after a thousand efforts of rhymeless lawlessness. Mr Lawrence never runs loose. You can call him immoral or even incontinent, but not licentious. He is no more licentious than a dervish. Moreover, his senses are too wakeful and proud. He sacrifices everything to a certain mood, emotion, or frame of mind, but nothing to fine lines, or to false emphasis. There are no 'fine' verses or lines of the usual sort, and the whole of a poem is intense and unchangeable like some of the beautiful single lines of old, when poets were still rhetoricians. Yet his separate phrases are often of a prose type.

If I were to quote a verse from one of the 'Schoolmaster' set of poems the reader might get an impression of prose, possibly of obscurity—and there is obscurity in the book, due to abruptness and lack of rhetorical flow. If I were to give the outline of a poem, he might say that it ought to have been a 'thing seen'. He would be wrong. But I have no space for his best, which are his longest, poems, though never more than a couple of pages long. If I quote one of the pieces short enough to be given whole, like 'Morning Work':

> A gang of labourers on the piled wet timber
> That shines blood-red beside the railway siding
> Seem to be making out of the blue of the morning
> Something fairy and fine, the shuttles sliding.
>
> The red-gold spools of their hands and faces shuffling
> Hither and thither across the morn's crystalline frame
> Of blue: trolls at the cave of ringing cerulean mining,
> And laughing with work, loving their work like a game—

it must not be supposed that he often describes appearances. What he does best might have been inspired by Browning and by a feeling that 'Parting at Morning', for example, is none the better for being shorn of particularity. Mr Lawrence's poems are not mere private disclosures of men and women, but all are particular, and do not offer themselves as symbolic or of general application. So honest and patiently vivid are they that no man can regard them as foreign to him.

Review of Love Poems and Others, DC, ? February 1913

The book of the moment in verse is Mr D. H. Lawrence's. He is remarkable for what he does not do and for what he does. Thus, he does not write smoothly, sweetly and with dignity; nor does he choose subjects, such as blackbirds at sunset, which ask to be so treated. For some time past it has been understood that verse is not best written in jerks of a line in length. Mr Lawrence goes further, and at times seems bent on insulting rhyme, as in this stanza from 'Dog-tired':

> The horses are untackled, the chattering machine
> Is still at last. If she would come,
> I would gather up the warm hay from
> The hill-brow, and lie in her lap till the green
> Sky ceased to quiver and lost its tired sheen.

Correspondingly, he writes of matters which cannot be subdued to conventional rhythm and rhyme—chiefly the intense thoughts, emotions, or gropings of self-conscious men or women set on edge by love or fatigue or solitude. If he trusts to make a general appeal, it is by faithful concentration on the particular—a woman receiving a lover straight from bloodshed, a man repulsed, standing like an 'insect small in the fur of this hill' in the night when 'The night's flood-winds have lifted my last desire from me,/And my hollow flesh stands up in the night abandonedly', and saying to the woman:

> And I in the fur of the world, and you a pale fleck from the sky,
> How we hate each other tonight, hate, you and I,
> As the world of activity hates the dream that goes on on high,
> As a man hates the dreaming woman he loves, but who will not
>   reply.

The last comparison would be a flaw were it not that Mr Lawrence sacrifices everything to intensity, particularly in amorousness. His triumph is, by image and hint and direct statement, to bring before us some mood which overpowers all of a sick, complex man save his self-consciousness. Mr Lawrence is fearless in treatment as in choice of subject. He will be exact in defining an intuition, a physical state, or an appearance due to the pathetic fallacy—herein resembling the man in 'We have bit no forbidden apple'. He will give us in dialect the plainest outlines of a working-class tragedy, and in careful abstract mono-logue a schoolmaster's moment of satisfaction when it is sweet in the morning to teach boys who are his slaves:

> Only as swallows are slaves to the eaves
> They build upon, as mice are slaves
> To the man who threshes and sows the sheaves.

Such moods he will sometimes follow with a painful curiosity that makes us rather sharers in a process than witnesses of a result. He does not refuse external things, a gang of labourers at work on timber, a picture by Corot, the Moon. A surprising number of his poems are tributary to the moon, but a moon of his own world, 'divesting herself of her golden shift', or bringing him a pang of reminiscence, or reddening:

> The moon lies back and reddens;
>   In the valley, a corncrake calls monotonously,
> With a piteous, unalterable plaint, that deadens
>   My confident activity:
> With a hoarse, insistent request that falls
>   Unweariedly, unweariedly,
> Asking something more of me,
>   Yet more of me.

I doubt if much of his effect is due to rhythm; verse aids him chiefly by allowing him to use a staccato shorthand which would be more uncomfortable in prose. But, whether the verse is always relevant or not, Mr Lawrence writes in a concentration so absolute that the poetry is less questionable than the verse.

Another review of *Love Poems and Others,* in review of new verse, etc.,
B, April 1913

RUPERT BROOKE

MR RUPERT BROOKE is a poet known only to those adventurers who look for poetry in the magazines, and find it. Of these five his book is the most interesting, as being a symptomatic quintessence of the rebellious attitude today. . . .

We should like to devote a volume to the poet who writes of those

> Wanderers, in the middle mist,
> Who cry for shadows, clutch, and cannot tell
> Whether they love at all, or, loving, whom,
> An old song's lady, a fool in fancy dress,
> Or phantoms, or their own face on the gloom;
> For love of Love, or from heart's loneliness.
> Pleasure's not theirs, nor pain. They doubt and sigh,
> And do not love at all. Of these am I.

This is the same poet who laments the day when

> Infinite hungers leap no more
> In the chance swaying of your dress;
> And love has changed to kindliness.

He envies the stars, and then, thinking how far away, looking at men,

> God out of Heaven may laugh to see
> The happy crowds; and never know
> That in his lone, obscure distress
> Each walketh in a wilderness—

he pities and loves the stars who 'in empty, infinite spaces dwell, disconsolate'. That is in perhaps his most perfect poem, if not his best. He writes of Helen, of London, of afternoon tea, of sleeping out, of seasickness. He experiments in choriambics. He is full of revolt, contempt, self-contempt, and yet of arrogance too. He reveals chiefly what he desires to be and to be thought. Now and then he gives himself away, as when, in three poems close together, he speaks of the scent of warm clover. Copies should be bought by everyone over forty who has never been under forty. It will be a revelation. Also, if they live yet a little longer, they may see Mr Rupert Brooke a poet. He will not be a little one.

Review of *Poems* in review of new verse, *DC*, 9 April 1912

On 23 April the poet Rupert Brooke died of sunstroke at Lemnos in his twenty-eighth year. He was a second lieutenant in the Royal Naval Division, on his way to the fighting in the Dardanelles. No poet of his age was so much esteemed and admired, or was watched more hopefully. His work could not be taken soberly, whether you liked it or not. It was full of the thought, the aspiration, the indignation of youth; full of the praise of youth. Many people knew the man or the reputation of his personal charm. Wherever he went he made friends, well-wishers, admirers, adorers. He was himself a friendly man, with humour and good humour added. Successful in many fields—he played in the eleven and the fifteen for Rugby school; he won a fellowship at King's College, Cambridge; he was celebrated as a golden young Apollo, in Mrs Cornford's phrase 'Magnificently unprepared/For the long littleness of life', his attractiveness included modesty and simplicity. He stretched himself out, drew his fingers through his waved, fair hair, laughed, talked indolently, and admired as much as he was admired. No one that knew him could easily separate him from his poetry: not that they were the same, but that the two inextricably mingled and helped one another. He was tall, broad, and easy in his movements. Either he stooped, or he thrust his head forward unusually much to look at you with his steady, blue eyes. His clear, rosy skin helped to give him the look of a great girl. The papers nearly all said something about his 'beauty', his good looks, his 'glamour', one said that he was one of the handsomest Englishmen of our time. And just before he died it happened that one of his last-published sonnets was quoted in St Paul's Cathedral by the Dean:

> If I should die, think only this of me:
> That there's some corner of a foreign field
> That is for ever England. There shall be
> In that rich earth a richer dust concealed;
> A dust whom England bore, shaped, made aware,
> Gave, once, her flowers to love, her ways to roam,
> A body of England's, breathing English air,
> Washed by the rivers, blest by suns of home.
>
> And think, this heart, all evil shed away,
> A pulse in the eternal mind, no less
> Gives somewhere back the thoughts by England given;
> Her sights and sounds; dreams happy as her day;

> And laughter, learnt of friends; and gentleness,
> In hearts at peace, under an English heaven.

So, instantly he took his share of the fame that comes to young poets dying conspicuously and unexpectedly, but not unprophesied by themselves.

In his lifetime he was not widely known for his one book, *Poems* (1911), the essays on Donne and John Webster published in *Poetry and Drama*, and the poems published in the same quarterly, in *Georgian Poetry*, in the four parts of *New Numbers*, and here and there in the newspapers.

His poems had referred a good deal to death, long before the war began. He was so eager for enjoyment and performance worthy of a very lofty conception of life and youth, that death, and old age, and the end of love, could not but confront him prodigiously. He varied between a Shelleyan eagerness and a Shelleyan despair. It was characteristic of him to apply the Shelleyan epithet 'swift' to a girl's hair. Sometimes it seemed to him he could not love; sometimes that so great was his love it would endure in his dust and haunt the mean lovers of later years:

> in that instant they shall learn
> The shattering ecstasy of our fire,
> And the weak passionless hearts will burn

> And faint in that amazing glow,
> Until the darkness close above;
> And they will know—poor fools, they'll know!—
> One moment, what it is to love.

He wrote a threnody for the 'Funeral of Youth', where 'fussy Joy', 'Passion, grown portly, something middle-aged', and 'Ardour, the sunlight on his greying hair', were among the mourners; but not Love—'Love had died long ago'. Like Shelley, he was metaphysical. One of his poems was the result of an effort to look at the world, another to see God, like a fish; while a third spoke of the cold life of the herring, but ended: 'He has his hour, he has his hour.'

The 'eternal instant', the 'immortal moment', troubled his mind. He was discontented with its rareness, and even in the midst of one such moment, before exclaiming 'Heart of my heart, our heaven is now, is won!', he must yet remember

> Through glory and ecstasy we pass;
> Wind, sun, and earth remain, the birds sing still,
> When we are old, are old. . . .

Yet he would turn from metaphysical Platonizing to very substantial enumeration of the things he loved:

> So, for their sakes I loved, ere I go hence,
> And the high cause of love's magnificence,
> And to keep loyalties young, I'll write those names
> Golden for ever, eagles, crying flames,
> And set them as a banner, that men may know,
> To dare the generations, burn, and blow
> Out on the wind of Time, shining and streaming. . . .

The list includes tea-cups and peeled sticks as well as rainbows.
 He celebrated the beauty and quiet of Grantchester, near Cambridge, and in a Berlin café thought of the honey for tea there. He was not going to stop short at youth any more than at vegetarianism, or walking barefoot in the dust, or bathing in the winter in the Cam. He was beginning not only to enjoy things as mortals do, but perhaps to be content to do so. It had long been true of him what he said of Donne: that 'humour was always at his command. It was part of his realism, especially in the bulk of his work, his poems dealing with love.' He turned to

> Lips that fade, and human laughter,
> And faces individual,
> Well this side of Paradise. . . .

and remarked 'There's little comfort in the wise.'
 He did not attain the 'Shelleyan altitude where words have various radiance rather than meaning', but perhaps no poet better expressed the aspiration towards it and all the unfulfilled eagerness of ambitious self-conscious youth. His promise is more generally spoken of, but it was a rare and considerable achievement to have expressed and suggested in so many ways the promise of youth.
 When the war came to Europe, apparently a minor peace came to his heart, not with imagined 'love's magnificence', but ridding him of 'all the little emptiness of love', in a new life of which he wrote:

> Oh! we, who have known shame, we have found release there,
> Where there's no ill, no grief, but sleep has mending,
> Naught broken save this body, lost but breath;
> Nothing to shake the laughing heart's long peace there
> But only agony, and that has ending;
> And the worst friend and enemy is but Death.

He felt safe, 'and if these poor limbs die, safest of all'. His reputation is safe: it was never greater than now, when he stands out clearly against that immense, dark background, an Apollo not afraid of the worst of life.

'Rupert Brooke', ER, June 1915

GEORGIAN POETRY

IT HAS FOR some time been debatable whether anything could be done for contemporary poetry which would leave a little less of its fate to chance. Anyone with £5 can get a book of verse printed. Reviewers and booksellers have not been able to keep their heads above this stream. But now there has been opened at 35 Devonshire Street, Theobald's Road, a Poetry Bookshop, where you can see any and every volume of modern poetry. It will be an impressive and, perhaps, an instructive sight.

The Poetry Bookshop has, as a good beginning, given us an anthology of the poetry published under George V. The editor, 'E M'—Mr Edward Marsh—introduces it with the remarks that 'English poetry is now once again putting on a new strength and beauty', and that this collection may help readers to see that 'we are at the beginning of another "Georgian period", which may take rank in due time with the several great poetic ages of the past'. The authors represented are Messrs Abercrombie, Bottomley, Brooke, Chesterton, Davies, de la Mare, Drinkwater, Flecker, Gibson, D. H. Lawrence, Masefield, Monro, Sturge Moore, Ronald Ross, E. B. Sargant, Stephens and R.C. Trevelyan. Not a few of these had developed their qualities under Victoria and Edward, and it cannot be said that any uncommon accession of power has very recently come to Messrs Chesterton, Davies, de la Mare, Sturge Moore and Trevelyan, though it has to Messrs Bottomley, Masefield and Gibson (whose 'Queen's Crags' in the current *English Review* is a fine thing and his best work). These three, together with Messrs Abercrombie, Brooke, Lawrence, Sargant and Stephens, have most of the Georgian tone, and would alone give a scientific critic material for defining that tone. Messrs Brooke, Lawrence and Sargant, are, as it were, the core of the group.

Most of the poets are well represented. The two hundred pages include the whole of Abercrombie's 'Sale of Saint Thomas', W. H. Davies's 'Child and the Mariner', Masefield's 'Biography', James Stephens's 'Lonely God', and the first part of Sturge Moore's 'Sicilian Idyll'. Room might have been made for several other writers whose work has lately appeared in books and magazines. There are writers more Georgian than half a dozen of these, and as worthy of inclusion. Then, to be precise, 'The Kingfisher' of Mr Davies, is Edwardian in date. But the volume is more representative and striking than if twice the number of poets had been drawn from. It shows much beauty, strength, and mystery, and some magic—much aspiration, less defiance, no revolt—and it brings out with great cleverness many sides of the modern love of the simple and primitive, as seen in children, peasants, savages, early men, animals, and Nature in general.

Everyone, except Messrs Davies and de la Mare, is represented either by narrative or by meditative verse, and by practically nothing else.

Review of *Georgian Poetry, 1911-1912, DC,* 14 January 1913

This book is a selection from the poetry published during the reign of George V especially by writers who then first became known or who then made some notable advance. It is the work of a comprehensive student who has no coterie to boom and no circulation to make absolutely safe. That it is very interesting goes without saying. Only those who are prejudiced against modern poetry—who are opposed at heart to the spirit of poetry—can fail to find what is beautiful as well as interesting in this great variety of lyric, narrative, meditative, and dramatic verse chosen from seventeen living and flourishing poets.

The book is more than a mere anthology. It is as much an independent living book as *England's Helicon* or any of the other anthologies of the Elizabethan age which still maintain their original form. It represents an age; in the main, the youth of an age. It has been so well compiled that the individuality of the age is, if anything, clearer than that of the majority of the men representing it. Perhaps only three men's work emerges new, beautiful, and complete above the rushing tide of the times, Messrs Sturge Moore, Walter de la Mare, and W. H. Davies. But all three are men whose work had culminated or had taken an unmistakable direction before the accession of George V. They achieve what the others are still fervently and loudly pursuing—some form of magic, rapture, or beauty.

First in the book comes Mr Lascelles Abercrombie, and in his 'Sale of St Thomas' he might seem to be preaching to his fellow-poets the one beatitude:

> But prudence, prudence is the deadly sin . . .
> Thou must not therefore stop thy spirit's sight
> To pore only within the candle-gleam
> Of conscious wit and reasonable brain;
> But search into the sacred darkness lying
> Outside thy knowledge of thyself, the vast
> Measureless fate, full of the power of stars,
> The outer noiseless heavens of thy soul.

The sermon, not now preached for the first time, has gone deep. In Mr Gordon Bottomley's 'End of the World', the lovers in the snowstorm rejoice 'To be so safe and secret at its heart/Watching the strangeness of familiar things.' Mr Rupert Brooke refers to a Cambridge sect who, 'When they get to feeling old,/They up and shoot themselves, I'm told.' Mr Drinkwater takes to his wings 'To greet the men who lived triumphant days,/And stormed the secret beauty of the world.' Two of Mr Gibson's heroes exclaim:

> We've left the fat and weatherwise
> To keep their coops and reeking sties,
> And eat their fill of oven-pies,
> While we win free and out again
> To take potluck beneath the sky
> With sun and moon and wind and rain.

Mr D. H. Lawrence concludes an amorous piece with 'And death I know is better than not-to-be.' Mr Masefield ends his 'Biography' saying: 'Best trust the happy moments. What they gave/Makes man less fearful of the certain grave. . . .' Mr Harold Monro hails the dawn, saying:

> Life, with thy breath upon my eyelids, seems
> Exquisite to the utmost bounds of pain.
> I cannot live, except as I may be
> Compelled for love of thee.
> Oh, let us drift. . . .

Mr E. B. Sargant has a long poem intended to convey the madness of panic glee in the forest. Mr James Stephens pictures a Creator and a human wife 'sowing jollity among the raving stars'.

All in some way adore Aphrodite, Mr Sturge Moore's 'Goddess of Ruin' or one of her priestesses, 'gay, invulnerable setters-at-naught of will and virtue'. Nearly all would give anything to be beyond good and evil. Messrs Davies and de la Mare alone have penetrated far into the desired kingdom, and that without having been certain of their goal or of their way, or possessing any guide or talisman known to anyone but themselves.

Another review of *Georgian Poetry*, ?, 15 January 1913

Whether it is or is not a compliment to publish all the poems, except the dramas, of the chief of living poets, at as low a price as if he were a classic, by a happy chance something more than a compliment is simultaneously paid by the dedication to him, on the part of editor and poets, of an anthology of Georgian Poetry. The poets are Messrs Abercrombie, Bottomley, Brooke, Chesterton, W. H. Davies, de la Mare, Drinkwater, Flecker, Gibson, D. H. Lawrence, Masefield, Monro, Sturge Moore, Ronald Ross, Sargant, Stephens, and R. C. Trevelyan; and if only Mr de la Mare among the number bears any obvious relationship to Mr Bridges, the dedication is the more remarkable, as showing from how many different young men—

dwelling in how different a world from that of 'I love all beauteous things' and 'I have loved flowers that fade'—his loveliness, his purity and his originality command homage.

Georgian Poetry contains 'beauteous things'. It includes for example long poems by Messrs Abercrombie, Davies, Masefield, Sturge Moore, and James Stephens. It includes the two most impressive of Mr Gordon Bottomley's recent poems, five remarkable pieces by Mr Rupert Brooke, and five representative poems from Mr de la Mare's *Listeners*. Altogether it is a brilliant selection from the poetry of 1911 and 1912. But it is less and more than that. It excludes many poems because it aims at showing what young men are typical and promising, what elder men notably reflect the spirit of the moment. Nobody not jaded by excess of poetry or starved for lack of it, will fail to see that there is such a spirit when he meets it thus concentrated. Compare it with a similar book of poetry from 1901 and 1902 and its novelty is apparent. There is, by the way, no anthology of 1901 and 1902, but if it is now too late to make one, it is to be hoped that similar volumes will henceforward be compiled decennially or even quinquennially. If they find editors as generous and impartial as 'E M' they will, like this Georgian anthology, be valuable and delightful.

Was there ten years ago such vividness—or such hectic and excited striving after vividness—as in Mr Abercrombie? In his new play—where he redresses the long-troubled balance by putting into the mouths of fishermen such poetry as used to be held too good for any but kings—a man speaks of a plague thus:

> The whole earth's peoples have been fiercely caught
> Like torn small papers in a wind, in this
> Great powerful ailing.

Another speaks of a sailor: 'With the ribs of his breast crusht like a trodden hamper,/Lying three days crampt in a boat, and he for ever groaning.'

Ten years ago Mr Chesterton was consoling and praising the ass by recalling the day when Christ rode one into Jerusalem. Today Mr Rupert Brooke sincerely and (so far as an unbewitched landsman can judge) powerfully endeavours to sympathize with a fish and its 'dark ecstasies' where:

> Those silent waters weave for him
> A fluctuant mutable world and dim,
> Where wavering masses bulge and gape . . . .

Ten years ago Mr Gordon Bottomley was not picturing the end of the world and the building of Babel in blank verse like the quintessence of G. W. Stevens's prose. Ten years ago nobody knew that Mr W. H.

Davies was a poet—not even himself. But then he is a fortunate accident that might have happened at any time, but did not. Ten years ago the surviving *Yellow Book* men would have been pleased with Mr D. H. Lawrence's subjects, enraged with his indifference to their execution. Nor would they alone have been enraged, and not only Mr Lawrence would have given offence. They would have contracted a chill from so much eagerness both to come at truth and to avoid the appearance of insincerity, the fidelity to crudest fact in Messrs Abercrombie, Gibson and Masefield, the fidelity to airiest fancy in Mr de la Mare, and to remotest intuition or guessing in Mr Brooke, the mixture everywhere of what they would have called realism and extravagance. They could not have endured the simplicity of Mr Abercrombie's 'Deborah' as here: 'Is it only a small thing to you, this/That once was David's? . . .', or the violent subtlety of his 'Sale of St Thomas?' as here:

> Gigantic thirst grieving our mouths with dust,
> Scattering up against our breathing salt
> Of blown dried dung, till the taste eat like fires
> Of a wild vinegar into our sheathed marrows . . . .

The anthology does not include all that is typical, or all that is best.

Another review of *Georgian Poetry* together with *The Poetical Works of Robert Bridges* and *Deborah: A Play in Three Acts* by Lascelles Abercrombie, in review of new verse, *B*, March 1913

EZRA POUND

CARELESSNESS OF SWEET sound and of all the old tricks makes Mr Pound's book rather prickly to handle at first. It was practically nothing but this prickliness that incited us to read his book through a second time. We read it a third time—it is less than sixty pages long—because it was good the second, and, nevertheless, still held back other good things. But we know from experience that it is impossible to show in a bit of a column that a new writer is good and in a new way. Nor will we trust him in the form of extracts to anyone's tender mercies, but give simply the one poem short enough for quotation. It is called 'The White Stag':

> I ha' seen them mid the clouds on the heather.
> Lo! they pause not for love nor for sorrow,
> Yet their eyes are as the eyes of a maid to her lover,
> When the white hart breaks his cover
> And the white wind breaks the morn.

'Tis the white stag, Fame, we're a-hunting.
Bid the world's hounds come to horn!

That will at least give you some idea of the way Mr Pound's work bursts upon the mind. All his poems are like this, from beginning to end, and in every way, his own, and in a world of his own. For brusque intensity of effect we can hardly compare them with any other work. Of course, this is due partly to his faults and to his pride in revolt, to his lack of all mere amiability, to his austerity, to his abruptness as of a swift beetle that suddenly strikes your cheek and falls stunned with its own force, to his use of a number of archaisms in the midst of a chaste and simple vocabulary.

But these faults have the same origin as his virtues, and are doubtless at present inseparable from them. He is so possessed by his own strong conceptions, that he not only cannot think of wrapping them up in a conventional form, but he must ever show his disdain for it a little; one of his poems is, in so many words, a revolt against the crepuscular spirit in modern poetry. But the disdain is the other side of a powerful love for something else, and it is usually either only implicit or entirely concealed. Yet, when we consider it, there is singularly little crudity, and practically no extravagance. It is mostly hard, naked, and grim.

Well, and what is this new thing? somebody is asking. It is only the very old, felt and said anew; the love of a man for the wild wood, for women, for his own songs, for his friend, for life. And in half at least the poet chooses to let men long dead utter his words—a troubadour of the Middle Ages, a companion of Villon's, an 'unknown writer' of the eighteenth century, a Saxon of the eighth, a Crusader, a poet in Nineveh!

Yet as we read we forget that it has been done before; we share something of the spirit of love that has entered him, and see all things anew. And, setting aside the archaisms, which do not count one way or the other, the method is so simple. No remarkable melody; no golden words shot with meaning; a temperate use of images, and none far-fetched; no flattering of modern fashions, in descriptions of Nature, for example; no apostrophe, no rhetoric, nothing 'Celtic'. It is the old miracle that cannot be defined, nothing more than a subtle entanglement of words, so that they rise out of their graves and sing. And part of our pleasure in reading the book has been the belief, in which we are confident, that the writer is only just getting under sail, that he will reach we know not where; nor does he, but somewhere far away in the unexplored.

Review of *Personae of Ezra Pound*, DC, 7 June 1909

It is easier to enjoy than to praise Mr Pound, easier to find fault with him, easiest to ridicule. His *Personae*, probably a first book, is strewn with signs of two battles not yet over, the battle with the world of a fresh soul who feels himself strong but alone, and the battle with words, the beautiful, the soiled, the rare, the antique words. It is not wonderful then that one coming up from the outside should be tempted for a moment to turn away from the battlefield with a promise to come back and see who and what is left. And yet such tumults are fascinating for themselves, especially if we know that sometimes when they are over, nothing, from the spectator's point of view, is left. In Mr Pound's case we feel sure there will be a great soul left. Also, in the meantime, the book is well worth having for itself and regardless of its vague large promise.

Let us straightway acknowledge the faults; the signs of conflict; the old and foreign words and old spellings that stand doubtless for much that the ordinary reader is not privileged to detect; the tricky use of inverted commas; the rhythms at one time so free as not to be distinguishable at first from prose, at another time so stiff that 'evanescent' becomes 'evan'scent'; the gobbets of Browningesque; and one piece of construction at the foot of p. 39 which we cannot unravel and are inclined to put down as not the only case of imperfect correction of proofs.

To say what this poet has not is not difficult; it will help to define him. He has no obvious grace, no sweetness, hardly any of the superficial good qualities of modern versifiers; not the smooth regularity of the Tennysonian tradition, nor the wavering, uncertain languor of the new, though there is more in his rhythms than is apparent at first through his carelessness of ordinary effects. He has not the current melancholy or resignation or unwillingness to live; nor the kind of feeling for nature that runs to minute description and decorative metaphor. He cannot be usefully compared with any living writers, though he has read Mr Yeats. Browning and Whitman he respects, and he could easily burlesque Browning if he liked. He knows mediaeval poetry in the popular tongues, and Villon, and Ossian. He is equally fond of strict stanzas of many rhymes, of blank verse with many unfinished lines, of rhymeless or almost rhymeless lyrics, of Pindarics with or without rhyme. But these forms are not striking in themselves, since all are subdued to his spirit; in each he is true in his strength and weakness to himself, full of personality and with such power to express it that from the first to the last lines of most of his poems he holds us steadily in his own pure, grave, passionate world.

It will appear paradoxical to say after this that the chief part of his power is directness and simplicity. A characteristic opening is this, put in the mouth of an Italian poet—'Italian Campagna, 1309, The Open Road':

> Bah! I have sung women in three cities,
> But it is all the same;
> And I will sing of the sun. . . .

or this, from 'A Villonaud: Ballad of the Gibbet; or the Song of the Sixth Companion of Villon':

> Drink ye a skoal for the gallows tree!
> François and Margot and thee and me,
> Drink we the comrades merrily
> That said us, 'Till then' for the gallows tree!

In the poem 'In Tempore Senectutis' the old man says to his old love:

> Red spears bore the warrior dawn
> > Of old.
> Strange! Love, hast thou forgotten
> The red spears of the dawn,
> The pennants of the morning?

The finest of his pieces are the love-poems. In 'Scriptor Ignotus: Ferrara, 1715' he astonishes us by using again the poet's claim, Ronsard's and Shakespeare's, to give immortality to a mistress by words, by 'A new thing as hath not heretofore been writ.' But it is not a playing upon an old theme as, for example, Locker-Lampson played on it. It is a piece of strong tender passion that happens to lean upon the old theme and to honour it. 'In Praise of Ysolt' is equally beautiful in an entirely different way, showing that the writer does not depend upon a single mood or experience. The beauty of it is the beauty of passion, sincerity and intensity, not of beautiful words and images and suggestions; on the contrary, the expression is as austere as biblical prose. The thought dominates the words and is greater than they are. It opens:

> In vain have I striven to teach my heart to bow;
> In vain have I said to him
> 'There be many singers greater than thou.'

> But his answer cometh, as winds and as lutany,
> As a vague crying upon the night
> That leaveth me no rest, saying ever,
> > 'Song, a song.'

In the 'Idyl for Glaucus' a woman hovers by the sea in search of Glaucus, who has tasted 'the grass that made him sea-fellow with the other gods'. Here the effect is full of human passion and natural magic, without any of the phrases which a reader of modern verse would expect in the treatment of such a subject. In 'From Syria' and 'From the Saddle' the thought is not new but it is made his own by genuineness, weakened only by allowing such a line as 'So if my line disclose distress.'

'And thus in Nineveh' we venture to quote in its entirety, not as the best but as the shortest of these love-poems, with this warning that, like the two last, it does not reveal Mr Pound neat, though we are confident that it will give conviction to our praise of his style: [poem quoted].

And on the same page is this wonderful little thing that builds itself so abruptly, swiftly, clearly into the air:

> I ha' seen them mid the clouds on the heather.
> Lo! they pause not for love nor for sorrow,
> Yet their eyes are as the eyes of a maid to her lover,
> When the white hart breaks his cover
> And the white wind breaks the morn.
> *'Tis the white stag, Fame, we're a-hunting,*
> *Bid the world's hounds come to horn!*

In taking leave of this admirable poet we should like to mention other poems we have particularly enjoyed, 'La Fraisne', 'Famam Librosque Cano' (a prophetic sketch of the kind of reader he will one day have), 'Ballad for Gloom,' 'For E. McC.' (these two last very brilliant and noble), 'Occidit', and 'Revolt against the Crepuscular Spirit in Modern Poetry'; and to apologize to him for our own shortcomings and to any other readers for that insecurity of modern criticism of which we feel ourselves at once a victim and a humble cause.

Another review of *Personae* in 'Two Poets', *ER*, June 1909

Mr Ezra Pound's verses look so extraordinary, dappled with French, Provençal, Spanish, Italian, Latin, and old English, with proper names that we shirk pronouncing, with crudity, violence and obscurity, with stiff rhythms and no rhythms at all, that we are tempted to think that they are the expression or at least the mask of an extraordinary man. It is a relief to us to turn from all but meaningless suavity and skill to something that appears to be individual. And doubtless no ordinary man could or would write like Mr Pound. But having allowed the turbulent opacity of his peculiarities to sink down we believe that we see very nearly nothing at all. Thus in the poem on Piere Vidal, the fool, who 'ran mad as a wolf because of his love . . . and how men hunted him with dogs', we find nothing which we cannot ourselves feel with the help of the introductory note in prose. The verses themselves show us only such things as the writer's effort to imagine what it would be like to be a wolf: 'God! how the swiftest hind's blood spurted hot/Over the sharpened teeth and purpling lips.'

In some of his poems he produces no effect at all, and we are at leisure to note the peculiar taste of the writer with astonishment, as, for example, the Irish turns in this verse:

> White Poppy, heavy with dreams,
> Though I am hungry for their lips
>> When I see them a-hiding
> And a-passing out and in through the shadows
> —and it is white they are—
> But if one should look at me with the old hunger in her eyes,
> How will I be answering her eyes?
>> For I have followed the white folk of the forest.

Here it may be that there was something to be expressed which failed to be, because it was difficult. But in the poem addressed to the beautiful women of London:

> I am aweary with the utter and beautiful weariness
> And with the ultimate wisdom and with things terrene;
> I am aweary with your smiles and your laughter,
> And the sun and the winds again
> Reclaim their booty and the heart o' me—

the thought is simple and plain enough, and interesting as a human fact, but it can hardly be claimed that it is expressed in a beautiful way or in any way which gives it an individual value as a cry of the heart. When Mr Pound has a subject, as in the 'Glaucus' of his first volume, he can treat it in a manner deserving attention, not always, but now and then. When he writes in the first person he is so obscure as to give some excuse for finding him incapable of self-expression. And both in personal and detached poems he is, as a rule, so pestered with possible ways of saying a thing that at present we must be content to pronounce his condition still interesting—perhaps promising—certainly distressing. If he is not careful he will take to meaning what he says instead of saying what he means.

Review of *Exultations of Ezra Pound*, DC, 23 November 1909

Mr Ezra Pound's *Spirit of Romance* deals with the poetry of the Latin races, roughly speaking, from the Provençals to Villon, Camoens, and Lope de Vega. It does not pretend to be exhaustive, but to express the opinions of Mr Pound upon certain representative poets. He is 'interested in poetry', both as a scholar and as a human being, and he writes probably for those who have more humanity than scholarship. His aim is to instruct, his ambition 'to instruct painlessly', and he confines himself to 'such mediaeval works as still possess an interest other than archaeological for the contemporary reader who is not a specialist'. His quotations are long and numerous; as they are often from little known or difficult writers they are valuable. Whatever may be thought of his opinions and his way of expressing them, there can be no doubt that his translations are in the main admirable, having the two qualities of intelligibility and of suggesting the superiority of the original. He says himself that his criticism has 'consisted in selection rather than in presentation of opinion'. If that were so we should have nothing but praise for the book, but it is not. It is restlessly opinionated. He has, or desires to have, an opinion upon everything; and if he has not then his eccentric speech makes it appear that he has. He relies, in fact, as much upon his personality as upon his learning. We are delighted to agree with him far more often than we disagree. On the subject of classic and romantic, for example, he says a number of true things, though he must admit that he is just as far as ever from the truth, even if he did not confound everything by saying: 'Certain qualities and certain furnishings are germane to all fine poetry; there is no need to call them either classic or romantic.'

He might have given more space than he does to proving that certain lines of Ovid are 'as haunted as anything in Ossian'. All he does is to show that the substance of these lines is very much like the substance of some 'Celtic' writer. This is not enough, and he seems to admit as much himself, when he speaks of Ovid's 'polished verse' and his demand for 'the definite'. Apuleius is far nearer to Ossian, and in him Mr Pound rightly perceives a different 'atmosphere', and the 'indefiniteness' of later writers, 'who speak of "the Duke Joshua" and "that good Knight Alexander of Macedon" '. It is altogether a question of atmosphere and style, and Mr Pound should not have plunged so heavily into disagreement without more circumspection. The same is true of his assertion that the 'Oedipus Coloneus' has 'all the paraphernalia of the "Romantic" school'. It is just conceivable that he is right, but his bare assertion of the contrary to received opinion is not enough to raise the question. The fact is that he is too much bent upon being interesting, upon being something more than a scholar. He is thus lured into digressions which could only be sustained by a strong personality. There is no reason why a writer of strong personality should not turn aside to abuse Whitman in a chapter upon 'Montcorbier, *alias* Villon'; but Mr Pound is not such a one. His personality is negative, and rises to the appearance of being positive only by contradition. His aim at being better than dryasdust by allowing his personality free play is therefore not so successful as it is laudable. At one moment he is a scholar writing in a way which is over the heads of the unlearned, and at another he is the free, courageous man wearing his learning lightly like a daisy. He cannot combine the scholar and the man. We regret to say this, because a point has been reached where men refuse to take works of learned dullness, and of this the learned are aware and they are considering their ways.

Mr Pound has considered his ways, but on the whole we had rather he confined himself to translation and the severest exposition. If he does so he will do extremely well, for already in this volume he has almost done what nobody else has done—given an account of the Provençal writers which to some extent accounts for Dante's admiration and their surviving repute.

Review of *The Spirit of Romance, MP*, 1 August 1910

THE IMAGISTS

There are in this book sixty-three pages, many of them only half-filled; yet it sticks out of the crowd like a tall marble monument. Whether it is real marble is unimportant except to posterity; the point is that it is conspicuous. Only Mr Ford Madox Hueffer, Miss Amy Lowell, and Mr James Joyce contribute pieces resembling ordinary poems. The rest, though divided into lines just like ordinary poems, are for the most part very different. A few are banterings of a private nature which hardly concern us. The majority fall into two classes. Either they are translations or paraphrases, or they are written in the manner of translations.

The best of the first class are Mr Allen Upward's 'Scented Leaves from a Chinese Jar', of which this is an example:

> My mother taught me that every night a procession of junks carrying lanterns moves silently across the sky, and the water sprinkled from their paddles falls to the earth in the form of dew. I no longer believe that the stars are junks carrying lanterns, no longer that the dew is shaken from their oars.

Mr John Cournos has a page, and 'after K. Tetmaier', suggesting a poetic original.

The second class forms the larger and more novel part of the book. The writers are Messrs Richard Aldington, Skipwith Cannell, William Carlos Williams, Ezra Pound, and 'H D', yet, as a rule, their work is not distinguishable, so much are they under one influence. Partly, no doubt, the influence is that of a common aim; partly, it may be, of some commanding personality. But the chief influence appears to have been the ordinary prose translation of the classics—in short, the crib. Burlesqued this had been already by Mr A. E. Housman and others. The Imagiste poets must have the credit of being the first to go to it for serious inspiration. On the whole, Mr Richard Aldington is most successful, and this is the more remarkable when we learn from poems like 'Beauty thou hast hurt me overmuch' that he has been endowed with exquisite sensibility. His 'Argyria' might be a prose translation, lacking all adornment except division into lines:

> O you,
> O you most fair,
> Swayer of reeds, whisperer
> Among the flowering rushes,
> You have hidden your hands
> Beneath the poplar leaves,
> You have given them to the white waters.
>
> Swallow-fleet,
> Sea-child cold from the waves,
> Slight reed that sang so blithely in the wind,
> White cloud the white sun kissed into the air;
> Pan mourns for you.
>
> White limbs, white song,
> Pan mourns for you.

Others of his poems must thrill anyone not wholly forgetful or disdainful of Bohn's first charm. 'H D' is equally good in the same way. It will be better, however, to quote one of Mr Skipwith Cannell's nocturnes written in the same style, but without a particularly Greek tinge:

> Thy feet are white
> Upon the foam of the sea;
> Hold me fast, thou bright swan,
> Lest I stumble,
> And into deep waters.

Probably it is simply out of a dislike for Tennyson, as well as contempt for natural history, that this swan has white feet, not 'swarthy webs'. Mr Pound, again, has seldom done better than here under the restraint imposed by Chinese originals or models. 'Ts'ai Chi'h' is very austere:

> The petals fall in the fountain,
> The orange-coloured rose leaves,
> Their ochre clings to the stone.

Here, also, is *ΔΩPIA*, the most impressive-looking poem in the whole book:

> Be in me as the eternal moods
>   Of the bleak wind, and not
> As transient things are—
>   Gaiety of flowers.
> Have me in the strong loneliness
>   Of sunless cliffs
> And of grey waters.
>   Let the gods speak softly of us
> In days hereafter.
>   The shadowy flowers of Orcus
> Remember Thee.

I do not see the meaning. I even doubt whether the words mean anything, and suspect a serious omission in the make-up of a writer who can slap in 'gaiety of flowers' like that; but it is an impressive-looking poem. The most attractive, on the other hand, are Mr F. S. Flint's pieces. They record a sincere and sensitive attempt to write poetry without admitting any commonplaces of verse, in form, language, or sentiment. They will interest readers as theorists, and touch them as men. They are the green ivy beginning to climb the tall marble monument, and may well outlast it.

Review of *Des Imagistes: An Anthology*, NW, 9 May 1914

ROBERT FROST

THIS IS ONE of the most revolutionary books of modern times, but one of the quietest and least aggressive. It speaks, and it is poetry. It consists of fifteen poems, from fifty to three hundred lines long, depicting scenes from life, chiefly in the country, in New Hampshire. Two neighbour farmers go along the opposite sides of their boundary wall, mending it and speaking of walls and of boundaries. A husband and wife discuss an old vagabond farm servant who has come home to them, as it falls out, to die. Two travellers sit outside a deserted cottage, talking of those who once lived in it, talking until bees in the wall boards drive them away. A man who has lost his feet in a saw-mill talks with a friend, a child, and the lawyer comes from Boston about compensation. The poet himself describes the dreams of his eyes after a long day on a ladder picking apples, and the impression left on him by a neglected woodpile in the snow on an evening walk. All but these last two are dialogue mainly; nearly all are in blank verse.

These poems are revolutionary because they lack the exaggeration of rhetoric, and even at first sight appear to lack the poetic intensity of which rhetoric is an imitation. Their language is free from the poetical words and forms that are the chief material of secondary poets. The metre avoids not only the old-fashioned pomp and sweetness, but the later fashion also of discord and fuss. In fact, the medium is common speech and common decasyllables, and Mr Frost is at no pains to exclude blank verse lines resembling those employed, I think, by Andrew Lang in a leading article printed as prose. Yet almost all these poems are beautiful. They depend not at all on objects commonly admitted to be beautiful; neither have they merely a homely beauty, but are often grand, sometimes magical. Many, if not most, of the separate lines and separate sentences are plain and, in themselves, nothing. But they are bound together and made elements of beauty by a calm eagerness of emotion.

What the poet might have done, could he have permitted himself egoistic rhetoric, we have a glimpse of once or twice where one of his characters tastes a fanciful mood to the full: as where one of the men by the deserted cottage, who has been describing an old-style inhabitant, says:

> 'As I sit here, and often times, I wish
> I could be monarch of a desert land
> I could devote and dedicate for ever
> To the truths we keep coming back and back to.
> So desert it would have to be, so walled
> By mountain ranges half in summer snow,
> No one would covet it or think it worth
> The pains of conquering to force change on.
> Scattered oases where men dwelt, but mostly
> Sand dunes held loosely in tamarisk
> Blown over and over themselves in idleness.
> Sand grains should sugar in the natal dew
> The babe born to the desert, the sand storm
> Retard mid-waste my cowering caravans—
>
> There are bees in this wall.' He struck the clapboards,
> Fierce heads looked out; small bodies pivoted.
> We rose to go. Sunset blazed on the windows.

This passage stands alone. But it is a solitary emotion also that gives him another which I feel obliged to quote in order to hint at the poetry elsewhere spread evenly over whole poems. It is the end of 'The Wood Pile':

> I thought that only
> Someone who lived in turning to fresh tasks
> Could so forget his handiwork on which

He spent himself, the labour of his axe,
And leave it there far from a useful fireplace
To warm the frozen swamp as best it could
With the slow smokeless burning of decay.

The more dramatic pieces have the same beauty in solution, the beauty of life seen by one in whom mystery and tenderness together just outstrip humour and curiosity. This beauty grows like grass over the whole, and blossoms with simple flowers which the reader gradually sets a greater and greater value on, in lines such as these about the dying labourer:

> She put out her hand
> Among the harp-like morning-glory strings
> Taut with the dew from garden bed to eaves,
> As if she played unheard the tenderness
> That wrought on him beside her in the night.
> 'Warren,' she said, 'he has come home to die:
> You needn't be afraid he'll leave you this time.'
> 'Home,' he mocked gently.
>   'Yes, what else but home?
> It all depends on what you mean by home.
> Of course, he's nothing to us, any more
> Than was the hound that came a stranger to us
> Out of the woods, worn out upon the trail.'
> 'Home is the place where, when you have to go there,
> They have to take you in.'
>   'I should have called it
> Something you somehow haven't to deserve.'

The book is not without failures. Mystery falls into obscurity. In some lines I cannot hit upon the required accents. But his successes, like 'The Death of the Hired Man', put Mr Frost above all other writers of verse in America. He will be accused of keeping monotonously at a low level, because his characters are quiet people, and he has chosen the unresisting medium of blank verse. I will only remark that he would lose far less than most modern writers by being printed as prose. If his work were so printed, it would have little in common with the kind of prose that runs to blank verse: in fact, it would turn out to be closer knit and more intimate than the finest prose is except in its finest passages. It is poetry because it is better than prose.

Review of *North of Boston*, DN, 22 July 1914

This is an original book which will raise the thrilling question, What is poetry? and will be read and re-read for pleasure as well as curiosity, even by those who decide that, at any rate, it is not poetry. At first sight, some will pronounce simply that anyone can write this kind of blank verse, with all its tame common words, straightforward constructions, and innumerable perfectly normal lines. Few that read it through will have been as much astonished by any American since Whitman. Mr Frost owes nothing to Whitman, though had Whitman not helped to sanctify plain labour and ordinary men, Mr Frost might have been different. The colloquialisms, the predominance of conversation (though not one out of fifteen pieces has been printed in dramatic style), and the phrase 'by your leave' (which is an excrescence), may hint at Browning. But I have not met a living poet with a less obvious or more complicated ancestry. Nor is there any brag or challenge about this.

Mr Frost has, in fact, gone back, as Whitman and as Wordsworth went back, through the paraphernalia of poetry into poetry again. With a confidence like genius, he has trusted his conviction that a man will not easily write better than he speaks when some matter has touched him deeply, and he has turned it over until he has no doubt what it means to him, when he has no purpose to serve beyond expressing it, when he has no audience to be bullied or flattered, when he is free, and speech takes one form and no other. Whatever discipline further was necessary, he has got from the use of the good old English medium of blank verse.

Mr Frost, the reader should be reminded, writes of what he or some country neighbour in New Hampshire has seen or done. Extraordinary things have not been sought for. There is but one death, one case of a man coming home to find the woman flown. There is a story of a doctor who has to share an inn bedroom with a stranger, and enters scared, and is at last terrified almost out of his wits, though the stranger is merely a talkative traveller offering him a hundred collars which he has grown out of. Two farmers talk as they repair the boundary wall between them. A husband and wife talk on the staircase about the child lying buried over there in sight of the house. An old woman discusses her daughter's running away from the man they kept house for. Here is no 'Lucy Grey', no 'Thorn', no 'Idiot Boy'. Yet it might be said that Mr Frost sometimes combines an effect resembling Wordsworth's, while he shows us directly less of his own feelings, and more of other people's, than Wordsworth did.

It is drama with a lyric intensity which often borders on magic. A line now and then can be quoted to prove Mr Frost capable of doing what other poets do, as in this description: 'Part of a moon was falling down the west,/Dragging the whole sky with it to the hills . . .', or:

'There are bees in this wall.' He struck the clapboards,
Fierce heads looked out; small bodies pivoted.
We rose to go. Sunset blazed on the windows.

or: 'Cottages in a row/Up to their shining eyes in snow.'

The pieces without dialogue rise up more than once to passages like
this about a deserted woodpile in the snow of a swamp:

> No runner tracks in this year's snow looped near it.
> And it was older sure than this year's cutting,
> Or even last year's or the year's before.
> The wood was grey and the bark warping off it,
> And the pile somewhat sunken. Clematis
> Had wound strings round and round it like a bundle.
> What held it though on one side was a tree
> Still growing, and on one a stake and prop,
> These latter about to fall. I thought that only
> Someone who lived in turning to fresh tasks
> Could so forget his handiwork on which
> He spent himself, the labour of his axe,
> And leave it there far from a useful fireplace
> To warm the frozen swamp as best it could
> With the slow smokeless burning of decay.

But the effect of each poem is one and indivisible. You can hardly
pick out a single line more than a single word. There are no show words
or lines. The concentration has been upon the whole, not the parts.
Decoration has been forgotten, perhaps for lack of the right kind of
vanity and obsession.

In his first book, *A Boy's Will*, when he was still a comparatively
isolated, egotistic poet, eagerly considering his own sensations more
than what produced them, he did things far more easily quotable, and
among them this piece, entitled 'Mowing':

> There was never a sound beside the wood but one,
> And that was my long scythe whispering to the ground.
> What was it it whispered? I knew not well myself;
> Perhaps it was something about the heat of the sun,
> Something, perhaps, about the lack of sound—
> And that was why it whispered and did not speak.
> It was no dream of the gift of idle hours,
> Or easy gold at the hand of fay or elf:
> Anything more than the truth would have seemed too weak
> To the earnest love that laid the swale in rows,
> Not without feeble-pointed spikes of flowers
> (Pale orchises), and scared a bright green snake.

> The fact is the sweetest dream that labour knows.
> My long scythe whispered and left the hay to make.

Those last six lines do more to define Mr Frost than anything I can say. He never will have 'easy gold at the hand of fay or elf' : he can make fact 'the sweetest dream'.

Naturally, then, when his writing crystallizes, it is often in a terse, plain phrase, such as the proverb, 'Good fences make good neighbours', or 'Three foggy mornings and one rainy day/Will rot the best birch fence a man can build', or 'From the time when one is sick to death,/One is alone, and he dies more alone', or 'Pressed into service means pressed out of shape.'

But even this kind of characteristic detail is very much less important than the main result, which is a richly homely thing beyond the grasp of any power except poetry. It is a beautiful achievement, and I think a unique one, as perfectly Mr Frost's own as his vocabulary, the ordinary English speech of a man accustomed to poetry and philosophy, more colloquial and idiomatic than the ordinary man dares to use even in a letter, almost entirely lacking the emphatic hackneyed forms of journalists and other rhetoricians, and possessing a kind of healthy, natural delicacy like Wordsworth's, or at least Shelley's, rather than that of Keats.

> Another review of *North of Boston, NW,* 8 August 1914

This is a collection of dramatic narratives in verse. Some are almost entirely written in dialogue: in only three is the poet a chief character, telling a story, for the most part, in his own words. Thus he has got free from the habit of personal lyric as was, perhaps, foretold by his first book, *A Boy's Will.* Already there he had refused the 'glory of words' which is the modern poet's embarrassing heritage, yet succeeded in being plain though not mean, in reminding us of poetry without being 'poetical'. The new volume marks more than the beginning of an experiment like Wordsworth's, but with this difference, that Mr Frost knows the life of which he writes rather as Dorothy Wordsworth did. That is to say, he sympathizes where Wordsworth contemplates. The result is a unique type of eclogue, homely, racy, and touched by a spirit that might, under other circumstances, have made pure lyric on the one hand or drama on the other. Within the space of a hundred lines or so of blank verse it would be hard to compress more rural character and relevant scenery; impossible, perhaps, to do so with less sense of compression and more lightness, unity, and breadth. The language ranges from a never vulgar colloquialism to brief moments of heightened and intense simplicity. There are moments when the plain language and lack of violence make the unaffected verses look like prose, except that the sentences, if spoken aloud, are most felicitously true in rhythm to the emotion. Only at the end of the best pieces, such as 'The Death of the Hired Man', 'Home Burial', 'The Black Cottage' and 'The Wood Pile', do we realize that they are masterpieces of deep and mysterious tenderness.

Another review of *North of Boston*, *ER*, August 1914

WAR POETRY

IF THEY ALSO SERVE who only sit and write, poets are doing their work well. Several of them, it seems to me, with names known and unknown, have been turned into poets by the war, printing verse now for the first time. Whatever other virtues they show, courage at least is not lacking—the courage to write for oblivion. No other class of poetry vanishes so rapidly, has so little chosen from it for posterity. One tiny volume would hold all the patriotic poems surviving in European languages, and originally written, as most of these are today, under the direct pressure of public patriotic motives. Where are the poems of Marlborough's wars? Where are the songs sung by the troops for Quebec while Wolfe was reading Gray's 'Elegy'? But for the wars against Napoleon English poetry would have been different, but how many poems directly concerning them, addressed to Englishmen at that moment, do we read now? One of the earliest, I believe, was Coleridge's 'Fears in Solitude: written in April 1798, during the alarm of an invasion'. But no newspaper or magazine, then or now, would print such a poem, since a large part of it is humble. He admits that abroad we have offended, and at home

> All individual dignity and power
> Engulf'd in courts, committees, institutions,
> Associations and societies,
> A vain, speech-mouthing, speech-reporting guild,
> One benefit-club for mutual flattery,
> We have drunk up, demure as at a grace,
> Pollutions from the brimming cup of wealth. . . .

He believes that

> (Stuffed out with big preamble, holy names,
> And adjurations of the God in heaven,)
> We sent our mandates for the certain death
> Of thousands and ten thousands. Boys and girls
> And women, that would groan to see a child
> Pull off an insect's leg, all read of war,
> The best amusement of a morning's meal . . . .

When he wrote this at Stowey, Coleridge was a solitary man who, if at all, only felt the national emotions weakly or,spasmodically. He was writing poetry, and the chances against the reading as against the writing of poetry early in a great war were overwhelming. The poem, one of the noblest of patriotic poems, has been omitted from most of the anthologies. Another odd thing is that a poem included in several anthologies, and perhaps the finest of English martial songs—I mean Blake's 'War Song to Englishmen'—was written in or before 1783, by one who became a red-capped Revolutionary and cared nothing for Pitt's England. What inspired him? The war with the American colonies? More likely, the history of England as he felt it when he saw the kings in Westminster Abbey and Shakespeare's plays. He wrote from a settled mystic patriotism, which wars could not disturb.

Another poet, touched by the outbreak of war, will be disturbed for some time: he will be more fit for taking up work from the past, if only for relief, though it is possible for a mature man who has seen other wars and is not shaken from his balance to seize the new occasion firmly. Mr Charles M. Doughty might have done so: Mr Hardy has done. The period of gestation varies, but few younger men who had been moved to any purpose could be expected to crystallize their thoughts with speed. Supposing they did, who would want their poems? The demand is for the crude, for what everybody is saying or thinking, or is ready to begin saying or thinking. I need hardly say that by becoming ripe for poetry the poet's thoughts may recede far from their original resemblance to all the world's, and may seem to have little to do with daily events. They may retain hardly any colour from 1798 or 1914, and the crowd, deploring it, will naturally not read the poems.

It is a fact that in the past but a small number of poems destined to endure are directly or entirely concerned with the public triumphs, calamities, or trepidations, that helped to beget them. The public, crammed with mighty facts and ideas it will never digest, must look coldly on poetry where already those mighty things have sunk away far into 'The still sad music of humanity'. For his insults to their feelings, the newspapers, history, they might call the poet a pro-Boer. They want something raw and solid, or vague and lofty or sentimental. They must have Mr Begbie to express their thoughts, or 'Tipperary' to drown them.

A patriotic poem pure and simple hardly exists, as a man who was a patriot pure and simple could not live outside a madhouse. Very seldom are poems written for occasions, great or small, more seldom for great than for small. But verses are, and they may be excellent. Virtually all hymns are occasional verses. They are written for certain people or a certain class. The writer of hymns or patriotic verses appears to be a man who feels himself always or at the time at one with the class, perhaps the whole nation, or he is a smart fellow who can simulate or exaggerate this sympathy. Experience, reality, truth, unless suffused or submerged by popular sentiment, are out of place. What we like is Mr J. A. Nicklin's city clerk (*And They Went to the War*) singing:

> When the air with hurtling shrapnel's all a-quiver
> And the smoke of battle through the valley swirls,
> It's better than our Sundays up the river,
> And the rifle's hug is closer than a girl's.

Mr Arthur K. Sabin's sonnet called 'Harvest Moon at Midnight', and dated 8 September (*War Harvest, 1914*), is equally the thing, though nearer truth—it ends:

> Ah, underneath this Moon, in fields of France,
> How many of our old companionship
> Snatch hurried rest, with hearts that burn and glow,
> Longing to hear the bugles sound *Advance!*
> To seize their weapons with unfaltering grip,
> And for old England strike another blow.

It reminds us all of what we thought or heard said during that moon. Here and there I have met a poem that I liked more than others, such as Mr Justin Huntly McCarthy's 'Ghosts at Boulogne':

> One dreamer, when our English soldiers trod
> But yesterday the welcoming fields of France,
> Saw war-gaunt shadows gathering, stare askance
> Upon those levies and that alien sod—
> Saw Churchill's smile, and Wellington's curt nod,
> Saw Harry with his Crispins, Chandos' lance,
> And the Edwards on whose breasts the leopards dance:
> Then heard a gust of ghostly thanks to God
> That the most famous quarrel of all time
> In the most famous friendship ends at last;
> Such flame of friendship as God fans to forge
> A sword to strike the Dragon of the Slime,
> Bidding St Denis with St George stand fast
> Against the Worm. St Denis and St George!

But this is not great poetry, nor is it what is wanted. It is the hour of the writer who picks up popular views or phrases, or coins them, and has the power to turn them into downright stanzas. Most newspapers have one or more of these gentlemen. They could take the easy words of a statesman, such as 'No price is too high when honour and freedom are at stake', and dish them up so that the world next morning, ready to be thrilled by anything lofty and noble-looking, is thrilled. These poems are not to be attacked any more than hymns. Like hymns, they play with common ideas, with words and names which most people have in their heads at the time. Most seem to me bombastic, hypocritical, or senseless; but either they go straight to the heart of the great public which does not read poetry, or editors expect them to, and accordingly supply the articles.

There is a smaller class of better or more honest work which can hardly last longer. I mean the work of true poets which has been occasioned by the war. A few men are in an exceptional position: Messrs Newbolt and Kipling belong to a professional class apart, and may be supposed to suffer less drastic modifications from the war. It was their hour, and they have not been silent. They have written as well as in times of peace. The one silence which can be felt is Mr Charles M. Doughty's. But it might easily have been forecast. He has lived through this time long ago, and *The Cliffs* and *The Clouds* show that modern warfare and German politics had no surprises for him. Other men who stood on old foundations of character and tradition were not suddenly transported out of themselves. Mr Bridges, Mr de la Mare, Mr Binyon, among others, remained themselves. Years before this they had proved themselves English poets. They have not done more now. Their private and social emotion does them credit, but with few exceptions, such as Messrs Binyon, Chesterton, and John Freeman, they have fallen various distances below their natural level. Nor am I surprised. I should have expected the shock to silence them, had it not been counterbalanced by a powerful social sense genuinely aroused. I have not liked any of these poems, but fancy tells me that they do for persons with more social sense than I, what the noisy stuff does for the man who normally lives without poetry. They are suddenly made old-fashioned: Mr Chesterton's 'Hymn of War', for example (*Lord God of Battles: a war anthology,* compiled by A. E. Manning Foster), is archaic and Hebraic, after this fashion:

> O God of earth and altar,
>   Bow down and hear our cry,
> Our earthly rulers falter,
>   Our people drift and die;
>
> The walls of gold entomb us,
>   The swords of scorn divide,
> Take not the thunder from us,
>   But take away our pride.

They revert, and they may be right, though I cannot follow them if I would. They seem excellent only by comparison with 'C W', a serious and well-read but ungifted versifier, who tells us (*1914*) that 'his offer of active service for his country being rejected on account of his advanced years, and not being able to turn his thoughts away from the tragic events of the day, he has put, in a more or less poetic form, his own thoughts on the circumstances which led to this war, and the consequences it may and ought to have'. At the same time the poets of whom I speak have done things not inferior to the similar work of men more famous. Of six *Patriotic Poems* by Tennyson not one is worthy of him or would have survived without his name. They have one distinction, that they are the work of one who had the right, and felt it, to address his countrymen as from an eminence. Two living men besides Mr Doughty might do the same, Messrs Hardy and Kipling. Mr Kipling has hardly done more than speak in echoes of himself. Mr Hardy has written an impersonal song which seems to me the best of the time, as it is the least particular and occasional. He may write even better yet. I should also expect the work of other real poets to improve as the war advances, perhaps after it is over, as they understand it and themselves more completely.

PD, II, 8, December 1914

4   Frontiers of Prose

THE FRONTIERS OF ENGLISH PROSE

THERE ARE MANY differences between the literatures of last century and of today. For example, an affectionate portraiture of *les dehors* has been added. But a most noticeable fact is the apparent destruction of the boundaries between poetry and prose, if not between verse and prose. The same writers work in both styles indifferently; for how many writers of the day have not produced at least one volume in each? That in itself is nothing new. Sidney, the Herberts, Spenser, and hundreds more did so. The point is that not only do most writers use verse and prose, but they treat also in both styles the same subjects, or subjects of the same class. In the last century no writer would have dreamt of describing in prose the riverside scene of Richard Feverel and Lucy Desborough. Whence, then, this audacity of prose? As was said above, it is traceable far back, but in particular to the work of great poets at the beginning of the century.

Of course, verse develops earlier than prose. It is the natural form of literature for men, when their joy is expressed by laughter, their sorrow by tears and sighs. Sappho's poetry is perfect; but certainly no contemporary wrote perfect prose. In England also, there is nothing in prose to compare with the ballads, except the *but-and-and* romances. From the first some fastidiousness was imposed by verse—by metre, by rhyme, perhaps. In Italy poetry had a sumptuous patrician vocabulary of its own, and so it had, to some degree, in England. Nor for a very long time would this vocabulary mix with the vulgar prose. Chaucer tried; but surely his intricate prose, though pure English, is a failure; and the nearest to triumph at any early date, is the romantic prose of 'Kitsun's' *Testament of Love*. Spenser's prose is not very significant. Shakespeare's is not; or that of the other poets of his day, except Sidney's, though the poets Du Bellay and Ronsard were then carving exquisite prose in France. As to Milton, for the form of prose he did little, indeed; but he swelled its vocabulary conspicuously, and in his liveliest work we see the possibility of what is to come. Sir T. Browne came, with the same splendour, but a wonderful delicacy and sweetness too, and with a full quiver of rhetoric, melody, and metaphor; and Dryden, with no striking matter, but a careful attempt at scholarship which produced a style so fastidious, that men like Chesterfield declared they would use no word that was not to be found in his work. Drummond of Hawthornden, Ben Jonson's friend, a true poet, ought not to be omitted; for part of the *Cypress Grove* is a philosophical rhapsody full of a modern opulence and melancholy. Then, in the eighteenth century, this line of development, that promised such magnificence ahead, was cut short. The spirit of prose—argumentative and partisan—entered into verse. The spirit of poetry breathed only in pensive Gray, pastoral Dyer, and homely religious Cowper.

But the air was highly charged at the junction of the eighteenth and nineteenth centuries: 1800 precisely is the date of Wordsworth's publication of the second volume of *Lyrical Ballads*. This volume contained 'Hartleap Well' and 'Poems on the naming of Places'; but it is the manifesto by way of preface that is of importance at present. That stirring piece contains an earnest and a prophecy of the character of much that is weightiest in the literature of our century.

> It would be [he says] a most easy task to prove that not only the language of a large portion of every good poem, even of the most elevated character, must necessarily, except with reference to the metre, in no respect differ from that of good prose, but likewise that some of the most interesting parts of the best poems will be found to be strictly the language of prose *when prose is well written.*

The opinion was startling if not new, and, as we have seen, the enunciation of it had been prepared for. Poetry had been too long and too harshly divided from prose. Life, like a lyre, had been touched in all her strings by poetry: while prose hung back. Take an example. The plays of Shakespeare contain innumerable pictures of natural beauty, which harmonize entirely, in their subtlety, mysticism, and feeling, with the attitude toward Nature as it finds expression today; but the prose of his time was leagues behind. As Wordsworth was writing this preface, prose had, in fact, after centuries of lagging, drawn level with poetry, whose birthright it claimed to divide. A notable fact! For in the literature of Rome and Greece, prose never went abreast with poetry. Let us hear Wordsworth again.

> It may be safely affirmed that there neither is, nor can be, any *essential* [the italics are his] difference between the language of prose and metrical composition. We are fond of tracing the resem-

blance between poetry and painting, and accordingly we call them sisters; but where shall we find bonds of connexion sufficiently strict to typify the affinity between metrical and prose composition. . . . The same human blood circulates through the veins of them both.

Wordsworth himself put life into his theory by actual prose of the kind suggested. Nor was he alone. Other poets, of whose verse the poetic quality is popularly more incontestable than his, from metre turned aside to prose, permanently or at intervals. Coleridge, the impassioned dreamer, received from Mill the title of 'the seminal mind of the century'. When the seed is of that kind, the fruit will be likewise, and hence the vague horizons, the generosity to doubt and idiosyncrasy, of this age; hence a *rapture* in all modes of prose composition, even philosophy. And yet more; confidently and successfully he treats matter as *poetical* as 'Kubla Khan' in prose. See, for instance, 'Allegoric Vision' in the *Poems* of 1834; and 'Over the Brocken' in Gillman's *Life of Coleridge*. Coleridge, too, has a passage very pertinent to the subject in hand. It is to be found in that volume of fragments which Mr E. H. Coleridge christened *Anima Poetae* (1895), and reads as follows:

> When there are few literary men, and one in a million of the population are ignorant, as was the case of Italy from Dante to Metastasio, from causes I need not here put down, there will be a poetical language; but that a poet ever uses a word as poetical, which he, in the same mood and thought, would not use in prose or conversation, Milton's prose works will assist us in disproving. But as soon as literature becomes common, and critics numerous, in any country, and a large body of men seek to express themselves habitually in the most precise, impassioned, sensuous words, the difference as to mere words ceases, as, for example, the German prose writers. The sole difference in style is that poetry demands a severe keeping—it admits nothing that prose may not often admit, but it often rejects.

Soon after Coleridge, other poets began writing notable prose. There is no unnatural gap between the versifying and prosifying periods of Scott's life, but a natural transition, involving not even a change of subject-matter. The loveliest passages in his fiction differ quite inessentially from his verse; the ballad scene between Bertram and the girl, in *Guy Mannering*, would fit (so to speak) the same bezil as many a scene in 'The Lady of the Lake' or 'Marmion'. Here was the beginning of the new romantic fiction, which expresses in prose many things for which another age would certainly have employed verse. Lyrical, idyllic, elegiac prose, all was henceforward possible; they have been realized by de Quincey, by Ruskin, by Pater, by the author of *Aylwin*, and by others.

Byron, again, despite his weakness for the eighteenth century, was not unmoved by the new spirit. His imitation of Ossian is well known. But most of all Shelley, in whose work the heat and purple of passion are more constant than with any one else, wrote prose such as Wordsworth had anticipated. It is fragmentary, indeed; and chiefly to be found in his letters, where, of course, a man can reasonably be auto-biographical and so have a store of unusual flame and colour at hand; but such pieces as the 'Defence of Poetry' and 'The Coliseum' and 'On Love' permanently extended the boundaries of our prose. [Three passages quoted.]

The change was wrought before Shelley died. Here, however, names become so numerous that most are of necessity left unmentioned. De Quincey, perhaps, is the most typical of all; and was conscious, as he himself boastfully records, of his revolution in prose, which, under his touch, possesses most of the beauties of verse—melody, passion, imagery. In Germany and elsewhere the same progress had been made, but more rapidly; and it acted considerably upon de Quincey, by way of Richter, whom he translated; still, on the whole, he was accurate in saying that he knew of no precedent in literature. As to France, the mere names of J. J. Rousseau, Ducis, Chateaubriand, Hugo, and their compeers will be more eloquent than brief criticism. Before de Quincey's death, his work had been followed by Ruskin's, with the addition of a minute and tender knowledge of natural things to the armoury of prose. Both these writers were also careful philo-logists, improving, defining our vocabulary, and thus continuing the work of Coleridge, who first made the study of words a beautiful and living thing. Their successors are innumerable, though their advance has been not unopposed; for we know how Matthew Arnold doubted whether Ruskin was not going beyond the limits of prose. The field has been won; prose shares it with verse, having in her grasp the lyre of life and claiming to touch every string by right, and to sing 'of man, of nature, and of human life'.

L, 23 September 1899

PERSONALITY IN LITERATURE

IT IS HARD to find one new and common element in modern books. But if such is to be found, it is the assertion of the individuality of the individual. The very variety of the literature of today proves the point. We are nearly all writers of books. Democracy has brought with it a discovery more important than that all men are equal; and that is, that all men are different. Writers do not nowadays pretend to legislate for the world. They do not divide the world into classes or claim to differentiate types. At most they have observed a few individuals and have diffidently described them. Their work, in a word, is to accumulate data that illustrate the individual. And hence arises the importance and popularity of the autobiographical essay and of lyrical poetry, in which many capable men and women have not dared to speak of any but themselves:

'I would,' says Mr Roberts, 'follow up my self, wheresoever I may be led to. I scorn the fashion and form of my fellows, and the paths they tread. The imbecility of imitation is contagious, and I desire not to rub elbows with such diseased personalities, not to be a trimmed box-tree in a Dutch garden. Rather would I be a wild hawk than one subdued to the falconer's wrist. I will catch for myself, and not be content with offal. For a proved personality is a perpetual freedom; I will run down hill like a torrent, and rise in natural mists to the heavens. I follow myself.'

And that is a forcible or savage expression of our point of view.

But personality in literature is another thing. For, as Mr Roberts admits, 'self portraiture is very difficult'. A man may be born with a personality which is more perfectly expressed in dress alone, or in conversation alone, or silence, or figure-skating: if he tries to write, such a man may very likely produce an article in the *Encyclopaedia Britannica*. That large work, let us at once declare, is inevitably full of personality. No man can escape self-expression. The difficulty lies in the imperfect capacities of his readers, who may be unable to perceive the self-expression. And we, at least, have been often unable to perceive the self-expression in *The Wingless Psyche*. In page after page, Mr Roberts seems to be recording his impressions as a solitary and sensitive observer of Nature, of men, and of himself. He has all the air of one whose writing is intensely subjective. The first personal pronoun is abundant everywhere. It is too abundant. He 'doth protest too much'. He seems to have set out to talk about himself, and to have felt that only those matters which were fit to be decorated by metaphor and rhetoric should be put down. He has not been drawn inevitably into self-expressions, but has selected and embellished and, in our opinion, invented.

From review of *The Wingless Psyche* by Morley Roberts, *DC*, 8 December 1903

There is an increasing fineness, an increasing subtlety of aim, a deepening of the palimpsest. New births there are, even in second-rate authors—births of thought or melody of which their greatest predecessors never dreamed or only dreamed.

Mannerisms increase, so that more and more the writing reflects not merely the main features of a man's character, but his moods, his smile, those things 'faint as are the phantasms that make a chrysom child to smile'. It was usual in earlier prose for a man to acquire a vocabulary, sentences, and cadences of a well-defined character, and to throw everything into the moulds thus made. Their mind was thus reflected, but their spirit did not move upon the surface, coming and going, as in some modern prose. Authors, with three exceptions, are now less public characters than they were, and the revelations which Hazlitt and de Quincey used to make of others are now made implicitly by the writers themselves. There is less and less writing which has even the air of infallibility and universal application. In every page by the modern writer it is clear that he, and perhaps he alone, feels or thinks this or that, and that he may soon think or feel differently. Great privacy and great publicity thus abet one another.

Nowhere is this more to be noticed than in descriptive writing. Compare Scott's with Stevenson's. Scott's landscape is a background which we know that he greatly loved, but of his own blood there is nothing in the colours used: he describes in such a manner that almost all readers admit that Nature is like that: in reading Stevenson's we must share his preferences to be able to see anything with his eyes. This is especially so in the purely rural literature, concerning sport, natural history, and the inhuman face of the earth. Gilbert White, an unfertile literary genius and an all-round countryman, in the course of his incomparable letters, had come—as it always appears, by accident—to express with perfect grace and humour his enjoyment and experience of life in the country. But he was in the first place a naturalist, and it is improbable that he had any contemporary influence except on naturalists: even Charles Lamb did not, I think, discover him. Few of his successors in the nineteenth century came near him for some generations.

From review of *Nineteenth Century Prose*, selected and arranged by
Mrs Laurence Binyon, *DC*, 9 May 1908

THE PROSE-POEM

'WHO OF US,' quotes Mr Symons from Baudelaire, 'has not dreamed in moments of ambition of the miracle of a poetic prose, musical without rhythm and without rhyme, subtle and staccato enough to follow in the lyric motions of the sun, the wavering outlines of meditation, the sudden starts of the conscience?' And to us it has always seemed remarkable that, although men of something like the poet's mind are not uncommon, who only lack his training in the use of verse and his impulse towards that form, yet the so-called prose-poem is very rarely attempted. Philostratus made it classical and venerable. Ossian, de Quincey, Baudelaire, Mallarmé, and some English writers of the *Yellow Book* period restored it, and even gave it popularity. We believe that Sir Thomas Browne was born for it, and that Lamb lost something by missing it. Today no one speaks of it; no writer of repute has anything to do with it.

It has never yet been accepted; it has never had a real vogue; certainly it has never been immersed in that bath of common practice out of which other forms have successfully emerged. Such prose-poems as survive are of so high an excellence that it may have seemed hard to their admirers to use a similar form without a similar material. The man who reads Milton and writes, however much he may wish to possess a blank-verse style not utterly unworthy of his master, has seldom any wish to write of man's first disobedience. But many who have read Baudelaire must have been at once moved to imitate both his medium and his material, though not many are born with his power of sincerely living on air.

And this seems to us to point to the beautiful way in which the prose poets have made their form and substance one. It is certainly true that the verse form is still a surprise to us. It is recognized as part of the decorations of an hierarchy, which the plain man may not use. There are few who could honestly say, after reading a great poem, that it could not have been equally great had the stanza form, for example, been different; to that extent we do distinguish between matter and form in poetry. Prose, on the other hand, is familiar to us. Everyone thinks that he can write prose, if only because he can write nothing else. Thus most of us come to prose with a predisposition to real enjoyment, and we should be inclined to think that here, then, is some encouragement to the poet in prose.

But familiarity breeds a hypocritical sort of contempt. It is so easy to read prose. A lazy man gets through the prose poet's thousand words or so without effort, but comes suddenly to the end and merely asks, 'Is that all?' Yet apparently it is true that any kind of literature which is to succeed must at least silence, if it does not please, the lazy man. Will the prose-poem ever silence him?

We believe that it will, and this book should be distributed by a charitable society with this end in view. We believe that a prose form as honest, as consistent, as impressionistic as Whistler's painting must arise. We have only to read a good novel to see that the mind of even a very clever man is not equal to such spacious work; we can often extract exquisite pages from it which are, as they stand, good prose poems.

Borrow really wrote about six prose-poems; yet he now wearies us with six bad books. So does de Quincey—and a hundred more. Economically, therefore, the prose-poem is to be recommended. Artistically, as Mr Symons shows in his perfect renderings of 'Which is true?', 'Be Drunken' and 'The Heroic Death', it is admirable. Also, it is natural and difficult, and it is an appropriate receptacle for most thoughts which are not of the highest kind. By a careful elimination of the obvious, the facile, the irrelevant, the prose poet may thus not only stay the multitudinous tide of books, but even silence the lazy man.

Review of *Poems in Prose*, from Charles Baudelaire, translated by
Arthur Symons, *DC*, 25 January 1906

J. M. SYNGE

THE FRESH BEAUTY of the speech appears with greater clearness in the book than on the stage. Mr Synge has used only one or two words which he has not heard 'among the country people of Ireland, or spoken in his own nursery before he could read the newspapers'. That might seem a needless handicap; but then he uses their arrangement of these words—their idiom, their directness, their fancy that seems to be partly a quality of the words themselves. Since *Lyrical Ballads* there has hardly been such a notable purification of the diction of English verse (and prose, too) as has come in the past generation, chiefly from Irishmen like Messrs Yeats and Synge. The best of the old ballads are not more direct. The quite unbookish phrases are like the speech of very young children of high courage, and yet have in them at times great subtlety and fitness to the moods of modern men. Mr Synge's play is a mine of those phrases. His characters being simple country people and not considerably moved, we need not expect a wide range or much subtlety. Yet when his innkeeper says: 'Where would I get a pot-boy? Would you have me send the bell-man screaming in the streets of Castlebar?'; when Christy says: 'It's well you know it's a lonesome thing to be passing small towns with the lights shining sideways when the night is down, or going in strange places with a dog noising before you and a dog noising behind, or drawn to the cities where you'd hear a voice kissing and talking deep love in every shadow of the ditch, and you passing on with an empty, hungry stomach failing from your heart', or: 'If the mitred bishops seen you that time, they'd be the like of the holy prophets, I'm thinking, do be straining the bars of Paradise to lay eyes on the Lady Helen of Troy, and she abroad, pacing back and forward, with a nosegay in her golden shawl', when the Widow Quin speaks of 'Looking out on the schooners, hookers, trawlers is sailing the sea, and I thinking on the gallant hairy fellows are drifting beyond, and myself long years living alone' we relish speech as a really thirsty man does water. Not many writers can hope to mend their writing by listening to Irish peasant girls through a thin floor, but a comparison of Mr Synge's prose with the leading article or literary criticism of today will perhaps knock some young men off their stilts before it is too late. By nature or by art, we must achieve a speech something like this which corresponds with the thought almost onomata-poetically, or fail.

From review of *The Playboy of the Western World*, B, August 1907

If the unworldly and un-English spirit of the play, with its obverse of superstition and childishness, is not Irish, we are much mistaken, and it is certainly as pleasing as if it were. Mr Synge has used 'one or two words only that I have not heard among the country people of Ireland, or spoken in my own nursery before I could read the newspapers'. He speaks, justly, of the striking and beautiful phrases ready to his hand as in the happy ages of literature they must have been; and he continues: 'In countries where the imagination of the people, and the language they use, is rich and living, it is possible for a writer to be rich and copious in his words, and at the same time to give the reality which is the root of all poetry, in a comprehensive and natural form.' A very true and new thought, and especially true of drama; and we know few plays of our day except his own and a few such as 'The Pot of Broth' where the talk has at once the character that seems almost to have caught an accent or brogue in it, and a poetry that has nothing to do with invention, but falls naturally out of the life of the speakers, as apples fall in a still night. The talk, all of it, is like poetry in its richness, its simplicity, its remoteness from the spoken print of towns. There is probably not a speech that might not have fallen from a peasant's lips, and yet Mr Synge has so arranged the talk that a hundred pages reveal more than a lifetime of evenings in a tap-room would reveal to most of us.

To Englishmen it ought to be as great a relief as *A Midsummer Night's Dream*. To all who care about life it will be a joy. Whether the life is Irish or straight out of Mr Synge's head, as his enemies will have us believe, does not matter; for it is life, and even without an actor there is human breath clinging to every word of it as it clings to a worn book or an old walking-stick. At each fragment of the dialogue, we exclaim that it must have been overheard; at the end of all we are equally confident that it is pure art.

From another review of *The Playboy, DC,* 13 September 1907

OSCAR WILDE

NO WRITER OF such reputation has in recent times equalled Wilde's versatility. But to connect one class of work with another there is little except the epigrams which he was so fond of repeating from book to book, instead of leaving them all in *Dorian Gray*. It can hardly be said that they contain a body of ideas, a philosophy gradually completing itself. The books have the appearance of being too deliberate— done to satisfy a belief that he could do this or that exceedingly well. That is not how they came to be written: to think so would be to accuse the writer of affectation, and who dares to bring that charge against any man who is not an imbecile? That they all sprang from the heart and brain of this man there is no doubt, and there is no more difficult or fascinating character study still left untouched than Wilde's. But it can with fairness be said that his works are works of fancy—fancy which has no divine call, but is free to choose between several paths— not of imagination, which is for ever engaged in continuing the work of the creation; works of wit, not of humour, certainly not of the comic spirit. His writings are clothes that reveal the man only in the dubious manner possible in an age when it is scarcely possible to be well dressed, but only to be usually or unusually dressed. 'Sleep, like all wholesome things, is a habit': so he wrote when discussing the prison life after he had shared it. Before that, he might have said a hundred things about habit, but this one was impossible.

He decorated. He never created but one thing in his life, *Salomé,* and that was in French, perhaps by way of tribute to Flaubert and M. Maeterlinck. *The Critic as Artist* is equal to almost anything that has been written about criticism by anyone since Coleridge; but then the writer's decorative instinct has actually made a sea of words to hide the pearls. Except *Salomé.* and *The Critic as Artist*, his writings raise him, indeed, to the position of the greatest rhetorician since de Quincey. But it was sad fate for one who thought so much of art and the artist that he should have been a signal example of the man who describes beautiful things, talks about beautiful things, as if that were the same as creating them. He used beautiful words about beautiful objects, and thought it art. It was a fitting punishment of one who could address Beauty as if she were a light woman:

There are a few
Who for thy sake would give their manlihood
And consecrate their being: I at least
Have done so, made thy lips my daily food,
  And in thy temples found a goodlier feast
Than this starved age can give me, spite of all
Its new-found creeds so sceptical and so dogmatical.

But with these limitations, how admirable he is; what exquisite patterns are his prose plays; how heavy and gorgeous and costly is *Dorian Gray, The House of Pomegranates,* and even the poems with all their wordiness, and their echoes of Arnold and Keats; what grace and abundance everywhere, what wit and dalliance! His writing can be like a dress wholly of jewels and fine gold, every part of it equally rich, but weighing the wearer to the ground and crushing her. Or it can be swift, sharp, and hard, logic and paradox, clad in complete steel. In either case it is on parade. It calls attention to itself. The words have a separate value from the things which they are meant to express. On paper, he seems often not affected, but incapable of sincerity. Thus, literature is made a craft rather than an art, related to wallpaper and carpets more than to life. It is a literature of the idle classes, for the idle, by the idle. Life flows past it, while it languidly watches the waves; only now and then there is a cry, and a watcher has fallen in and gone down; and still life flows past, regardless of the voice repeating 'Experience, the name we give to our mistakes', or 'I am dying beyond my means', or 'Merely to look at the world will always be lovely'.

From review of *The Works of Oscar Wilde, DC,* 13 April 1908

ALGERNON CHARLES SWINBURNE

MR SWINBURNE was a scholar of equal learning and intuition, but in this essay, or, as it might well be called, this oration, on Shakespeare he kept both learning and intuition out of sight and relied upon his command of words and prose-rhythms. Perhaps no other piece of his prose is so purely a work of art as this. . . .

. . . It is, indeed, characteristic of his poetry that his words have no value beyond their face value. In his prose often, and perhaps always in this specimen of it, they have not even that value. When he says of *A Midsummer Night's Dream* that, it is 'beautiful', that word is valueless. So is 'sweet' used of Perdita and 'adorable' of Imogen. When he says that *As You Like It* is 'one of the most flawless examples of poetic and romantic drama . . . that ever cast its charm upon eternity' those last seven words are of no use except that they lengthen the sentence and make it more high-flown. The style suggests nothing but the sonorous lips of the rhetorician; it falls without an echo into the brain. The writer was one of those of whom there are so few, if any, among the great, who seem to shape their thought in order that it may fit a certain favourite type of sentence instead of allowing the thought to govern the form of the sentence. It could probably be shown that every writer tends to use certain kinds of rhythms in their sentences rather than others. But we picture Mr Swinburne as having had a number of moulds, and not a great number, into which he forced his thoughts, and whereas the good writer's prose seems to be the thought made visible and audible his appears to have as much resemblance to the thought as a sideboard has to a walnut tree. Carlyle said that Tennyson wrote poetry because he had acquired the habit of versification at school. It may well prove that Mr Swinburne's prose is due to an unforgettable amount of Latin prose composition at an age when it was praiseworthy to write, not well, but in a dignified manner, upon a broomstick. In this supreme example of his prose style it is necessary to be able to divorce manner from matter before the one possible pleasure is extracted from it.

From review of *Shakespeare*, *MP*, 9 September 1909

LAFCADIO HEARN

EACH STORY [in *Some Chinese Ghosts*] cost 'months of hard work and study', as Hearn has told us, and it can be believed; for he adopted a style for them which had to be deliberately maintained. The style apparently did not grow out of his speech or his letters, but was a loftier ceremonious medium which became a second or a third nature. It cannot be analysed here sufficiently. But a few isolated points should be noticed and considered. Thus on page 31 he speaks of 'savage flowers', where he means '*wild* flowers'; but 'wild' was too familiar and he did not see, in his unreal tower of composition, that 'savage' was a mere synonym and an unsuitable one. So on page 65 he calls the autumn light 'aureate' for no better reason. In every story description abounds, and it is of such a kind that the words call attention to themselves, and are possibly admired, but ultimately fail to produce any effect beyond themselves. For example, in 'the great citron-light of the sunset faded out', either the mind will think only of citrons, or it will painfully discover for itself a resemblance between one of the sunset colours and the colour of a citron, leaving the words of the writer a merely accurate statement incapable of producing a pure impression related to its context. This is far too often the reader's fortune. When he reads about an ear and a cheek in this style: *'O the jewel in her ear!* What lotus bud more dainty than the folded flower of flesh, with its dripping of diamond fire! Again he saw it, and the curve of the cheek beyond, luscious to look upon as beautiful brown fruit', he finds it hard to think of human beauty, so confused is he by words and by flowers and fruit. The utmost reward of such writing is an admiration near akin to fatigue, and more often we feel that the writer has forgotten the woman and lost any possible power to suggest her by the time he has decided upon the sentence: 'All suddenly he felt glide about his neck the tepid smoothness of a woman's arm.' Such writing fails because it is dictated by an ideal that is not deep enough in the writer's spirit, the ideal of 'one thing, one word'—one word chosen deliberately as if it were dead and still and powerless to retaliate and live alone. Much of Hearn's care must have gone to make the eloquence of his opening and closing sentences, like: 'Thrice had spring perfumed the breast of the land with flowers, and thrice had been celebrated that festival of the dead which is called *Siu-fan-ti*, and thrice had Tong swept and garnished his father's tomb and presented his five-fold offerings of fruits and meats.' The pity of it is that such eloquence rarely has any natural sweet cadence, and Hearn's has not. When he wrote a letter about something he cared for and understood, his words had a flow which was inseparable from their sense; but in this entirely self-conscious writing the spirit is never free to make music, or if one good cadence emerges the next will clash with it. Where this curious writing is most successful is in catalogues, such as this from the 'Tale of the Porcelain God:' 'The vases with orifices belled like the cups of flowers, or cleft like the bills of birds, or fanged like the jaws of serpents, or pink-lipped as the mouth of a girl; the vases flesh-coloured and purple-veined and dimpled, with ears and with earrings; the vases in likeness of mushrooms, of lotus-flowers, of lizards, of horse-footed dragons woman-faced; the vases strangely translucid, that simulate the white glimmering of grains of prepared rice, that counterfeit the vapoury lace-work of frost, that imitate the efflorescences of coral.' Life is not expected in a catalogue; connexion is unnecessary; and blind attention to isolated detail can work no harm. Hearn knew this: his books are full of such catalogues and they were sometimes useful receptacles for the products of his games of skill with words.

The effect of *Chinese Ghosts* is therefore a mixed one: the story and the treatment are always separable. Hearn's contribution is decoration. He overlays the simple and beautiful outline though without concealing it. According to the reader's power of enjoying words that are without a spirit will be his enjoyment of the tales as a whole. He will be continually in the neighbourhood of the spirit of beauty, as in 'The

Story of Ming-Y', but he will be aware that Hearn who found the beauty also caged it, with words pretending to be equivalent to things as well as more than names.

Two long stories followed in 1889 and 1890, 'Chita' and 'Youma'. They belong to the same period of his art as *Chinese Ghosts*. They are beautiful stories full of beautiful elements, but the treatment is the conspicuous thing. There is the story and there is the eloquent description of tropical nature, not exactly separable but not perfectly united by the mind which loved them both. 'Chita', for example, contains much mere eyesight and unvitalized notes of description, sometimes in the favourite form of a catalogue. The writing tends constantly towards a superhuman level of eloquence, such as may be indicated by the passage: 'But she saw and heard and felt much of that which, though old as the heavens and the earth, is yet eternally new and eternally young with the holiness of beauty—eternally mystical and divine—eternally weird: the unveiled magnificence of Nature's moods—the perpetual poem hymned by wind and surge—the everlasting splendour of the sky.' It is relevant to ask why he should have dragged the girl Chita into such description of what he admired in nature. But even when he has not the excuse of writing about Nature in her augustness, he makes the same ceremonious approach to his subject, as in 'the progressively augmenting weariness of lessons in deportment, in dancing, in music, in the impossible art of keeping her dresses unruffled and unsoiled'. He translates 'On with the dance' into 'Better to seek solace in choreographic harmonies, in the rhythm of gracious motion and of perfect melody.' Much of the description of beautiful things is nearly as good as possible of its kind, and the rhapsodies are likely to interest and charm students of the eloquence of Browne, de Quincey or Ruskin. But its power is halved because the writer has not chosen the right opportunity for such exercises, and exercises they remain, instead of essential elements in a work of art. The book is not without humanity, but the attitude towards human things, the most tragic and the most simple, is usually spectatorial. He describes, for example, the jetsam of a storm which destroyed an island and all its holiday population: the sheep, casks, billiard tables, pianos, children's toys, clothes, and dead bodies. The impression given by the passage is that Hearn had never got beyond the point of view that this scene was a good subject for description. He was writing as a detached aesthetic artist and this cold figure is as conspicuous as the storm and its havoc. In a different key is the description of yellow fever which ends the book. Hearn himself had nearly died of the disease in New Orleans: in 'Chita' it kills a man but it gives some life to the style, because the author is writing of what he knows and has mastered too well to regard it as a subject for decoration, or for felicities like 'the stridulous telegraphy of crickets', and 'a soporific murmur made of leaf-speech and the hum of gnats'.

Lafcadio Hearn, 45-52

WALTER PATER

Point of View

[PATER] lived the celibate and sedentary life of the ordinary don. Except in his inner life, so far as is known, he met with no adventures, ran no risks, never suffered. He was never before the County Court, never benighted on a mountain, never horse-whipped. What happened to him 'happened in the heart', which was inaccessible. When he speaks in dreamy monologue about the beauty of the Reserved Sacrament and how it gives the Roman churches all the sentiment of a house where a dead friend lies, it arouses curiosity as to whether Pater had experienced the loss of a friend. The phrase suggests 'a dead friend' as part of the stock-in-trade of an artist—like a rustic bridge or a crescent moon. This suggestion may delude us, and it certainly will if it persuades us to think of Pater as callous or unreal in an extraordinary degree.

For the last hundred years ideas and the material of ideas have come to the reading classes mainly through books and bookish conversation. Their ideas are in advance of their experience, their vocabulary in advance of their ideas, and their eyelids 'are a little weary'. They think more of cold than those who have to feel it. They are aware of all the possible vices by the time their blood has chilled and they have understood that they are old. The passions seem to them to belong to a golden age of the past, and it is of their ghosts that they sing. Since everything is an illusion they have no illusions. Not even beauty deceives them. Beauty, says Pater in the preface to *The Renaissance*, is like all other qualities presented to human experience: it is relative. He is, above all men, 'the aesthetic critic', willing—or compelled—to give up the common grey or purple-patched experience for one that clicks incessantly with maybe faint but certainly conscious sensations. He regards everything, in art, nature and human life, 'as powers or forces producing pleasurable sensations'. He writes for those whose education becomes complete in proportion as their susceptibility to these sensations increases in depth and variety. His qualification is that he has a temperament which is 'deeply moved by the presence of beautiful objects'; his end is reached when he has disengaged the virtue by which a thing in art, nature or human life, produced its impression of beauty or pleasure. It is not enough to be capable of leaving his mistress' arms to write a sonnet about her eyebrow. In fact, such a one would hardly be an aesthetic critic at all; it would be better that he should first write the sonnet and then proceed to her arms for verification. The aesthetic critic will hardly have time for the passions except of others. There is an austerity about his life. His virtues and his vices must be fugitive and cloistered. He must beware of the bestial waste of nature, the violent, brief passion and the long languors following.

Walter Pater, 68-70

What is... surprising [in Pater's essay on Giorgione] is a passage where he speaks of 'the unexpected blessedness' of moments in life, when our everyday consciousness is relaxed and we are more receptive of the 'happier powers' in things without us. This receptivity is for most people not to be cultivated or counted on. To admit the importance of it is to cast suspicion on Pater's conscious quest of sensation, to make absurd his advice to be sure that your passion is passion, and that it pays for itself by 'this fruit of a quickened, multiplied consciousness'. These fortunate evasive moods of receptivity may be discovered to yield the fruit, but they have little to do with the art which comes to us proposing frankly to give nothing but the highest quality to the moments of life, 'simply for those moments' sake'; to the artists themselves the moods may be priceless, to the aesthetic spectator with a stop-watch they should seem either wasteful or barbarous. It may be significant that they should first be mentioned or suggested in an essay written ten years after the Conclusion to *The Renaissance*. Yet an essay on Romanticism, of almost the same date, couples with artists 'those who have treated life in the spirit of art'. It may be said of *The Renaissance* that it suggests a writer who treats life in the spirit of art. The same phrase occurs in his *Diaphaneité* and his *Wordsworth*. That the end of life is contemplation, not action, being, not doing, is, he says, 'the principle of all higher morality'. He connects poetry and art with this principle because they 'by their very sterility are a type of beholding for the joy of beholding'. Thus he thinks they encourage the treatment of life 'in the spirit of art'; and to identify the means and the ends of life is to do this. He calls it 'impassioned contemplation', and poets the experts in it, withdrawing our thoughts from 'the mere machinery of life' to the spectacle of men and nature in their grandeur. To witness this spectacle with appropriate emotions, he says, 'is the aim of all culture'.

It is impossible not to regard this aim, as Pater expressed it, as a kind of higher philately or connoisseurship. He speaks like a collector of the great and beautiful. He collected them from books, and pictures, not from life. He is on the look out for them; he knows them by certain signs; on his pages they appear only at his desire, never taking us by surprise as they do in Nature and in poetry. Thus he tends to conventionalize the strange, to turn all things great and small into a coldly pathetic strain of music. He refines upon the artists who have refined upon the Lord of Lords.   94-6

Style

It is not known what the Old Mortality society thought of *Diaphaneité* when they heard it in 1864. I can only say that I think I know what Pater meant by it. Not being certain of his meaning it is with diffidence that I say anything about his method of expressing it. There can be no doubt that he had taken great pains with the expression; no doubt at all that he did not write as he spoke. The interjected 'Well' near the end is the one obvious tinge of speech; there is perhaps another in the lack of connecting links which intonation supplies. The attempt at exactness has achieved a notable colourlessness. The language is colourless, and from beginning to end each word has a mere dictionary value, and not one conferred by the context and the writer's personality. The essay has no gesture, no advancing motion, and is painful to read aloud. In spite of a kind of hard lucidity it is not anywhere easily intelligible. . . .

. . . Contemporary gossip credited him with a 'wonderful style'. It was obviously a style which aimed consciously at accuracy and a kind of perfection; unconsciously, perhaps, at a hard purity and dignity. It abhorred paraphrase, anything like padding even for the purpose of connection, all looseness, repetition, emphasis and personal accent. It had not attained to being a 'wonderful style' except by causing wonder. It was obscure and almost without grace. It was wonderful particularly in its detachment. For it retained no sign of an original impulse in it. If there had been a strong impulse the after elaboration had worn it completely away. This detachment made language seem to be as hard and inhuman a material as marble, and like marble to have had no original connection with the artist's idea. It was shy but decided, as well as stiff. It suggested the desire of a narrow, intense perfection both in language and in life. . . .

It might be suspected that a mere dread of vulgarity and commonplace had forced this shy and rigid spirit into such isolation. Speaking of Coleridge's *Aids to Reflection, The Friend,* and *Biographia Literaria,* he calls them 'bundles of notes', the 'mere preparation for an artistic effect which the finished literary artist would be careful one day to destroy','efforts to propagate the volatile spirit of conversation into the less ethereal fabric of a written book'. That kind of weakness was impossible to Pater: fear of it carried him to an opposite weakness that might prove as dangerous. He avoided obscurity more and more, by dealing chiefly with the concrete and with the ideas and images of other men. The stiffness, the lack of an emotional rhythm in separate phrases, and of progress in the whole, the repellent preoccupation with an impersonal and abstract kind of perfection, did not disappear. The rarity of blank verse in his prose is the chief mark of its unnaturalness. When his prose sounds well it is with a pure sonority of words that is seldom related to the sense. He expresses himself not by sounds, but by images, ideas, and colours.

I have noticed already how he came to repeat words expressing what was pleasant or in some way fascinating. 'Strange' begins in *Diaphaneité*. Words expressing refinement followed in large numbers, so that one page contains '*finesse*', 'nicety' twice, 'daintiness', 'light aerial delicacy', 'simple elegance', 'gracious', 'graceful and refined' and 'fair, priestly'; they continually remind us of the author's delight in delicacy, elegance, etc., and his always obviously conscious use of language does the same. When he has to say that Leonardo was illegitimate, he uses eight words: 'The dishonour of illegitimacy hangs over his birth.' He at once makes the 'dishonour' a distinction with some grandeur: he almost makes it a visible ornament. Whenever he can, he seeks the visible, insisting, for example, that Pico della Mirandola was buried 'in the hood and white frock of the Dominican order'. Even his ideas appeal as much as possible to the eye. Thus, in *Winckelmann*, alluding to the growth and modification of religions, he says that they 'brighten under a bright sky' and 'grow intense and shrill in the clefts of human life, where the spirit is narrow and confined, and the stars are visible at noonday'. His very words are to be seen, not read aloud; for if read aloud they betray their artificiality by a lack of natural expressive rhythm. His closely packed sentences, pausing again and again to take up a fresh burden of parenthesis, could not possibly have a natural rhythm. . . .

Nearly every one of the essays in *The Renaissance* opens abruptly. Pater cannot wind into our confidence. He is a shy man, full of 'it may be' and 'we may think', and he has the awkward abruptness of a shy man. But this sudden entry is due also to his disdain of mere connections and of any words that are under weight. He will have nothing 'common or mean'. If he has to mention the pleasure of a cold plunge in summer, he speaks of 'the moment of delicious recoil from the flood of water in summer heat'. 'The flood of water' is very foreign. His sentences must not only be essential and perfectly fitting parts of a whole, but they must be somehow exquisite of themselves, certainly in form, if possible in content.

As he says that not the fruit of experience, but experience itself, is the end of life, so he would wish to have every sentence, every clause, every word, conspicuously worthy, apart from the sum and effect of all. Here is still another reason for doing without connections, props, padding, and whatever is of itself unimportant. No writer can be skipped less easily. The lack of progressive movement, the lack of a clear and strong emotional tone such as makes for movement, forbids us to take for granted more than a sentence now and then at long intervals. Every inch has the qualities of the whole. Open any essay at any page: it will yield some beautiful object or strange thought presented in the words of a learned and ceremonious lover. He says of the school of Giorgione that the air in their painting 'seems as vivid as the people who breathe it, and literally empyrean, all impurities being burnt out of it . . .'; and in another place speaks of 'a singular charm of liquid air, with which the whole picture seems instinct'. Such an air, though not as vivid, is the atmosphere of Pater's work. It is far from producing the 'wind-searched brightness and energy' of which Pater goes on to speak: it is rather a chilly unchanging light as of a northward gallery. It has not ease or warmth or music, but dignity, ceremony, educated grace. Above all, it is choice. Pater is at all points an eclectic. Several times he insists upon the necessity of separating what is touched with 'intense and individual power' in a man's work from what has 'almost no character at all'. In art, in life, the best of whatever kind will delight him. He loves the spectacle of 'brilliant sins and exquisite amusements'. The strong, the magnificent, the saintly, the beautiful, the cruel, the versatile, the intense, the gay, the brilliant, the weary, the sad-coloured, everything but the dull, delights him. From religion, philosophy, poetry, art, Nature, human life, he summons what is rich and strange. He delivers it in choicest language because it has to be worthy of his own choicest moments of enjoyment. For here also he is an eclectic, ignoring the ordinary, the dull, the trite.

Thus his prose embalms choice things, as seen at choice moments, in choice words. . . . It is not the style of ecstasy such as can be seen in Jefferies' *Story of My Heart*, or Sterne's Journal to Eliza, or Keats' last letter to Fanny Brawne. Hardly does it appear to be the style of remembered ecstasy as in Traherne's *Centuries of Meditation* or Wordsworth's 'Tintern Abbey'. It is free from traces of experience. All is subtilized, intellectualized, 'casting off all debris'. It is a polished cabinet of collections from history, Nature, and art; objects detached from their settings but almost never without being integrated afresh by Pater's careful arrangement, whether they are pictures, books, landscapes or personalities. It fulfils Pater's own condition of art by putting its own 'happy world' in place of 'the meaner world of our common days'.

97-109

Again and again [in Pater's Greek essays] we are made aware that the writer accepts no word or arrangement of words as a matter of course, and that if he has an impulse he opposes it with inflexible austerity. For example, he wishes to appeal to those who have touched the earth of a vineyard in August that they may corroborate his suggestion that wine is to the other 'strengths' of the earth as lightning is to light. He writes: 'And who that has rested a hand on the glittering silex of a vineyard slope in August, where the pale globes of sweetness are lying, does not feel this?'

The words 'pale globes of sweetness' remind us that grapes are pale, globular, and sweet; they do not vividly suggest or represent grapes, but rather the mind of a man who has pondered the subject of the relation between things and words, and has come to no inspiring conclusion. What he often succeeds in doing is to refuse to himself, and even to the reader, all the conventional associations of a subject or of a word. Here, for example, in *The Bacchanals of Euripides*, is Dionysus armed with the thyrsus:

> The pine-cone at its top does but cover a spear point; and the thing is a weapon—the sharp spear of the hunter Zagreus—though hidden now by the fresh leaves, and that button of pine-cone (useful also to dip in wine, to check the sweetness) which he has plucked down, coming down through the forest, at peace for a while this spring morning.

Nothing here has any value except what Pater gives it. It is an attempt to build up a scene out of sterilized words in a vacuum. All is strange, even to the colloquial tinge of the dubious 'thing' and 'at peace for a while this spring morning', and the interjected information about the pine-cone. We are forced to regard the words as words, and only in part able to think of the objects denoted by them.   124-5

The Essay on Style

Pater's sense of the importance of personality in art is emphatically expressed in his essay on Style. He says that a writer is an artist, and his work fine art, in proportion as he transcribes, not the world, or mere fact, 'but his sense of it'. The essay is, and has come to be regarded as, of central significance in Pater's work. A really skilled anatomist could build up the whole of that work from the hints in this small part. Here, for example, not for the first time, he calls art a refuge, 'a sort of cloistral refuge, from a certain vulgarity in the actual world', for scholars and all 'disinterested lovers' of books. Here he repeats that music is the ideal of all art, because in it form cannot be distinguished from matter, or subject from expression. Thence he moves to the opinion that literature finds its specific excellence in the 'absolute correspondence of the term to its import'. He means the same thing as when he says that 'the essence of all good style, whatever its accidents may be, is expressiveness'. The world agrees with him. It does not go very far, but it is common sense.

There is more than common sense in the essay. For though Pater admits that the facility of one man and the difficult elaboration of another may be equally good art, his own preference is clear. He insists that literary artists are 'of necessity' scholars, and seems to think of them as all writing for the 'scholarly conscience', for the reader who will follow them 'warily, considerately, though without consideration for them'. Thus he is forced to allow that a man can be a great writer without being an artist. He credits readers with finding one of their greatest pleasures in 'the critical tracing out of conscious artistic structure, and the pervading sense of it' as they read. Pater himself was one of these readers, as he shows in writing of Flaubert and Flaubert's masterly sentences; that these sentences fit their meaning with absolute justice, he says, 'will be the judgment of immediate sense in the appreciative reader'. With Flaubert, he is willing to believe that the problem of art is to find the one word or phrase, or sentence, for what is to be expressed. It is certain, however, that men have written well without knowing this. . . .

I shall not argue the question whether perfection is to be compassed by malice aforethought. Certainly deliberateness and patience alone can hardly make any writing perfect, unless it be a notice to trespassers or a railway guide. I doubt if they could adequately frame an advertisement of a fowl-house for sale. There must be an impulse before deliberate effort and patience are called in, and if that impulse has not been powerful and enduring the work of its subordinates will be too apparent.

It might be taken for granted that the writer's workshop ought not to be visible through his words. Even the note-taking of Tchekov's story writer, though it gave him a dog's life, may not have betrayed him in print. But Pater is one of the few writers who have emerged from obscurity with a frank desire that their words should give a view of the workshop. He thought that a writer would wish his reader to seek, and to be able to find, the history of his choice of certain words. . . .

I have no wish to plead for the 'natural eloquence of ordinary conversation, the language in which we address our friends, wives, children, and servants, and which is intended only to express our thoughts, and requires no foreign or elaborate ornament'. It is for most people easier to speak as they write, or more or less as journalists write, than to write as they speak. Nor do I consider the matter settled by Mr Arnold Bennett's dicta:

Style cannot be distinguished from matter. When a writer conceives an idea he conceives it in a form of words. That form of words
constitutes his style, and it is absolutely governed by the idea. . . .
When you have thought clearly you have never had any difficulty in
saying what you thought, though you may have some difficulty in
keeping it to yourself.

This amounts to nothing more than that no man can escape self-
expression in the presence of a sufficiently intelligent listener or
reader, though it also implies an exclusive acquaintance with very
ready speakers and writers. It is certain that there is a kind of unconscious self-expression which no man escapes. Thus Pater expressed
something in himself which made John Addington Symonds revolt as
from a civet-cat. Some have thought that his style reveals his use of
gilt-edged note-paper. Style, even in Pater, is not a 'mere dress' for
something which could be otherwise expressed and remain the same.
A thing which one or a thousand men would be tempted to express in
different ways is not one but many, and only after a full realization of
this can we agree with Pater's statement that in all art 'form, in the full
signification of the term, is everything, and the mere matter nothing':
we can agree and yet wonder how Pater could say also that 'form
counts equally with, or for more than, the matter'. Even carelessness
or conventionality of language has its value as expression, though if it
ends in a pale, muddy, or inharmonious style, the value will be very
little in this world. That two men possess walking-sticks of the same
kind is not nearly so important as that one twirls and flourishes it,
while the other regularly swings it once in every four steps—unless, of
course, the observer is a manufacturer, or retailer, or connoisseur,
of walking-sticks. Literature is not for connoisseurs. Is there no
difference but in length and sound between 'It has not wit enough to
keep it sweet' and 'It has not vitality enough to preserve it from putre-
faction'? or between 'Under the impression that your peregrinations
in this metropolis have not as yet been extensive, and that you might
have some difficulty in penetrating the arcana of the Modern Babylon
in the direction of the City Road' and the form of that idea which Mr
Micawber introduced with the words 'In short'? It is not satisfactory,
then, to say that we think with words, or that 'the best words generally
attach themselves to our subject, and show themselves by their own
lights'. John Hawkins spoke with feeling and spoke truly when he
ended the account of his third voyage with these words: 'If all the
miseries and troublesome affairs of this sorrowful voyage should be
perfectly and thoroughly written, there should need a painful man
with his pen, and as great a time as he that wrote the lives and deaths of
the martyrs.' . . .

Somewhere in *Wilhelm Meister*, Goethe says that a man will not think clearly unless he talks. Mr George Moore, after quoting Numa Roumestan's 'I cannot think unless I talk', says: 'I often find my brain will not work except in collaboration with my tongue: when I am composing a novel I must tell my ideas; and as I talk I formulate and develop my scheme of narrative and character.' Many a man has said or written much as Goldsmith did: 'To feel your subject thoroughly, and to speak without fear, are the only rules of eloquence.' When Coleridge wishes to praise Southey's style, he says: 'It is as if he had been speaking to you all the while.' But he does not say that Southey's writing was the same as his speech; for a mere copy of speech might have a different effect from the spoken words, in the absence of the individual voice and its accompaniment of looks and gestures.

It is the last thing that many writers would think of, to write as they speak: and the more solitary and learned the writer, the less likely is he to attempt so unnatural a thing.... Yet it has been said that in Elizabeth's time 'men wrote very much as they spoke; the literary language has probably never stood nearer to the colloquial, and, consequently, it was peculiarly adapted to express the exuberant thought and feeling of the age.... And when,' continues Professor Earle, 'we fully see the importance of this social principle, we may be in a position to do justice to the great services which have been rendered to English prose by the newspaper press. That large and influential order of men, which daily provides news and comments upon public affairs, is animated by one highly developed professional instinct, and that instinct is the social sense of its relation to the public. Under the salutary influence of this honourable sentiment continued through the tradition of generations, our English prose has (more than by any other means) ascertained the right pitch of elevation, and the most available means of attaining lucidity accompanied with the relief of variety.'

'The hunters are up in America', and in Fleet Street grace and dignity are being added to what inherited neither, and there is more space and less time than could be filled by writing like speech. Men could be found there who would think Locke's style 'a disgusting style, bald, dull, plebeian, giving indeed the author's meaning, but giving it ungraced with any due apparatus or ministry', and they would also consent to decorate it with due apparatus or ministry. The phrase is from Professor Saintsbury's introduction to *Specimens of English Prose and Style*, and caused Pater to protest against the implied separation of form and matter.

The reason why Professor Earle was pleased with this Prose Diction, and why Mr W. B. Yeats believes that 'in this century he who does not strive to be a perfect craftsman achieves nothing', is that men understand now the impossibility of speaking aloud all that is within them, and if they do not speak it, they cannot write as they speak. The most they can do is to write as they would speak in a less solitary world. A man cannot say all that is in his heart to a woman or another man. The waters are too deep between us. We have not the confidence in what is within us, nor in our voices. Any man talking to the deaf or in darkness will leave unsaid things which he could say were he not compelled to shout, or were it light; or perhaps he will venture once—even twice—and a silence or a foolish noise prohibits him. But the silence of solitude is kindly; it allows a man to speak as if there were another in the world like himself; and in very truth, out of the multitudes, in the course of years, one or two may come, or many, who can enter the solitude and converse with him, inspired by him to confidence and articulation. . . . Much good poetry is far from the speech of any men now, or perhaps at any recorded time, dwelling on this earth. There would be no poetry if men could speak all that they think and all that they feel. Each great new writer is an astonishment to his own age, if it hears him, by the apparent shrillness and discordancy of the speech he has made in solitude. It has to become vulgarized before common ears will acknowledge the sweetness and wisdom of it. Pater still astonishes men with his falsetto delicacy, but may lift posterity up to him.

The more we know of any man the more singular he will appear, and nothing so well represents his singularity as style. Literature is further divided in outward seeming from speech by what helps to make it in fact more than ever an equivalent of speech. It has to make words of such a spirit, and arrange them in such a manner, that they will do all that a speaker can do by innumerable gestures and their innumerable shades, by tone and pitch of voice, by speed, by pauses, by all that he is and all that he will become. . . .

. . . The most and the greatest of man's powers are as yet little known to him, and are scarcely more under his control than the weather: he cannot keep a shop without trusting somewhat to his unknown powers, nor can he write books except such as are no books. It appears to have been Pater's chief fault, or the cause of his faults, that he trusted those powers too little. The alternative supposition is that he did not carry his self-conscious labours far enough. On almost every page of his writing words are to be seen sticking out, like the raisins that will get burnt on an ill-made cake. It is clear that they have been carefully chosen as the right and effective words, but they stick out because the labour of composition has become so self-conscious and mechanical that cohesion and perfect consistency are impossible. The words have only an isolated value; they are labels; they are shorthand: they are anything but living and social words. What, for example, is the value of 'extorted by circumstance', applied to the first edition of *Religio Medici*? If the reader happens to know the circumstance he

smiles at the phrase: if he does not know he smiles, if at all, at Pater. . . .
His colloquialism, or deliberate easing of manner, is practically
always ineffectual, like swearing in a stilted talker. He produces only a
blush or a cold shudder by his 'ah' or 'can't'. Nor does he gain by the
measure of hoisting a popular phrase amid inverted commas; or by
spelling a word so as to remind readers of its true meaning—as in
'aweful', or by explaining one word by another—as 'illustrate' by
'lustre'. And in *Sir Thomas Browne* did he split an infinitive in pure
self-denial?

'Scholarship,' says the Pateresque Lionel Johnson, 'is the only
arbiter of style.' It may be so, and it may also be that scholarship
will in the end convert posterity to 'gibbous towns'. In the meantime
'gibbous' remains a word not sufficiently full and exact to be of
scientific value, and, having no other value in this place, is but a label.

Pater was, in fact, forced against his judgment to use words as bricks,
as tin soldiers, instead of flesh and blood and genius. Inability to
survey the whole history of every word must force the perfectly self-
conscious writer into this position. Only when a word has become
necessary to him can a man use it safely; if he try to impress words by
force on a sudden occasion, they will either perish of his violence or
betray him. No man can decree the value of one word, unless it is his
own invention; the value which it will have in his hands has been
decreed by his own past, by the past of his race. It is, of course, impossible to study words too deeply, though all men are not born for this
study: but Pater's influence has tended to encourage meticulosity in
detail and single words, rather than a regard for form in its largest
sense. His words and still less his disciples' have not been lived with
sufficiently. Unless a man write with his whole nature concentrated
upon his subject he is unlikely to take hold of another man. For that
man will read, not as a scholar, a philologist, a word-fancier, but as a
man with all his race, age, class and personal experience brought to
bear on the matter. . . .

When words are used like bricks they are likely to inflict yet another
punishment on the abuser, so making it more than ever impossible that
they will justly represent 'the conscious motions of a convinced
intelligible soul'. They refuse to fall into the rhythms which only
emotion can command. The rhythms satisfactory to the mere naked
ear are of little value: they will be so much sonority or suavity. How
rhythm is commonly regarded may be shown by the following: 'The
sentence can have two other qualities, rhythm and a certain cadence,
light or grave, or of some other kind, in harmony with its meaning.
These graces of the sentence are best regarded as refinements added to
its essential and indispensable qualities.'

Here again appears the necessity for the aid of speech in literature.

Nothing so much as the writer's rhythm can give that intimate effect 'as if he had been talking'. Rhythm is of the essence of a sincere expressive style. . . .

. . . It is, of course, true that writing stands for thought, not speech, and there is a music of words which is beyond speech; it is an enduring echo of we know not what in the past and in the abyss, an echo heard in poetry and the utterance of children; and prose, if 'born of conversation', is 'enlivened and invigorated by poetry'. But is it true there is a harmony which the ear cannot acknowledge? Has not the eye the power to act as a ghostly messenger to the ear? I doubt whether Pater's sidelong, pausing sentences have any kind of value as harmony, heard or unheard. It might be retorted, in the words of Joubert, that 'he who never thinks beyond what he says, nor sees beyond what he thinks, has a downright style', that there is 'a vulgar naturalness, and an exquisite naturalness' and no one would expect of Pater a downright style or a vulgar naturalness. It may be retorted again that Pepys is often intimate without aid of rhythm. But a diary, more or less in shorthand, is no argument. And if it is a question of naturalness, even an exquisite naturalness is hard to attain, when the writing, disturbed by protuberant words, has no continuous rhythm to give it movement and coherence. What Pater has attained is an exquisite unnaturalness.

196-220

5 Country Books

SOME COUNTRY BOOKS

In the cool of the evening, when the low sweet whispers waken,
  When the labourers turn them homeward, and the weary have
    their will,
When the censers of the roses o'er the forest aisles are shaken,
  Is it but the wind that cometh o'er the far green hill?

ALFRED NOYES

READING LAMB the other day, I could not but envy his pure love
of the country and contrast it with our own, and especially when I
came to the conclusion of 'Blakesmoor': 'Mine too—whose else?—thy
costly fruit garden, with its sun-baked southern wall; the ampler
pleasure-garden, rising backwards from the house in triple terraces,
with flower-pots now of palest lead, save that a speck here and there,
saved from the elements, bespake their pristine state to have been gilt
and glittering; the verdant quarters backwarder still; and stretching
still beyond, in old formality, thy firry wilderness, the haunt of the
squirrel and the day-long murmuring wood-pigeon, with that antique
image in the centre, God or Goddess I wist not; but child of Athens or
old Rome paid never a sincerer worship to Pan or to Sylvanus in their
native groves, than I to that fragmental mystery. . . .'

Call it a passing tenderness or what you will; but where in modern
books can we find an attitude as happy, sincere, unquestioning, and
intelligible as that?

We protest too much today. We have reached, perhaps, the edge of a
great mystery, and we are querulous and chattering as swallows before
dawn. No class of books is now exempt from announcements of our
affection for the country, but there are, excluding the scientific, two
classes, not very well defined, which contain little else.

The first class is composed of books by naturalists and sportsmen,
who may write very well, but pretend chiefly to share their know-

ledge, and incidentally their love of the country, with their readers. The second class is composed of books by literary men and women, who may know much of natural history, but aim chiefly at expressing their own emotions in the presence of wild life. The best of each class approach one another very closely in character.

Knowledge of the country life abounds; never more so, if one may judge from the number of sandwich papers found lying in the remotest parts of the earth; but men seem not to have progressed so much as might have been expected in the art of setting down observation. Dull records of facts that mean nothing when they are dull are multiplied continually. But even they have their beauty when compared with the similar records which are garnished with jaunty sentiments and hastily chosen words. A sense of arrangement is very rare. A clear motive is rare; thousands rush to inform the world that they have found a bird's nest or seen a vole climbing the tender shoots of young ash trees. In mere bulk such books are remarkable, and a proof that many persons of modest talents become well acquainted with the country today. But at the head of this class there is a small number of books which stand high, as literature, in comparison with any other books of our time. In the best of them, the modern attitude reaches something like its best expression. They have a sound knowledge of the facts of Nature, coupled, as it has hardly been at any other time, with a deep and sometimes passionate and mournful love of all that takes place in the open air and in the human mind under its influence. They have, too, a curious interest in character—the character of birds, for example, of snakes, of places. Thus, at their best, these books add considerably to pure knowledge; and (by the sense of the poetry of life) appeal to any one with an intellectual and spiritual life, whether naturalist or not; and they give an interesting view of the mind of our age, and continue the revelation which Jefferies began in *The Story of My Heart*. To this class should be added the gardening books which abound in information, but, in spite of much sentiment and quotation from Bacon and Marvell, hardly succeed in rising out of the rank of guide-books, to which rank they do honour.

The second class is equally large today, for it includes half the essayists and half the writers of verse. In their work, form is less the result of accident than in the first class. Observation, for its own sake, is less conspicuous, and the mind of the author expresses itself rather through the moods which certain objects produce, than through a careful record of the objects themselves. The worst of this class are worse than the worst of the other, because they are derivative in form and manner, and without any fresh observation. There are also a number of considerably gifted people who do nothing but continue or weaken in verse the attitude of Shelley, for example, or of Keats, sometimes with the addition of a vaguer mournfulness and a less intelligible choice of words, which may mean that they write for posterity.

In prose, these writers have their equals in some very sweet-voiced persons who use material already well known to us through Jefferies and Kingsley, and the rest, in a manner which differs little from theirs, except that it has less sincerity, more whims, and a much more poetical vocabulary. On a somewhat higher level than these, but not very high, stand those of a frankly town-bred attitude, who tell us, with some wit and some felicity, the joys of walking, of fishing, of country inns, and thus produce a literary form of bread-and-cheese and ale.

Higher in aim, but not always successful, are those men of reading and much musing, who express a mystical attitude in lyrics and songs which use Nature as a symbol, as a background, as a pigment for use in self-portraiture. Even these at the best are apt to write after Wordsworth and Thoreau, or to differ from them chiefly in a wilful use of the pathetic fallacy or in a vague religious sentimentality. Here, as in the other ranks of country books, too many writers give infinite attention to detail, but no thorough kneading to the whole, a weakness which seems to be due to the lack of a philosophical or individual attitude in minds much influenced by books.

Higher still are the books which really show, in verse or prose, the inseparableness of Nature and Man, with an inevitable tendency to dwell upon the power which Nature derives from her mystery—a romance like *Green Mansions*, the supreme example; a poem like 'The Rout of the Amazons'.

In these the differences from nineteenth-century work are not always easy to define. But I find in them subtler rhythms, a diminution of man's importance in the landscape, the use of the visible and tangible things as symbols of the unseen, and a great love of detail that is perhaps due to a belief that if only a scene is clearly drawn in words, the effect of the scene will be gained. Knowledge, love and art are not wanting. But one may conjecture that scientific discoveries and theories, while they feed and in no way impede the outdoor literature, yet tend to break it up, to confuse its aims, and to make impossible a grand concerted advance like that which accompanied the French Revolution.

It is not surprising, therefore, that many go back with a high zest or a great sense of peace to the old books that reveal a sensitiveness to Nature that is quite unlike our own, and to some later books between whose lines we may insert our dreams, like rose leaves, undisturbed. There is nothing in books, for example, to surpass the tale of Guiscardo and Ghismonda, read on a hot May morning, when you have just caught enough trout in a little chalk stream. It might be argued that, under those circumstances, the book does not matter; but he who could argue so is no true lover of joy or of books. A page of Chaucer, of Parkinson, of Temple, of Malory, of Goldsmith, of Keats, will please this one or that, as well. And, for my part, I have found myself pretty often in May going back to a passage in a certain famous book, which begins thus:

> To take a boat in a pleasant evening, and with musick to row upon the waters, which Plutarch so much applauds, Aelian admires upon the river Peneus, in those Thessalian fields beset with green bays, where birds so sweetly sing that passengers, enchanted as it were with their heavenly musick, forget forthwith all labours, care and grief: or in a Gondola through the Grand Canal in Venice, to see those goodly Palaces, must needs refresh and give content to a melancholy dull spirit. Or to see the inner rooms of a fair built and sumptuous edifice, as that of the Persian Kings so much renowned by Diodorus and Curtius, in which all was almost beaten gold, chairs, stools, thrones, tabernacles, and pillars of gold, plane trees and vines of gold, grapes of precious stones, all the other ornaments of pure gold . . . with sweet odours and perfumes, generous wines, oviparous fare, etc., besides the gallantest young men, the fairest virgins. . . .

It is not easy to like our modern authors as well, however gracious in spirit and in body rich.

British Country Life in Autumn and Winter, The Book of the Open Air,
(ed. E T), 196-200

GILBERT WHITE

[GILBERT WHITE] had, in fact, made a book which had three extraordinary merits. It contained valuable and new observations; it over-flowed with evidence of a new spirit—a spirit of minute and even loving inquiry into the life and personality of animals in their native surroundings—that was coming into natural history; and, thirdly, it had style or whatever we like to call the breath of life in written words, and it was delightfully and easily full of the man himself and of the delicate eighteenth-century southern countryside which he knew. But the observations are no longer new; the new spirit has been renovated by the gunless naturalists from Thoreau to Mr W. H. Hudson of our own day. The man himself is still fresh to succeeding generations, and thousands, who care not at all how many willow-wrens there be, delight to read these letters from a man so happy and remote from our time that he thought the dying fall of the true willow-wren 'a joyous easy laughing note'. We are always pleasantly conscious of the man in his style, which strikes us as the lines and motions of a person's face strike us for good or for bad, and, even so, in a manner that defies analysis. His quack who ate a toad, his boys twisting the nests out of rabbit-holes with a forked stick, his love of the 'shapely-figured aspect of the chalk hills' above that of the 'abrupt and shapeless' mountains, his swallows feeding their young and treading on the wing, his friendly horse and fowl, his prodigious many-littered half-bred bantam sow that proved, when fat, good bacon, juicy and tender, his honey-loving idiot, his crickets ('a good Christmas fire is to them like the heats of the dog-days')—these things have in his pages a value which can only be attributed to his literary genius, by which his book survives.

A Literary Pilgrim in England, 114-15

WILLIAM COBBETT

WILLIAM COBBETT is one of those names which have come to symbolize the bearer's character to perfection. It is now impossible to say how much of the character of the name was given to it by this one man in his seventy-two years of life (1762-1835). It was an altogether English name to begin with, thoroughly native and rustic; and English it remains, pure English, old English, merry English—a name all but impossible in a writer of this generation, though, with a difference, it was borne of late by a very hearty sporting writer, Martin Cobbett, a collateral descendant of William. William Cobbett is the only Cobbett in the *Dictionary of National Biography,* but through him speak a thousand Cobbetts, too horny-handed to hold a pen, hairy, weather-stained, deep-chested yeomen and peasants, yet not one of them, I dare say, a better man than this Farnham farmer's boy, whose weapons included the sword, the spade, the voice, and the pen. . . .

. . . He studied English when he was a private at sixpence a day, writing Lowth's *Grammar* out two or three times and repeating it all through from memory while on sentinel duty: one of his earliest writings was *Tuteur Anglais* based on his experience in teaching English to French refugees in America. He was out of the army before he was thirty, and indignation made him an author with a pamphlet called 'The Soldier's Friend; or Considerations on the late pretended Augmentation of the Subsistence of the Private Soldier'. What with Lowth, and Swift, and George and Ann Cobbett, he could write from the first in sentences that express a plain thought or feeling as clearly and swiftly as the flash of an eye or a bang of the fist on a table. Hence his advice to a nephew on the subject of prose composition:

The order of the matter will be, in almost all cases, that of your thoughts. Sit down to write what you have thought, and not to think what you shall write. Use the first words that occur to you, and never attempt to alter a thought; for that which has come of itself into your mind is likely to pass into that of another more readily and with more effect than anything which you can, by reflection, invent.

Never stop to make choice of words. Put down your thoughts in words just as they come. Follow the order which your thoughts will point out; and it will push you on to get it upon the paper as quickly and as clearly as possible.

Thoughts come much faster than we can put them upon paper. They produce one another; and this order of their coming is in almost every case the best possible order that they can have on paper; yet, if you have several in your mind, rising above each other in point of force, the most forcible will naturally come the last upon paper.

This was the man who held single-stick matches at Botley for the Wiltshire and Hampshire players, and thought one of his fellow-soldiers, a private, the wittiest man he ever knew, comparing him favourably with Sheridan. He died four years before the birth of that other stylist who advised writers to 'make time to write English more as a learned language'—Walter Pater.

To the age of Pater Cobbett's style is something of a curiosity. But it is an age of tolerant connoisseurs and does not despise Cobbett even though he does soil the carpet with his thick shoes. He is puritan, humorist, sportsman, enthusiast, all in one. It seems improbable that we shall behold his like again in print, any more than we shall see a house like his at Botley, where they say 'everything was excellent, everything was abundant' according to 'the largest idea of a great English yeoman of the old time'. He is one of the few thorough-going countrymen in our literature. Like Jefferies, he began as a Tory, and to the end he had a Tory's hate of 'nonsense' both good and bad. But he remained a practical man, with the prejudices of the practical man instead of visions. Simplicity kept him sweet through the muck of journalism and politics. His open-air scenes take us back to Chaucer. Yet he is, of course, not a countryman pure and simple. It was characteristic of him that he never touched intoxicating liquors while he was in the army. He always spoke with respect of beer, especially in comparison with tea, but he was no beef-and-beer man. On one of his rides he says that he fed on apples and nuts, and that he could be very well content to live on nuts, milk, and home-baked bread. His morals were not beef-and-beer morals. It might be shown too that his style, with all its open-air virility, is yet lean and hard and undecorated, in accordance with his shrewd puritanism.

But what a thing that style is! What descriptions, what opinions, what campaigns of words! It is like watching a man, a confident, free-speaking man, with a fine head, a thick neck, and a voice and gestures peculiarly his own, standing up in a crowd, a head taller than the rest, talking democracy despotically. *Rural Rides*, written straight after long days in the saddle when Cobbett was past fifty, is a good book to reprint. It is not necessary, as has been done in the only cheap reprint, to cut down the political diatribes. Not a hundred people, it is true, will understand them like a contemporary. It would be hard to ask more troublesome questions than, Who was 'the Stern-path-of-duty Man'? and 'the Great Hole-Digger'? and what was Cobbett's 'Gridiron Policy'? But no matter: Cobbett is such a man and such a writer that names and phrases once full of dire and immediate significance have now something of the value of names in Ossian or the Prophetic Books of the Bible. The Barings, the Stock-jobbers, the Seed of Abraham, are classic. It is true that this man was an out and out contemporary, violently given up to things of the moment, and with ideas exclusively devoted to those things; that a really well-edited Cobbett would make one of the most valuable histories of the early nineteenth century. But he lives now by the personal force which is almost independent of his subject matter and ideas. He comes to us offering, as only a few other men do, the pleasure of watching a fighter whose brain and voice are, as it were, part of his physical and muscular development. The movement of his prose is a bodily thing. His sentences do not precisely suggest the swing of an arm or a leg, but they have something in common with it. His style is perhaps the nearest to speech that has really survived. Borrow's has the effect of speech without the method; Cobbett's is like speech in its method and effect, and carries with it on every page a reminder of the 'elderly, respectable-looking, red-faced gentleman, in a dust-coloured coat and drab breeches with gaiters, tall and straightly built, with sharp eyes and a round and ruddy countenance, smallish features, and a peculiarly cynical mouth', who sat in the Parliament of 1832. 'Cynical mouth', however, must be wrong: it must be Lord Dalling's misinterpretation of an enthusiast with a sense of humour. It were too difficult an inquiry to discover how Cobbett was able to project himself thus physically into his work. In part, no doubt, the continually awakened consciousness of his publicity helped him; at least, that is suggested when he tells us that, while hunting over some dangerous ground, he thought once or twice of his neck, how his enemy, Lord Sidmouth, would like to see him; and when he describes a stormy meeting of Sussex farmers where it was moved that he should be put out of the room—'I rose,' says Cobbett, 'that they might see the man they had to put out.' He was then sixty. In part, also, this effect is due to his colloquial words and phrases, to his italics, and to his very personal references to himself and others. He was always the boy of eight who trailed a herring over Moor Park to puzzle the harriers and a brutal huntsman. The best part of his education he considered to have been rolling down a sandhill with his brothers. He went to see this sandhill with his son, 'to return to it my thanks for the ability which it probably gave me to be one of the greatest terrors to one of the greatest and most powerful bodies of knaves and fools that ever was permitted to afflict this or any other country', Cobbett's pen, at any rate, was as good as a sword, a short, thick sword, with a point as well as an edge.

From Introduction to *Rural Rides,* vii-xi

GEORGE BORROW

BORROW WAS a writing man; he was sometimes a friend of jockeys, of Gypsies and of pugilists, but he was always a writing man; and the writer who is delighted to have his travels in Spain compared with the rogue romance, *Gil Blas,* is no innocent. Photography, it must be remembered, was not invented. It was not in those days thought possible to get life on to the paper by copying it with ink. Words could not be the equivalents of acts. Life itself is fleeting, but words remain and are put to our account. Every action, it is true, is as old as man and never perishes without an heir. But so are words as old as man, and they are conservative and stern in their treatment of transitory life. Every action seems new and unique to the doer, but how rarely does it seem so when it is recorded in words, how rarely perhaps it is possible for it to seem so. A new form of literature cannot be invented to match the most grand or most lovely life. And fortunately; for if it could, one more proof of the ancient lineage of our life would have been lost. Borrow did not sacrifice the proof.

George Borrow, 40

He is, as it were, himself substantial, richly-coloured, strange and with big strokes and splashes he suggests the thing itself. There have been writers since Borrow's day who have thought to use words so subtly that they are equivalent to things, but in the end their words remain nothing but words. Borrow uses language like a man, and we forget his words on account of the vividness of the things which they do not so much create as evoke. I do not mean that it can be called unconscious art, for it is naively conscious and delighting in itself. The language is that of an orator, a man standing up and addressing a mass in large and emphatic terms. He succeeds not only in evoking things that are very much alive, but in suggesting an artist that is their equal, instead of one, who like so many more refined writers, is a more or less pathetic admirer of living things. In this he resembles Byron. It may not be the highest form of art, but it is the most immediate and disturbing and genial in its effect. Finally, the whole book [*The Zincali*] has body. It can be browsed on. It does not ask a particular mood, being itself the result of no one mood, but of a great part of one man's life. Turn over half a dozen pages and a story, or a picture, or a bit of costume, or of superstition, will invariably be the reward. It reads already like a book rather older than it really is, but not because it has faded. There was nothing in it to fade, being too hard, massive and unvarnished. It remains alive, capable of surviving the Gypsies except in so far as they live within it and its fellow books.   162

His English geography is far vaguer than his Spanish. He creeps— walking or riding—over this land with more mystery. The variety and difficulties of the roads were less, and actual movement fills very few pages [of *Lavengro*]. He advances not so much step by step as adventure by adventure. Well might he say, a little impudently, 'there is not a chapter in the present book which is not full of adventures, with the exception of the present one, and this is not yet terminated'—it ends with a fall from his horse which stuns him. There is an air of somnambulism about some of the travel, especially when he is escaping alone from London and hack-writing. He shows great art in his transitions from day to day, from scene to scene, making it natural that one hour of one day should have the importance of the whole of another year, and one house more than the importance of several days' journeys. It matters not that he crammed more than was possible between Greenwich and Horncastle fairs, probably by transplanting earlier or later events. Time and space submit to him: his old schoolfellows were vainly astonished that he gave no chapters to them and his years at Norwich Grammar School. Thus England seems a great and a strange land on Borrow's page, though he does not touch the sea or the mountains, or any celebrated places except Stonehenge. His England is strange, I think, because it is presented according to a purely spiritual geography in which the childish drawling of 'Witney on the Windrush manufactures blankets', etc., is utterly forgot. Few men have the courage or the power to be honestly impressionistic and to say what they feel instead of compromising between that and what they believe to be 'the facts'.   228-9

It may be said of this [extract from *The Romany Rye*] that it is the style of the time, modified inexplicably at almost every point by the writer's character. The Bible and the older-fashioned narrative English of Defoe and Smollett have obviously lent it some phrases, and also a nakedness and directness that is half disdainful of the emotions and colours which it cannot hide. Still further to qualify the Victorianism which he was heir to, Borrow took over something from the insinuating Sterne. . . .

But innumerable are the possible styles which combine something from the Bible, Defoe, and Sterne, with something else upon a Victorian foundation. Borrow's something else, which dominates and welds the rest, is the most important. It expresses the man, or rather it allows the man's qualities to appear, his melancholy, his independence, his curiosity, his love of strong men and horses. Of little felicities there are very few. It has gusto always at command, and mystery also. We feel in it a kind of reality not often associated with professional literature, but rather with the letters of men who are not writers and with the speech of illiterate men of character. The great difference between them and Borrow is that their speech can rarely be represented in print except by another genius, and that their letters only now and then reach the level which Borrow continues at and often rises above.   250-1

As a master of the living word, Borrow's place is high, and it is unnecessary to make other claims for him. He was a wilful roamer in literature and the world, who attained to no mastery except over words. If there were many Romany Ryes before Borrow, as there were great men before Agamemnon, there was not another Borrow, as there was not another Homer.

He sings himself. He creates a wild Spain, a wild England, a wild Wales, and in them places himself, the Gypsies, and other wildish men, and himself again. His outstanding character, his ways and gestures, irresistible even when offensive, hold us while he is in our presence. In these repressed indoor days, we like a swaggering man who does justice to the size of the planet. We run after biographies of extraordinary monarchs, poets, bandits, prostitutes, and see in them magnificent expansions of our fragmentary, undeveloped, or mistaken selves. We love strange mighty men, especially when they are dead and can no longer rob us of property, sleep, or life: we can handle the great hero or blackguard by the fireside as easily as a cat.

Borrow, as his books portray him, is admirably fitted to be our hero. He stood six-feet-two and was so finely made that, in spite of his own statement which could not be less than true, others have declared him six-feet-three and six-feet-four. He could box, ride, walk, swim, and endure hardship. He was adventurous. He was solitary. He was opinionated and a bully. He was mysterious: he impressed all and puzzled many. He spoke thirty languages and translated their poetry into verse. . . .

In these days when it is a remarkable thing if an author has his pocket picked, or narrowly escapes being in a ship that is wrecked, or takes poison when he is young, even the outline of Borrow's life is attractive. Like Byron, Ben Jonson, and Chaucer, he reminds us that an author is not bound to be a nun with a beard. He depicts himself continually, at all ages, and in all conditions of pathos or pride. Other human beings, with few exceptions, he depicts only in relation to himself. He never follows men and women here and there, but reveals them in one or two concentrated hours; and either he admires or he dislikes, and there is no mistaking it. Thus his humour is limited by his egoism, which leads him into extravagance, either to his own advantage or to the disadvantage of his enemies.

He kept good company from his youth up. Wistful or fancifully envious admiration for the fortunate simple yeomen, or careless poor men, or noble savages, or untradesmanlike fishermen, or unromanized *Germani*, or animals who do not fret about their souls, admiration for those in any class who are not for the fashion of these days, is a deep-seated and ancient sentiment, akin to the sentiment for childhood and the golden age. Borrow met a hundred men fit to awaken and satisfy this admiration in an age when thousands can over-eat and over-dress in comfort all the days of their life. Sometimes he shows that he himself admires in this way, but more often he mingles with them as one almost on an equality with them, though his melancholy or his book knowledge is at times something of a foil. He introduces us to fighting men, jockeys, thieves, and ratcatchers, without our running any risk of contamination. Above all, he introduces us to the Gypsies, people who are either young and beautiful or strong, or else witch-like in a fierce old age. . . .

. . . Borrow's Gypsies are wild and uncoddled and without sordidness, and will not soon be superseded. They are painted with a lively if ideal colouring, and they live only in his books. They will not be seen again until the day of Jefferies' wild England, 'after London', shall come, and tents are pitched amidst the ruins of palaces that had displaced earlier tents. Borrow's England is the old England of Fielding, painted with more intensity because even as Borrow was travelling the change was far advanced, and when he was writing had been fulfilled. And now most people have to keep off the grass, except in remotest parts or in the neighbourhood of large towns where landowners are, to some extent, kept in their place. The rivers, the very roads, are not ours, as they were Borrow's. We go out to look for them still, and of those who adventure with caravan, tent, or knapsack, the majority must be consciously under Borrow's influence. . . .

He is best when he is without apparent design. As a rule if he has a design it is too obvious: he exaggerates, uses the old-fashioned trick of reappearance and recognition, or breaks out into heavy eloquence of description or meditation. These things show up because he is the most 'natural' of writers. His style is a modification of the style of his age, and is without the consistent personal quality of other vigorous men's, like Hazlitt or Cobbett. Perhaps English became a foreign language like his other thirty. Thus his books have no professional air, and they create without difficulty the illusion of reality. This lack of a literary manner, this appearance of writing like everybody else in his day, combines, with his character and habits, to endear him to a generation that has had its Pater and may find Stevenson too silky.

More than most authors Borrow appears greater than his books, though he is their offspring. It is one of his great achievements to have made his books bring forth this lusty and mysterious figure which moves to and fro in all of them, worthy of the finest scenes and making the duller ones acceptable. He is not greater than his books in the sense that he is greater than the sum of them: as a writer he made the most out of his life. But in the flesh he was a fine figure of a man, and what he wrote has added something, swelling him to more than human proportions, stranger and more heroical. So we come to admire him as a rare specimen of the *genus homo*, who had among other faculties that of writing English; and at last we have him armed with a pen that is mightier than a sword, but with a sword as well, and what he writes acquires a mythical value. Should his writing ever lose the power to evoke this figure, it might suffer heavily. We today have many temptations to over praise him, because he is a Great Man, a big truculent outdoor wizard, who comes to our doors with a marvellous company of Gypsies and fellows whose like we shall never see again and could not invent. When we have used the impulse he may give us towards a ruder liberty, he may be neglected; but I cannot believe that things so much alive as many and many a page of Borrow will ever die.   317-22

RICHARD JEFFERIES

RICHARD JEFFERIES was born at Coate Farm, in the north Wiltshire hamlet of Coate and the parish of Chisledon, on 6 November 1848. There he dwelt for the greater part of the first thirty years of his life; there and thereabouts, and in the neighbouring county of

Gloucestershire, dwelt his ancestors for several, perhaps many, generations. This country and its people was the subject of half his work, and the background, the source, or the inspiration, of all but all the rest. He, in his turn, was the genius, the human expression, of this country, emerging from it, not to be detached from it any more than the curves of some statues from their maternal stone.

Richard Jefferies, 1

Such, then, is the surface of this land, such the genial reticence of its fat leazes, its double hedges like copses, its broad cornfields, its oaks and elms and beeches, its unloquacious men, its immense maternal downs. Jefferies came to express part of this silence of uncounted generations. He was, as it were, a rib taken out of its side in that long sleep last disturbed by the cannon at Aldbourne Chase.   20

All this—the hunting, the reading, the brooding—was filling his brain, clearing and subtilizing his eye. The clearness of the physical is allied to the penetration of the spiritual vision. For both are nourished to their perfect flowering by the habit of concentration. To see a thing as clearly as he saw the sun-painted yellow-hammer in Stewart's Mash is part of the office of the imagination. Imagination is no more than the making of graven images, whether of things on the earth or in the mind. To make them, clear concentrated sight and patient mind are the most necessary things after love; and these two are the children of love. With the majority, love, accompanying and giving birth to imagination, reaches its intensity only once, and that briefly, in a life-time; and if they are ever again to know imagination, it is through fear, as when a tall flame shoots up before the eyes, or through sudden pain or anger giving their faces an honest energy of expression, and their lips, perhaps, a power of telling speech. Yet more rare is the power of repeating these images by music or language or carved stone. It is those who can do so who alone are, as a rule, aware that human life, nature, and art are every moment continuing and augmenting the Creation—making today the first day, and this field Eden, anni-hilating time—so that each moment all things are fresh and the sun has not drunken the blessed dew from off their bloom. The seeing eye of child or lover, the poet's verse, the musician's melody, add thus con-tinually to the richness of the universe. Jefferies early possessed such an eye, such an imagination, though not for many years could he reveal some of its images by means of words. In fact, he was very soon to bear witness to the pitiful truth that the imagination does not supply the words that shall be its expression; he was to fill much paper with words that revealed almost nothing of his inner and little more of his outer life.   44-5

In [Jefferies' first country essays] nature and country things are described from the point of view of one who is not merely a sportsman, or a naturalist, or an agriculturist, or an archaeologist, though he may play all those parts; but of a human being, sensuous, observant, reflective, who enjoys 'doing nothing' out of doors. Jefferies had many predecessors. Gilbert White, an unfertile literary genius and an all-round countryman, in the course of his incomparable letters to Pennant and Barrington, had come, as it always appears, by accident or divine grace, to express with perfect felicity his experience and enjoyment of life in the country. But his book has to carry with it a considerable dead weight of what is or was only matter of fact. He was in the first place a naturalist; and it was improbable that, if he had any contemporary influence, it would be felt except by naturalists. Few of his successors approach him in literary importance. Waterton, a gentleman of good family, whose *Essays on Natural History* appeared in 1838, had the charm of a genuine zeal and affection for wild life. His notes on the rook, for example, are in the spirit of the plainest passages in Jefferies' *Wild Life*. They state matters of fact of no great significance in a manner showing that he has enjoyed observing them himself; yet he can attract few not specially interested in birds. His affection does not involve the whole man, but is in the nature of a hobby, however much time it may have filled. St John (who knew Wiltshire as a boy, and trapped wheatears on the downs) is an intelligent, healthy, outdoor man, fond of scenery, and with an eye for such things as a party of Gaels bringing bright fish to the piny shore of a highland lake under the moon. His enjoyment was probably great, but it is not a great element in his book, however much we may import into it from our liking for him. He is a fine man, but he is not an artist, and the reader does half the work of producing his admirable effects. His *Short Sketches of the Wild Sports and Natural History of the Highlands* appeared in 1846. In the next year came Edward Jesse's *Favourite Haunts and Rural Studies*. This author would like to give the cottagers 'a stake in this country worth fighting for'. He likes to see them on Sunday having tea in the garden; and there is a real satisfaction in his picture of the interior of a cottage, the flitch of bacon on the rack, the dried pot-herbs and string of onions, the warming-pan shining in the corner. His *Month of May—a Rural Walk*, with his mowers and haymakers and birds singing, is one of the earliest pieces of the kind in prose; but if it sprang from a real delight in the country, no soul or blood has suffused the words, and they are dead. Two years later, in

1849, appeared Knox's *Ornithological Rambles in Sussex*. He is an ornithologist and sportsman. There is a careless charm, not incomparable to that of Jefferies' earlier work, about his descriptions of shooting in the weald, and of the lane from Petworth to Parham, and of the wild open country, the nightingales in the little copses of blackthorn and dwarf oak, the common which provides the best sport a man could desire 'on this side of Tweed'. Buckland, whose *Curiosities of Natural History* was published in 1857, is simply a curious, chatty naturalist with some stories to tell; and when he does not appeal to naturalists, as in *Whitmonday at Harting,* he has not enough humanity to appeal to any one else. Kingsley, in his *Prose Idylls* of 1873, is sportsman, naturalist, historian, clergyman, and country gentleman. They are in dialogue, and they are bluff, hard, and superficial; but they belong to the same class as Jefferies' essays, from which they differ chiefly in this: that while his lead us to the writer's personality through nature, Kingsley's lead us to nature through the writer's personality, and if that is not liked by the reader, his pictures, etc., are unendurable.

In these early essays of 1875 and 1876 Jefferies sets himself the unusual and difficult task of reflecting in prose the solitary enjoyment of nature, without any of the resources of these predecessors in sport or natural history, without the aid even of any passion, as of love, except what nature herself inspires. In *Marlborough Forest* he mentions the Civil War, saying that it did not touch the forest; but he relies for his effect upon the leaves and fruits, the pathless bracken, the woodpeckers and jays, the pack of stoats, the fighting stags, the beech avenue, and the inhuman quiet. As he says himself, 'The subtle influence of Nature penetrates every limb and every vein, fills the soul with a perfect contentment, an absence of all wish except to lie there half in sunshine, half in shade for ever, in a Nirvana of indifference to all but the exquisite delight of simply *living*.' But he fails as yet to convey that influence, to produce more than a readable article which only the careless townsman or unobservant countryman can much enjoy.   98-100

He had already begun to write short sketches of the country, of the men, the wild life, and the landscape; but it was only after reaching Surbiton that he began to concentrate himself upon his work. London thrilled and delighted and repelled him, and probably stimulated him. He certainly found a market there for his work, which was readily printed in newspapers and magazines, and afterwards published with applause in the form of books. With little arrangement, but with the charm of exuberance and freshness, he poured out his stores of country knowledge. There had been unlettered men who knew much that he knew; there had been greater naturalists and more experienced sportsmen, more magical painters—at least, in verse—of country things; but no one English writer before had had such a wide knowledge of labourers, farmers, gamekeepers, poachers, of the fields, and woods, and waters, and the sky above them, by day and night; of their inhabitants that run and fly and creep, that are still and fragrant and many-coloured. No writer had been able to express this knowledge with such a pleasing element of personality in the style that mere ignorance was no bar to its enjoyment. When he wrote these books— *The Amateur Poacher* and its companions—he had no rival, nor have they since been equalled in purity, abundance, and rusticity. The writer was clearly as much of the soil as the things which he described. In his books the things themselves were alive, were given a new life by an artist's words, a life more intense than they had had for any but the few before they were thus brought on to the printed page. Here was the life of man and animal, the crude and lavish beauty of English country life in the nineteenth century, with glimpses of the older life remembered by the men and women who still ploughed or kept sheep in Wiltshire and Surrey. In writing these four books, Jefferies was mainly drawing upon his memory and his Wiltshire notes, depicting things as he had seen and known them in his childhood and youth. The expression is mature, indeed, but the matter simple, the spirit, as a rule, one of wholesome old-fashioned enjoyment, the reflection contented and commonplace.

When these books had been written his good health was at an end, and when, in *Nature near London,* he came to describe scenes which he had not known as a young man, there was a new subtlety in the observation, at once a more microscopic and a more sensuous eye, more tenderness, a greater love of making pictures and of dwelling upon colours and forms. There was no more of the rude rustic content to be out rabbiting and fishing. The tall countryman who knew and loved all weathers as they came was bending, and spring was now intensely spring to his reawakened senses. The seasons, night and day, heat and cold, sun and rain and snow, became more sharply differentiated in his mind, and came to him with many fresh cries of joyous or pathetic appeal. In the early books the country lies before us very much as it would have appeared to James Luckett or old John Jefferies. They would have recognized everything in them, if they had had the luck to read them; the sport, the poaching, the curious notes on wild things, the old customs and pieces of gossip—these stand out clear and unquestionable as in an old woodcut. It was a priceless gift, smelling of youth and the days before the steam plough. But how different these later essays! Pain, anxiety, fatigue, had put a sharp edge on life—a keen edge, easily worn out. He was still glad to be with a shepherd, to hear about the sport, but it was a characteristic of the new period that he should watch a trout for days and years, and be careful lest any one should rob the pool of it; that he should love the old wooden plough with no machine-made lines, and discover the 'bloom' in the summer atmosphere; and confess that he often went to London with no object, and, arriving there, wandered wherever the throng might carry him. In these later essays there is often much observation that may be read for its own sake. But something was creeping into the style, staining it with more delicate dyes. The bloom in the atmosphere, the hues on an old barn roof, were in part his own life blood. In the earlier work we think only of the author where he is explicitly autobiographical, though we may exercise our fancy about him in an irrelevant way. Many had seen nature just so, though he was alone in so writing of it. In the later he was more and more a singular man, a discoverer of colours, of moods, of arrangements. This was the landscape of sensuous, troubled men; here were most rare, most delicate, most fleeting things. The result was at once portraiture and landscape. Perhaps the mystic element in Jefferies, unintentionally asserted, gave its new seriousness to this work. Except in the last words of *The Poacher*, there had been little sign of it; but now, in the fanciful narrative of *Wood Magic* and the autobiographical story of *Bevis*, the mystic promise was clear in those passages where the child Bevis talked to the wind or felt with his spirit out to the stars and to the sea. For a long time Jefferies must have been imperfectly conscious of the meaning of his mystic communion with nature. It was as a deep pool that slowly fills with an element so clear that it is unnoticed until it overflows. It overflowed, and Jefferies wrote *The Story of my Heart* in a passion.

Here for the first time was the whole man, brain, heart, and soul, the body and the senses, all that thought and dreamed and enjoyed and aspired in him. At every entrance the universe came pouring in, by all the old ways and by ways untrodden before. The book is the pledge of the value of Jefferies' work. It reveals the cosmic consciousness that had become fully developed in him soon after he turned thirty. Such acute humanity as is to be found in *The Story of my Heart* gives us confidence that what its possessor did in his prime, before and after it, is not to be neglected of those who are touched by mortal things. To past, present, and future he offers a hand that is not to be denied. Having tasted of physical, mental, and spiritual life, and aware of the diverse life of the world, in man, in beast, in tree, in earth, and sky, and sea, and stars, he comes to us as from a holy feast, face flushed, head crowned. He was discontented to some purpose with our age, with modernity, and not merely discontented, for he unsealed a new fountain of religious joy, and in the books that followed, whether he wrote of men or of nature, he gave a rich, sensuous, and hearty pleasure, lofty delights of the spirit, a goad to a bolder, more generous life in our own inner deeps and in our social intercourse; he pointed to an everlasting source of truth and joy; he created a woman, Felise, whom it is a divine inspiration to know, and others, men and women, scarred, mournful, but undespairing, whose ordinary humanity, as in *Amaryllis*, was drawn with such minuteness and love that we enjoy while we suffer, and rise ourselves with a useful discontent and an impulse towards what is more beautiful and true. *The Story of my Heart* gathered up into itself all the spiritual experiences which had been dimly hinted at in the early novels and outdoor books. As an autobiography it is unsurpassed, because it is alone. It is a bold, intimate revelation of a singular modern mind in a style of such vitality that the thoughts are as acts, and have a strong motive and suggestive power. . . .

The mystic consciousness which gave the original impulse to *The Story of my Heart* did not die away, though it was but seldom distinctly expressed after *The Dewy Morn*. It was diffused through his maturest essays, nevertheless, such as *The Pageant of Summer, Meadow Thoughts, Nature in the Louvre,* and *Winds of Heaven,* effecting a greater seriousness, a wider ramification of suggestion, a deeper colouring; while in the semi-scientific essays it is to be found in the increased imagination, and in the essays criticizing agricultural conditions it takes the form of deeper sympathies and more advanced thought. It gave a more solemn note to the joy which is the most striking thing in all his books, whether it is the joy of the child, the sportsman, the lover, the adventurer, the mystic, the artist, the friend of men. Against this his ill-health is nothing to record, except as something triumphed over by the spirit of life. His sadness came of his appetite for joy, which was in excess of the twenty-four hours day and the possible threescore years and ten. By this excess, resembling the excess of the oak scattering its doomed acorns and the sun parching what it has fostered, he is at one with nature and the forces of life, and at the same time by his creative power he rescues something of what they are whirling down to oblivion and the open sea, and makes of it a rich garden, high-walled against them. . . .

Few men have put themselves into words with such unconsidered variety. He expressed the whole range of a man's experience in the open air. This was not done without risks and some loss. He commented on many matters of his day and country. His lonely, retiring, and yet emphatic egoism made a hundred mistakes, narrow, ill-considered, splenetic, fatuous. He was big enough to take these risks, and he made his impression by his sympathies, his creation, not by his antipathies. He drew nature and human life as he saw it, and he saw it with an unusual eye for detail and with unusual wealth of personality behind. And in all of his best writing he turns from theme to theme, and his seriousness, his utter frankness, the obvious importance of the matter to himself, give us confidence in following him; and though the abundance of what he saw will continue to attract many, it is for his way of seeing, for his composition, his glowing colours, his ideas, for the passionate music wrought out of his life, that we must chiefly go to him. He is on the side of health, of beauty, of strength, of truth, of improvement in life to be wrought by increasing honesty, subtlety, tenderness, courage, and foresight. His own character, and the characters of his men and women, fortify us in our intention to live. Nature, as he thought of it, and as his books present it, is a great flood of physical and spiritual sanity, 'of pure ablution round earth's human shores', to which he bids us resort. Turning to England in particular, he makes us feel what a heritage are its hills and waters; he even went so far as to hint that some of it should be national. It is he who, above all other writers, has produced the largest, the most abundant, and the most truthful pictures of southern English country, both wild and cultivated. . . .

. . . He enjoyed, simply and passionately, his own life and the life of others, and in his books that enjoyment survives, and their sincerity and variety keep, and will keep, them alive; for akin to, and part of, his gift of love was his power of using words. Nothing is more mysterious than this power, along with the kindred powers of artist and musician. It is the supreme proof, above beauty, physical strength, intelligence, that a man or woman lives. Lighter than gossamer, words can entangle and hold fast all that is loveliest, and strongest, and fleetest, and most enduring, in heaven and earth. They are for the moment, perhaps, excelled by the might of policy or beauty, but only for the moment, and then all has passed away; but the words remain, and though they also pass away under the smiling of the stars, they mark our utmost achievement in time. They outlive the life of which they seem the lightest emanation—the proud, the vigorous, the melodious words. Jefferies' words, it has been well said, are like a glassy covering of the things described. But they are often more than that: the things are forgotten, and it is an aspect of them, a recreation of them, a finer development of them, which endures in the written words. These words call no attention to themselves. There is not an uncommon word, nor a word in an uncommon sense, all through Jefferies' books. There are styles which are noticeable for their very lucidity and naturalness; Jefferies' is not noticeable even to this extent. There are styles more majestic, more persuasive, more bewildering, but none which so rapidly convinces the reader of its source in the heart of one of the sincerest of men. Sometimes it is slipshod—in sound often so, for he had not a fine ear. It comes right, as a rule, by force of true vision and sincerity. On a moving subject, and amidst friends, he would speak much as he wrote. He did not make great phrases, and hardly any single sentence would prove him a master. He could argue, describe visible things and states of mind; he could be intimate, persuasive, and picturesque. No one quoted so rarely as he. He drew many sides of indoor and outdoor rustic life, human and animal, moving and at rest, and in his words these things retain their pure rusticity. Later, the neighbourhood of London made him dwell more sensuously than before on the natural beauty which contrasted with the town. Later still, the sensuous was merged and mingled with the spiritual, and the effect was more and more poetic—it might be said religious; and his style expanded to aid these larger purposes, thus being able in turn to depict nature from the points of view of the countryman, of the sensuous painter, of the poet of humanity. So, too, with human life. Whether he touched it lightly and pictorially, as in *Round about a Great Estate,* or with love and fire, as in *The Dewy Morn,* or with minute reconstruction of acts, thoughts, conversation, and environment, as in *Amaryllis,* he was equal to the different demands upon his words. Though he had read much, it was without having played the sedulous ape that he found himself in the great tradition, an honourable descendant of masters, the disciple of none, and himself secure of descendants; for he allied himself to nature, and still plays his part in her office of granting health, and hearty pleasure, and consolation, and the delights of the senses and of the spirit, to men.

291-9

GEORGE BOURNE

THERE IS ONE notable weakness in nearly all books concerning 'Nature'. They are over-burdened by a more or less vivid consciousness of an object to be attained. Their writers seem to be holding a brief and sometimes to be pleading with the querulousness of a supposed minority. In Richard Jefferies, for example, this is very conspicuous; at his worst, he tries to persuade men and women to go out into the fields, with the fervour of an auctioneer. Thoreau is more at his ease, but the weakness is there, and he is occasionally lured into unveracity by a desire of contrast. And so it is with all the prose-writers. The poets are less questionable; for they have been in possession of the theme for more generations. Still, Wordsworth and even Shelley may be assailed. Keats, almost alone, entirely lacks inartistic intention. Hence his perfect beauty, and, if we may say so, his urbanity. Gilbert White has very little of the modern spirit, and he, too, is urbane, and should more often be a model, especially in style. Of these who have gone to Nature full of the modern spirit nearly every one has no doubt been bowed and made tremulous by the wonderful experience. This intensity of emotion is admirable, but it is strange that by a year or two in Arcadia their English should be weakened and confused. The adventure seems to be too fresh, as if the descriptive writer had just left 'La Belle Dame Sans Merci': 'And I awoke and found me here/On the cold hill-side.'

The result is, as we have said, that this school is usually either didactic or oracular. It says, 'Come and see this beautiful thing', or 'Hush! we have dreamed dreams.' We look therefore in vain for writing in this kind that has the intimacy, the simplicity, and the mellowness which Lamb shows in another sphere. Meantime a near approach to perfection, or at least a delightful substitute, will be found in *The Bettesworth Book*, by Mr George Bourne. Bettesworth is a Surrey peasant, and the book is almost entirely a record of his conversations. The author now and then gives us the setting of his words quite unobtrusively. After reading it, the book seems to be full of summer and winter, and the ceremonial of the valleys and all the hills; it is as suggestive as an eagle's feather, a hazel-cluster of a long-past autumn, or an old coat.

From review of *The Bettesworth Book, DC,* 25 November 1901

I looked in vain for a statue of Cobbett in Farnham. Long may it be before there is one, for it will probably be bad and certainly unnecessary. So long as *Rural Rides* is read he needs not to share that kind of resurrection of the just with Queen Anne and the late Dukes of Devonshire and of Cambridge. The district has bred yet another man who combines the true countryman and the writer. I mean, of course, George Bourne, author of *The Bettesworth Book*, a volume which ought to go on to the most select shelf of country books, even beside those of White, Cobbett, Jefferies, Hudson, and Burroughs. Bettesworth was a Surrey labourer, a neighbour and workman of the author's. He was an observant and communicative man: his employer took notes from time to time, and the book is mainly a record of conversations. George Bourne gives a brief setting to the old man's words, yet a sufficient one. Pain and sorrow are not absent, and afar off we see a gray glimpse of the workhouse; but the whole is joyful. Even when Bettesworth 'felt a bit Christmassy' there is no melancholy; his head merely seems 'all mops and brooms'. His wife tells him that he has been laughing in his sleep. 'I was always laughing, then,' he says, 'until I was sore all round wi' it.' We have Bettesworth's own words in most cases, and George Bourne never interferes except to help. There is no insipid contrast with the outer world, though here and there we have an echo from it; we hear of railways as not particularly convenient, and a dull way of travelling; and of cut-purses, 'got up they was, ye know, reg'lar fly-looking blokes, like gentlemen'. Nothing is omitted but what had to be. Bettesworth cleaned cesspools at times, and the best things in the book centre round his 'excellent versatility in usefulness'. Well-sinking, reaping, lawn-mowing, pole-pulling in the hop garden, mending of roofs and steeples, and all the glorious activities connected with horses, had come into his work: as for adventure, he drove his first pair of cart horses from Staines to Smithfield Market. He had been a wanderer, too. During a long absence from friends he wrote to a brother, enclosing a gift; but on the way to the post he met an acquaintance, 'and I ast'n if he'd 'ave a drink. So when he says yes, I took the letter an' tore out the dollar an' chucked the letter over the hedge. An' we went off an' 'ad a bottle o' rum wi' this dollar. An' that's all as they ever heerd o' me for seven year.'

But the conversations themselves were held while Bettesworth was laying turf, or during the quite genial fatigue following a fifteen-hour day. 'Laying Turf' is one of the most charming pieces in the world. The old steeple-mender, reaper, and carter was laying turf under continuous rain and in an uncomfortable attitude, and made the unexpected comment: 'Pleasant work this. I could very well spend my time at it, with good turfs.'

The Bettesworth Book appeared in 1901. *Memoirs of a Surrey Labourer*, the record of Bettesworth's last years—1892-1905— appeared in 1907. At first the book may seem tame, a piece of reporting which leaves the reader not unaware of the notebooks consulted by the author. But in the end comes a picture out of the whole, painfully, dubiously emerging, truthful undoubtedly, subtle, not easy to understand, which raises George Bourne to a high place among observers. Apart from his observation, too, he shows himself a man with a ripe and generous, if staid, view of life, and a writer capable of more than accurate writing: witness his picture of frozen rime on telegraph wires, of Bettesworth's 'polling beck' or potato fork, and phrases like this: 'Near the beans there were brussels sprouts, their large leaves soaked with colour out of the clouded day.'

Bettesworth had fought in the Crimea, and during sixty years had been active unceasingly over a broad space of English country— Surrey, Sussex, and Hampshire—always out of doors. His memory was good, his eye for men and trades a vivid one, and his gift of speech unusual, 'with swift realistic touch, convincingly true'; so that a picture of rural England during the latter half of the nineteenth century, by one born in the earlier half and really belonging to it, is the result. The portrait of an unlettered pagan English peasant is fascinating. He lived in a parish where people of urban habits were continually taking the place of the older sort who dropped out, but he had himself been labourer, soldier, 'all sorts of things; but . . . first and last by taste a peasant, with ideas and interests proper to another England than that in which we are living now', and perhaps unconscious of the change since the days when he saw four men in a smithy making an axe-head: 'Three with sledge-'ammers, and one with a little 'ammer, tinkin' on the anvil . . . There was one part of making a axe as they'd never let anybody see 'em at.'

The talk, and George Bourne's comments, reveal this man's way of thinking and speaking, his lonely thoughts, and his attitude in almost every kind of social intercourse. They show his physical strength, his robust and gross enjoyment, his isolation, his breeding and independence, his tenderness without pity, his courage, his determination to endure. No permissible amount of quotation can explain the subtle appeal of his talk, for example, whilst turf-laying,

> Half unawares it came home to me, like the contact of the garden mould, and the smell of the earth, and the silent saturation of the cold air. You could hardly call it thought—the quality in this simple prattling. Our hands touching the turfs had no thought either; but they were alive for all that; and of such a nature was the life in Bettesworth's brain, in its simple touch upon the circumstances of his existence. The fretful echoes men call opinions did not sound in it; clamour of the daily press did not disturb its quiet; it was no bubble puffed out by learning, nor indeed had it any of the gracefulness which some mental life takes from poetry and art; but it was still a genuine and strong elemental life of the human brain that during those days was my companion. It seemed as if something very real, as if the true sound of the life of the village had at last reached my dull senses.

It will now reach duller senses than George Bourne's. No one has told better how a peasant who has not toned his other virtues with thrift is deserted in the end by God and even the majority of men. The *Memoirs* are shadowed from the first by the helplessness of Bettesworth's epileptic wife. The whole of his last year was a dimly lighted, solitary, manly agony. . . . Now, a statue of Frederick Bettesworth might well be placed at the foot of Castle Street, to astonish and annoy, if a sculptor could be found.

In Pursuit of Spring, 83-8

CONTEMPORARY READERS AND WRITERS

FOR THE VILLA residents and the more numerous others living 'in London and on London' who would be or will be villa residents, all our country literature is written; for them Mr [Stewart Edward] White has disturbed the untrodden solitudes of the mountains. Many are the varieties of this literature and its degrees of merit. It includes books of natural history and of topography, minute or general, some dry, some decorated, some alive; of sports treated in an instructing or an enjoying manner; histories, descriptions innumerable; books about houses and gardens; several thousand volumes annually of verse up to the neck in the country, used as a subject or as a source of imagery. They broaden our horizon by introducing us to trees, animals, gypsies, peasants, and romantic vagabonds.

A few of these books are the result of a genuine impulse towards literary expression; crowds are written to order by men, women, and others, in flats, villas, farmhouses, cottages, and tents. They reveal many kinds of satisfaction in the country, which the writers regard as a source of rest, relief, stimulation, a kind of religion, poetry, cash: as a refuge for thinkers, poets, lovers, children, tired workers or players. For some the country is hardly more than an alternative to theatres, exhibitions, clubs, or pills. A large number find in a country mixture of sport, natural history, archaeology, and vagabondage, in the society of the lonely sea, what most calls out and contents their deeper genial instincts: on the hills or in forests they do not feel themselves to be mere spirits fettered to restless but heavy bodies, or mere bodies with starving spirits, but can, for 'moments big as years' and even for some weeks, feel only a little lower than the animals as well as the angels. The country gives them more encouragement to moods or ease and a sense of unity with life, more obvious opportunities than the town for self-reliance and freedom from the confounding paraphernalia of civilization. Other men, like that Italian of the Renaissance, have shed tears at the sight of noble trees and waving cornfields, and a long landscape has cured their sickness. To these and some others the country is the principal reality outside themselves: there only are they at home, and the city seems to them an accident, perhaps an unnecessary one. They do not care the less for individual men, they are not indifferent to movements affecting multitudes, they may even have become entangled in one or another kind of social net, but they recognize only two great things, Nature and the heart of man. The extinction of a bird may rouse them, as it has done the poet, Mr Ralph Hodgson, to sorrow both for the loss of beauty and for the wound given to an ancient order which passes man's understanding. In others the freedom and simplicity connected by them with some forms of country life foster that cultivation of the instinctive and primitive which is the fine flower of a self-conscious civilization, turning in disgust upon itself.

The Country, 36-9

'WELL-KNOWN BRANDS'

THESE ARE all country books of fairly well-known brands. The first is by a vivacious journalist; the second, by a not ill-natured not unintelligent, but superficial and impatient wife of a clergyman; the third, by an exceedingly clever observer, who knows a fine piece of English country as well as a man knows his oldest coat.

They contrast with one another in one amusing way. For the first two know little of the country: they write because almost everyone else is writing, and the residue are supposed to read, country books; they help to perpetuate a fashion. Mr Tregarthen, on the other hand, has little to do with fashion. He is simply a keen and skilful sporting observer, who, in these versatile days, has discovered that a pen may be used agreeably when guns and dogs are far off.

Miss Leith has a glib and not entirely feeble pen, and to those who have never really cared for the country, but have liked to hear it talked about, the story of her search for a cottage, the discovery, the restoration, and the occupation, will perhaps be attractive. She tells us that she had long 'yearned for a cottage': 'A long procession of cottages, rustic, wooded, river-brinked, remote on breezy common or heather hill, thatched, timbered, mossy-tiled, deep-eaved, flower-embowered and green-swarded, passed alluringly before my fevered vision.'

An old and empty cottage, within thirty miles of London, was not easily to be found, but never would she have given up 'the lovely quest until compelled to do so by infirmity and decrepitude'. Suddenly she found a dejected cottage, recommended to her by its bacon loft, brick-oven, and ingle-nook, its convenient situation near golf and 'shopping in a good Surrey town'. She bought the cottage and its half-acre garden for £500. She spent £300 in making it habitable, and £60 in furniture. She tells us what furniture she bought, and no doubt it was very Caldecotty, and all that. But unless we except these facts, there is nothing 'useful and interesting to the practical housewife', such as is promised in the preface.

The book is a chatty narrative of what Miss Leith and her friends did with and in the cottage, with interspersed reflections like these: 'Oh, ugliness is dull, dull, dull! It has no redeeming quality, and alas! it persists even after its misguided perpetrators have been laid to rest 'neath the green beautiful earth they did their best to spoil. . . .' Her most original power is that of transporting the atmosphere of a flat to the country.

As Miss Leith surveys the country from the height of a London flat, so 'Deborah Primrose' surveys the country people from a parsonage. Of scenery, by the way, she is an intelligent appreciator, as when she remarks, 'How wonderfully like the sea' are the Downs. But she has made it her business here to write of men and women, and she fails because she has no charity and is not clever enough for satire. She appears to be one of many women who are compelled to spend a great part of their lives among and with the rustic poor, only because they have married clergymen. The most conspicuous features of her book are two faults; first, she says many things that we already know or are supposed to know, e.g., that 'the idylls of country life are over', or that the girls 'are becoming too grand for service', or that organ-blowers eat apples, or that the people are (through somebody's folly) ill-educated. Second, she writes with an irritated and negligent contempt, because the people are, for better or for worse, not as she is.

She says, for example, that 'Romance is dead within us, for we see them as they are.' In one place, she is surprised that the children, when asked to write an answer to the question, 'What they would like to be when they grew up' did not choose to be farm labourers and servants. She sets out to catalogue the virtues of her parishioners, and admits them to be clean, honest and independent, and after alluding to their vices, repeats benevolently, 'Be tender to ignorance as to all forms of poverty', and briefly allows that for centuries they have not had the best opportunities. One day the choir went wrong owing to the stupidity of the vicar, and his wife tells us that he and she 'had to turn our backs on them, that we might laugh unobserved': and 'with blushing hypocrisy' she once thanked the children for a song she detested. Yet she is surprised that she hears fewer comments on the sermon than she could wish. And while she remarks that 'much of our usual Sunday service is strangely ill-adapted to our ignorant grown-up children', she has no time to think of the difficult, obvious remedy.

But she has two or three chapters dealing with things which she seems to care about—a village 'Saint' and her own home. The Saint was probably a noble old woman. Our author's account of her is indifferent. It is just enough to suggest what an artist could have made of her. The parsonage she calls 'the Oasis'. 'Where love is, home is,' we are told; as also that even a garret may be a true home. She goes on to say that the house is large, and she gives four pages to a ludicrous account of her fear of burglars. Then she grumbles about the poverty of the living, and the amount of 'Dilapidations'. The garden is nice; but she sometimes longs to hear an organ-grinder or a muffin man.

Mr Tregarthen's book is almost wholly excellent. He is not an artist, and in the stores of his memory there are things which only an artist could save from dullness in the telling. But to pass from *The Book of the Country Cottage* and *A Modern Boeotia* is like passing out of town, through the suburbs, and into the excellent country, with its men and women and trees and waters. He writes of fox, otter, badger, hare, seal, fish, and birds, and of the men whose work or leisure is concerned with them. For example, imagination waiting upon exquisite knowledge has enabled him to give a wonderful account of an otter hunt. Neither Kingsley nor Jefferies could have done it better—the slow preparation of the earth-stopper on the night before, keeping the otter from leaving the inland waters for the coast; then the anxious quest, the fast and slow pursuit, and finally the satisfaction (to all but the earth-stopper) of calling off the hounds from the highly-gifted but exhausted beast. And, by the way, a trait we like in Mr Tregarthen is his love of the animals which he hunts.

From review of *The Book of the Country Cottage* by Emma S. Leith; *A Modern Boeotia* by Deborah Primrose; *Wild Life at the Land's End* by J. C. Tregarthen, *DC*, 18 June 1904

W. H. HUDSON

ONCE UPON A TIME there was much talk about the supposed incompatibility of science with poetry. In a few years, if it was not already dead, the poetry was to die of eating from the tree of knowledge. One of the best rebukes to this talk was the case of Mr W. H. Hudson, author of *Idle Days in Patagonia, The Naturalist in La Plata, Birds and Man, Nature in Downland, Hampshire Days, The Land's End, Afoot in England;* also of *Green Mansions: A Romance of the Tropical Forest,* and *The Purple Land.* For Mr Hudson is a poet and a man of science. His work on South America was described by Dr Russel Wallace as 'a storehouse of facts and observations of the greatest value to the philosophic naturalist, while to the general reader it will rank as the most interesting and delightful of modern books on natural history'; he has also written some of the most romantic stories of this age, and a great body of books depicting English wild life with an exactness and enthusiasm both unrivalled and in combination unapproached. But although generation after generation of schoolboys know his *British Birds,* and everyone remembers *Idle Days in Patagonia,* because it seems an odd place to be idle in, Mr Hudson has so far concealed himself from the public almost as successfully as he conceals himself from both birds and men out of doors.

Mr Hudson began by doing an eccentric thing for an English natura-

list. He was born in South America. He opened his study of birds on
the Pampas, and as a boy discovered a species which has since been
named after him. When he had been twenty-six years in England, he
could still see with his mind's eye two hundred birds of La Plata and
Patagonia as distinctly as he could the thrush, the starling, and the
robin, and could hear with his mind's ear the voices of a hundred and
fifty. That was thirteen years ago. And he is still indignant at the loss of
the great birds, especially the soaring birds, which he knew in South
America, and can never see here. But forty years in England, and
English blood on both sides—though on the mother's side it was
Americanized—have not turned Mr Hudson into the sort of Englishman that it is a pleasure to make a lion of. Himself has told us, and has
oftener made us feel, that he is one of 'a dying remnant of a vanished
people', 'strangers and captives' in a world where language and
customs and thoughts are not theirs. 'The blue sky, the brown soil
beneath, the grass, the trees, the animals, the wind, and rain, and sun,
and stars, are never strange to me,' he says in *Hampshire Days*; he has
none of 'that "world-strangeness" which William Watson and his
fellow-poets prattle in rhyme about'; he feels the strangeness where
men with 'pale civilized faces', eagerly talking about things that do not
concern him, are crowded together, while he feels a kinship with 'the
dead, who were not as these; the long, long dead, the men who knew
not life in towns, and felt no strangeness in sun and wind and rain'.
Jefferies also evoked these men from their graves upon the downs, but
Mr Hudson is perfectly original, and makes those prehistoric figures
with 'pale furious faces' more alive than Jefferies did. Nor is this a
whim of Mr Hudson's. A passage in his last book, *Adventures among
Birds*, shows how ready he is to enter into prehistoric life. There it is
for the sake of the various and innumerable birds of the undrained fens
of Lincolnshire and Somersetshire that he travels 'by devious ways
over the still water, by miles and leagues of grey rushes and sedges
vivid green, and cat's-tail and flowering rush and vast dark bulrush
beds, and islets covered with thickets of willow and elder and trees of
larger growth'. His vision of that great sonorous nation of birds is
beautiful. It is not the less wonderful that he is a man with a really
potent sense of historical time, so potent that he seems to possess, and
to employ most grimly at times, 'a consciousness of the transitoriness
of most things human', as when he sees without sadness or anger 'the
wild ancient charm' of Salisbury Plain partially exiled. Nevertheless,
his taste is for 'better, less civilized days'. He is, in fact, one of the few
writers who could be called a child of Nature without offending either
him or the other children, one of the few who could speak of 'earth
which is our home', without rhodomontade. So much does he know of
men and beasts on the earth and under the earth. He is even a little

grim, as towards the 'pale civilized people', towards the 'ordinary unobservant' man.

But he is equally impatient of the romantic who has been nourished on books alone. For example, he quotes a gipsy's words: 'You know what the books say, and we don't. But we know other things that are not in the books, and that's what we have. It's ours, our own, and you can't know it.' But he will not have it that there is anything mysterious in the gipsy's faculty: it is 'the animal's cunning, a special, a sublimated cunning, the fine flower of his whole nature', and has 'nothing mysterious in it'. Then he laughs: 'It is not so much the wind on the heath, brother, as the fascination of lawlessness, which makes his life an everlasting joy to him; to pit himself against game-keeper, farmer, policeman, and everybody else, and defeat them all; to flourish like the parasitic fly on the honey in the hive and escape the wrath of the bees.' What pleases him in the gipsy is his gipsyism, the very root of those differences which, superficially or romantically observed, give rise to 'the romance and poetry which the scholar-gipsy enthusiasts are fond of reading into him'. He professes himself a naturalist in these formidable terms. 'He' (the gipsy) 'is to me a wild, untameable animal of curious habits, and interests me as a naturalist accordingly.'

But there are naturalists and naturalists. In Mr Hudson curiosity is a passion, or, rather, it is part of the greater passion of love. He loves what things are. That is to say, he loves life, not merely portions selected and detached by past generations of writers. Take, for example, what he says of insects in *Hampshire Days*. He has pronounced 'the society of indoor people unutterably irksome' to him on account of the 'indoor mind', which sees most insects as pests. But, says he, without insects, without 'this innumerable company that each "deep in his day's employ" are ever moving swiftly or slowly about me, their multitudinous small voices united into one deep continuous Aeolian sound, it would indeed seem as if some mysterious malady or sadness had come upon Nature. Rather would I feel them alive, teasing, stinging, and biting me; rather would I walk in all green and flowering places with a cloud of gnats and midges ever about me.' He so loves the humming-bird hawk-moth that he retains in his mind a lovely picture of the insect 'suspended on his misty wings among the tall flowers in the brilliant August sunshine'. The image came up as he was introduced to a 'lepidopterist' who proceeded to tell him that this season he had only seen three humming-bird hawk-moths, and that he had 'secured' all three. In the presence of this super-moth he calls himself 'a simple person whose interest and pleasure in insect life the entomologist would regard as quite purposeless'.

What he reverences and loves is the earth, and the earth he knows is, humanly speaking, everlasting. He is at home wherever grass grows, and he has hardly a trace of an amiable 'weakness' for particular places. In fact, at times he is detached enough to be a connoisseur, as when he says that the Wiltshire Downs may be neglected, 'since, if downs are wanted, there is the higher, nobler Sussex range within an hour of London'. Yet in Hampshire he speaks of villages on the Test and Itchen where he could spend 'long years in perfect contentment'; and in Wiltshire, among those very downs, he experienced a home feeling—the vast, undulating vacant land won him through its resemblances to his early home: 'I can note,' says he in *A Shepherd's Life*, 'many differences, but they do not deprive me of this home feeling; it is the likenesses that hold me, the spirit of the place, one which is not a desert with the desert's melancholy or sense of desolation, but inhabited, although thinly, and by humble-minded men whose work and dwellings are unobtrusive. The final effect of this wide green space with signs of human life and labour in it, and sight of animals—sheep and cattle—at various distances, is that we are not aliens here, intruders or invaders on the earth, living in it but apart, perhaps hating and spoiling it, but with the other animals are children of Nature, like them living and seeking our subsistence under her sky, familiar with her sun and wind and rain.' And, again, in *Afoot in England,* he mentions that the lowing of cattle, on account of early association, is more to him than any other natural sound.

Once he admits that 'the West Country has the greatest attraction' for him; but he writes of all the southern counties, and does not disdain the eastern or the midland counties. During these forty years he has seen England as few writers have since Cobbett. He has written about counties as far apart as Kent and Cornwall, Derbyshire and Dorsetshire, Norfolk and Monmouthshire. In all counties he has been at home with the wild life. He has visited places connected with his predecessors—White, Cobbett, and Jefferies. But I should not say that his 'country' embraces all the counties. Thus, Cornwall is foreign to him. His *Land's End* is an uncomfortable, unsympathetic book, though every page is interesting, and many a one beautiful, as where he pictures the fishing fleet going out from St Ives. The people were alien to him. He was annoyed by what he considered their childishness or savagery, and 'their occasional emotional outbreaks, which when produced by religious excitement are so painful to witness'. Unlike the gipsies, they seem not to have been interesting to him as a naturalist. In fact, he was not at his best with them. Thus, when he wished to find 'that rarity in Cornwall, a man with a sense of humour', he asked a man, who was digging stones in a very stony field, where they got stone for building houses, and having been told to 'use your own eyes', and obliged to explain that the question was in fun, he related the incident to six people in Cornwall without amusing them. There were too many

Cornishmen in Cornwall. What he would have liked would have been an odd, isolated one in Kent or Wiltshire.

On the whole I think Mr Hudson is most at home in Hampshire. True, he has experienced a home feeling among the downs, and two of his best books, *Nature in Downland* and *A Shepherd's Life*, are based on observations among the downs of Wiltshire and Sussex. But he has been chiefly a rambler in those counties. In Hampshire he has apparently been at least a migrant with a temporary narrow range. Here he may be seen at home with adders, absorbed in contemplating or thinking about them. Above all, *Hampshire Days* reveals him at home with insects. His corner of the New Forest not only abounded in insect life, but there 'the kings and nobles of the tribe'—the humming-bird hawk-moth, the White Admiral butterfly, the fairest and mightiest of the dragon-flies, the hornet, the great green grasshopper—were to be met with. His intimacy with the insects of Hampshire suggests residence. The book would have been different had he not spent successive summers in the same district. Here, again, there is a recollection of South America, where he says of the hornet: 'As he comes out of the oak-tree shade and goes swinging by in his shining gold-red armature, he is like a being from some other hotter, richer land, thousands of miles away from our cold, white cliffs and grey seas.' This book is full, like the others, of a profound love; but it is, I think, the happiest of them, partly because he was fortunate in the houses that received him. One old house, in the south of the New Forest, had more of Nature in and about it than any other human habitation 'in a land whose people are discovered dwelling in so many secret, green, out-of-the-world places'. Another was a cottage on the Itchen, between Winchester and Alresford, which he had to himself, without dog, cat, child, or chick—only the wild birds for company.

Hampshire, then, is Mr Hudson's 'country'. I could add many codicils, but I shall be content with one, from *Birds and Man*, from the chapter on 'Daws in the West Country' where he says:

> Of all the old towns which the bird loves and inhabits in numbers, Wells comes first. If Wells had no birds, it would still be a city one could not but delight in. There are not more than half a dozen towns in all the country where (if I were compelled to live in towns) life would not seem something of a burden; and of these two are in Somerset—Bath and Wells.... Wells has the first place in my affections, and is the one town in England the sight of which in April and early May, from a neighbouring hill, has caused me to sigh with pleasure.

Scattered over his rambling books are passages that give an intense, and even magical, but quite unfanciful, life to many of the towns and villages, as well as the rivers, woods, and hills, of England. They have the beauty of discoveries and the sufficingness of what is genuinely imagined. But whether he is a rambler or a sojourner, it is seldom as a traveller that he interests us. He lays little stress on his walking or cycling. They are means to an end, and his end is to be still, somewhere in the sun or under trees where birds are.

Primarily his search has been for birds. When, for example, he found himself at Chepstow, and was disappointed in his hope of seeing a rare species near by, he tells us that he had 'to extract what pleasure he could' out of the castle, the Wye, and Tintern Abbey. These things had already been discovered, and he knew it. He does not positively refuse to like what others are well known to have liked; for example, he likes a vast range of English poets from Swinburne to Bloomfield; but he must always be discovering. He discovered Swinburne by his own side-track, I have no doubt. So he discovered the city of Wells, which he informs us is the one city in the kingdom where you will hear that 'woodland sound', the laughter of the green woodpecker; and also the city of Bath, 'a city that has a considerable amount of Nature in its composition, and is set down in a country of hills, woods, rocks, and streams, and is therefore, like the other, a city loved by daws and by many other wild birds'. He has gone about without dictionaries of literature, and practically without maps or guides. The scenes which he can best or most happily remember are those discovered by chance, which he had not heard of, or else had heard of and forgotten, or which he had not expected to see. His books now contain, fortunately, an almost countless number of these scenes, each one of them peopled, made alive, made (I should say) next to immortal, by the presence of some extraordinary or beautiful living thing, by a child, an adder, a vast ringing and echoing and re-echoing of bells, a cowman, a fox, a poet, a river, a memory, a legend, above all by birds, together with his own personality that withdraws itself, at times, far from vulgar error as from poetic illusion, but seldom far from profound humanity or natural magic, and, if it eludes our sympathy, never our wonder, curiosity, and admiration.

A Literary Pilgrim in England, 190-9

[*Adventures among Birds*] is one of [Mr Hudson's] best country books. It is, in fact, the best book entirely about birds that is known to me. The naturalist may hesitate to admit it, though he knows that no such descriptions of birds' songs and calls are to be found elsewhere, and he cannot deny that no other pages reveal English birds in a wild state so vividly, so happily, so beautifully. Mr Hudson is in no need of recommendation among naturalists. This particular claim of his is mentioned only in order to impress a class of readers who might confuse him with the fancy dramatic naturalists, and the other class who will appreciate the substantial miracle of a naturalist and an imaginative artist in one and in harmony.

Were men to disappear they might be reconstructed from the Bible and the Russian novelists; and, to put it briefly, Mr Hudson so writes of birds that if ever, in spite of his practical work, his warnings and indignant scorn, they should cease to exist, and should leave us to ourselves on a benighted planet, we should have to learn from him what birds were.

Many people, even 'lovers of Nature', would be inclined to look for small beer in a book with the title of *Adventures among Birds*. If they are ignorant of Mr Hudson's writings, they are not to blame, since bird books are, as a rule, small beer. Most writers condescend to birds or have not the genius to keep them alive in print, whether or not they have the eternal desire 'to convey to others', as Mr Hudson says, 'some faint sense or suggestion of the wonder and delight which may be found in Nature'. He does not condescend to birds, 'these loveliest of our fellow-beings', as he calls them, 'these which give greatest beauty and lustre to the world'. He travels 'from county to county viewing many towns and villages, conversing with persons of all ages and conditions', and when these persons are his theme he writes like a master, like an old master perhaps, as everybody knows, who has read his *Green Mansions, The Purple Land* and *South American Sketches*. It might, therefore, be taken for granted that such an artist would not be likely to handle birds unless he could do so with the same reality and vitality as men. And this is what he does....

There is a very large variety in his enjoyment. It is exquisite and it is vigorous; it is tender and at times almost superhuman in grimness. It is a satisfaction of his senses, of his curious intelligence, and of his highest nature. The green eggs of the little bittern thrill him 'like some shining supernatural thing or some heavenly melody'. He is cheerful when his binoculars are bringing him close to birds 'at their little games'—a kestrel being turned off by starlings, a heron alighting on another heron's back, a band of starlings detaching themselves from their flock to join some wild geese going at right angles to their course; for 'the playful spirit is universal among them'. The songs of blackbird, nightingale, thrush, and marsh warbler delight him, and yet at other times the loss of the soaring species, eagles and kites, oppresses him, and he speaks contemptuously of 'miles on miles of wood, millions of ancient noble trees, a haunt of little dicky birds and tame pheasants'. His vision of the Somerset of the lake-dwellers, of 'the paradise of birds in its reedy inland sea, its lake of Athelney', makes a feast for the eyes and ears. Moreover, he is never a mere bird man, and the result of this variety of interest and pleasure on the part of a man of

Mr Hudson's imagination, culture, and experience, is that while his birds are intensely alive in many different ways, and always intensely birdlike, presenting a loveliness beyond that of idealized or super-naturalized women and children, yet at the same time their humanity was never before so apparent. The skylark is to him both bird and spirit, and one proof of the intense reality of his love is his ease in passing, as he does in several places, out of this world into a mythic, visionary, or very ancient world. This also is a proof of the powers of his style. At first sight, at least to the novice who is beginning to distin-guish between styles without discriminating, Mr Hudson's is merely a rather exceptionally unstudied English, perhaps a little old-fashioned. Nothing could be farther from the truth. It is, in fact, a combination, as curious as it is ripe and profound, of the eloquent and the collo-quial, now the one, now the other, predominating in a variety of shades which make it wonderfully expressive for purposes of narrative and of every species of description—precise, humorous, rapturous, and sub-lime. And not the least reason of its power is that it never paints a bird without showing the hand and the heart that paints it. It reveals the author in the presence of birds just as much as birds in the presence, visible or invisible, of the author.

In Pursuit of Spring, 244-50

6 Nature and England

YARROW BLOSSOMING from the stones of the field-roads, and at path-sides: cocks-comb out in the thin mowing grass.

Elder in flower, its scent thickest after rain when the petals whiten the sward under: the flower-clusters were noticeable, bosomed in young leaf, as soon as the March buds burst.

Hemlock in flower along the brook.

House-martins beginning to lay: thus late, because earlier nests had been blown down.

Lesser field convolvulus in flower: braiding the driest paths, even on ploughed land, unsown: and creeping about the barren sea-beach.

Common mallow flowering in dry places.

Blackberry-bramble blossoming; humming already with many bees.

Cuckoo sings, but broken-voicedly.

Wild parsnip flowering: found more in the midst of the fields than at the hedges, like parsley.

Curious crying of the young rooks—a faltering 'ka-wa-wa', in attempting the grave 'caw'.

Bee, burying himself in the larkspur blooms, each one of which he looks into in turn.

Meadow-sweet flowering: at the margins of canal and brook—sometimes actually in the water, with the lesser skullcap and its upturned leaves.

Common arrowhead in blossom; growing in dense beds, where the moorhen builds, and under which the pike lurk: its leaves and tough, easily penetrable stems, hold the angler's line or hooks.

Nightingale hatches her eggs under a bramble: and her mate stops singing and begins to scold with a harsh 'bit-bit' or a wistful 'wheet-torr', in which both birds join deep in the underwood.

Spotted orchis blossoming with poppy, tormentil, chamomile, and coltstail, among the railway metals on dry soil.

Shivering drawl of the common bunting, as if the dust of the road-sides, which he loves, had got into his throat: he sings on the telegraph wires or bare posts by preference: quite a short song, betraying his relationship to the reed-bunting, and in a lesser degree to the larks.

A Diary In English Fields and Woods', 7-17 June 1895,
The Woodland Life, 180-2

One evening I heard a man who had served twenty years' imprisonment in a London office and was not yet done with it, trying to prove by autobiography that all was over for him and the world because of this servitude. He was a country-bred man with a distinct London accent. Once upon a time, it seems, he had charmed a snake, caught a tench of five pounds and lost a bigger one, and, like Jefferies, heard the song of the redwing in England; now he kept somebody's accounts and wore the everlasting mourning of clerks: hence these tears. 'Science,' he said, in dreary anger, 'Science is wearing out its eyes with staring, and soon the best spectacles in the world will avail her nothing. Science is not final, or absolute. It is only a recent method of looking at things, and it will pass away like the method which made it not only possible but necessary to believe in witches. And what will have been its effect?

'Take, for example, a matter in which Science is supposed to have wrought a great and beneficial or at any rate ennobling change—the sense of time and space, the feeling for eternity and infinity. I believe that the average educated or partly educated man, as well as the uneducated man, now holds the story of Adam and Eve untrue, and thinks that man was only made in the image of God a little before the Reform Bill. Myths have been destroyed which helped to maintain a true and vivid acknowledgment of the mystery of the past. Science has not left us without a substitute. It has given us figures and innumerable statements, and the newspapers cannot overpraise the substitute. And so with space. Formerly no one had any idea that the stars were a certain number of million miles away. They entered into human life: they were beautiful and useful, and mythology made them more human but not less god-like. Now they are inferior to gas and electric light. Our way of humanizing them is to say that the railway metals of Great Britain, if placed on end, would reach to the moon, or would do so if they were a little longer. We gape and gasp, and the railway is not any more divine or the moon any more human. The sky is now a very large dome pricked through by a number of lights so small as to be practically useless, and if we catch ourselves sighing at them the sigh is deepened by the thought that we are still suffering from a discredited but not extinct superstition. That the universe has been enlarged is somehow supposed to be not incompatible with the fact that the telegraph, etc., have annihilated space.

'The peasant who saw his lord ride home with apes and ivory and peacocks had the means for as sublime a view of the glories of the world as the schoolboy who could tell you the diameter of the earth. How long will it take the truths of Science to pass out of the stage of facts and figures into realities or living falsehoods? The poet Francis Thompson is one of the few who have even pretended to possess such realities. He speaks of the Earth, "a joyous David", dancing before God, and of a mighty Spirit unknown "that swingeth the slow earth before the embannered Throne". But this is not the living reality or falsehood of imagination: it is the shadowy half-truth of fancy. Poets who believed the earth and man to be two or three thousand years old had not less regard for "the dark backward and abysm of time" than poets who are geologists.

'But let me speak for myself. I am a man of the English middle class, as my people have been for several generations. We have moved among our kind. We have travelled and read. We have not been altogether dull and blind. Yet, though we accept the statement that the earth is round, and have watched the apparent motion of the firmament and seen Capella rise and set in a summer night, though we have seen ships sink out of sight over the rim of the world—we treat the earth as flat, we point with a horizontal arm towards America, and if with a vertical arm to New Zealand, then with no more understanding than if we pointed upwards to heaven. To me who have not travelled, India is a small coloured place on a map; if I think of its mighty rivers that place fades out of sight and I see floods larger than the land itself. The lesser stars are white sparks to me, the great are cups of fire spilt but never emptied: I distinguish them from dew-drops or glow-worms by their position overhead. The moon is something which resembles a hundred different things, from a shaving of silver or a dried Honesty seed to a dinted golden shield. The sublimest thing I know is the sea, and after that London, vast, complex, ancient, restless, and incalculable: I pass through it at night and hear its noises like the wrath and sorrow of lions raving in bondage, and when I look up the starry sky is like a well in the forest of the city. . . . I wonder how many others feel the same, that we have been robbed—all but Mr Charles M. Doughty—of the small intelligible England of Elizabeth and given the word Imperialism instead. Apollo, Woden, Jehovah, have been put away for the sake of unsectarian education. No wonder we are languid, fretful, and aimless.

'*There is nothing left for us to rest upon,* nothing great, venerable, or mysterious, which can take us out of ourselves, and give us that more than human tranquillity now to be seen in a few old faces of a disappearing generation. To be a citizen of infinity is no compensation for the loss of that tranquillity. When we grow old what will grant any of us that look? Certainly not statistics and the knowledge that we have lived through a time of progress unparalleled in history.

'As for myself, I can only hope that when I am old, "in this our pinching cave", I shall remember chiefly the valley of the river Uther where I was born, and the small old house half encircled and half shadowed by an enormous crescent of beech-covered hills. That is my world in spite of everything. Those fifteen or twenty square miles make the one real thing that I know and cannot forget, in spite of a hundred English scenes wantonly visited and forgotten, in spite of London unforgotten and unintelligible.'

And much he had to say of that old house shadowed and smothered in leaves, and of himself doing as he liked in it and in the woods, and of the farmers, the labourers, the inn-keeper, the squire, and other well-preserved fragments of old England, and in particular of the only man he had ever met in those huge woods on the hills above his home.

'Once only,' he said, 'I met a man in the woods. I was reaching the top of the hill, and the hounds had just streamed past me, when a shrill voice like a bull's filled the air. A cough close by soon afterwards told me that it was a man. I looked round, and there, sitting on a beech-stump in the sun, was an old, old man, and he was leaning on a stick. His face was like a wrinkled red apple, and yet I have seen boys of twelve with older faces. It told you the boy he had been eighty years before—the dullest of boys at his books, one who was not good either at leading or obeying other boys—a mischievous, too daring, indiscreet boy, who would do anything and submit to any punishment, but was likely all of a sudden to lower his head and run at a bully, knock him down, and fall over him in a heap. All the mischief had not yet gone out of his face, though his eyes were a rheumy blue and resembled shell-fish. It was a merry face. I know now that he was probably made by hard work, beer, and women, but I should like to live another seventy years to see if this generation produces anything as fit for living on the earth. "I work for all," says the labourer on the inn-sign of the Five Alls; and yet, I think, looking back at that old man, he often had the laugh of all the others. You may be sure there were hundreds like him in Shakespeare's time and in Wordsworth's, and if there aren't a good sprinkling of them, generation after generation, I do not know what we shall come to, but I have my fears. I warrant, every man who was ever any good had a little apple-faced man or woman like this somewhere not very far back in his pedigree. Where else will he get his endurance, his knowledge of the earth, his feeling for life and for what that old man called God? When a poet writes, I believe he is often only putting into words what such another old man puzzled out among the sheep in a long lifetime. You cannot persuade me that the peak-faced poets think of all those things about earth and men by themselves.'

He concluded by saying that he had had ten years in that house and those woods, that then his father died, he went away to school and afterwards into an office. Those ten years were the only reality in his life. Everything since had been heavy illusion without rest. 'There is nothing to rest on,' he said, 'nothing to make a man last like the old man I met in the woods.'

This man's story could probably be paralleled thousands of times today. I have given it because unintentionally it refutes his statement that nothing is left for us to rest on. There was something firm and very mighty left even for him, though his melancholy, perverse temper could reach it only through memory. He had Nature to rest upon. He had those hills which were not himself, which he had not made, which were not made for man and yet were good to him as well as to myriads of other races, visible and invisible, that have been upon the earth and in the air, or will be in some other moment of eternity.

To put it less equivocally, he had the country to rest on. For Nature includes Fleet Street as well as the Milky Way, Whitechapel as well as the valley of the Towy or the valley of the Wylye. There are eyes, and at least one pair of human eyes, that look with as much satisfaction on a lamp-post as on a poplar-tree, and see towns as beautiful birds' nests. For most of us this visionary or God-like view is impossible except in a few particular and irrecoverable moments. We cannot make harmony out of cities: often we think it a great triumph to become blind and deaf to them and without sense of smell; or we are proud that the rain on the windy 'bus-top has kissed us exactly as on Old Winchester Hill or Sir John's Hill at Laugharne and has brought them to mind. Roughly speaking, we still accept Cowper's hard-and-fast distinction between God-made country and man-made town. We may feel the painful splendour of our humanity in the town, but it is in the country more often that we become aware, in a sort of majestic quiet, of the destiny which binds us to infinity and eternity. Old as the towns are so plainly—often stiff and rotten with age—we know and deeply feel that the oldest of them are as grass in the sight of the wind, the moon, even the hills. We know that it was all once 'country': we know without the help of 'After London' that it will all once again be 'country'. I like to see grass and flowers come down softly to take possession of any London soil that is, for a month or two, allowed to feel the sun, wind, and rain. With all their inhuman grace, lightness, and silence, the flowers and grass are related to me as the bricks, mortar, and iron are not, and I have a kind of far-off share in their victories. On the other hand I am not dismayed at a house building in a field. It can do no harm; moreover it is adventuring, it is going to mix with high, strange company, and to learn something from clouds and stars, from the long bays of corn and grass among the woods at the bases of the hills, which it will look down on perhaps for many generations. But all towns have committed something of the sin of Babel. They are complicated and divided; they end in confusion. Before super-human eyes, no doubt, they are not confused in themselves, nor out of harmony with what is about and above them: yet for most of us Cowper's distinction is true. It was Varro's also: eighteen hundred years before Cowper he remarked that the country life was more ancient than the town life, that the country was made by divine Nature, the towns by human art.

The Country, 1-13

Mr Hueffer has undoubtedly been in Arcady. So have very many of us. Along with a million others he wishes to be back in Arcady, and in a shrill voice he cries for it. We think, however, that the manners of that blissful place are still largely unknown to him, or they would have somewhat softened his speech. He is, in fact, one of the society for organizing a return to Nature. Such societies, as we know, are not infallible; and in common with many of the band, he makes, we think, a desert in order to cry in it; too often the voice announces nothing more than a reed that is shaken by the wind. The return to Nature is by many paths. It can now be managed by train, by steamboat, and from the suburbs by motor car and three-penny bus. But it is strange that if people are bound for Arcady they never see anyone else on the way, and come back with a desire that it should be advertised. Mr Hueffer, too, seems to believe that he is pleading a lost cause, which we can only regret, wishing that he would not scream when he saw a man.

From review of *In Arcady and Out*, by Oliver Madox Hueffer, *DC*, 21 May 1901

Men and women talk much today about a return to Nature; and they mean, very often, a flight from the city to the fields. There everything will be more simple, more just, and beautiful, they think; there they will easily be able to make terms with life. John Burroughs, in his last book, claimed to have proved it. As if, in an age that is not at all simple, it were possible, even were it good, to be simple, except in clothing and food! Society makes character; solitude makes soul; and it is just possible that life in the country may give a wise man the opportunity for that combination of character and soul which a good man possesses. But a country life is neither more easy nor more simple than a city life. If it were, the world would now be ruled by the brewers, bankers, and journalists who are taking the place of hops in Kent.

And just as, in thinking about life, we cry out for a return to Nature and her beneficent simplicity, so we are apt to cry out for a return to simplicity in literature. Men ask us to look at the *Odyssey,* and see how large and simple, how moving even, today it is. A critic has lately spoken of *Tom Jones* and *Pendennis* as unrolling 'the infinite variety of human nature' before us, and has compared Mr Meredith most unfavourably with them. They are simpler, and they do not disturb. Nothing could be more false than this attitude. If it were also strong, it might endanger much that is most characteristic of our age. If a reply were necessary, we need but point out how much less simple the *Argonautica* and the *Aeneid* are than the *Iliad*; how much less simple the *Divine Comedy* than its predecessors, and *Paradise Lost* than them all. The *Henriade* is simple, but it is not therefore great.

Here, before us, are many views which would seem to have been inspired by a cunning search for simplicity. These men are trying to write as if there were no such thing as a Tube, Grape Nuts, love of Nature, a Fabian Society, A Bill for the reform of the Marriage Laws; nor do they show that they are in possession of any grace or virtue which can be set up against those wonders of our age.

From review of new verse, *DC*, 30 August 1905

I had left behind me most cyclists from London, but I was now continually amongst walkers. There were a few genial muscular Christians with their daughters, and equally genial muscular agnostics with no children; bands of scientifically-minded ramblers with knickerbockers, spectacles, and cameras; a trio of young chaps singing their way to a pub.; one or two solitaries going at five miles an hour with or without hats; several of a more sentimental school in pairs, generally chosen from both sexes, disputing as to the comparative merits of Mr Belloc and Mr Arthur Sidgwick: and a few country people walking, not for pleasure, but to see friends seven or eight miles away, whom perhaps they had not visited for years, and, after such a Good Friday as this, never will again.

These travellers gave me a feeling that I had been forestalled (to put it mildly). . . .

In Pursuit of Spring, 68

NATURE-STUDY

WHAT IS to come of our Nature-teaching in schools? What does it aim at? Whence does it arise? In part, no doubt, it is due to our desire to implant information. It is all very well for the poet to laugh 'When

Science has discovered something more / We shall be happier than we were before;' but that is the road we are on at a high rate of speed. If we are fortunate we shall complete our inventory of the contents of heaven and earth by the time when the last man or woman wearing the last pair of spectacles has decided that, after all, it is a very good world and one which it is quite possible to live in. That, however, is an end which would not in itself be a sufficient inducement to push on towards it; still less can such a vision have set us upon the road.

Three things, perhaps, have more particularly persuaded us to pay our fare and mount for somewhere—three things which are really not to be sharply distinguished, though it is convenient to consider them separately. First, the literary and philosophical movement imperfectly described as the romantic revival and return to Nature of the eighteenth and nineteenth centuries. Poets and philosophers need private incomes, State porridge and what not, but literature and philosophy is a force, and for a century it has followed a course which was entered in the period of the French Revolution. This literature shows man in something like his true position in an infinite universe, and shows him particularly in his physical environment of sea, sky, mountain, rivers, woods, and other animals. Second, the enormous, astonishing, perhaps excessive, growth of towns, from which the only immediate relief is the pure air and sun of the country, a relief which is sought by the urban multitudes in large but insufficient numbers and for too short a time. Third, the triumph of science, of systematized observation. Helped, no doubt, by the force of industrialism—to which it gave help in return—science has had a great triumph. At one time it was supposed to have fatally undermined poetry, romance, religion, because it had confused the minds of some poets and critics.

These three things considered, Nature-study is inevitable. Literature sends us to Nature principally for joy, joy of the senses, of the whole frame, of the contemplative mind, and of the soul, joy which if it is found complete in these several ways might be called religious. Science sends us to Nature for knowledge. Industrialism and the great town sends us to Nature for health, that we may go on manufacturing efficiently, or, if we think right and have the power, that we may escape from it. But it would be absurd to separate joy, knowledge and health, except as we separate for convenience those things which have sent us out to seek for them; and Nature-teaching, if it is good, will never overlook one of these three. Joy, through knowledge, on a foundation of health, is what we appear to seek.

There is no longer any need to hesitate in speaking of joy in connection with schools, yet might we not still complain, as Thomas Traherne did two hundred and fifty years ago:

There was never a tutor that did professly teach Felicity, though that be the mistress of all other sciences. Nor did any of us study these things but as aliena, which we ought to have studied as our enjoyments. We studied to inform our Knowledge, but knew not for what end we so studied. And for lack of aiming at a certain end we erred in the manner.

If we cannot somehow have a professor of Felicity we are undone. Perhaps Nature herself will aid. Her presence will certainly make for felicity by enlarging her pupil for a time from the cloistered life which modern towns and their infinite conveniences and servitudes encourage. Tolstoy has said that in the open air 'new relations are formed between pupil and teacher: freer, simpler and more trustful'; and certainly his walk on a winter night with his pupils, chatting and telling tales (see *The School at Yasnaya Polyana*, by Leo Tolstoy), leaves an impression of electrical activity and felicity in the young and old minds of that party which is hardly to be surpassed. And how more than by Nature's noble and uncontaminated forms can a sense of beauty be nourished? Then, too, the reading of great poetry might well be associated with the study of Nature, since there is no great poetry which can be dissevered from Nature, while modern poets have all dipped their pens in the sunlight and wind and great waters, and appeal most to those who most resemble them in their loves. The great religious books, handed down to us by people who lived in closer intercourse with Nature than many of us, cannot be understood by indoor children and adults. Whether connected with this or that form of religion or not, whether taken as 'intimations of immortality' or not, the most profound and longest remembered feelings are often those derived from the contact of Nature with the child's mind.

Of health, though there are exactly as many physicians as patients, it is unnecessary to say anything, except that one of the pieces of knowledge—I do not speak of information—which science has left to us is that movement and the working of the brain in pure air and sunlight is good for body and soul, especially if joy is aiding.

Knowledge aids joy by discipline, by increasing the sphere of enjoyment, by showing us in animals, in plants, for example, what life is, how our own is related to theirs, showing us, in fact, our position, responsibilities and debts among the other inhabitants of the earth. Pursued out of doors where those creatures, moving and still, have their life and their beauty, knowledge is real. The senses are invited there to the subtlest and most delightful training, and have before them an immeasurable fresh field, not a field like that of books, full of old opinions, but one with which every eye and brain can have new vital intercourse. It is open to all to make discoveries as to the forms and habits of things, and care should be taken to preserve the child from the most verbose part of modern literature, that which repeats in multiplied ill-chosen words stale descriptions of birds and flowers, etc., coupled with trivial fancies and insincere inventions. Let us not take the study, the lamp and the ink out of doors, as we used to take wild life—having killed it and placed it in spirits of wine—indoors. Let us also be careful to have knowledge as well as enthusiasm in our masters. Enthusiasm alone is not enthusiasm. There must, at some stage, be some anatomy, classification, pure brain-work; the teacher must be the equal in training of the mathematician, and he must be alive, which I never heard was a necessity for mathematicians. But not anatomy for all, perhaps; for some it might be impossible, and a study of colours, curves, perfumes, voices—a thousand things—might be substituted for it.

Yet Nature-study is not designed to produce naturalists, any more than music is taught in order to make musicians. If you produce nothing but naturalists you fail, and you will produce very few. The aim of study is to widen the culture of child and man, to do systematically what Mark Pattison tells us in his dry way he did for himself, by walking and outdoor sports, then—at the late age of seventeen—by collecting and reading such books as *The Natural History of Selborne,* and finally by a slow process of transition from natural history into 'the more abstract poetic emotion . . . a conscious and declared poetical sentiment and a devoted reading of the poets'. Geology did not come for another ten years, 'to complete the cycle of thought, and to give that intellectual foundation which is required to make the testimony of the eye, roaming over an undulating surface, fruitful and satisfying. When I came in after years to read *The Prelude* I recognized, as if it were my own history which was being told, the steps by which the love of the country boy for his hills and moors grew into poetical suscep- tibility for all imaginative presentations of beauty in every direction.' The botany, etc., would naturally be related to the neighbourhood of school or home; for there is no parish or district of which it might not be said, as Jefferies and Thoreau each said of his own, that it is a micro- cosm. By this means the natural history may easily be linked to a pre- liminary study of hill and valley and stream, the positions of houses, mills and villages, and the reasons for them, and the food supply, and so on, and this in turn leads on to—nay, involves—all that is most real in geography and history. The landscape retains the most permanent marks of the past, and a wise examination of it should evoke the begin- nings of the majestic sentiment of our oneness with the future and the past, just as natural history should help to give the child a sense of one- ness with all forms of life. To put it at its lowest, some such cycle of knowledge is needed if a generation that insists more and more on living in the country, or spending many weeks there, is not to be bored or to be compelled to entrench itself behind the imported amusements of the town.   *The South Country*, 141-6

THE SOUTH COUNTRY

The name of 'South Country' is taken from a poem by Mr Hilaire Belloc, beginning:

> When I am living in the Midlands,
>   That are sodden and unkind,
> I light my lamp in the evening,
>   My work is left behind;
> And the great hills of the South Country
>   Come back into my mind.

The name is given to the south of England as distinguished from the Midlands, 'North England', and 'West England' by the Severn. The poet is thinking particularly of Sussex and of the South Downs. In using the term I am thinking of all that country which is dominated by the Downs or by the English Channel, or by both; Cornwall and East Anglia have been admitted only for the sake of contrast. Roughly speaking, it is the country south of the Thames and Severn and east of Exmoor, and it includes, therefore, the counties of Kent, Sussex, Surrey, Hampshire, Berkshire, Wiltshire, Dorset, and part of Somerset. East and west across it go ranges of chalk hills, their sides smoothly hollowed by Nature and the marl-burner, or sharply scored by old roads. On their lower slopes they carry the chief woods of the south country, their coombes are often fully fledged with trees, and sometimes their high places are crowned with beech or fir; but they are most admirably themselves when they are bare of all but grass and a few bushes of gorse and juniper and some yew, and their ridges make flowing but infinitely variable clear lines against the sky. Sometimes they support a plateau of flint and clay, which slopes gradually to the level of the streams. Sometimes they fall away to the vales in well-defined ledges—first a long curving slope, then a plain of cornfield, and below that a steep but lesser slope covered with wood, and then again grassland or sandy heaths and rivers. Except on the plateau, the summits have few houses and very small hamlets; the first terrace has larger villages and even a town or two; but most of the towns are beneath on the banks of the rivers, and chiefly where they are broadest near the sea, or on the coast itself. The rivers flow mainly north and south, and can have but a short course before they enter the sea on the south or the Thames on the north. Those I remember best are the Stours, the two Rothers, but especially the one which joins the Arun, the Medway, the Len, the Eden, the Holling, the Teise, the Ouse, the

Itchen, the Meon, the Wey, the Mole, the Kennet, the Ray, the Winterbournes, the Wiltshire Avon, the Wylye, the Ebble, and many little waters running gold over New Forest gravel or crystal over the chalk of Hampshire. . . .

Most of the towns are small market towns, manufacturing chiefly beer; or they are swollen, especially in the neighbourhood of London, as residential quarters on lines of railway or as health and pleasure resorts on the sea. But any man used to maps will be wiser on these matters in an hour than I am. For what I have sought is quiet and as complete a remoteness as possible from towns, whether of manufactures, of markets or of cathedrals. I have used a good many maps in my time, largely to avoid the towns; but I confess that I prefer to do without them and to go, if I have some days before me, guided by the hills or the sun or a stream—or, if I have one day only, in a rough circle, trusting, by taking a series of turnings to the left or a series to the right, to take much beauty by surprise and to return at last to my starting-point. On a dull day or cloudy night I have often no knowledge of the points of the compass. I never go out to see anything. The signboards thus often astonish me. I wish, by the way, that I had noted down more of the names on the signboards at the cross-roads. There is a wealth of poetry in them, as in that which points—by a ford, too—first, to Poulner and Ringwood; second, to Gorley and Fordingbridge; third, to Linwood and Broomy: and another pointing to Fordingbridge, to Ringwood, and to Cuckoo Hill and Furze Hill: and another in the parish of Pentlow, pointing to Foxearth and Sudbury, to Cavendish and Clare, and to Belchamps and Yeldham.

Castles, churches, old houses, of extraordinary beauty or interest, have never worn out any of my shoe leather except by accident. I like to come upon them—usually without knowing their names and legends—but do not lament when chance takes me a hundred times out of their way. Nor have I ever been to Marlow to think about Shelley, or to Winterslow for Hazlitt's sake; and I enter Buriton many times without remembering Gibbon. They would move me no more than the statue of a man and a fat horse (with beribboned tail) which a grateful countryside erected to William III in the market square at Petersfield. I prefer any country church or chapel to Winchester or Chichester or Canterbury Cathedral, just as I prefer 'All round my hat', or 'Somer is icumen in', to Beethoven. Not that I dislike the cathedrals, or that I do not find many pleasures amongst them. But they are incomprehensible and not restful. I feel when I am within them that I know why a dog bays at the moon. They are much more difficult or, rather I am more conscious in them of my lack of comprehension, than the hills or the sea; and I do not like the showmen, the smell and look of the museum, the feeling that it is admiration or nothing, and all the well-dressed and flyblown people round about. I sometimes think that religious architecture is a dead language, majestic but dead, that it never was a popular language. Have some of these buildings lived too long, been too well preserved, so as to oppress our little days with too permanent an expression of the passing things? The truth is that, though the past allures me, and to discover a cathedral for myself would be an immense pleasure, I have no historic sense and no curiosity. I mention these trivial things because they may be important to those who read what I am paid for writing. I have read a great deal of history—in fact, a university gave me a degree out of respect for my apparent knowledge of history—but I have forgotten it all, or it has got into my blood and is present in me in a form which defies evocation or analysis. But as far as I can tell I am pure of history. Consequently I prefer the old brick houses round the cathedral, and that avenue of archaic bossy limes to the cathedral itself with all its turbulent quiet and vague antiquity. The old school also close at hand! I was there after the end of the term once, and two boys were kicking a football in a half-walled court; it was a bright, cold, windy April afternoon; and the ancient brick was penetrated with their voices and the sound of the ball, and I thought there could be nothing lovelier than that court, the pleasant walls, and the broad playing fields in sight of a smooth noble hill and a temple of dark firs on top. I was not thinking of Winchester or of any one older than the fondest son of that 'mother, more than mother', and little of him; but was merely caught up by and with the harmony of man and his work, of two children playing, and of the green downs and windy sky.

And so I travel, armed only with myself, an avaricious and often libertine and fickle eye and ear, in pursuit, not of knowledge, not of wisdom, but of one whom to pursue is never to capture. Politics, the drama, science, racing, reforms and preservations, divorces, book clubs—nearly everything which the average (oh! mysterious average man, always to be met but never met) and the superior and the intelligent man is thinking of, I cannot grasp; my mind refuses to deal with them; and when they are discussed I am given to making answers like, 'In Kilve there is no weathercock.' I expect there are others as unfortunate, superfluous men such as the sanitation, improved housing, police, charities, medicine of our wonderful civilization saves from the fate of the cuckoo's foster-brothers. They will perhaps follow my meanders and understand. The critics also will help. They will misunderstand—it is their trade. How well they know what I ought, or at least ought not, to do. I must, they have said, avoid 'the manner of the worst oleographs'; must not be 'affected', though the recipe is not to be had; must beware of 'over-excitation of the colour sense'. In slow course of years we acquire a way of expression, hopelessly inadequate, as we plainly see when looking at the methods of great poets, of beautiful women, of athletes, of politicians, but still gradually as fitted to the mind as an old walking-stick to the hand that has worn and been worn by it, full of our weakness as of our strength, of our blindness as of our vision—the man himself, the poor man it may be. And I live by writing, since it is impossible to live by not writing in an age not of gold but of brass.

Unlearned, incurious, but finding deepest ease and joy out of doors, I have gone about the South Country these twenty years and more on foot, especially in Kent between Maidstone and Ashford and round Penshurst, in Surrey between London, Guildford and Horley, in Hampshire round Petersfield, in Wiltshire between Wootton Bassett, Swindon and Savernake. The people are almost foreign to me, the more so because country people have not yet been thrown into quite the same confusion as townspeople, and therefore look awkwardly upon those who are not in trade—writing is an unskilled labour and not a trade—not on the land, and not idle. But I have known something of two or three men and women, and have met a few dozen more. Yet is this country, though I am mainly Welsh, a kind of home, as I think it is more than any other to those modern people who belong nowhere. Here they prefer to retire, here they take their holidays in multitudes. For it is a good foster-mother, ample-bosomed, mild and homely. The lands of wild coast, of mountains, of myriad chimneys, offer no such welcome. They have their race, their speech and ways, and are jealous. You must be a man of the sea or of the hills to dwell there at ease. But the South is tender and will harbour any one; her quiet people resent intrusion quietly, so that many do not notice the resentment. These are the 'home' counties. A man can hide away in them. The people are not hospitable, but the land is.

Yet there are days and places which send us in search of another kind of felicity than that which dwells under the Downs, when, for example, the dark wild of Ashdown or of Woolmer, some parcel of heathery land, with tufted pines and pale wandering roads, rises all dark and stormy out of the gentle vale, or on such an evening as when the sky is solemn blue save at the horizon where it is faint gold, and between the blue and the gold, across the north-west, lies an ashen waste of level cloud. This sky and its new moon and evening star below, is barred by the boles of beeches; through them the undulations of deserted ploughland are all but white with dewy grass and weed. Underfoot winds a disused path amid almost overlapping dog's mercury. The earth is like an exhausted cinder, cold, silent, dead, compared with the great act in the sky. Suddenly a dog-fox barks—with melancholy and malice in the repeated hoarse yells—a sound that a-wakens the wildest past out of the wood and the old path. He passes by me at a trot, pausing a little to bark. He vanishes, but not his voice, into the wood, and he returns, still barking, and passes me again, filling the wood and the coombe below with a sound that has nothing to match it except that ashen waste in the beech-barred, cold blue and golden sky, against which the fox is carved in moving ebony. Or again, when a rude dark headland rises out of the mist of the plain into the evening sky. The woods seem but just freed from the horror of primeval sea, if that is not primeval sea washing their bases. Capella hangs low, pale, large, moist and trembling almost engulfed between two horns of the wood upon the headland, the frailest beacon of hope, still fluttering from the storm out of which the land is emerging. Then, or at home looking at a map of Britain, the West calls, out of Wiltshire and out of Cornwall and Devon beyond, out of Monmouth and Glamorgan and Gower and Caermarthen, with a voice of dead Townsends, Eastaways, Thomases, Phillipses, Treharnes, Marendaz, sea men and mountain men. . . .

This, then, is my South Country. It covers the North Downs and the South Downs, the Icknield Way and the Pilgrims' Way, and the cross-roads between them and the Thames and the sea, a land of hops, fruit, corn, high pasture, meadow, woodland, heath and shore. But there is no man of whose powers I stand more in awe than the topographical writer, from Mr A. G. Bradley or Mr E. V. Lucas downwards. I shall not attempt to compete with them. I should only be showing my ignorance and carelessness were I to label every piece of country which I chance to mention or describe. Any one can point out my omissions, my blindness, my exaggeration. Nor can I bring myself to mention the names of the places where I walked or sat down. In a sense this country is all 'carved out of the carver's brain' and has not a name. This is not the South Country which measures about two hundred miles from east to west and fifty from north to south. In some ways it is incomparably larger than any country that was ever mapped, since upon nothing less than the infinite can the spirit disport itself. In other ways it is far smaller—as when a mountain with tracts of sky and cloud and the full moon glass themselves in a pond, a little pond.

The South Country, 1-11

HISTORY AND THE PARISH

SOME DAY there will be a history of England written from the point of view of one parish, or town, or great house. Not until there is such a history will all our accumulations of information be justified. It will begin with a geological picture, something large, clear, architectural, not a mass of insignificant names. It must be imaginative: it might, perhaps, lean sometimes upon Mr Doughty's *Dawn in Britain*. The peculiar combination of soil and woodland and water determines the direction and position and importance of the ancient trackways; it will determine also the position and size of the human settlements. The early marks of these—the old flint and metal implements, the tombs, the signs of agriculture, the encampments, the dwellings—will have to be clearly described and interpreted. Folk-lore, legend, place-names must be learnedly, but bravely and humanly used, so that the historian who has not the extensive sympathy and imagination of a great novelist will have no chance of success. What endless opportunities will he have for really giving life to past times in such matters as the line made by the edge of an old wood with the cultivated land, the shapes of the fields, with their borders of streams or hedge or copse or pond or wall or road, the purpose and interweaving of the roads and footpaths that suggest the great permanent thoughts and the lesser thoughts and dreams of the brain. . . . As the historic centuries are reached, the action of great events, battles, laws, roads, invasions, upon the parish—and of the parish upon them—must be shown. Architecture, with many of its local characteristics still to be traced, will speak as a voice out of the stones of castle, church, manor, farm, barn and bridge. The birds and beasts cannot be left out. The names of the local families—gentle and simple—what histories are in them, in the curt parish registers, in tombstones, in the names of fields and houses and woods. Better a thousand errors so long as they are human than a thousand truths lying like broken snail-shells round the anvil of a thrush. If only those poems which are place-names could be translated at last, the pretty, the odd, the romantic, the racy names of copse and field and lane and house. What a flavour there is about the Bassetts, the Boughtons, the Worthys, the Tarrants, Winterbournes, Deverills, Manningfords, the Suttons: what goodly names of the South Country—Woodmansterne, Hollingbourne, Horsmonden, Wolstanbury, Brockenhurst, Caburn, Lydiard Tregoze, Lydiard Millicent, Clevancy, Amesbury, Amberley (I once tried to make a beautiful name and in the end it was Amberley, in which Time had forestalled me); what sweet names Penshurst, Frensham, Firle, Nutley, Appleshaw, Hambledon, Cranbrook, Fordingbridge, Melksham, Lambourne, Draycot, Buscot, Kelmscot, Yatton, Yalding, Downe, Cowden, Iping, Cowfold, Ashe, Liss. . . . Then there are the histories of roads. Every traveller in Hampshire remembers the road that sways with airy motion and bird-like curves down from the high land of clay and flint through the chalk to the sand and the river. It doubles round the head of a coombe, and the whole descent is through beech woods uninterrupted and all but impenetrable to the eye above or below except where once or twice it looks through an arrow slit to the blue vale and the castled promontory of Chanctonbury twenty miles south-east. As the road is a mere ledge on the side of a very steep hill the woods below it hurry down to a precipitous pit full of the glimmering, trembling and murmuring of innumerable leaves and no sight or sound of men. It is said to have been made more than half a century ago to take the place of the rash straight coach road which now enters it near its base. . . .

There are many places which nobody can look upon without being consciously influenced by a sense of their history. It is a battlefield, and the earth shows the scars of its old wounds; or a castle or cathedral of distinct renown rises among the oaks; or a manor house or cottage, or tomb or woodland walk that speaks of a dead poet or soldier. Then, according to the extent or care of our reading and the clearness of our imagination, we can pour into the groves or on the turf tumultuous or silent armies, or solitary man or woman. It is a deeply-worn coast; the spring tide gnaws the yellow cliff, and the wind files it with unceasing hiss, and the relics of every age, skull and weapon and shroudpin and coin and carven stone, are spread out upon the clean, untrodden sand, and the learned, the imaginative, the fanciful, the utterly unhistoric and merely human man exercises his spirit upon them, and responds, if only for a moment. In some places history has wrought like an earthquake, in others like an ant or mole; everywhere, permanently; so that if we but knew or cared, every swelling of the grass, every wavering line of hedge or path or road were an inscription, brief as an epitaph, in many languages and characters. But most of us know only a few of these unspoken languages of the past, and only a few words in each. Wars and parliaments are but dim, soundless, and formless happenings in the brain; toil and passion of generations produce only an enriching of the light within the glades, and a solemnizing of the shadows. . . .

But because we are imperfectly versed in history, we are not therefore blind to the past. The eye that sees the things of today, and the ear that hears, the mind that contemplates or dreams, is itself an instrument of an antiquity equal to whatever it is called upon to apprehend. We are not merely twentieth-century Londoners or Kentish men or Welshmen. We belong to the days of Wordsworth, of Elizabeth, of Richard Plantagenet, of Harold, of the earliest bards. We, too, like Taliesin, have borne a banner before Alexander, have been with our Lord in the manger of the ass, have been in India, and with the 'remnant of Troia', and with Noah in the ark, and our original country is 'the region of the summer stars'. And of these many folds in our nature the face of the earth reminds us, and perhaps, even where there are no more marks visible upon the land than there were in Eden, we are aware of the passing of time in ways too difficult and strange for the explanation of historian and zoologist and philosopher. It is this manifold nature that responds with such indescribable depth and variety to the appeals of many landscapes.   147-52

WORDS AND PLACES

MR J. H. ROUND has a wholesome warning for the learned in his *Notes on the Systematic Study of our English Place Names*. He suggests that two generations hence antiquaries may be seeking the origin of a name which was in fact given by a speculative builder to honour his daughter; and Canon Taylor mentions 'Flos, Tiny, and other townships which a late Canadian governor named after his wife's lap dogs.' Mr Round also mentions the case of Stowe Maries, which is known to take its name from the family of Marice or Morice. It is now assuming the title of Stowe St Mary, as the old East Cow and West Cow in the Isle of Wight have become slyly plural as East Cowes and West Cowes. Remembering the 'too ingenious antiquary' and the fearless folk etymology which created the 'liver' for Liverpool, Mr Round disputes the philologist's claim to explain place names by his laws, because, like the laws of political economy, 'they ignore the human element'. But they ignore only what is incalculable, and when they confess defeat they are bowing partly to darkest antiquity and partly to this very human element. Mr Round is more troublesome when he points out that two identical names side by side may undergo very different changes. The 'Biseleye' of Domesday becomes 'Bisley' in Gloucestershire, but 'Bushey' in Worcestershire ten miles away.

Imitating the old-style antiquarian, a writer in the *Saturday Review* derived Lambeth from the Mongolian word 'lama', meaning a chief priest, and the Semitic 'beth' a house—'the chief priest's house', or the archbishop's palace. But there were once upon a time men who grimly derived the 'Crick' in 'Cricklade' from 'Greek' and attributed a university to the little place to dilute the wonder. William Stukeley, an eighteenth-century antiquarian, was a master of wonders in this kind. He explained 'Hackpen' as serpent's head, by a combination of Hebrew and ancient British. 'Pen' was simple and meant 'head', while 'Hack' was the same as the 'Ochim' (Isaiah xiii. 21) which is rendered 'doleful creatures' by our translators and as 'serpents' by St Jerome. Stukeley was as high-handed as his name—somehow—suggests. He found a 'King Barrow' above Wilton and straightway presumed that King Carvilios was buried there. Kings, he declared, often took their names from their people or their country: Cassibelan, for example, was King of the Cassii. Well then, 'Where should Carvilius live but at Carvilium, now Wilton, or where be buried but in the most conspicuous place near his palace?' These were the men who made England great, fearing neither man nor God nor philology. There are some such still with us. As Stukeley heard the people at Beckhampton calling the Roman road the 'French Way', so in the year of Admiral Rodjetsvensky's victory in the North Sea I found a sturdy fellow sitting on Offa's Dyke in Monmouthshire who told me that the mound was 'Dogger's Bank'. We have need of men like that to explain 'Eggpie' Lane near the village of Sevenoaks Weald, or Tumbling Bay in a neighbouring parish far inland. It was no rustic but a clergyman who took in the *Hibbert Journal* that told me Ludcombe was named after King Lud of Ludgate Hill.

Better pure imagination than rash science in handling place names. It is with philology as with poetry—'the imagination of a boy is healthy, and the mature imagination of a man is healthy. . . .' And fortunately science cannot destroy the imagination which kindles at the majestic 'Caernarvon', the romantic 'Schiehallion', and at the infinite variety of significance in names like Baydon, Tregonebris, Shepherdswhim, Castell-y-Dail, Castell-y-Gwynt, Kingly Vale, Noar Hill, Thorpe Constantine, Stoke Charity, Palfrey Green, Happersnapper Hanger, Jenny Pink's Copse, Amesbury, Bynoll, Ryme Intrinseca. Studies like Canon Taylor's can only feed the roots of the imagination; they can colour or shape the flowers only by means beyond anticipation or estimate. Mr Max Beerbohm has shown that our impression of a street is created chiefly by its character, not by its deliberately given name; that 'Oxford' cannot exalt a street, nor 'Manchester' depress a square. This is truer to life than the romantic's flighty praise for the rococo mixture of suburban street and house names, which might lead future antiquaries to suppose Lyndhurst a holy place, and to form a wild opinion of our standard of scenery from the prevalence of 'Belle Vue'. Association is as strange as life: it absolutely distinguishes 'guitar' from 'catarrh', and helps to make the gulf between Amberley and Anerley. It was not until I remembered the rhyme of rapier and Napier that I knew how I had given the finest edge and point of chivalry to that soldier name. Sometimes contrast alone is powerful, as when we take pleasure in Forest Hill, Gypsy Hill, Lambourn Street, or Seven Kings, in a world of chimneys and east wind.

From Introduction to *Words and Places* by Isaac Taylor, viii-x

ON ROADS AND FOOTPATHS

MUCH HAS been written of travel, far less of the road. Writers have treated the road as a passive means to an end, and honoured it most when it has been an obstacle; they leave the impression that a road is a connection between two points which only exists when the traveller is upon it. Though there is much travel in the Old Testament, 'the way' is used chiefly as a metaphor. 'Abram journeyed, going on still toward the south,' says the historian, who would have used the same words had the patriarch employed wings. Yet to a nomadic people the road was as important as anything upon it. The earliest roads wandered like rivers through the land, having, like rivers, one necessity, to keep in motion. We still say that a road 'goes' to London, as we 'go' ourselves. We point out a white snake on a green hill-side, and tell a man: 'That is going to Chichester.' At our inn we think when recollecting the day: 'That road must have gone to Strata Florida.' We could not attribute more life to them if we had moving roads with platforms on the side-walks. We may go or stay, but the road will go up over the mountains to Llandovery, and then up again over to Tregaron. It is a silent companion always ready for us, whether it is night or day, wet or fine, whether we are calm or desperate, well or sick. It is always going: it has never gone right away, and no man is too late. Only a humorist could doubt this, like the boy in a lane who was asked: 'Where does this lane go to, boy?' and answered: 'I have been living here these sixteen years and it has never moved to my knowledge.' Some roads creep, some continue merely; some advance with majesty, some mount a hill in curves like a soaring sea-gull.

   Even as towns are built by rivers, instead of rivers being conducted past towns, so the first settlements grew up alongside roads which had formerly existed simply as the natural lines of travel for a travelling race. The oldest roads often touch the fewest of our modern towns, villages, and isolated houses. It has been conjectured that the first roads were originally the tracks of animals. The elephant's path or tunnel through the jungle is used as a road in India today, and in early days the wild herds must have been invaluable for making a way through forest, for showing the firmest portions of bogs and lowland marshes, and for suggesting fords. The herd would wind according to the conditions of the land and to inclinations of many inexplicable kinds, but the winding of the road would be no disadvantage to men who found their living by the wayside, men to whom time was not money. Roads which grew thus by nature and by necessity appear to be almost as lasting as rivers. They are found fit for the uses of countless different generations of men outside cities, because, apart from cities and their needs, life changes little. If they go out of use in a new or a changed civilization, they may still be frequented by men of the most primitive habit. All over England may be found old roads, called Gypsy Lane, Tinker's Lane, or Smuggler's Lane; east of Calne, in Wiltshire, is a Juggler's Lane; and as if the ugliness of the 'uggle' sound pleased the good virtuous country folk, they have got a Huggler's Hole a little west of Semley and south of Sedgehill in the same county: there are also Beggar's Lanes and roads leading past places called Mock Beggar, which is said to mean Much Beggar. These little-used roads are known to lovers, thieves, smugglers, and ghosts.

Even if long neglected they are not easily obliterated. On the fairly even and dry ground of the high ridges where men and cattle could spread out wide as they journeyed, the earth itself is unchanged by centuries of traffic, save that the grass is made finer, shorter, paler, and more numerously starred with daisies. But on the slopes down to a plain or ford the road takes its immortality by violence, for it is divided into two or three or a score of narrow courses, trenched so deeply that they might often seem to be the work rather of some fierce natural force than of slow-travelling men, cattle, and pack-horses. The name Holloway, or Holway, is therefore a likely sign of an old road. So is Sandy Lane, a name in which lurks the half-fond contempt of country people for the road which a good 'hard road' has superseded, and now little used save in bird's-nesting or courting days. These old roads will endure as long as the Roman streets, though great is the difference between the unraised trackway, as dim as a wind-path on the sea, and the straight embanked Roman highway which made the proverb 'Plain as Dunstable Road', or 'Good plain Dunstable'—for Watling Street goes broad and straight through that town. Scott has one of these ghostly old roads in *Guy Mannering.* It was over a heath that had Skiddaw and Saddleback for background, and he calls it a *blind road*—'the track so slightly marked by the passengers' footsteps that it can but be traced by a slight shade of verdure from the darker heath around it, and, being only visible to the eye when at some distance, ceases to be distinguished while the foot is actually treading it.'

   The making of such roads seems one of the most natural operations of man, one in which he least conflicts with nature and the animals. If he makes roads outright and rapidly, for a definite purpose, they may perish as rapidly, like the new roads of modern Japanese enterprise, and their ancient predecessors live on to smile at their ambition. These are the winding ways preferred by your connoisseur today. 'Give me,' says Hazlitt, 'the clear blue sky over my head and the green turf beneath my feet, a winding road before me, and a three-hours' march to dinner—and then to thinking!' These windings are created by the undulating of the land, and by obstacles like those of a river—curves such as those in the High Street of Oxford, which Wordsworth called 'the stream-like windings of that glorious street'. The least obstacle might bring about a loop, if nothing more, and as even a Roman road curled round Silbury Hill, so the path of the Australian savage is to be seen twisting round bush after bush as if it enjoyed the interruption, though it cannot purl like the river at a bend. Probably these twists, besides being unconsciously adapted to the lie of the land, were, as they are still, easeful and pleasant to the rover who had some natural love of journeying. Why go straight? There is nothing at the end of any road better than may be found beside it, though there would be no travel did men believe it. The straight road, except over level and open country, can only be made by those in whom extreme haste and fore-thought have destroyed the power of joy, either at the end or at any part of its course. Why, then, go straight? The connoisseur had some- · thing of the savage in him when he demanded a winding road.

The Icknield Way, 1-5

THE INN

The night was dark and solid rain tumultuously invested the inn. As I stood in a dim passage I could see through the bar into the cloudy parlour, square and white, surrounded by settles, each curving about a round table made of one piece of elm on three legs. A reproduction of 'Rent Day' and a coloured picture of a bold Spanish beauty hung on the wall, which, for the rest, was sufficiently adorned by the sharp shadows of men's figures and furniture that mingled grotesquely. All the men but one leaned back upon the settles or forward upon the tables, their hands on their tankards, watching the one who sang a ballad—a ballad known to them so well that they seemed not to listen, but simply to let the melody surge about them and provoke what thoughts it would. . . .

. . . of all music, the old ballads and folk songs and their airs are richest in the plain, immortal symbols. The best of them seem to be written in a language that should be universal, if only simplicity were truly simple to mankind. Their alphabet is small; their combinations are as the sunlight or the storm, and their words also are symbols. Seldom have they any direct relation to life as the realist believes it to be. They are poor in such detail as reveals a past age or a country not our own. They are in themselves epitomes of whole generations, of a whole countryside. They are the quintessence of many lives and passions made into a sweet cup for posterity. A myriad hearts and voices have in age after age poured themselves into the few notes and words. Doubtless, the old singers were not content, but we, who know them not, can well see in their old songs a kind of immortality for them in wandering on the viewless air. The men and women—who hun-dreds of years ago were eating and drinking and setting their hearts on things—still retain a thin hold on life through the joy of us who hear and sing their songs, or tread their curving footpaths, or note their chisel marks on cathedral stones, or rest upon the undulating church-yard grass. The words, in league with a fair melody, lend themselves to infinite interpretations, according to the listener's heart. What great literature by known authors enables us to interpret thus by virtue of its subtlety, ballads and their music force us to do by their simplicity. The melody and the story or the song move us suddenly and launch us into an unknown. They are not art, they come to us imploring a new lease of life on the sweet earth, and so we come to give them something which the dull eye sees not in the words and notes themselves, out of our own hearts, as we do when we find a black hearthstone among the nettles, or hear the clangour of the joyous wild swan, invisible overhead, in the winter dawn.

In the parlour of the inn the singer stood up and sang of how a girl was walking alone in the meadows of spring when she saw a ship going out to sea and heard her true love crying on board; and he sailed to the wars and much he saw in strange countries, but never came back; and still she walks in the meadows and looks out to sea, though she is old, in the spring. He sang without stirring, without expression, except in so far as light and darkness from his own life emerged enmeshed among the deep notes. He might have been delivering an oracle of solemn but ambiguous things. And so in fact he was. By its simplicity and remoteness from life the song set going the potent logic of fancy which would lead many men to diverse conclusions. It excluded nothing of humanity except what baseness its melody might make impossible. The strangeness and looseness of its framework allowed each man to see himself therein, or some incident or dream in his life, or something possible to a self which he desired to be or imagined himself to be, or perhaps believed himself once to have been. There were no bounds of time or place. It included the love of Ruy Blas, of Marlowe, of Dante, of Catullus, of Kilhwch, of Swift, of Palomides, of Hazlitt, of Villon. . . . And that little inn, in the midst of mountains and immense night, seemed a temple of all souls, where a few faithful ones still burnt candles and remembered the dead.

The Heart of England, 196-9

BALLADS

I CANNOT HELP wondering whether the great work done in the last century and a half towards the recovery of old ballads in their integrity will have any effect beyond the entertainment of a few scientific men and lovers of what is ancient, now that the first effects upon Wordsworth and his contemporaries have died away. Can it possibly give a vigorous impulse to a new school of poetry that shall treat the life of our time and what in past times has most meaning for us as freshly as those ballads did the life of their time? It is possible; and it is surely impossible that such examples of simple, realistic narrative shall be quite in vain. Certainly the more they are read the more they will be respected, and not only because they often deal with heroic matters heroically, but because their style is commonly so beautiful, their pathos so natural, their observation of life so fresh, so fond of

particular detail—its very lists of names being at times real poetry.
 Sometimes the style is equal and like to that of the most accomplished poetry, as in the stanza:

> The Ynglyshe men let ther boys (bows) be,
> And pulde owt brandes that were brighte;
> It was a hevy syght to se
> Bryght swordes on basnites lyght.

Or in:

> God send the land deliverance
> Frae every reaving, riding Scot!
> We'll sune hae neither cow nor ewe,
> We'll sune hae neither staig nor stot.

It is equally good in passages where the poet simply expresses his
hearty delight in something which his own eyes have seen among his
neighbours, as in:

> He had horse and harness for them all,
> Goodly steeds were all milke-white:
> O the golden bands an about their necks,
> And their weapons, they were all alike. . . .

 And, by the way, do not touches like these often reveal the stamp of
individuals upon pieces which are loosely said to have been 'composed by the folk'? They quite do away with the notion that ballads
were composed by a number of people, after the fashion of a story in
the game of Consequences. In fact, it is one of the pleasures of reading
ballads to watch for those things which show us the heart of one man
who stands out by himself. Such a one was the man who said: 'I dreamt
I pu'd the heather green/Wi' my true love on Yarrow.'

The South Country, 241-3

MR STODHAM SPEAKS FOR ENGLAND

SOMEONE with a precocious sneer, asked if England was now anything more than a geographical expression, and Mr Stodham preached
a sermon straight away:
 'A great poet said once upon a time that this earth is "where we have
our happiness or not at all". For most of those who speak his language
he might have said that this England is where we have our happiness or
not at all. He meant to say that we are limited creatures, not angels, and
that our immediate surroundings are enough to exercise all our faculties of mind and body: there is no need to flatter ourselves with the

belief that we could do better in a bigger or another world. Only the bad workman complains of his tools.

'There was another poet who hailed England, his native land, and asked how could it but be dear and holy to him, because he declared himself one who (here Mr Stodham grew very red and his voice rose, and Lewis thought he was going to sing as he recited):

> From thy lakes and mountain-hills,
> Thy clouds, thy quiet dales, thy rocks and seas,
> Have drunk in all my intellectual life,
> All sweet sensations, all ennobling thoughts,
> All adoration of the God in nature,
> All lovely and all honourable things,
> Whatever makes this mortal spirit feel
> The joy and greatness of its future being.
> There lives nor form nor feeling in my soul
> Unborrowed from my country. O divine
> And beauteous island! thou hast been my sole
> And most magnificent temple, in the which
> I walk with awe, and sing my stately songs,
> Loving the God that made me!

'Of course, I do not know what it *all* means,' he muttered, but went on: 'and that other poet who was his friend called the lark: "Type of the wise who soar but never roam,/True to the kindred points of heaven and home." Well, England is home and heaven too. England made you, and of you is England made. Deny England—wise men have done so—and you may find yourself some day denying your father and mother—and this also wise men have done. Having denied England and your father and mother, you may have to deny your own self, and treat it as nothing, a mere conventional boundary, an artifice, by which you are separated from the universe and its creator. To unite yourself with the universe and the creator, you may be tempted to destroy that boundary of your own body and brain, and die. He is a bold man who hopes to do without earth, England, family, and self. Many a man dies, having made little of these things, and if he says at the end of a long life that he has had enough, he means only that he has no capacity for more—*he* is exhausted, not the earth, not England.

'I do not think that a man who knows many languages, many histories, many lands, would ask if England was more than a geographical expression. Nor would he be the first to attempt an answer to one that did ask.

'I do not want you to praise England. She can do without receiving better than you can without giving. I do not want to shout that our great soldiers and poets are greater than those of other nations, but they are ours, they are great, and in proportion as we are good and intelligent, we can respond to them and understand them as those who are not Englishmen cannot. They cannot long do without us or we without them. Think of it. We have each of us some of the blood and spirit of Sir Thomas More, and Sir Philip Sidney, and the man who wrote *Tom Jones*, and Horatio Nelson, and the man who wrote *Love in the Valley*. Think what we owe to them of joy, courage, and mere security. Try to think what they owe to us, since they depend on us for keeping alive their spirits, and a spirit that can value them. They are England: we are England. Deny England, and we deny them and ourselves. Do you love the Wilderness? Do you love Wales? If you do, you love what I understand by "England". The more you love and know England, the more deeply you can love the Wilderness and Wales. I am sure of it. . . .'

At this point Mr Stodham ran away. Nobody thought how like a *very good* rat he was during this speech, or, rather, this series of short speeches interrupted by moments of excitement when all that he could do was to light a pipe and let it out. Higgs, perhaps, came nearest to laughing; for he struck up 'Rule Britannia' with evident pride that he was the first to think of it. This raised my gorge; I could not help shouting 'Home Rule for Ireland'. Whereupon Higgs swore abominably, and I do not know what would have happened if Ann had not said: 'Jessie, my love, sing "Land of my Fathers" ', which is the Welsh national anthem; but when Jessie sang it—in English, for our sakes—everyone but Higgs joined in the chorus and felt that it breathed the spirit of patriotism which Mr Stodham had been trying to express. It was exulting without self-glorification or any other form of brutality. It might well be the national anthem of any nation that knows, and would not rashly destroy, the bonds distinguishing it from the rest of the world without isolating it.

Aurelius, who had been brooding for some time, said: 'I should never have thought it. Mr Stodham has made me a present of a country. I really did not know before that England was not a shocking fiction of the journalists and politicians. I am the richer, and, according to Mr Stodham, so is England. But what about London fog? what is the correct attitude of a patriot towards London fog and the manufacturers who make it what it is?'

The Happy-Go-Lucky Morgans, 220-5

This is an anthology from the work of English writers rather strictly so called. Building round a few most English poems like 'When icicles hang by the wall'—excluding professedly patriotic writing because it is generally bad and because indirect praise is sweeter and more profound—never aiming at what a committee from Great Britain and

Ireland might call complete,—I wished to make a book as full of English character and country as an egg is of meat. If I have reminded others, as I did myself continually, of some of the echoes called up by the name of England, I am satisfied.

Note to *This England*

ENGLAND

IN TIMES of peace and tranquillity the vocabulary of patriotism is not much used. The old songs are sung occasionally without question; in speeches, lectures, and leading articles, where men are licensed, the old forms are repeated. Many a man who is at all particular about meanings of words leaves alone patriotic and religious phrases, with or without a reservation that there are times when they have meant something and will mean something again. Trouble changes this. The most touching phrase of patriotism in *The Anglo-Saxon Chronicle* occurs where the chronicler, writing, I imagine, amid the troubles of the Conquest, records the death of Edward the Confessor. He speaks of Edward dwelling in exile while 'the Danes wielded the dear realm of England.' When Edward the Martyr was murdered at Corfe Castle the chronicler remarked: 'Never was a worse deed done to the English than this was since they first sought Britain.' If England lies like a vast estate calm around you, and you a minor, you may find faults without end. If England seems threatened you feel that in losing her you would lose yourself; she becomes plainly and decidedly 'this dear realm of England'; if you are in exile you may understand how the Roman Emperor in the *Mabinogion* had Roman earth brought to Britain that he might sleep, sit, and walk upon it and keep in health. The old phrases come back alive in war-time. I have heard a farmer's wife refer to England as She. At an ordinary time Henley would say: 'Beef, beer, horses, *Moll Flanders*, and the Church of England, the King, and the *Newgate Calendar*—what is there, what could there be more typically English than these?' But writing *Pro Rege Nostro* the same man saw England 'with glorious eyes austere, as the Lord were walking near', and addressed her as 'You whose mailed hand keeps the keys/Of such teeming destinies. . . .' In print men become capable of anything. The bards and the journalists say extraordinary things. I suppose they do it to encourage the others. They feel that they are addressing the world; they are intoxicated with the social sense. But it is a curious thing that they do not talk like this in private, or I am exceptionally unfortunate in meeting the wrong sort of bards and journalists. In a newspaper a bard, and a young one, will address 'The "Nut" who did not go':

You're a hero bold,
  My gallant son,
Though you do not hold
  A soldier's gun.
For you wave a little flag
Which is quite a bally fag,
Though, perhaps, it is a 'rag'
  And rather fun.

But I never happened to hear bard, journalist, clergyman, or woman using this kind of patriotic phrase in private. I have heard a man say, 'The soldiers are splendid, aren't they? Aren't they all splendid?' I heard a woman say: 'I don't quite know what they mean by England. Sometimes I feel proud, but more often ashamed, though certainly I can't say there is any other country to which I would rather belong.' And I am not sure that love of country can go much farther in words, except under the influence of alcohol or a crowd; that is, among those who only stand and wait. It is, perhaps, curious also that I never was in company where any man or woman said that somebody else ought to enlist. When they have expressed an opinion, soldiers and civilians have said that they cannot understand anyone pointing out his duty to another. I do not conclude that 'my country' and the like are literary phrases, and that men no more use them in real life than they call their mistresses 'Lady' in the style of bards of the 'nineties; but I understand the temptation to this conclusion.

While I was trying to learn from other people what they meant by 'England' and 'my country', I went to a friend who knows his England and is not ignorant of Europe. I did not say, 'Why do you love your country?' but I must have used words to that effect. I wanted to know what he felt. Instead he told me what he thought, now that I asked him. He said: 'What quaint idea is this? Reasons why I love England? Do I love England? If I *prefer* England I expect it is merely that I am accustomed to it, that my material welfare is bound up more or less with that of the whole country, that the greater number of beautiful sensations I have enjoyed are associated with its scenery and its people. These reasons would hold good for any other country, if I had chanced to be born elsewhere.' (He carelessly forgot that if he had been born somewhere else he would have been a different person, and so on.) 'In any case these reasons are not sufficient to make me conscious of any active love of England, in the sense that it would be impossible for me to be quite as happy in any other country—excepting always the loss of old associations.' (He forgot to consider how much he possessed apart from associations.)

'All my material interests are here, and since the war started I have frequently been in a blue funk that I should be left destitute.' (He forgot to consider how much that would matter, if associations counted for comparatively little; for his country would have provided him with food, drink and shelter.) 'So I am patriotic—in the sense that I want the Germans to be smashed.

'I am conscious most of my love of myself; that is, not self-approval, but a *constant* solicitude as to my getting and doing what I like and what I think good for me. Are not all Western people like this? We love ourselves, not our country. If I owned a bit of land I think it might make a great difference to my feelings.' (Here is a chance for a landowner who wants to manufacture patriots.) 'But I don't own any, and in common with the forty-four millions of the dispossessed, I know that I am never likely to. The dice are cogged against us by the capitalists and other cunning monopolists, who, in their turn, love no country but only what they own in it.

'I listened yesterday to a prosperous middle-aged man bullying a booking-office clerk, because our fast evening train from town is temporarily suspended. He was furious about it, as it would mean the loss of, say, half an hour every evening to him. What did he care that the Government wanted extra railway accommodation for a time, in order to ship troops and ammunition in huge quantities? All he was conscious of was that his habits would be interfered with, his dinner a little late every evening.

'This man is a patriot. He says so himself. He has an immense contempt for any enemies of England, and his ignorant, blatant jingoism is an offence to any decent man who happens to share the same compartment in the train with him.

'Are there other, finer kinds of patriots? I don't know them. If by patriots we mean men who wish good to their own country at the expense of no matter what other country, I hope not. For such patriotism is only a high-sounding name for self-interest, self-preservation.' (He forgot that this was what he himself was chiefly conscious of. He was capable of anything, in this mood for applying superhuman standards to everybody.) '*My* instinct is to apply to the whole world Marcus Aurelius's words: "That which is not for the interest of the whole swarm is not for the interest of a single bee."

'In the present crisis I distinguish. I think the good German peoples have been mistaught and misled. Their moral standard is lower than that of their enemies; their victory would mean reaction. I want them, for the sake of the whole world, to be beaten.'

I am sure nobody that he or I would bother about can question his patriotism. But he was eager to dissociate himself from sentiment which he thought false. He is a stickler for the meanings of words. 'Love of England' seemed to him to mean so much that he denied it to himself and apparently to most others. Being naturally a just man he tried to be supernaturally just with his head. Fortunately I knew even more of his feelings than can be gathered from his last sentences. For example, when he was abroad, he was frequently shocked by the table manners of foreigners, and although he is not supernaturally squeamish in conversation when it is a question of amusement, I remember him condemning the French severely because they used as a technical term for a certain machine, and in print, too, a word invoking an obvious gross image. An Englishman would laugh at the image. A Frenchman was not ashamed to use it seriously, and was condemned for it by the Englishman. Also, I have heard this same man say that often he can't help feeling that our men are the best in the field, though he is anxious not to be deceived by that sort of talk. That is to say, he prefers England and English ways when it comes to a comparison. It would not be rash to class him with the other man who said that England was a place where 'one isn't forbidden to do what one wants to do or forced to do what somebody else wants', and that in spite of gamekeepers; for who ever met a landowner in a wood?

I take this to be the foundation of patriotism. It begins with security. When a woman with a child could cross the country safely patriotism began to be certain. Before that, England was 'the island of Britain', 'the land of the English race', rather than England, though 'England' was used almost as early for this island as 'Britain', and the two terms are mixed in the early Chronicle as in the authorized version of the French Yellow Book, which says: 'The statement regarding the intervention of the English fleet is binding on the British Government.' The poem on the Battle of Brunanburh speaks of Edward the Elder's sons defending 'our land, our treasure, and our homes'. In the poem on the Battle of Maldon, the earl facing the Danes with his levy says they will defend 'this homeland, the country of Ethelred my prince, the people and their ground'. Here already is what Wordsworth expressed for the Tyrolese:

> The land we from our fathers had in trust,
> And to our children will transmit, or die:
> This is our maxim, this our piety;
> And God and Nature say that it is just!
> That which we *would* perform in arms—we must!
> We read the dictate in the infant's eye;
> In the wife's smile; and in the placid sky;
> And, at our feet, amid the silent dust
> Of them that were before us.—Sing aloud
> Old songs, the precious music of the heart!
> Give, herds and flocks, your voices to the wind!

> While we go forth, a self-devoted crowd,
> With weapons grasped in fearless hands, to assert
> Our virtue, and to vindicate mankind.

By the time of the Battle of Maldon men had long possessed and often defended irreplaceable things in England. Out of England the same men would have had nothing unless they had a sword. They had begun to realize that without England they were little or nothing: that with England they were 'greater than they knew', since, according to their strength and their affection they were part of what Milton says a commonwealth should be, 'one huge Christian personage, one mighty growth and stature of an honest man, as big and compact in virtue as in body'. Men forgot that the English race came once upon a time to Britain and made it England. They were preparing to think of Britain as rising out of the sea at Heaven's command, with the sovereignty of the sea, as Edward III says in Blake's play:

> That Heaven gave
> To England, when at the birth of nature
> She was seated in the deep; the ocean ceased
> His mighty roar, and fawning played around
> Her snowy feet, and owned his awful Queen.

Two little things in early English history suggest England more vividly to me than bigger things. One is the very stunted hawthorn round which the battle of Ashdown mainly clashed, between the Danes and King Ethelred with his brother Alfred and the Christian host, 'fighting for life, and their loved ones, and their native land'. Two kings and five earls of the 'pagans' fell there, says Asser, who tells the tale; and he had with his own eyes seen the tree. Incidentally I know by this that the Berkshire down-top there by the Ridgeway was no more wooded then than it is now. But above all it tells me of the making of landmarks and the beginning of historic places. Of such things has England gradually been made, not lifted at one stroke by Heaven's command out of the azure main. The other little thing is the hoar apple tree where Harold's host met the Conqueror near Hastings. Here I have a foretaste of the England of Chaucer and of Langland, who, in one book, could speak confidently of such widely separated parts of England as London, Walsingham, Banbury, and the Malvern Hills, and of so many parts of London as Cornhill, East Cheap, Shoreditch, Stratford, Tyburn, and Southwark. There was a man, half-Londoner, half-Worcestershireman, and all Englishman. Even so was Walton, three centuries later, half-Londoner, half-countryman, as he shows in many a passage like this:—'When I go to dress an Eel thus, I wish he were as long and as big as that which was caught in Peterborough river in the year 1667; which was a yard and three-quarters long. If you will not believe me, then go and see at one of the coffee-houses in King Street in Westminster.'

Many of the early kings and earls, in the same way, were partly Kentish or Hampshire men, partly, on great occasions, Englishmen. Already, before Langland, a Gloucester man, Robert of Gloucester, had called England 'merry' in his chronicle: 'England is a right merry land, of all on earth it is best,/Set in the end of the world, as here, all in the west.' It was the Merry England of the English people, 'full of mirth and of game, and men oft-times able to mirth and game, free men of heart and with tongue'. Whether it would have seemed Merry England if Robert had been writing in Sussex or Northumberland is not certain. For I take it that England then as now was a place of innumerable holes and corners, and most men loved—or, at any rate, could not do without—some one or two of these, and loved all England, but probably seldom said so, because without it the part could not exist. The common man was like a maggot snug in the core of an apple: without apples there are no cores he knew well, nor apples without cores. Giraldus Cambrensis put this beautifully in speaking of his birthplace, Manorbier in Pembroke. Demetia, he said, was the most beautiful as well as the most powerful part of Wales, Pembroke the finest part of Demetia, Manorbier the most delightful part of Pembroke: 'it is evident, therefore, that Manorbier is the pleasantest spot in Wales.'

Throughout English history you have the two elements combined inseparably, love of the place where you 'have your happiness or not at all', and a more fitfully conscious love of the island, and glory in its glories. On the one hand Edward Leigh, who lived a hundred years in the sixteenth and seventeenth centuries, quotes at the end of his advice to travellers these words of Sir Benjamin Rudyard: 'France is a good country to ride through, Italy a good country to look upon, Spain a good country to understand, but England a good country to live in.' For an Englishman England was the snuggest place under the sun, and he imagined it made for him like a house. Cowper called it the Heaven-protected isle

> Where Peace and Equity and Freedom smile,
> Where no volcano pours his fiery flood,
> No crested warrior dips his plume in blood. . . .

Everything centres round such an isle. Wordsworth calls the evening star, seeing it from Calais as it sets over England, 'star of my country'. To Hazlitt England was the place for bells and nonsense. 'Bells,' he says, 'are peculiar to England'; and 'I flatter myself that we are almost the only people who understand and relish *non*sense.' England was, for Blake, 'the primitive seat of the Patriarchal Religion': for (or therefore) 'All things begin and end in Albion's ancient Druid rocky shore.'

On the other hand, there is a more active patriotism of comparison and aggression. The patriot scorns other lands which he does not know and could not live in: he delights to discover and assert that foreigners living in different houses on different food are inferior to his countrymen. Raleigh answers the question whether the Roman or the Macedonian were the better warrior by saying: 'The Englishman.' But stay-at-home Englishmen treat their neighbours across the bridge or the hill not much better. The Wiltshireman says that Hampshire is where they held the pig up to see the band go by, and the Hampshireman says that Wiltshire is where they buried the donkey on his back with his feet out of the ground so that they could polish his shoes. The very villages have been honoured thus by satirical neighbours: Aldbourne in Wiltshire is where they tried to drown the moorhen, and Wroughton (I think) is where they gave the pig a watch to see when it was time to eat.

A happy nation luxuriates in its differences and distinctions, as a county does in its Selsey cockle, Chichester lobster, Arundel mullet, and Amberley trout. The people of such a nation can taste and enjoy the patriotism of another people, like the Tyrolese, or a bygone patriotism defeated in its own land, as Wordsworth did the patriotism of the Ancient Britons:

> Mark, how all things swerve
> From their known course, or vanish like a dream;
> Another language spreads from coast to coast;
> Only perchance some melancholy Stream
> And some indignant Hills old names preserve,
> When laws, and creeds, and people all are lost.

The more differences a nation has had freedom to preserve or to develop, I should say, the greater the variety of affections it will concentrate from time to time, and as civilization advances the more complicated will be the affections felt towards it by those who know more than one or two holes and corners, by those with the purest culture. There comes a thrill, today at least, on hearing so complete an Englishman as Walton say out of the fullness of his knowledge that 'certain fields near Leominster, a town in Herefordshire, are observed to make the sheep that graze upon them more fat than the next and also to bear finer wool; . . . which I tell you, that you may the better believe that I am certain, if I catch a trout in one meadow he shall be white and faint, and very like to be lousy; and, as certainly, if I catch a trout in the next meadow, he shall be strong, and red, and lusty, and much better meat'.

Englishmen are more different from one another than from foreigners who all seem alike: they will quarrel together like husband

and wife who know one another's weaknesses yet will turn as one upon the outsider who interferes. For we have gone so far in security, and the idiosyncrasy and pride born of it, that we can criticize and attack not only one another but even the whole, which is at one time a jealous God and at another a kindly nurse; there is no need to be always blindly shouting like schoolboys at a football match.

I suppose a time comes when shouting and waving a flag is the best or only thing worth doing if you are not being shouted or waved for, when one of our national growths, men or ideas, has triumphed. For if there is a patriotism that does not lose its savour by being carried too far over the sea it is one like Milton's where he first praises 'the stout and manly prowess of the German disdaining servitude; the generous and lively impetuosity of the French; the calm and stately valour of the Spaniard; the composed and wary magnanimity of the Italian', and then beholds 'the nations of the earth recovering that liberty which they so long had lost; and the people of this island transporting to other countries a plant of more beneficial qualities, a more noble growth, than that which Triptolemus is reported to have carried from region to region, disseminating the blessings of freedom and civilization among citizens, kingdoms, and nations'. In time of war the differences get sunk, though still one regimental band plays 'The Lincolnshire Poacher' and another 'Ap Shenkin'; and either we see or fancy some one of our virtues, our beefsteak or our liberty or our regard for small nationalities, being acknowledged in a practical manner by the enemy; or we become excessively conscious of our weaknesses, misdeeds, shortcomings, as Coleridge did when he was in fear of an invasion in 1798, or as Mr Horatio Bottomley does in the lines:

Come, comrade, we must answer—and let our answer be—
Why is the red blood flowing?—*To chasten you and me.*

But right or wrong, if it is a question of existence, it is hardly easier for a man to imagine his country beaten down than to imagine himself dead, and I have heard reasonable, anxious, and careful men say they never have any doubt that we shall win.

A writer in *The Times* on patriotic poetry said a good thing lately: 'There may be pleasanter places; there is no *word* like home.' A man may have this feeling even in a far quarter of England. One man said to me that he felt it, that he felt England very strongly, one evening at Stogumber under the Quantocks. His train stopped at the station which was quite silent, and only an old old man got in, bent, gnarled, and gross, a Caliban; 'but somehow he fitted in with the darkness and the quietness and the smell of burning wood, and it was all something I loved being part of.' We feel it in war-time or coming from abroad, though we may be far from home: the whole land is suddenly home.

Wordsworth felt it in the valley near Dover immediately after landing in August 1802, when he wrote the sonnet beginning:

> Here on our native soil we breathe once more.
> The cock that crows, the smoke that curls, that sound
> Of bells;—those boys who in yon meadow-ground
> In white-sleeved shirts are playing; and the roar
> Of the waves breaking on the chalky shore;—
> All, all are English. . . .

Some books can give the same feeling. I took up the *Compleat Angler* the other day, and felt it there. Since the war began I have not met so English a book, a book that filled me so with a sense of England, as this, though I have handled scores of deliberately patriotic works. There, in that sort of work, you get, as it were, the shouting without the crowd, which is ghastly. In Walton's book I touched the antiquity and sweetness of England—English fields, English people, English poetry, all together. You have them all in one sentence, where the Milkwoman, mother of Maudlin the milkmaid, is speaking to Piscator and Venator: 'If you will but speak the word, I will make you a good syllabub of new verjuice: and then you may sit down in a haycock, and eat it; and Maudlin shall sit by and sing you the good old song of the "Hunting in Chevy Chase", or some other good ballad, for she hath store of them: Maudlin, my honest Maudlin, hath a notable memory, and she thinks nothing too good for you, because you be such honest men.' They are all in two sentences of Piscator's: 'And now look about you and see how pleasantly that meadow looks; nay, and the earth smells so sweetly, too. Come, let me tell you what holy Mr Herbert says of such days and flowers as these, and then we will thank God that we enjoy them, and walk to the river and sit down quietly, and try to catch the other brace of trout': then he quotes Herbert's 'Sweet day, so cool, so calm, so bright. . . .'

This man knew England and the men who knew England best—Camden and Michael Drayton. Drayton, the author of *Polyolbion* and the ballad of Agincourt, was Walton's 'honest old friend'. There is one other passage which I shall quote, though my subject is not the *Compleat Angler*, because it reminds us how much a man may be lord of that he does not possess. He is speaking of some fields which belonged to a rich man with many lawsuits pending, yet he who 'pretended no title' to them could take a sweet content in them: 'For I could sit there quietly, and looking on the water see some fishes sport themselves in the silver streams, others leaping at flies of various shapes and colours; looking on the hills, I could behold them spotted with woods and groves; looking down the meadows could see, here a boy gathering lilies and ladysmocks, and there a girl cropping culverkeys and cowslips, all to make garlands suitable to this present month of May: these and many other field-flowers so perfumed the air that I thought that very meadow like that field in Sicily of which Diodorus speaks, where the perfumes arising from the place make all dogs that hunt in it to fall off, and to lose their hottest scent. I say, as I thus sat, joying in my own happy condition, and pitying this poor rich man that owned this and many other pleasant groves and meadows about me, I did thankfully remember what my Saviour said, that the meek possess the earth. . . .' I believe the man who thought it a 'quaint' idea to love England would feel very much as I do about these passages and about Walton altogether. I believe that England means something like this to most of us; that all ideas of England are developed, spun out, from such a centre into something large or infinite, solid or aëry, according to each man's nature and capacity; that England is a system of vast circumferences circling round the minute neighbouring points of home.   *The Last Sheaf,* 91-111

I should like to know what the old soldier meant by 'England', if it was anything more than some sort of a giant with Gloucestershire for its eyes, its beating heart, for everything that raised it above a personification. His was a very little England. The core and vital principle was less still, a few thousand acres of corn, meadow, orchard, and copse, a few farms and cottages; and he laughed heartily over a farmer's artfulness who had hid away some horses wanted by the War Office. If England was against Germany, the parish was against Germany, England, and all the world. Some of his neighbours, not so fearless, went even greater lengths in their parochialism. They had made up their minds about invasion. They not only imagined themselves suffering like Belgian peasants, but being specially attacked in the Forest of Dean by German aeroplanes. Napoleon, a hundred years ago, was expected to sail up the Severn and destroy the Forest: now it was feared that the Germans were coming.
                  From 'It's a Long, Long Way', *The Last Sheaf,* 136

TIPPERARY

To the tune of 'It's a long, long way to Tipperary' I have just travelled through England, from Swindon to Newcastle-on-Tyne, listening to people, in railway carriages, trams, taverns, and public places, talking about the war and the effects of it. They were people, for the most part, who worked with their hands, and had as little to do with the pen as with the sword. The period was from 29 August to 10 September, when everybody in town and village, excepting as a rule, the station-master, was discussing the transport of Russian troops down the country—'if they were not Russians, then they were Canadians or else

Indians', as a man said in Birmingham. I shall write down, as nearly as possible, what I saw and heard, hoping not to offend too much those who had ready-made notions as to how an Imperial people should or would behave in time of war, of such a war, and while the uncertainty was very dark. For their sakes I regret that men should everywhere be joking when our soldiers were fighting and our poets writing hard. Though not magnificent, it is war. At Coventry a fat man stepped stately off a weighing machine. Seventeen stone, accumulated in peace. A lean man with a duck's-bill nose at once attacked him. 'You're the sort of man that stays behind, while a lot of fine young fellows go to fight for their country. I suppose you stay to take care of the ladies. When the Kaiser reaches Coventry he'll see a lot like you. You ought to be ashamed of yourself. You will be.'

Every one had his joke. The porter who dropped something and caused another to jump, covered up his fault by exclaiming, 'Here come the Germans.' Precisely the same remark was made when small boys let off crackers after dark. The hostess with the false hair, being asked if her husband had gone to the war, and how she liked the idea of his being in Paris, replied with a titter that she did not fear—'the gay girls have all left Paris.' More serious, but not more satisfactory, were the thousands of young men streaming away from the football ground at Sheffield on a Saturday afternoon. Yet even at a football match recruiting can be done and the hat sent round. Some professionals were paying five per cent. of their wages to the Relief Fund, as men in a number of factories were contributing 2*d.* or 3*d.* a week. And a man in blue overalls said to me in Birmingham, 'If a man doesn't fight, he will do better to go to a football match than to drink in a pub or stay indoors moping.' On the other hand, every one seemed to acknowledge that the war was the great thing; at the free library a hundred shuffling coughers were studying war to one that concentrated on Aston Villa.

The most cheerful man I met was reading the *British Weekly*, and continually saying rotund and benignant things. 'The Irish,' he would pronounce, 'have responded manfully. In fact, this unfortunate business has bound people together more than anything else could have done.' A young Northumbrian recruit was the most wretched. He had walked twenty-six miles to enlist. 'I wish to God I was back again in the village,' he said, 'though it is a cock-eyed little place. Since I came here I haven't had a wash or a brush or changed my clothes. If I were you I would sit farther off. I have had a cement floor for a bed, and some of them singing till three in the morning. We have to be out at six. The food's all right, but it's worse than a dog's life. I wish I could get back, and I will too.' Here a recruit of slightly longer standing, and already wearing a uniform, cut in with, 'I wish I had your chance, I'd be off. We have been moved fifteen times since July.'

'You'll be all right in a day or two,' said a decent, wooden-legged man, flicking away this fly from the jam of patriotism.

Most men fell short of the recruit in wretchedness and the reader of the *British Weekly* in benignity. Unless the Kaiser was mentioned they used, as a rule, the moderate language of sober hope or philosophic doubt. The one act of violence I witnessed was an oldish man, with a head like a German Christ, knocking down a sot who persisted in saying, 'You look like a—German.' More typical was the man I overheard at Ardwick, talking of the black and white pig he was fattening for Christmas, regardless of the fact that the Kaiser had God 'magnificently supporting him'.

Wherever I went I was told that employers—'the best firms'—were dismissing men, the younger unmarried men, in order to drive them to enlist. 'Not exactly to drive them,' said one, 'but to encourage.' Nobody complained. They suggested that the 'Government' had put the employers up to it, or that 'It don't seem hardly fair', or 'It comes near conscription, and only those that don't care will give up good wages and leave their wives to charity.' One old man at Sheffield remarked that it used to be, 'Oh, you're too old' for a job; now it's 'You're too young.' It was added that the men's places were to be kept open for them; they were to receive part of their wages; if rejected by the doctor, they would be taken back. 'They *have* to like it,' said one man. These were not the only men who had lost their work. The jewellery-makers of Birmingham, for example, young or old, could not expect to be employed in war-time. Collieries near Newcastle that used to supply Germany were naturally idle, and many of the lads from these pits enlisted. Factories that supplied Russia were not busy either, and Russian debts looked like bad debts. Some trades were profiting by the war. Leicester was so busy making boots for the English and French armies that it had to refuse an order from the Greek army. Harness-makers had as much work as they could do at Walsall. The factories for explosives at Elswick the same. Publicans were flourishing though still ambitious; one public-house at Manchester had these 'Imperial Ballads' printed on a placard:

> What plucks your courage up each day;
> What washes all your cares away?
> What word do you most often say?
> Why, Imperial!

the reference being to a drink of that name. But these successes were extraordinary. Already it was said at Newcastle that shop-assistants were serving for longer hours at reduced pay. Men in motor-car works were on short time. A photographer at Manchester had to resort to this advertisement:

> Gone to the front!
> A beautiful enlargement of any photo of our brave comrades
> may be had at a discount of 25 per cent.

Where relief was being given, a queue of women stood along a wall in the sun.

For the women the sun was too hot, but not for the corn, the clover-hay, the apples, of this great summer, nor for the recruits sleeping out. The sun gilded and regilded the gingerbread. Everybody that could, made an effort to rise to the occasion of the weather. The parks and the public gardens were thronged. The public-houses overflowed, often with but a single soldier as an excuse. Bands played in the streets—at Newcastle bagpipes—to quicken recruiting. A crowd listened to a band at Birmingham outside the theatre before going in to hear Mr Lewis Waller recite 'Kipling and Shakespeare', and the first remark to break the ensuing silence was, 'It's by far the best band in Birmingham, by far.' Street meetings having no connection with the war were held. Men in the Bull Ring at Birmingham one afternoon argued furiously on faith and works, quoting Scripture amid eager onlookers. At the top of Oldham Street, Manchester, two knots of men on a Sunday evening debated what would or would not happen under Socialism, while one in the centre of a looser knot shouted, 'Oh, my friends, God wants all of you.' The war, in fact, was the one subject that was not debated in public. A man breaking this rule was branded a Socialist. For instance, near the statue of James Watt at Birmingham a man had got into an argument about the provision for soldiers' wives. Moistening dry lips with dry tongue, he declared that the working class made fifty times the sacrifice of the upper class. He met nothing but opposition, and perhaps only persevered because he was wedged tight among his enemies and could not for ever keep his eyes downcast. At length a vigorous elderly man in a grey suit stepped in with fists clenched, said he was a working man himself, and laid it down that every one's business was to fight, to sink class, and to avoid quarrelling. His wife, smiling behind him, told the heretic that he ought to be ashamed. Someone chipped in, saying that as a matter of fact many wives were better off with their one-and-twopence than when the men were working. 'God help them before!' ejaculated the solitary man. Then another said he was going himself, and would go if his wife was penniless. 'Hear, hear!' said several; and others muttered, 'These here Socialists.' Of course, class feeling did exist. A workman in Birmingham hoped that not too many of the well-to-do would go to the front, because they were needed to give employment and to control it. The rich and the working-class, said a Coventry man, were doing their duty, but not the middle class—he called it the 'second class'—'these young fellows who are neither man nor girl, and think about their socks all day'.

The war was not debated, but every one was bound to turn into it as into a main road of conversation, bound also to turn out of it. It could not be avoided. The newspapers issued edition after edition without reason. Pavement artists were strong on admirals, generals, and ships. Portraits of General French and Admiral Jellicoe adorned the entrances to picture palaces. Someone had chalked on a pavement at Manchester: 'See no sports. Fight the good fight.' Young men going to work by train began talking about the Russians. One interjected that he *was* glad to receive his salary in full at the end of the month. Another looked up from his paper saying, 'Kitchener's getting his second hundred thousand.' A Socialist was quoted as having said that 'we might as well be exploited by Germans as by British'. Gradually they drifted into stories about public men, into indecent stories about anybody, until running into a fog at Birmingham one exclaimed: 'It's a bombardment. We must be careful what we do and say today. It's a warning.' Older men going out to the Peak for Sunday, zigzagged from fishing yarns to 'uncreditable' tales told by a German in the Secret Service, on to the moorland appetite that makes you eat three-quarters of a pound of ham at a meal, and back again to 'I haven't had a day off except Sunday since the war began.' 'You durstn't.' The street roar of Newcastle or Sheffield was compounded of hoofs, boots, wheels, gongs, a thousand voices interwoven and one shouting, 'Fourth edition', one whispering, 'If Turkey . . .'

Conversations definitely on the subject of the war, fed on the abstract diet which the Press provided, were much of a muchness. A man began reading: 'This bloke says the rapidity of the German advance on Paris fairly stupefied the French', or he reminded his friend that 'this war has often been predicted in this very place'. A man interrupted his game of dominoes to say: 'I thought before now we were going to cut the German communications.' A man stands silent for a long time among his mates, and suddenly blurts out: 'What I want to know is, are these bombs' (he means mines) 'made of iron?' A favourite opening was, 'There's some great move coming.' The end of a conversation about the retreat was: 'The English have always been cool, calm, and collected.'

All kinds of abstract legends were current, as that the Germans were cowards, that the Kaiser was mad; but not many concrete ones. There was the Russian legend. Then there was a tale earlier in the war that British wounded were arriving at Grimsby, and the town was like a shambles. One man actually in Grimsby, answering an inquiry on the telephone, said that this was so; but another was able to deny it on good evidence.

One of the legends was that England was careless and slack. In the levelling of this charge I think there was a certain fondness as well as indignation. Men liked to think that we could play bowls and win a battle in the same day. 'England is too good-hearted,' said a man at Swindon. He came into the bar asking for 'Down where the water-lilies grow' on the gramophone, and, being disappointed, he sighed and began to speak of his 'month of misery'; for he had three sons and five nephews, or, as he sometimes put it, five sons and three nephews, at the front. 'The English are too good-hearted. Here, look 'ee. If any damned foreigner comes into this bar we give him a penny as soon as if he was an Englishman. Now I thinks and studies a lot. You recollect the manoeuvres at Faringdon? Well, there was all nations there, Germans, Italians, Russians, French, Egyptians, and I don't know what—fifteen nations. Do you think they wasn't taking notes? Of course they were. And the Kaiser—the mad bull—didn't he come over and kiss King Edward, and wouldn't he as soon have knocked him down?' There was a man at Birmingham who began by talking about the Russians and Ostend, two millions of them, he believed. Oh, yes, they had certainly come down through England by night. He thought the Russians would repay the Germans for their atrocities. Nor do I think he minded. Yet he drew satisfaction from the faith that the English themselves would not retaliate. No, he said, the English are 'easy'. A Sheffield man who was advocating the bloodiest treatment for the Kaiser said that, 'If English soldiers fired at the Red Cross, Lord Kitchener would blow their brains out, he would.' Men were bloody-minded, to judge by their talk. They would have had no patience with the gentle person who had his favourite horse shot to save it from the battle-field. More intelligible to them would have been the gentleman of Cromwell's time who sent orders to have the sucking foals slaughtered that the mares might become chargers.

Such men had a strong, simple idea of a perfidious barbaric Germany. 'They have been preparing for this war ever since old Queen Vic died, and before that. I'd turn all the Germans out of England, same as they would turn us out.' 'I wouldn't; I would shoot the lot of them.' 'These nationalized Germans—you don't know what they are up to. Double-faced, they're all double-faced. They're savages, killing children and old men. I'd like to get at the Kaiser. I wouldn't kill him. I'd just turn him loose. . . .' 'I wouldn't. If I could get at him, I'd . . . and choke him with them.' Thus spoke two workmen in Coventry. An old woman at Swindon—one of thousands—wanted to 'get at the Kaiser'. Everywhere men were drinking health—with a wink and 'You know what I mean'—to the Kaiser or the 'King of Proosher'. A very sober workman of fifty in Newcastle who was working short time simply did not know what epithets to give the man, and had to relapse on 'that tinker' (with much expression). Almost the only judicious reference to him that I heard was: 'Either the Kaiser is mad or he has found a new explosive.' People varied a little more in their attitude towards the German nation. 'They have got to be swept out of Europe,' said a man at Sheffield. A gentle old man was going to Harrogate with 'nerves run down' and 'distorted views', and he had got it into his head that he had eaten a German sausage. The man with the *British Weekly* was consoling him: 'Oh, you may depend upon it, it did not come from Germany. There's nothing coming from there now. They make a great quantity at Leeds. They don't call it German sausage either.' A Tyneside Scot, after pronouncing the Kaiser mad to make war on 'all nations', said: 'The Germans are a rotten lot. They won't stand and fight like any other nation. They keep moving all the time.' Others regarded the German army as a sort of ridiculous bully and coward, with this one grace, that it would probably shoot the Kaiser. A few praised German strategy and organization. One youth at Manchester even ventured to think 'they must be a fine race of soldiers'. A man at Sheffield held up a pair of German nail-scissors, lamenting that now he could not buy anything so neat at fourpence-halfpenny. A man at Manchester was asking: 'Where shall we get our gas mantles?' It was a Coventry man who went so far as to say that the German people were as good as ourselves and not so very different. 'They don't want war. It's not the Kaiser either. It's the aristocracy. Still, the Kaiser must not come here, like other deposed monarchs.'

This man, like every one else, was sure of victory. Some expected Paris to fall, but . . . They only laughed at any doubter. Most held the opinion that in retiring on Paris the Allies were leading the enemy into a trap. They did not stomach the idea of English soldiers retiring and retiring, and they imagined it must be deliberate. Open boasting had gone out of fashion, unless the man is a boaster who says on a black day that an Englishman is equal to five Germans. Patriotism took subtler forms. It was reported that one of the new Territorials weighed nineteen stone. 'Oh, but he will soon lose four or five stone, don't you fear. It's a healthy life, a grand life.' 'What I most rejoice at,' said a man at Swindon, 'is that we did not want the war.' Scores said something like it. It was 'the greatest war of all time', said all sorts of people. In Sheffield a solitary pessimist was content to think it the ruin of Europe, a great sudden movement in 'evolution'. The dirtiest man in Sheffield, with the most rasping voice, talking among his mates on a Saturday afternoon about rights of way, dukes, corporations, trespassing, and poaching, jerked out the remark: 'The capitalist is forking out now to save his own property.' A printer in the same town said: 'We are not soldiers or politicians; we are workmen. We have our trades, it is not for us to fight. That is another trade: let the soldiers fight. That is what I used to say; but it won't do now. All I can say is that I don't feel like fighting, myself. There is a great deal of loyalty everywhere, and I hope we shall win.'

Peace was not much talked about. A man at Swindon was figuring a reconstruction of Europe after the war. 'Why,' he asked, 'why shouldn't all the countries be bound together like the United States? There are a lot of nationalities over there, and they agree very well, I fancy.' Probably many were using the same phrases as the Birmingham chess-player: 'The pity of it, when you think of all the education in England and Germany. *We* don't go out into the street and fight if we have a difference. It sets a bad example to the nation.' 'It's man's nature to fight.' 'It isn't mine.' 'Your move.'

Only one eloquent militarist did I hear, a Manchester Irishman. He, too, declared it man's nature to fight. From Cain and Abel, having demolished and labelled as un-Christian the suggestion that we were descended from monkeys, he branched out to the animals. 'It's the same everywhere,' he said. 'They must hit out. Until they have hit out, they don't know themselves. To hit out is a man's very life and nature, the best he can do, his greatest pleasure, what he was made for. Most of us have to obey the law, if we can. But the soldier is a hired law-breaker and murderer, and we must let him enjoy himself sometimes. Don't you go pitying the poor soldier. Poor soldier! This is the time he has been waiting for. He is in a passion, and nothing hurts him. Sudden death is a glorious thing.'

This was not a soldier. He was a workman, a looker-on, one of the thousand loitering workers and unemployed who stare at the hundred recruits between the statues of Watt and Edward VII at Birmingham, and in squares or by-streets all over the country. The soldier has another style. A crippled pensioner at Birmingham said simply that if he was fit they would not have to call him twice; then he gossiped of the Burmah war, of catching and killing your own mutton before eating it, of an immortally tough bullock, of having a foot cut off by a Dacoit, of how far better off today's soldier is with his bacon and jam and tea for breakfast. A soldier's father at Swindon just said his son was glad to go, but wished it had been with Buller. These were men who would not be hurt till they were struck, and I do not know how much then. The Irishman was not one to squander himself on a battlefield; his duty to his country was to preserve his tongue without having to hold it. But he was a patriot.

Probably there are two kinds of patriot; one that can talk or write, and one that cannot; though I suspect that even the talkers and writers often come down in the end to 'I do not understand. I love.' It must happen more than once or twice that a man who can say why he ought to fight for his country fails to enlist. The very phrase, 'to fight for one's country', is a shade too poetical and conscious for any but non-combatants. A man enlists for some inexplicable reason which he may translate into simple, conventional terms. If he has thought a good deal about it, he has made a jump at some point, beyond the reach of his thought. The articulate and the inarticulate are united in the ranks at this moment by the power to make that jump and come to the extreme decision. I heard a mother trying to persuade—pretending she was trying to persuade—a young man against enlisting. She said: 'I would not risk my life for anybody. It isn't yours, for one thing. Think of Mary. I would sooner go to America. . . .' She found a hundred things to say, few of them quite genuine, since it was her desire to overpower him, not to express herself. In argument he was overpowered. His reasons he could not give. Nevertheless, if he passed the doctor he was going; if the doctor rejected him, he rather hoped some girl would taunt him—she would have to produce a champion to justify her. Had the eleven or twelve thousand recruits from Birmingham written down their reasons, I dare say they would not have been worth much more than the pen, ink, and paper. That is, assuming they included no poets, and I do not see that they were more likely to prove poets than the men, women, and children who made haste to send in their verses to the papers. Out of the crowd at Newcastle the dissatisfied one spoke best. If any at Coventry or elsewhere were kept waiting so long outside the recruiting office that they changed their minds and went away, they might speak better still. Some men of spirit may have kept back to spite their interfering persuaders. Why, the lowest slut in the town, fetching her beer at eleven-thirty, would look after a procession of recruits and say: 'So they ought to. Lord! look what a lot of fellows hang about the corners. They ought to fight for their country.'

There was really no monotony of type among these recruits, though the great majority wore dark clothes and caps, had pale faces tending to leanness, and stood somewhere about five foot seven. It was only the beginning, some thought, of a wide awakening to a sense of the danger and the responsibility. Clean and dirty—some of them, that is, straight from the factory—of all ages and features, they were pouring in. Some might be loafers, far more were workers. I heard that of one batch of two hundred and fifty at Newcastle, not one was leaving less than two pounds a week. Here and there a tanned farm labourer with lighter-coloured, often brownish, clothes, chequered the pale-faced dark company. The streets never lacked a body of them or a tail disappearing. Their tents, their squads drilling this way and that, occupied the great bare Town Moor above Newcastle. The town was like a vast fair where men were changing hands instead of cattle. The ordinary racket of tramcar and crowd was drowned by brass instruments, bagpipes, drums and tin boxes beaten by small boys, men in fifties and in hundreds rounding a corner to the tune of 'It's a long, long way to Tipperary'. Thousands stood to watch them. With crowds on the kerbstones, with other crowds going up and down and across, with men squatting forward on the pavement, it was best to have no object but to go in and out. The recruits were the constant, not the only attraction. The newest ones marching assumed as military a stiff uprightness as possible. The older ones in uniform were slacker. Some stood at corners talking to girls; others went in and out of 'pubs' attended by civilians; more and more slouched, or staggered, or were heavy-eyed with alcohol. Everyone was talking, but the only words intelligible were 'Four o'clock winner' and 'It's a long, long way to Tipperary'. At nightfall the boys who beat the drums and tins began to carry around an effigy and to sing 'The Kaiser, the Kaiser' or

> And when we go to war
> We'll put him in a jar,
> And he'll never see his daddy any more.

  Companies of recruits were still appearing. Perhaps their faces were drawn and shining with drink, fatigue, and excitement, but they remained cheerful even when a young officer with a dry, lean face and no expression said 'Good night' without expression and rode off. His was the one expressionless, dead calm face in the city, the one that seemed to have business of its own, until I crossed the river and saw the women on the doorsteps of the steep slum, the children on pavement and in gutter. They were not excited by the fever in Clayton Street and Market Street, any more than by St Mary's bells banging away high above slum and river, or by the preacher at the top of Church Street bellowing about 'the blessed blood of Jesus Christ'. In an almost empty tavern a quiet old man was treating a lad in a new uniform, and giving him advice: 'Eat as much as you can, and have a contented mind.' It was a fine warm evening. But what could the great crowd do to spend its excitement? As a crowd, nothing. In a short time it was doubled. For at nine o'clock the public-houses had to be emptied and shut. The burly bell of St Nicholas tolled nine over thousands with nothing to do. Those who had not taken time by the forelock and drunk as much as they would normally have done by eleven, stood about aimlessly. A man took his stand in Bigg Market and sang for money. It was not what people wanted. Several youths got together at a short distance and tried to bawl down the singer. Even that was not what people wanted. Even the temperance man was only half pleased when he reflected that what he had long agitated for in vain had been done by one stroke of the military pen. There was nothing to be done but to go to bed and wait for the morning papers.   113-34

SOLDIERS EVERYWHERE

THE FIRST MAN I met this morning was a soldier. He was riding and shouting 'Son of a bitch!' after a runaway horse which I expected to run me down in the narrow road. But the horse dislikes hurting anyone but an enemy, and as he approached me he slowed up. 'Stop him!' shouted the soldier in a Welsh accent. 'Rise your hand; he won't come at you then.' I raised my hand, and the horse stopped. The soldier rode cautiously towards him. When he was within a dozen yards he gave up threats and insults, saying very respectfully: 'Come on, Thomas.' The horse stood still, with his head towards the hedge. A few yards more, and the Welshman addressed him in an affectionate tone, almost endearingly: 'Come on, Tom; come along.' But as he leant out to seize the halter, up went Tom into the air, twice his former length and half his height, with two legs, as it seemed, over one hedge and two over the other, yet without kicking anything. Then away he went like the wind, but with more noise, followed by the soldier's warning, 'You wicked ——! I'll warm you when I get you!' After these stages had thrice been gone through the horse was caught, which gave the Welshman so much satisfaction that he forgot to perform his promise.

The railway carriage was almost packed by two sailors lying at length upon the seats, sober and tired out. I managed, however, to slip into one corner by the door, and a young farmer into the other, and so we travelled some distance. At each station, whenever someone was about to enter the carriage, the farmer winked and jerked his head towards the sailors; if necessary, he added: 'Best leave them to have their sleep out.' Thus the sailors were not disturbed until we reached a station near a big camp. The platform was crowded. Two navvies stumbled in upon us, good-humouredly protesting against the sailors changing position, but sitting down as good-humouredly. They began to talk about the camp. Bread was sixpence a loaf there at the canteen, and matches a halfpenny a box; their breakfast, dinner, and tea on Sunday had cost them three and sixpence a head. One of them had picked up a fragment of some unidentifiable instrument with figures on it, and wanted to know if the sailors, or the farmer, or I could tell him if it was part of an aeroplane and what it was worth. The other navvy laughed when he read out the figures, 8 to 12, and explained that they meant 'the time you have got to meet the young woman'. The finder went on trying to read the maker's name. As he had only one good eye, he made slow progress. But he was proud both of the good and the other eye. That he had lost in the Boer War. The survivor, he said, was good enough for a soldier. He laid me five shillings that he could read as well with his one as I with two. He did not know that I had good sight and was accustomed to reading, and he lost the bet (but not the money). Three times, he said, he had offered to re-enlist. They were getting used to him. Last time he went the porter just shouted 'Here's that one-eyed bloke again'; and the doctor just shouted back 'Turn him out!' He was too indignant over this to be very sad. He and his mate were both past forty. They had the spirits of schoolboys, of unattached workmen.

At the big station these men and the sailors left the train. Two sergeants of regulars came in and sat in opposite corners. A bulky cattle-dealer in a greasy box-cloth overcoat sat between one of them and me. An Army Medical private and a civilian sat on the other side, and in the fourth corner a great broad old man, who said nothing. The platforms were crowded with soldiers. 'Soldiers everywhere,' remarked the cattle-dealer, looking out sideways over his spectacles. 'It's all right. If the German Emperor could see what's getting ready for him, he wouldn't smile again. The man must be mad! I said so right at the beginning of the war. There, look! there's some young ones!'

Here one of the sergeants spoke. He was trying to persuade an injured thigh into a comfortable position. He was wretched. His grey eyes seemed incapable of seeing things except as they were. 'If you knew,' said he, 'what I know, you wouldn't like to see those young ones. They will get killed, most likely. We don't want many of their sort in the trenches. They can't keep still and smoke. They are too excited and restless, and keep bobbing about, and they get shot. And don't you make a mistake: if some of these men were to go out now, the Germans would die of laughing.'

'That's a fact,' said the other sergeant. 'Soldier's clothes don't make a soldier.'

'Quite true,' said the cattle-dealer, disconcerted, but glad to have a generalization to agree with. From that point onward he agreed with everything the sergeant said, until he fell asleep, which he did in spite of the fact that I did not put the window up for him. For the sergeant—the unwounded one: the wounded did not speak again—was truculent and three parts drunk. He was a pioneer sergeant on his way up to see his colonel, hoping to be made regimental sergeant.

The war, he said, was hell. Nobody who had been out there once wanted to go a second time. It was hell: there was no other word for it. After an interval the red cross on the arm of the RAMC man—a meek, quiet young man—roused him. 'What did you join that for?' asked the sergeant, grinning; 'was it to shun the bullets?' The young man had a bad voice, and, what with nervousness, made no audible reply. But the sergeant did not mind; he was set going now. He announced that it was every man's duty—every man's—to go and have a taste of it. The upper classes had done their duty. The poor classes had done their duty. But the middle classes had not. They ought to be made to go. Varicose veins! Sprains! He had got sprains in both legs.

The civilian who wanted to agree with him, a man with half a mouthful of teeth like agates, said:

'Yes, and teeth too. You don't shoot with your teeth. That's what I say.'

'But you eat with your teeth, don't you?' said the sergeant with his grin. He was not going to have any interruption. 'I have done my share,' he continued. 'I was wounded in the Boer War. I was wounded on the Marne in this war. I have done my share, and others ought to do theirs.'

The wounded sergeant looked at him, but only readjusted his thigh. The great broad old man looked at him, and, moreover, did not take his eyes off him, which, I think, was the reason why the sergeant began to feel the bit, and possibly why he got out at the next station. 'I was a soldier before he was born,' said the old man. 'Some people don't know when to keep their mouths shut. He made a great mistake for a recruiter. He said right off that it was hell. Then he said everyone ought to be sent out for a taste. If he was in the Boer War, why doesn't he wear his medal? It's a crime not to in these times. Well, a man with no more sense than he has got will never make a regimental sergeant. He ought to be on the stage.'

By the time we were all standing up to get out at the terminus the cattle-dealer woke, and, seeing the soldiers on the platform, said as before: 'Soldiers everywhere. It's all right.'

NS, 8 May 1915

7   'And myself, too'

WHEN I penetrate backward into my childhood I come perhaps sooner than many people to impassable night. A sweet darkness enfolds with a faint blessing my life up to the age of about four. The task of attempting stubbornly to break up that darkness is one I have never proposed to myself, but I have many times gone up to the edge of it, peering, listening, stretching out my hands, and I have heard the voice of one singing as I sat or lay in her arms; and I have become again aware very dimly of being enclosed in rooms that were shadowy, whether by comparison with outer sunlight I know not. The songs, first of my mother, then of her younger sister, I can hear not only far off behind the veil but on this side of it also. I was, I should think, a very still listener whom the music flowed through and filled to the exclusion of all thought and of all sensation except of blissful easy fullness, so that too early or too sudden ceasing would have meant pangs of expectant emptiness. The one song which, by reason of its repetition or of some aptitude in me, I well remember, was one combining fondness with tranquil if peevish retrospection and regret in a soft heavy twilight. I reach back to it in that effort through a thousand twilights lineally descended from that first one and from the night which gave it birth. If I cried or suffered pain or deprivation in those years nothing remains to star the darkness. Either I asked no question or I had none but sweet answers. I was at peace with life. Indoors, out of the sun, I seem never to have been troubled by heat or cold strong enough to be remembered. But out of doors, somewhere at the verge of the dark years, I can recall more simply and completely than any spent indoors at that time one day above others. I lay in the tall grass and buttercups of a narrow field at the edge of London and saw the sky and nothing but the sky. There was some one near, probably a servant, necessary but utterly insignificant. I was alone and happy to be so, just as indoors I was happy among people and shadows between walls. Was it one day

or many? I know of no beginning or end to it; but an end I suppose it
had an age past.

The Childhood of Edward Thomas, 13-14

Games

The Common and the streets leading up to it were the scene of our
principal game. It was played chiefly on Saturday, our whole holiday.
We assembled, for example, at the top of the road in the well-trodden
garden of a doctor who had a rowdy son; each bringing a weapon
or several weapons, wooden swords and pikes, or daggers, shields,
pistols, bows, arrows, and with horns and trumpets, and perhaps some
bread and cheese and an apple or orange. There sides were chosen.
One side went out to seek a fort, in some one's garden or among the
gorse bushes. Ten minutes later the other set forth, often in two
divisions. Sometimes stealth was the rule of expedition; we advanced
whispering and in some order. Sometimes everyone was shouting for
his own plans and against another's. At other times the methods alter-
nated: the stealth would become wearisome, we began to chatter and
disagree; or the riot of anarchy would suddenly strike us as wrong,
everyone said 'hush', and for some minutes we modelled ourselves on
Sioux, Mohicans, or Hurons, crouching, pausing, trying to hush the
sound of our breathing. We forgot everything in this Indian ideal.
Nevertheless, the enemy had to be found. Nor were they loth.
Someone was sure to show himself and wave defiance, or to leap out on
us, supposing we passed by. If seen at a distance they might change the
stronghold and there would be a chase. If they were content to stand a
storm, the second army would gather all its numbers together and,
with yells and counter-yells, batter and push them out or be battered
and pushed out itself. The struggle was one of character, not weapons.
The side possessing the fiercest and most stubborn boys won. The
winners would then in turn fortify themselves and sustain an attack;
and so it went on, until a mealtime, or nightfall, or rain, or a serious
quarrel, finished the war.

At long intervals fiercer battles were waged. The boys of a neighbouring school of the grammar-school standard looked down upon the
Board-school boys, or 'Boardy Blags' (i.e. blackguards). The Board-
school boys resented this. The feud was usually hardly in so much as a
smouldering condition, and so far as I know must have been all but
forgotten. Then suddenly it would flame out. A loose army of Board-
school boys several score strong moved along the Grove at the edge of
the Common towards the enemy's school. The army was continually
being swelled from the side streets. With all the smaller or more timid
boys hanging on its fringes, more angry than warlike, more curious

than angry, the numbers were considerable. Stones were the long-distance weapons. But rarely, I think, did both sides muster a fairly equal army at the same time. When they came in sight of one another they began to throw stones. They halted, odd stones were thrown here and there, the hangers-on disappeared. I doubt if both sides ever advanced and clashed in hand-to-hand conflict. Usually after some challenging shouts, some wavering and dissension, the victors knew themselves and set up a shout and moved forward confidently. The smaller army broke and fled down the streets; the larger broke and pursued. Here and there a group kept together and set upon any solitary enemy it could discover. I, who was too small to be in the army, was content to hang on the outer outskirts, pick up the news, and occasionally insult one of the enemy if I remembered that he was one.

As a relaxation we hung about in corners smoking cigarettes of rolled brown paper. Making these, lighting them, puffing them, coughing, relighting them, asking one another if they were alight, and silently enjoying the act and the seclusion, filled hours.

Our sense of discipline was slight and transient. It was not encouraged by doing lessons, a few ridiculous exercises under the eye of an unsleeping master, and playing mostly individualist games in the playground. Being in a little mob increased our boldness and also our ease and safety. According to our tempers, I think we hoped that the others would either shelter us or support us in doing signal deeds. As member of the army, any one of us could most likely insult a passing outsider with impunity: if, however, there had been any swift retaliation the victim of it would often have been left to suffer alone.

Therefore the armies did not always wait for a formal order of disbandment. The Common, for example, offered many temptations to more irregular games and aimless rovings. For it was an uneven piece of never cultivated gravelly land. Several ponds of irregular shape and size, varying with the rainfall, had been hollowed out, perhaps by old gravel diggings. It was marshy in other places. Hawthorn and gorse clustered tall and dense in great and in little thickets. Tall elms and poplars stood about irregularly. And the level spaces suitable for cricket, football and tennis were not many. With this variety the Common, even though the railway ran through it parallel to Bolingbroke Grove and only two or three hundred yards away from it, was large enough to provide us with many surprises and discoveries for years. We could spend a day on it without thinking it small or having to retrace our steps. We wandered about it with or without our hoops. For any kind of hiding and hunting game the thickets were excellent. We played the other games in the open spaces. The ponds were for paddling in. One of them, a shallow irregular one, weedy and rushymargined, lying then in some broken ground between the Three Island and the railway, was full of effets and frogs. Bigger boys would torture the frogs, by cutting, skinning or crushing them alive. The sharp penknives sank through the skin and the soft bone into the wood of the seat which was the operating table. This seat and the earth under and about it would be strewn with fragments, pale bellies slit up, and complete frogs seeming to be munching their own insides. At that time I could not have done it myself, but my horror lacked pity and turned into a kind of half-shrinking, half-gloating curiosity. . . .

The streets were a playground almost equal to the Common. The labyrinth of them, all running at right angles and parallel to one another, with some *culs de sac*, could be mastered but indefinitely extended; every month or two I should think I added a street or two to my knowledge. Alone or with others I bowled my hoop up and down them either in purposeless pleasure or on some errand for my mother. Best of all errands was to the blacksmith's to have a broken hoop mended. The smithy was a primeval forest cave that broke a line of ordinary shops. The bellows snored, the sparks spouted up, and the pallid, gaunt, bare-armed man made the anvil ring its double or its single song. When it was very cold I ran along with hands in pockets striking sparks out of the rough kerbstone with my ironshod heel. At night we often played games of hide and seek with lanterns. We picked up sides, fixed the boundaries which were not to be exceeded, and laid down rules against hiding in our own houses. One side went out to hide, to be followed in a few minutes by most of the other side, except one or two who were left behind to guard the home, which the other side had to reach without being touched. Setting out with bull's-eye shining and a good companion, and exposing the others behind laurel bushes and catching them after a chase; or ourselves being the quarry and eluding capture for the whole evening whether with constant obedience to rules or not—these were great joys. If the game became monotonous we rang people's bells and ran away, or we went into shops and asked for sweets with ridiculous names just invented by ourselves.

36-42

Holidays

Swindon was a thousand times better [than Brighton]. It was delicious to pass Wantage, Challow, Uffington, Shrivenham, to see the 75th, 76th mile marks by the railwayside, to slow down at last to the cry of 'Swindon' and see my grandmother, my uncle or my aunt waiting. My aunt was an attendant in the refreshment bar, and sometimes gave me a cake or sandwich to eat amid the smell of spirits, or took me to the private apartments, talking in a high bright voice and showing me

round to various other neat women in black with high bright voices
and nothing but smiles and laughs. My uncle was a fitter in the Great
Western Railway works and knew everybody. He was tall, easy-going,
and had a pipe in his mouth and very likely a dog at his heels. I was
proud to be with him as he nodded to the one-legged signalman and
the man with a white apron and a long hammer for tapping the wheels
of all the carriages.

The look of the town pleased me altogether. I could think no ill of
houses built entirely of stone instead of brick, especially as they
seemed to exist chiefly to serve as avenues by which I happily
approached to my grandmother's. It was for me a blessed place. The
stonework, the flowers in the gardens, the Wiltshire accent, the rain if
it was raining, the sun if it was shining, the absence of school and
schoolmaster and of most ordinary forms of compulsion—everything
was paradisal. No room ever was as cosy as my grandmother's kitchen.
Its open range was always bright. There was a pair of bellows frequently in use. A brass turnspit hung from under the mantelpiece. The
radiant steel trivet was excellent in itself but often bore a load of girdle
cakes or buttered toast or more substantial things. An old brown
earthenware teapot stood eternally upon the hob. Tea-caddies, brass
candlesticks, clay pipes and vases full of spills, stood on the mantelpiece. On its walls hung coloured engravings entitled 'Spring' and
'Summer' and painted in England some time before the Fall, and
photographs of me and Mr Gladstone's Cabinets and Mr Gladstone,
of Belle Bitton, and of an uncle who had died long before I was born.
There were chairs and there was an old mahogany table piano at one
side. The smell of 'Westward Ho' tobacco hung about the room. My
uncle got us chatting instantly. He seemed grown up, yet a boy, by the
way he laughed, whistled and sang a bit of a gay tune. At supper, with
our bread and cheese, or cold bacon, or hot faggots, or chitterlings, and
pickles, he would now and then give us a little tumbler, or 'tot', of ale.

My grandmother being all important, omnipotent, omnipresent if
not omniscient, she stood out less. She marketed, cooked, cleaned, did
everything. She made pies with pastry a full inch thick, and many different undulant fruit tarts on plates. Above all, she made doughy
cakes, of dough, allspice and many raisins, which were as much better
than other cakes as Swindon was better than other towns, and always
as much better than other so-called doughy cakes. She knew, too,
where to get butter which taught me how divine a thing butter can be
made. On the other hand, she was a Conservative and a church-
woman. Without her, these holidays would have been impossible, and
she gave me countless pleasures. But if I loved her it was largely
because of these things, not instinctively or because she loved me. She
was marvellously kind and necessary but we were never close together;

and, when there was any quarrel, contempt mingled with my hate of her inheritance from semi-rural Wales of GeorgeIV's time. She was bigoted, worldly, crafty, narrowminded, and ungenerous, as I very early began to feel. She read her Bible and sang hymns to herself, sometimes in Welsh. She also sang Welsh songs that were not hymns, in particular one that an old beggar used to sing at Tredegar when she was a girl, something about a son whom the mother was begging not to be married. When she wanted to warn me against going fishing some miles off with a strange man she hinted that he might be Jack the Ripper.

She first took me to church. Clad in those uncomfortable clothes, I walked beside her, who looked more uncomfortable in her layers of black. I felt that everyone enjoyed being stiff, solemn, black, except myself. On entering the church she bent forward to pray, dragging me down with her to blur my sight for a similar period. I rose with an added awkwardness in gazing at the grim emotionless multitudes of hats, bonnets, and bare heads. It was an inexplicable conspiracy for an hour's self-torture. The service was a dreary discomfort in which the hymns were green isles. When all was over, we crept with a shuffle, a pause, a shuffle, a pause, out to the tombstones and the astonishing fresh light. . . .

But my strongest and most often considered memory of this period was my second visit to Wales at the age of nine. It is associated with an incident which preceded and almost frustrated it. One evening after tea I went up on to Wandsworth Common with some bigger boys and sat on the seat by the Box Pond. A cigar was produced, lit and given to me to smoke. A few minutes afterwards I was crawling down the road by giddily clinging to the railings of garden after garden. I slunk into the house neglecting my mother's question 'What's the matter?' but soon answering it by deeds not words. My father said that I should not go to Wales. Nevertheless, I went. I remember the names of the stations, 'Risca', 'Cross Keys' . . . I walked through a park among great trees that stood at stately distances from one another: there were long-horned shaggy cattle about. I saw the river Ebbw racing over stones, and mountain ash trees on rough rising ground. I saw chimneys and smoke and ruins and whitewashed walls. I stopped at Abertillery with friends and met Welsh people who spoke no English. Above all I remember a house alone on a hill with a parrot and a dark girl named Rachel, pretty and dirty, who was down on her knees scrubbing the kitchen hearth. I made friends with the boy and the girl of the house in Abertillery and played with them among rolls of stuff in a dark shop. With my mother I drove out along a road among trees and above running water to Pontypool. I went to Aberbeg. . . . That is all the stuff of an abiding memory. These things joined forces with the street in

Caerleon, the river and the Round Table, and also with phrases and images from *The Adventures of the Knights of the Round Table*, and a curious illusion of a knight with a shield kneeling at the foot of a pillar in the photograph at home of Tintern Abbey.

45-55

But a more entertaining and lasting acquaintance [than others in Swindon] was an old man whom I called Dad, in the Wiltshire style, almost from the first day. I remember him first as a stiff straight man, broad-shouldered and bushy bearded, holding his rod out and watching his float very intently. Suddenly up went the rod and a little roach flew high over his head into the hedge behind. 'Daddy bin and caught one!' shouted the boy with me. We laughed and the old man laughed too. As every day he fished not far from me and Fred or whoever was my companion, we began to chat. We used to sit and eat our dinner together. He being toothless had to chew prodigiously, his nose and his beard almost meeting at each bite, to get through his brown bread and watercress. The bread he brought with him, the watercress he gathered from the brooks. His eating grimace amused me, his gravity, the simplicity of the meal, and his thanks to God for it impressed me. At that time he lived with his wife under the roof of a son who was in the factory. The rod and half a loaf helped him to fill up his time with obvious satisfaction, and what he caught he kept, however small. Very soon I sought him out and got him to walk with me when I was tired of fishing. I shared my doughy cake with him, or if we had a meal at a village shop I paid for the tea and bread and butter and egg and lardy cake. He knew the names of most birds and could imitate their cries: his imitations of the jackdaw calling his name, and of the young rook crying and swallowing a worm at the same time, were wonderful. The flowers, too, he knew, both the common pretty flowers and those whose virtues he had read of in Culpeper's *Herbal*. With dried and powdered dock root and with extracts of leaves, flowers or bark, he composed dark medicinal-looking draughts. His ointment made of lard scented with elder flower was delicious. Then he had a way with country people. He spoke to everyone. All the old men to him were 'Dad' and the old women 'Granny' and the younger men 'young man'. He would stop by a stonebreaker to say, 'How many ups and downs o' that to a pound of mutton, young man?' The pity was that he was too poor to get friendly with keepers. If we were caught trespassing he was no good. Out we had to go, the old man muttering, 'We beant poaching', and the keeper retorting, 'Looks very much like it wi' they thick sticks.' He was a much better hand with the labourers and especially the women with whom he had an ineffably grave knowing manner: many times they gave us tea and an egg which the fowl had just laid in the cupboard; and the son would tell us perhaps where there was a magpie's nest. The only man he seemed to feel himself above was the yellow half-bred gypsy youth, the 'diddikai', who used to slouch by us sometimes. Dad had done some poaching in his younger days. Odd-job man under a wood-ward, militiaman, and latterly outdoor assistant to grocers, he had not had time to become very respectable. So he was the first man old enough to be my grand-father with whom I was on thoroughly good easy terms. He did not hide anything or invent a moral code for my benefit. He would say of the round-shouldered sour man living alone in the sham-Gothic house with the orchard, 'It's the women has put old Dicky's back up', and leave me to make what I could of it. Or he shook his head solemnly as he saw the once decent middle-aged gaffer from the works going up the canal-side with an obvious loose woman and later on emerging from the ash copse. It merely amused me. Sex was alluring and amusing, whenever it was revealed, because the whole grown-up world for the benefit of the young was endeavouring to keep up the appearance of doing without sex. Thus Dad's extraordinary freedom was equally amusing and alluring. At first I supposed him to be a wicked old man until I came to believe that all men were radically like him but most of them inferior in honesty. He was not in the least unseemly or obtrusive, but grave and roused very rarely to his Shakes-pearian laughter and the words, 'Well, well, what a thing it is!'

129-32

Walking and Reading

Whenever I was not bound to play in a football match I spent my half-holidays with John, walking, to Merton or Wimbledon, or taking the train to South Croydon and exploring southwards and eastwards. We had no single definite object now that no eggs were to be found. Talking, and looking at the earth and the sky, we just walked about until it was dark. Students we were not: nothing was pursued to the uttermost. We merely became accustomed to the general life of the common birds and animals, and to the appearances of trees and clouds and everything upon the surface that showed itself to the naked eye. Some rare thrush or robin we might stop to listen to; or we might watch a wren threading a bush or a tit on a birch-spray, or look at a mossy greenfinch's nest or climb up with some sort of unfounded hope to a big nest which had escaped us in spring; but for the most part we were moving and usually fast. When it froze we were content with what we saw as we stalked up and down the rough ice of Beverley Brook. Only at night did we join the throng of skaters pure and simple. If the weather was bad and we were not together and no school work had to be done, I read books of travel, sport and natural history. I remember those of Waterton, Thomas Edward, Buckland, Wallace, Charles Kingsley, but above all Richard Jefferies. If I say little of Jefferies it is because not a year passed thereafter without many copious draughts of him and I cannot pretend to distinguish amongst them. But very soon afterwards I was writing out in each one of his books and elsewhere—as in a cousin's album—when I had the opportunity, those last words of *The Amateur Poacher:* 'Let us get out of these indoor narrow modern days, whose twelve hours somehow have become shortened, into the sunlight and the pure wind. A something that the ancients thought divine can be found and felt there still.' They were a gospel, an incantation. What I liked in the books was the free open-air life, the spice of illegality and daring, roguish characters—the opportunities so far exceeding my own, the gun, the great pond, the country home, the apparently endless leisure—the glorious moments that one could always recapture by opening *The Poacher*—and the tinge of sadness here and there as in the picture of the old moucher perishing in his sleep by the lime kiln, and the heron flying over in the morning indifferent. Obviously Jefferies had lived a very different boyhood from ours, yet one which we longed for and supposed ourselves fit for. He had never had to wear his best clothes for twelve or fourteen hours on Sunday. Enforced attendances at church and Sunday school could not have been known to him. The crowd parading in their Sunday-best clothes along the walks of the Commons were impossible in that southern county.

133-5

HOW I BEGAN

TALKING prose is natural to most of the species; writing it is now almost as common, if not as natural; having it published when written is the third step which distinguishes an author from the more primitive minority of mankind. No author, I suppose, except Miss Helen Keller, has varied this method of progress. Every one begins by talking, stumbles into writing, and succumbs to print.

The first step is the most interesting and the most difficult to explain and describe. I shall leave it alone. The second step is very interesting, and less difficult to explain and describe, yet I can remember little of it. I can only remark here that the result of teaching a child to read before it can write is that it begins and usually ends by writing like a book, not like a human being. It was my own experience. From the age of one, I could express by words and inflections of the voice all that ever sought expression within me, from feelings of heat, cold, hunger, repletion, indigestion, etc., to subtle preferences of persons and things. But when I came to write the slowness of that unnatural act decimated and disconcerted my natural faculties. I laboriously covered a square foot of notepaper, communicating nothing much beyond the fact that I had begun to hold a pen, and to master English grammar.

That the best of fountain-pens is slow, does not entirely account for the inexpressiveness of that square foot of notepaper. The slowness made it practically impossible to say what I was thinking, even if I had tried. I did not try hard. I do not believe that it was by any means my sole or chief aim to write what I was thinking, or what I should have spoken had my correspondent been in the same room with me. I felt it to be highly important that I should use terms such as I had met in books, seldom if ever in speech. Nor do I remember hearing it said that I could, or should, write as I thought or as I spoke.

Until the age of eight or nine, therefore, all my writing was painful and compulsory, and I knew well that it displayed a poorer creature than the severest critic could judge me. But at that age I was given a small notebook in a cover as much like tortoiseshell as could be made for a penny. In this I wrote down a number of observations of my own accord, though I dare say the notebook had been designed as a trap; if there was a separate bait, I have forgotten it. All that I can remember is that I pronounced the houses of Swindon to be 'like bull-dogs, small but strongly built'. They were of stone, and I was accustomed to brick. Stone seemed to be a grander material. Hence the note. The sententious form was, no doubt, due to a conscious desire to be impressive, that is to say, adult. It was not the last time I experienced this desire, but I shall not trouble you with more instances.

With short intervals, from that time onwards I was a writer by choice. I began several diaries, carrying on the entries in some of them as far as February. By the time I was fourteen or fifteen, I did more; I kept a more or less daily record of notable events, the finding of birds' nests, the catching of moles or fish, the skinning of a stoat, the reading of Richard Jefferies and the naturalists.

These notes aimed at brevity: they were above syntax and indifferent to dignity. I was now, however, permitted to forget syntax or dignity. I was obliged to write essays on Imperial Federation, the Greek Colonization of Sicily, Holidays, etc., where I gave myself up to an almost purely artistic rendering of such facts as I remembered, and such opinions as I could concoct by the help of memory, fancy, and the radical and the free-thinking influence of home. Thus, like nearly every other child, I virtually neglected in my writing the feelings that belonged to my own nature and my own times of life—an irreparable loss, whether great or not. If I wrote about what really pleased or concerned me, like a walk all day or all night in Wiltshire, I had in view not the truth but the eyes of elders, and those elders clothed in the excess and circumstance of elderliness regularly assumed in the presence of children. I was considered to excel in this form of rhetoric. So seriously, too, did I take myself in it, that from the time I was sixteen I found myself hardly letting a week pass without writing one or two descriptions—of a man, or a place, or a walk—in a manner largely founded on Jefferies' *Amateur Poacher*, Kingsley's *Prose Idylls*, and Mr Francis A. Knight's weekly contributions to the *Daily News*, but doubtless with tones supplied also by Shelley and Keats, and later on by Ruskin, de Quincey, Pater, and Sir Thomas Browne. I had quite a number of temptations to print, and at the age of fifteen easily gave way. At seventeen, some of those descriptions were printed in the *Speaker* and the *New Age*, and soon afterwards took the form of a book.

While I was afflicted with serious English composition and English literature, I was reading Scott, Fenimore Cooper, Henty, and the travellers, because I loved them; I was also thinking and talking in a manner which owed little to those dignified exercises, though the day was to come when I spoke very much as I wrote. Presently, also, myself and English, as she is taught in schools, came to a conflict, and gradually to a more and more friendly agreement through the necessity of writing long letters daily to one who was neither a schoolboy nor an elder, the subject of the letters being matters concerning nobody else in the world. Now it was that I had a chance of discarding or of adapting to my own purpose the fine words and infinite variety of constructions which I had formerly admired from afar off and imitated in fairly cold blood. There is no doubt that my masters often lent me dignity and subtlety altogether beyond my needs.

Both in these letters and in papers intended for print, I ravaged the language (to the best of my ability) at least as much for ostentation as for use, though I should not like to have to separate the two. This must always happen where a man has collected all the colours of the rainbow, 'of earthquake and eclipse', on his palette, and has a cottage or a gasometer to paint. A continual negotiation was going on between thought, speech and writing, thought having as a rule the worst of it. Speech was humble and creeping, but wanted too many fine shades and could never come to a satisfactory end. Writing was lordly and regardless. Thought went on in the twilight, and wished the other two might come to terms for ever. But maybe they did not and never will, and, perhaps, they never do. In my own case, at any rate, I cannot pronounce, though I have by this time provided an abundance of material for a judgment.

The Last Sheaf, 15-20

'THE OTHER MAN'

FROM [Farleigh Hungerford Castle] the Other Man would have me turn aside to see Tellisford. This is a hamlet scattered along half a mile of by-road, from a church at the corner down to the Frome. Once there was a ford, but now you cross by a stone footbridge with white wooden handrails. A ruined flock-mill and a ruined ancient house stand next to it on one side; on the other the only house is a farm with a round tower embodied in its front. Away from this farm a beautiful meadow slopes between the river and the woods above. This grass, which becomes level for a few yards nearest the bank, was the best possible place, said the Other Man, for running in the sun after bathing at the weir—we could see its white wall of foam half a mile higher up the river, which was concealed by alders beyond. He said it was a great haunt of nightingales. And there was also a service tree; and, said he, in that tree sang a thrush all through May—it was the best May that ever was— and so well it sang, unlike any other thrush, that it made him think he would gladly live no longer than a thrush if he could do some one thing as right, as crisp and rich, as the song was. 'I suppose you write books,' said I. 'I do,' said he. 'What sort of books do you write?' 'I wrote one all about this valley of the Frome. . . . But no one knows that it was the Frome I meant. You look surprised. Nevertheless, I got fifty pounds for it.' 'That is a lot of money for such a book!' 'So my publisher thought.' 'And you are lucky to get money for doing what you like.' 'What I like!' he muttered, pushing his bicycle back uphill, past the goats by the ruin, and up the steps between walls that were lovely with humid moneywort, and saxifrage like filigree, and ivy-leaved toad-flax. Apparently the effort loosened his tongue. He rambled on and on about himself, his past, his writing, his digestion; his main point being that he did not like writing. He had been attempting the impossible task of reducing undigested notes about all sorts of details to a grammatical, continuous narrative. He abused notebooks violently. He said that they blinded him to nearly everything that would not go into the form of notes; or, at any rate, he could never afterwards reproduce the great effects of Nature and fill in the interstices merely—which was all they were good for—from the notes. The notes—often of things which he would otherwise have forgotten—had to fill the whole canvas. Whereas, if he had taken none, then only the important, what he truly cared for, would have survived in his memory, arranged not perhaps as they were in Nature, but at least according to the tendencies of his own spirit. 'Good God!' said he. But luckily we were by this time on the level. I mounted. He followed.

In Pursuit of Spring, 218-20

MR TORRANCE

HE WROTE at an aged and time-worn black bureau, from which he could sometimes see the sunlight embracing the apple tree. But into that room the sunlight could not enter without a miracle, or by what so seldom happened as to seem one—the standing open of an opposite window just so that it threw a reflection of the late sun for about three minutes. Even supposing that the sunlight came that way, little could have penetrated that study; for the French windows were ponderously draped by tapestry of dark green with a black pattern, and on one side the bureau, on the other a bookcase, stood partly before the panes. No natural light could reach the ceiling or the corners. Instead of light, books covered the walls, books in a number of black-stained bookcases of various widths, all equal in height with the room, except one that was cut short by a grate in which I never saw a fire. The other few interspaces held small old pictures or prints in dark frames, and a dismal canvas darkened, probably, by some friendly hand. Most of the books were old, many were very old. The huge, blackened slabs of theology and drama emitted nothing but gloom. The red bindings which make some libraries tolerable had been exorcised from his shelves by the spirits of black and of darkest brown.

The sullen host of books left little room for furniture. Nevertheless, there was a massive table of ancient oak, always laden with books, and apparently supported by still other books. Six chairs of similar character had long succeeded in retaining places in front of the books, justifying themselves by bearing each a pile or a chaos of books. Dark as wintry heather were the visible portions of the carpet. The door was hung with the same black and green tapestry as the windows; if opened, it disclosed the mere blackness of a passage crowded with more books and ancestral furniture.

Yet Mr Torrance smiled whenever a visitor, or his wife, or one or all of his children, but, above all, when Aurelius entered the room. No doubt he did not always smile when he was alone writing; for he wrote what he was both reluctant and incompetent to write, at the request of a firm of publishers whose ambition was to have a bad, but nice-looking, book on everything and everybody, written by some young university man with private means, by some vegetarian spinster, or a doomed hack like Mr Torrance. Had he owned copies of all these works they would have made a long row of greens and reds decorated by patterns and lettering in gold. . . .

His books are not the man. They are known only to students at the British Museum who get them out once and no more, for they discover hasty compilations, ill-arranged, inaccurate, and incomplete, and swollen to a ridiculous size for the sake of gain. They contain not one mention of the house under the hill where he was born.

The Happy-Go-Lucky Morgans, 120-7

MORGAN RHYS

I SHOULD like to win some charity for Morgan Rhys, the descendant of a prince, a bard and a tin-plater. Charity it must be; for, in truth, he is something of a Celt in the bad, fashionable sense of that strange word, and is somewhat ridiculous beside the landlord of the Cross Inn. An orphan, he lived as the only child in the large house of a distant relative, reading everything, playing half-heartedly at games, yet now and then entering into them with such enthusiasm that he did what he liked and won a singular reputation. He went seldom to a chapel, and when he went, did something more than escape boredom, by the marvellous gift of inattention which enabled him to continue his own chain of thought or fancy from beginning to end of the service. He was quite unhindered by hymn, prayer, or sermon, and accepted what he heard, as elderly persons accept fairies, without even curiosity. The death of others made him helpless for a time, but he did not reason about the fact: his own death he at all times contemplated without fear; what he feared, if anything, was the fear of death.

These things would not be remarkable, if he had not been at the same time an impressionable, submissive child, incapable of listening to argument, indeed, but of an unsatisfied sentimentality that might have been made much use of by a priest. His abstraction from things to which he was indifferent was wonderful. He was delighted and fascinated by abstraction itself, and finding a thing uninteresting, he could at once withdraw into a sweet, vaporous, empty cave. Thus, he was praised at school for his calmness during punishment, which, he says, on many occasions he never felt at all.

When a child of five he had been left alone for half a day in a remote chamber of a great house, and at nightfall was found sitting at a window that commanded an orchard and a lawn, and when he did not rise to greet his friends, and was questioned, merely said 'Look!' Nobody could see anything, or rather, they saw everything as usual: nor could he explain. He always remembered the incident, and could not explain it. There was no fairy, no peculiar light or gloom. Yet he admitted that he was intoxicated by the mere trees and the green lawn. In the same way he was often found listening to silence. He did not pretend to hear strange music. It was the voluptuousness of sheer silence. At home, in the fields, at school, he would cry: 'There!' So far as any one could see, there was nothing. To shut his eyes was not to see amply and clearly, but to see infinite purple darkness, which he vastly loved. He would ask friends whether they remembered this place or that on a certain day, and if they did, could never have them share his pleasure at the recollection; and for this whim he was scolded and ridiculed.

But at the age of sixteen or seventeen, poetry gave him a second world in which he thenceforward moved with a rapture which I do not often observe in the religious, while in religious matters he remains so pure a sceptic that he has never yet learned that there is anything about which to be sceptical. This so-called matter-of-factness in combination with a rich imaginativeness is perhaps a Welsh characteristic. I remember a farmer in Cardiganshire, with the blood of a lamb on his wrist, singing a fine hymn very nobly; and though I cannot like such a mystic, I admire him. In the same way will Rhys turn from ribaldry to a poem by Mr Yeats. But he valued poetry not so much because it was full of music for ear and spirit, though that he loved; not so much because it was the first discoverer of Nature and Man, though that he well knew, as because it revealed to him the possibility of a state of mind and spirit in which alone all things could be fully known at their highest power, and that state was his most cherished aim, and poetry helped him to achieve it. Along with love of poetry went a curious study of appearances and illusions. He was never tired of considering them; of trying to elucidate the impressionism of the eyes and the other senses; of trying to know what there was in tree or face or flower which many measurements, scientific descriptions, photographs, and even pictures did not exhaust. So many trees he saw were scarcely more than nothing, though close by and in clear air: what were they, he asked. He had never any answer. 'If only we could think like that!' he said once, pointing to a fair, straight hawthorn that stood, with few branches and without leaves, on the mountain side. And he came to hope for a state in which he and the trees and the great estuary near his house, the flowers, the distant white cottages, should become all happily arranged in as perfect a pattern as that made with iron dust by a magnet—all filling their places, all integral parts of a whole, and important because they were.

One evening he came into the farmhouse in deep excitement because (as he said) he had been part of the music of the spheres. He had walked through village after village, over the mountains and along the rivers, under great motionless white clouds. The air had been so clear that every straw of the thatch gleamed separately. He had passed through the lonely places with a sense of passing through a crowd because the rich spring air had been so much a presence. The men labouring or idling in the fields had seemed to be seraphic and majestic beings; the women smiling or talking by the gates were solemn and splendid. When at last he descended into this valley, he saw the wood smoke rising gently and blue from all the houses, as if they had been a peaceful company smoking pipes together. He had looked at the sky, the flushed mountain sheep, the little stony lanes that led steeply up to farmyard and farm, the jackdaw making suitable music high up in the cold bright air, the buzzard swirling amidst the young bracken, and he had approved, and had been approved, in ecstasy. And on that day the mazes of human activity had been woven into a rich pattern with the clouds and the hills and the waters for the pleasure of the gods, and were certainly for once fitted to the beauty and harmony of the universe. Thus he spoke in ejaculations, to our great joy, though not without giving us a fear that he would spoil it by something inapposite. But merely remarking that he had seen the parson feeding his boar and that the harmony between them also was complete, he became silent, and for a time the whole world shimmered and darkened as if it had been some tapestry which Rhys had made. The most pious member of the party, a Christian if ever there was one, remarked that he 'wished he had felt like that sometimes'. To which Rhys replied that he could not possibly wish that, as he would then be damned like himself: and the other agreed.

On days like this, he stepped over the edge of the world and saw the gods leaning from the stars among the clouds, and perhaps the loneliness that followed appalled him. For these days flew fast. And so he tried to fortify himself by mingling warmly with the life of every day in the village, where his reputation was for generosity, hard drinking, and perfect latitude of speech. He stimulated the trade-unionist, the parson, the minister, the bard. But he could not live both lives. The worldly one was the more difficult and he gave it up, and only made spasmodic and gross attempts to return to it. He began to shrink not only from all men but from all outward experience, and to live, as only too easily he could, upon his own fantasy. He was 'surprised' when he saw men in the street. A million people, all different and their differences so much the more difficult because they were not acknowledged, frightened him. So his advocacy of certain humane measures and his support of some enthusiasms sounded as if they came from an angel, a fiend, or a corpse. As will happen with men who love life too passionately, he was often in love with death. He found enjoyment in silence, in darkness, in refraining from deeds, and he longed even to embrace the absolute blank or death, if only he could be just conscious of it; and he envied the solitary tree on a bare plain high up among the hills, under a night sky in winter where the only touch of life and pleasure was the rain. And now, with his fantastic belief that the corpse is life's handiwork and its utmost end, he is humanized only by a dread of the blank to which he is going:

> When we shall hear
> The rain and wind beat dark December, how,
> In that our pinching cave, shall we discourse
> The freezing hours away?

He has made a heaven and he fears it.

Beautiful Wales, 88-95

THE ATTEMPT

SEVERAL seasons had passed since Morgan Traheron had so much as looked at his fishing tackle, and now he turned over, almost indifferently, the reels and lines and hooks and flies which had been carefully put away in an old tool box of his great-grandfather's. He looked at the name 'Morgan Traheron' cut neatly inside the lid, and shivered slightly during the thought that one of his own name had bought it in 1776 at the ironmonger's and brazier's under the sign of the 'Anchor and Key' near Charing Cross, and that the owner had been dead nearly a hundred years. Cold, cold, must he be! Even as cold would be the younger bearer of that name, and he anticipated, in a kind of swoon, the hundred years that would one day submerge himself from all known friendliness of sun, earth, and man.

He was seeking, not any of the fishing tackle, but a revolver that lay amongst it, and a small green box containing only one ball cartridge. He had often thought of throwing the revolver away. His wife always looked wonderingly at him when he cleaned it once every year or so, but if she had urged him to throw it away he would have scoffed at the fear which he detected, all the more heartily because the sign of her concern inflated his vanity. She, lest she should provoke his mood in some way which even her consideration could not foresee, remained silent or asked him to tell again how he shot the woodpigeon fifty yards off, actually within sight of the gamekeeper's cottage. It was a thrilling and well-told tale, albeit untrue.

It was not a mere accident that one ball cartridge was left.

Morgan took out the revolver and the cartridge and shut the box. The lock was stiff and the chambers would not revolve without the use of both hands. To fire it off, it would therefore be necessary to twist the loaded chamber laboriously round to its place and then force back the hammer to full cock. The barrel was brown from rust, but probably the ball would force its way through as it had done before. It was a cheap, ugly, repulsive weapon; it impressed him with unsuitableness. He did not stay to oil it, but putting it in a pocket and the cartridge in another, he prepared to leave the house.

'Won't you take Mary with you, Morgan?' said his wife.

'Yes,' said Mary, his little daughter, laughing not so much because there was anything to laugh at as because she must either laugh or cry, and certainly the chance of a walk was nothing to cry for: 'Take me with you, father.'

'Oh no, you don't really want to come, you only say it to please me,' said Traheron, mild but hard.

'Yes, I am sure she . . . Goodbye, then,' said his wife.

'Goodbye,' said he.

The thought of kissing his daughter turned him back for a moment. But he did not; the act occurred to him more as a part of the ceremony of this fatal day than as a farewell, and he feared to betray his thought. She was the immediate cause of his decision. He had spoken resentfully to her for some fault which he noticed chiefly because it disturbed his melancholy repose; she had then burst out crying with long, clear wails that pierced him with self-hate, remorse, regret, and bitter memory.

Why should he live who had the power to draw such a cry from that sweet mouth? So he used to ask in the luxurious self-contempt which he practised. He would delay no more. He had thought before of cutting himself off from the power to injure his child and the mother of his child. But they would suffer; also, what a rough edge would be left to his life, inevitable in any case, perhaps, but not lightly to be chosen. On the other hand, he could not believe that they would ever be more unhappy than they often were now; at least, the greater poverty which his death would probably cause could not well increase their unhappiness; and settled misery or a lower plane of happiness was surely preferable to a state of faltering hope at the edge of abysses such as he often opened for them. To leave them and not die, since the child might forget him and he would miss many a passing joy with her, was never a tolerable thought; such a plan had none of the gloss of heroism and the kind of superficial ceremoniousness which was unconsciously much to his taste. But on this day the arguments for and against a fatal act did not weigh with him. He was called to death.

He was called to death, but hardly to an act which could procure it. Death he had never feared or understood; he feared very much the pain and the fear that would awake with it. He had never in his life seen a dead human body or come in any way near death. Death was an idea tinged with poetry in his mind—a kingly thing which was once only at any man's call. After it came annihilation. To escape from the difficulty of life, from the need of deliberating on it, from the hopeless search for something that would make it possible for him to go on living like anybody else without questioning, he was eager to hide himself away in annihilation, just as, when a child, he hid himself in the folds of his mother's dress or her warm bosom, where he could shut out everything save the bright patterns floating on the gloom under his closed eyelids. There was also an element of vanity in his project; he was going to punish himself and in a manner so extreme that he was inclined to be exalted by the feeling that he was now about to convince the world he had suffered exceedingly. He had thus taken up the revolver, and blurred the moment of the report by thinking intently of the pure annihilation which he desired. The revolver was the only accessible weapon that entered his mind, and he had armed himself with it without once having performed in thought what he had committed himself to do in fact before long.

As he mounted the hill by a white path over the turf, he felt the revolver strike against his hip at each stride. He was in full view of anyone who happened to be looking out from his home, and he pressed on lest the wavering of his mind should be seen. Recalling the repulsiveness of the weapon, the idea of a rope crossed his mind, not because it was preferable, but because it was something else, something apart from his plans which now had a painful air of simplicity.

When he was among some bushes that concealed him and yet still gave him a view of his house, he paused for breath. He half-longed for an invasion of sentiment at the sight of his home; but he was looking at it like a casual stranger, and without even the pang that comes when the stranger sees a quiet house embowered in green against which its smoke rises like a prayer, and he imagines that he could be happy there as he has not until now been happy anywhere. The house was mere stones, nothing, dead. He half wished that Mary would run out into the garden and compel him to a passionate state. His will and power of action were ebbing yet lower in his lifeless mood. He moved his eyes from the house to the elder hedgerow round it, to the little woods on the undulations beyond, to the Downs, and, above them, the cloudy sun perched upon a tripod of pale beams. Nothing answered his heartless call for help. He needed some tenderness to be born, a transfigured last look to keep as a memory; perhaps he still hoped that this answer that was not given to him could save him from the enemy at his side and in his brain; even so late did he continue to desire the conversion, the climacteric ecstasy by which life might solve its difficulty, and either sway placidly in harbour or set out with joy for the open sea.

He mounted the upper slopes and passed in among the beeches. He turned again, but again in vain. There was little in him left to kill when he reached the top and began to think where exactly he should go. He wished that he could hide away for ever in one of the many utterly secret mossy places known to him among beech and yew in the forsaken woods; the foxhounds might find him, but no one else. But he must go farther. The sound of the discharge must not be heard in that house below. Almost with tenderness he dreamed of the very moment when his wife would hear the news and perhaps see his body at the same time; if only that could be put off—the announcement must not come today, not under this sun in which the world was looking as he had always seen it, though more dull and grey, but on some day he had not known, a black, blind day yet unborn, to be still-born because of this event so important to him. Who would find him? He did not like the thought that some stranger who knew him by sight, who had never spoken to him, should come across the body, what was left of him, his remains, and should suddenly become curious and interested, perhaps slightly vain of the remarkable discovery. If only he could fade away rapidly. Several strangers with whose faces he was familiar passed him in a lane, and he assumed a proud, hard look of confidence, as he hoped.

He quickened his steps and turned into a neglected footpath where he had never met anybody. He took out the revolver and again looked at it. It was just here that he had come in the hottest of the late summer to show his daughter cinnabar caterpillars, tigerish yellow and black, among the flaming blossoms of ragwort. The ragwort was dead now, blossom and leaf. He recalled the day without comment.

He was now hidden, on one side by a dense wood, on the other by the steep slope of a hill, and before and behind by windings of the path which skirted the wood. He inserted the cartridge and with difficulty forced it into position; the brass was much tarnished. Now he revolved the chambers in order that the cartridge should be under the hammer, but by mistake he turned them too far; he had to try again, and, losing count of the chambers, was again defeated. Where the cartridge was he could not be sure, and he looked to see; its tarnished disc was hostile and grim to his eye, and he hid the weapon.

Moving on, he now looked down upon a steep wood that sloped from his feet, and then rose as steeply up an opposite hill. They were beech woods with innumerable straight stems of bare branchwork that was purple in the mass. Yews stood as black islands in the woods, and they and the briers with scarlet hips close to his eye were laced with airy traveller's joy, plumy and grey.

Traheron now turned the muzzle to his temple, first letting the hammer down for fear of an accident. He had only one shot to fire, and he could not feel sure that this would enter his brain. His ear, his mouth—the thought was horrible, impossible. His skin ached with the touch of the steel which was very cold. Next he turned the weapon to his breast, and saw that he had better pull the trigger with his thumb. The hammer was now at full cock, the cartridge in place. The hideous engine looked absurdly powerful for his purpose. The noise, the wound, would be out of proportion to the little spark of life that was so willing, so eager, to be extinguished. He lowered the weapon and took a last sight of the woods, praying no prayer, thinking no thought, perfectly at ease, though a little cold from inaction.

Suddenly his eye was aware of someone moving above the opposite wood, half a mile away, and at the same moment this stranger raised a loud halloo as if he had sighted a fox, and repeated it again and again for his own delight, feeling glad, and knowing himself alone. Traheron had been watching the wood with soul more and more enchanted by the soft colour, the coldness, the repose. The cry rescued him; with shame at the thought that he might have been watched, he raised the revolver and turned it to his breast, shut his eyes and touched the trigger, but too lightly, and breathless, in the same moment, he averted the barrel and hurled it into the wood, where it struck a bough without exploding. For a moment he dreamed that he had succeeded. He saw the man who found him pick up the revolver and examine it. Finding but one cartridge in the chambers he concluded that the dead man was a person of unusual coolness and confidence, with an accurate knowledge of the position of the heart. Then, for he was cold, Traheron moved rapidly away, his mind empty of all thought except that he would go to a certain wood and then strike over the fields, following a route that would bring him home in the gentleness of evening.

He opened the door. The table was spread for tea. His wife, divining all, said: 'Shall I make tea?'

'Please,' he replied, thinking himself impenetrably masked.

Light and Twilight, 160-73

AURELIUS, THE SUPERFLUOUS MAN

AURELIUS was gone, then. It cannot have surprised anyone. What was surprising was the way he used to reappear after long absences. While he was present everyone liked him, but he had something unreal about him or not like a man of this world. When that squire's agent called his under-gardener a superfluous man, he was a brute and he was wrong, but he saw straight. If we accept his label there must always have been some superfluous men since the beginning, men whom the extravagant ingenuity of creation has produced out of sheer delight in variety, by-products of its immense process. Sometimes I think it was some of these superfluous men who invented God and all the gods and godlets. Some of them have been killed, some enthroned, some sainted, for it. But in a civilization like ours the superfluous abound and even flourish. They are born in palace and cottage and under hedges. Often they are fortunate in being called mad from early years; sometimes they live a brief, charmed life without toil, envied almost as much as the animals by drudges; sometimes they are no more than delicate instruments on which men play melodies of agony and sweetness.

The superfluous are those who cannot find society with which they are in some sort of harmony. The magic circle drawn round us all at birth surrounds these in such a way that it will never overlap, far less become concentric with, the circles of any other in the whirling multitudes. The circle is a high wall guarded as if it were a Paradise, not a Hell, 'with dreadful faces thronged and fiery arms': or it is no more than a shell border round the garden of a child, and there is no one so feeble but he can slip over it, or shift it, or trample it down, though powerless to remove it. Some of these weaker ones might seem to have several circles enclosing them, which are thus upset or trampled one by one as childhood advances. Everybody discovers that he can cross their borders. They do not retaliate. These are the superfluous who are kept alive to perform the most terrible or most loathsome tasks. Rarely do their tyrants see their eyes gleaming in their dungeons, and draw back or hurl a stone like a man who has almost trodden upon a fox.

But the superfluous are not always unfortunate; we who knew Aurelius would never call him unfortunate. There are some—and more than ever in these days when even the strongest do not condemn outright, and when deaths less unpleasant to the executioner have been discovered—some who escape the necessity to toil and spin for others, and do not spend their ease in manacles. Many of the women among the hunted are not slaughtered as soon as caught. They are kept in artfully constructed and choicely decorated cages where their captors try to force them to sing over and over again the notes which were their allurement at first; a few survive to wear white locks and trouble with a new note the serenity of the palaces where their cages are suspended. The superfluous have been known to learn the ways of their superiors, to make little camps unmolested in the midst of the foreign land, to enjoy a life admired of many and sometimes envied, but insincerely.

The Happy-Go-Lucky Morgans, 48-51

The air was now still and the earth growing dark and already very quiet. But the sky was light and its clouds of utmost whiteness were very wildly and even fiercely shaped, so that it seemed the playground of powerful and wanton spirits knowing nothing of earth. And this dark earth appeared a small though also a kingly and brave place in comparison with the infinite heavens now so joyous and so bright and out of reach. I was glad to be there, but I fell in with a philosopher who seemed to be equally moved yet could not decide whether his condition was to be described as happiness or melancholy. He talked about himself. He was a lean, indefinite man; half his life lay behind him like a corpse, so he said, and half was before him like a ghost. He told me of just such another evening as this and just such another doubt as to whether it was to be put down to the account of happiness or melancholy. He said that he had been digging all day in a heavy soil, often jarring the fork against immovable flints, lifting more often than not a weight of clay only just short of the limit of his strength. He had thought and thought until his brain could do nothing but remain aware of dull misery and the violent shocks of the hard work. But his eyes saw the sun go down with a brief pomp of crimson soon covered up by funereal drifts, and these in their turn give way to a soft blue, full of whitest stars and without one cloud. They saw the far hills once more take on their night look of serene and desolate vastness, and felt the meadows of the valley become dark and uncertain, the woods much duller but distinct. The woods immediately below him on the hill-side thickened and appeared more wild and impossible; the road winding up between them like a long curl of smoke was wholly concealed. Slowly the solid world was whittled away. The lights of the small town half-way across the valley, towards the hills, came out.

As an owl in the woods announced the triumph of night with one large, clear note, he straightened himself slowly and painfully among the clods. It would have been easier to continue his toil than to do this, but he did it, and then cleaned the prongs of his upright fork with the toe of his boot, prolonging the action as if he either hoped to arrive now at some significant conclusion with its help or feared the next step that had to be taken. When he could no longer clean the prongs he raised his head and looked out beyond the woods over the valley to the far hills. The quiet, the magnitude of space, the noble lines of the range a little strengthened his spirit. He remained still. The surface of his hands was dry to brittleness; he was stiff and yet unsatisfied with the result of his labour; he felt the dullness of his eyes; and no thing or person in the world or out of it came into his mind with any conscious delight or quickness; yet he still looked along the ridges of the hills from one end to the other, from star to star, without a thought save the sleeping, underlying one that he was growing old.

A motor-car climbed nervously up the invisible hill-road, the lamps of it darting across a hundred little spaces between one tree and another of the vague woods. It left the silence stronger than ever.

The man leaned with his chest upon his hands, which were upon the handle of his fork. Only a few years ago—either three or four—he could not have ascertained by any searching of memory—he had been young, and treated with contempt or with pitiful kindness by those of more years. But now he had come by unknown ways to feel that he differed from mature men, not by anything positive that could be called youth, but only by some undefinable lack which condemned him to a kind of overblown immaturity. Thus when he consciously or unconsciously demanded a concession such as might be due to youth for some act or attitude, he met, in the individual or in society in some corporate form or other, a blankness or positive severity at which he recoiled with open but as yet uncertainly comprehending eyes. Of young men he was now sometimes jealous; of middle-aged men afraid and no longer defiant. Towards the contemporaries with whom he had shared thought and experience for some years he felt jealousy, if he seemed to have outstripped them in the unwilling race; fear, if it was himself that lagged; and towards only one or two a fair and easy freedom, and that only intermittently. Therefore no more destitute and solitary man looked that night on the stars. Yet they were as bright and the hills under them as noble as those we saw today on the road from Dunstable.

The Icknield Way, 137-41

I lay awake listening to the rain, and at first it was as pleasant to my ear and my mind as it had long been desired; but before I fell asleep it had become a majestic and finally a terrible thing, instead of a sweet sound and symbol. It was accusing and trying me and passing judgment. Long I lay still under the sentence, listening to the rain, and then at last listening to words which seemed to be spoken by a ghostly double beside me. He was muttering: The all-night rain puts out summer like a torch. In the heavy, black rain falling straight from invisible, dark sky to invisible, dark earth the heat of summer is annihilated, the splendour is dead, the summer is gone. The midnight rain buries it away where it has buried all sound but its own. I am alone in the dark still night, and my ear listens to the rain piping in the gutters and roaring softly in the trees of the world. Even so will the rain fall darkly upon the grass over the grave when my ears can hear it no more. I have been glad of the sound of rain, and wildly sad of it in the past; but that is all over as if it had never been; my eye is dull and my heart beating evenly and quietly; I stir neither foot nor hand; I shall not be quieter when I be under the wet grass and the rain falls, and I of less account than the grass. The summer is gone, and never can it return. There will never be any summer any more, and I am weary of everything. I stay because I am too weak to go. I crawl on because it is easier than to stop. I put my face to the window. There is nothing out there but the blackness and sound of rain. Neither when I shut my eyes can I see anything. I am alone. Once I heard through the rain a bird's questioning watery cry—once only and suddenly. It seemed content, and the solitary note brought up against me the order of nature, all its beauty, exuberance, and everlastingness like an accusation. I am not a part of nature. I am alone. There is nothing else in my world but my dead heart and brain within me and the rain without. Once there was summer, and a great heat and splendour over the earth terrified me and asked me what I could show that was worthy of such an earth. It smote and humiliated me, yet I had eyes to behold it, and I prostrated myself, and by adoration made myself worthy of the splendour. Was I not once blind to the splendour because there was something within me equal to itself? What was it? Love . . . a name! . . . a word! . . . less than the watery question of the bird out in the rain. The rain has drowned the splendour. Everything is drowned and dead, all that was once lovely and alive in the world, all that had once been alive and was memorable though dead is now dung for a future that is infinitely less than the falling dark rain. For a moment the mind's eye and ear pretend to see and hear what the eye and ear themselves once knew with delight. The rain denies. There is nothing to be seen or heard, and there never was. Memory, the last chord of the lute, is broken. The rain has been and will be for ever over the earth. There never was anything but the dark rain. Beauty and strength are as nothing to it. Eyes could not flash in it.

I have been lying dreaming until now, and now I have awakened, and there is still nothing but the rain. I am alone. The unborn is not more weak or more ignorant, and like the unborn I wait and wait, knowing neither what has been nor what is to come, because of the rain, which is, has been, and must be. The house is still and silent, and those small noises that make me start are only the imagination of the spirit or they are the rain. There is only the rain for it to feed on and to crawl in. The rain swallows it up as the sea does its own foam. I will lie still and stretch out my body and close my eyes. My breath is all that has been spared by the rain, and that comes softly and at long intervals, as if it were trying to hide itself from the rain. I feel that I am so little I have crept away into a corner and been forgotten by the rain. All else has perished except me and the rain. There is no room for anything in the world but the rain. It alone is great and strong. It alone knows joy. It chants monotonous praise of the order of nature, which I have disobeyed or slipped out of. I have done evilly and weakly, and I have left undone. Fool! you never were alive. Lie still. Stretch out yourself like foam on a wave, and think no more of good or evil. There was no good and no evil. There was life and there was death, and you chose. Now there is neither life nor death, but only the rain. Sleep as all things, past, present, and future, lie still and sleep, except the rain, the heavy, black rain falling straight through the air that was once a sea of life. That was a dream only. The truth is that the rain falls for ever and I am melting into it. Black and monotonously sounding is the midnight and solitude of the rain. In a little while or in an age—for it is all one—I shall know the full truth of the words I used to love, I knew not why, in my days of nature, in the days before the rain: 'Blessed are the dead that the rain rains on.'

280-3

THIS ENGLAND

IT WAS a part of the country I had never known before, and I had no connections with it. Once only, during infancy, I had stayed here at a vicarage, and though I have been told things about it which it gives me, almost as if they were memories, a certain pleasure to recall, no genuine memory survives from the visit. All I can say is that the name, Hereford, had somehow won in my mind a very distinct meaning; it stood out among county names as the most delicately rustic of them all, with a touch of nobility given it long ago, I think, by Shakespeare's 'Harry of Hereford, Lancaster, and Derby'. But now I was here for the third time since the year began. In April here I had heard, among apple trees in flower, not the first cuckoo, but the first abundance of day-long-calling cuckoos; here, the first nightingale's song, though too far-off and intermittently, twitched away by gusty night winds; here I found the earliest mayblossom which by May Day, while I still lingered, began to dapple the hedges thickly, and no rain fell, yet the land was sweet. Here I had the consummation of Midsummer, the weather radiant and fresh, yet hot and rainless, the white and the pink wild roses, the growing bracken, the last and best of the songs, blackbird's, blackcap's. Now it was August, and again no rain fell for many days; the harvest was a good one, and after standing long in the sun it was gathered in and put up in ricks in the sun, to the contentment of men and rooks. All day the rooks in the wheat-fields were cawing a deep sweet caw, in alternating choirs or all together, almost like sheep bleating, contentedly, on until late evening. The sun shone, always warm, from skies sometimes cloudless, sometimes inscribed with a fine white scatter miles high, sometimes displaying the full pomp of white moving mountains, sometimes almost entirely shrouded in dull sulphurous threats, but vain ones.

Three meadows away lived a friend, and once or twice or three times a day I used to cross the meadows, the gate, and the two stiles. The first was a concave meadow, in April strewn with daffodils. There, day and night, pastured a bay colt and a black mare, thirty years old, but gay enough to have slipped away two years back and got herself made the mother of this 'stolen' foal. The path led across the middle of the meadow, through a gate, and alongside one of the hedges of the next, which sloped down rather steeply to the remnant of a brook, and was grazed by half a dozen cows. At the bottom a hedge followed the line of the brook and a stile took me through it, with a deep drop, to a plank and a puddle, and so to the last field, a rough one. This rose up as steeply and was the night's lodging of four cart horses. The path, having gradually approached a hedge on the left, went alongside it, under the horse-chestnut tree leaning out of it, and in sight of the house, until it reached the far hedge and the road. There, at another stile, the path ceased. The little house of whitened bricks and black timbers lay a few yards up the road, a vegetable garden in front with a weeping ash and a bay-tree, a walnut in a yard of cobbles and grass behind, a yew on the roadside, an orchard on the other.

How easy it was to spend a morning or afternoon in walking over to this house, stopping to talk to whoever was about for a few minutes, and then strolling with my friend, nearly regardless of footpaths, in a long loop, so as to end either at his house or my lodging. It was mostly orchard and grass, gently up and down, seldom steep for more than a few yards. Some of the meadows had a group or a line of elms; one an ash rising out of an islet of dense brambles; many had several great old apple or pear trees. The pears were small brown perry pears, as thick as haws, the apples chiefly cider apples, innumerable, rosy and un-eatable, though once or twice we did pick up a wasp's remnant, with slightly greasy skin of palest yellow, that tasted delicious. There was one brook to cross, shallow and leaden, with high hollow bare banks. More than one meadow was trenched, apparently by a dried water-course, showing flags, rushes, and a train of willows.

If talk dwindled in the traversing of a big field, the pause at gate or stile braced it again. Often we prolonged the pause, whether we actually sat or not, and we talked—of flowers, childhood, Shakespeare, women, England, the war—or we looked at a far horizon, which some dip or gap occasionally disclosed. Again and again we saw, instead of solid things, dark or bright, never more than half a mile off, the complete broad dome of a high hill six miles distant, a beautiful hill itself, but especially seen thus, always unexpectedly, through gaps in this narrow country, as through a window. Moreover, we knew that from the summit, between the few old Scots firs and the young ones of the plantation, we could command the Severn and the Cotswolds on the one hand, and on the other the Wye, the Forest of Dean, the island hills of North Monmouthshire, dark and massive, the remote Black Mountains pale and cloud-like, far beyond them in Wales. Not that we often needed to escape from this narrow country, or that, if we did, we had to look so far. For example, the cloud and haze of a hot day would change all. As we sat on a gate, the elms in a near hedge grew sombre, though clear. Past them rose a field like a low pitched roof dotted over with black stooks of beans and the elms at the top of that rise looked black and ponderous. Those in farther hedges were dimmer and less heavy, some were as puffs of smoke, while just below the long straight ridge of the horizon, a mile or two away, the trees were no more than the shadows of smoke.

Lombardy poplars rose out from among the elms, near and far, in twos and threes, in longer or shorter lines, and at one point grouping themselves like the pinnacles of a cathedral. Most farm-houses in the neighbourhood, and even pairs of cottages, possessed a couple or more. If we got astray we could steer by this or that high-perched cluster, in which, perhaps, one tree having lost a branch now on one side, now on the other, resembled a grass stalk with flowers alternating up it. When night came on, any farm-house group might be transmuted out of all knowledge, partly with the aid of its Lombardy poplars. There was also one tree without a house which looked magnificent at that hour. It stood alone, except for a much lesser tree, as it were, kneeling at its feet, on the long swooping curve of a great meadow against the sky; and when the curve and the two trees upon it were clear black under a pale sky and the first stars, they made a kind of naturally melodramatic 'C'est l'empereur' scene, such as must be as common as painters in a cypress country.

Whatever road or lane we took, once in every quarter of a mile we came to a farm-house. Only there by the two trees we tasted austere inhuman solitude as a luxury. Yet a man had planted the trees fifty or sixty years back. (Who was it, I wonder, set the fashion or distributed the seedlings?) It was really not less human a scene than that other one I liked at nightfall. Wildly dark clouds broke through the pallid sky above the elms, shadowy elms towering up ten times their diurnal height; and under the trees stood a thatched cottage, sending up a thin blue smoke against the foliage, and casting a faint light out from one square window and open door. It was cheerful and mysterious too. No man of any nation accustomed to houses but must have longed for his home at the sight, or have suffered for lacking one, or have dreamed that this was it.

Then one evening the new moon made a difference. It was the end of a wet day; at least, it had begun wet, had turned warm and muggy, and at last fine but still cloudy. The sky was banded with rough masses in the north-west, but the moon, a stout orange crescent, hung free of cloud near the horizon. At one stroke, I thought, like many other people, what things that same new moon sees eastward about the Meuse in France. Of those who could see it there, not blinded by smoke, pain, or excitement, how many saw it and heeded? I was deluged, in a second stroke, by another thought, or something that overpowered thought. All I can tell is, it seemed to me that either I had never loved England, or I had loved it foolishly, aesthetically, like a slave, not having realized that it was not mine unless I were willing and prepared to die rather than leave it as Belgian women and old men and children had left their country. Something I had omitted. Something, I felt, had to be done before I could look again composedly at English landscape, at the elms and poplars about the houses, at the purple-headed wood-betony with two pairs of dark leaves on a stiff stem, who stood sentinel among the grasses or bracken by hedge-side or wood's-edge. What he stood sentinel for I did not know, any more than what I had got to do.

The Last Sheaf, 215-21

Notes

NOTES TO INTRODUCTION

1   *MP*, 17 November 1910.
2   R. George Thomas (ed.), *Letters from Edward Thomas to Gordon Bottomley* (Oxford University Press, 1968), 107, letter dated 26 April 1906.
3   Review of *His People*, by R.B. Cunninghame Graham, *DC*, 15 January 1907.
4   Review of *Punctuation: its principles and practice*, by T.F. and M.F.A. Husband, *A*, 23 September 1905.
5   *Beautiful Wales*, 44.
6   *Letters to Gordon Bottomley*, 85, letter dated 13 June 1905.
7   Ch.7 of *Edward Thomas: a critical biography* (Faber & Faber, 1970).
8   *Letters to Gordon Bottomley*, 87, letter dated 30 June 1905.
9   *Letters*, 90, letter dated 24 July 1905.
10 *Letters*, Introduction, 9.
11 Ibid. The war accelerated a decline in Thomas's reviewing market, as well as drying up commissions. The enforced leisure may have played a part in releasing his poetry: 'There is little work that has to be done, so I do the other kind.' *Letters to Gordon Bottomley*, 240, letter dated 19 December 1914.
12 Thomas continues: 'As soon as one publisher has brought out a charming edition of an old poet in a blue cover, another brings one out in red, which is followed rapidly by editions in green, in parchment, and in pink, and probably another in blue. Phineas Fletcher, Cowley, Crashaw, Sedley, Prior, Butler, Crabbe, Drayton, and a great many more who are better known, have appeared during the last year or two.' Review of *Poetical Works of Thomas Traherne*, ed. Bertram Dobell; *De Flagello Myrteo*, by Richard Garnett; *Poetical Works of Tennyson*, 5 vols.: *DC*, 15 August 1906. Working chiefly for Everyman's Library, Thomas himself added Dyer, Herbert, Marlowe, and prose by Borrow, Jefferies and Cobbett, to this cascade.

13 *B*, December 1917.

14 Review of *Rio Grande's Last Race, and Other Verses*, by A.B. Paterson (an Australian), *DC*, 8 February 1904.

15 Review of *Walt Whitman: the man and the poet*, by James Thomson ('BV'), *MP*, 12 September 1910.

16 Reviewed *DC*, 24 April 1914.

17 Review of *Heretics*, *A*, 24 June 1905.

18 *The Dyer's Hand* (Faber & Faber, 1963), 11.

19 Review of new verse, *DC*, 16 February 1904.

20 *Poetry and Drama*, I, 1, March 1913, 33-42. The essay includes the recommendation that her works 'will move an elephant and will not hurt a child'.

21 Review of *Actions and Reactions*, *Saturday Review*, 16 October 1909.

22 Reviewed *DC*, 28 December 1911.

23 Review of *The Centaur's Booty, The Rout of the Amazons, The Gazelles and other Poems, Pan's Prophecy*, by T. Sturge Moore, *WS*, 1 October 1904.

24 Review of *French Profiles*, *The World*, 7 February 1905.

25 Reviewed *DC*, 29 January 1906.

26 Reviewed *The Speaker*, 4 August 1906.

27 Reviewed *MP*, 19 August 1909.

28 Review of *William Blake*, vol. I, with an introduction by Laurence Binyon, *MP*, 17 December 1906.

29 Reviewed *DC*, 3 May 1905. Earlier in his review of *The Poetical Works of Percy Bysshe Shelley* (pp.23-4) Thomas quotes a characteristic footnote with the comment: 'We need Shelley's pages undefiled; we resent a page like that just mentioned, as we should resent a lily with a page from Hooker's Botany tied to its stem or a microscope left in its chalice.'

30 Review of two volumes of *The Writings of Matthew Prior*, ed. A.R. Waller, *DC*, 15 August 1907.

31 Review of *The New Laokoon*, by Irving Babbitt, *DC*, 5 October 1910.

32 Ibid.

33 Reviewed *DC*, 16 April 1909.

34 Review of edition by J. Shawcross, *DC*, 8 June 1908.

35 Review of *Poems by John Clare*, ed., with an introduction, by Arthur Symons, *DC*, 19 December 1908. Thomas defended Symons to Bottomley: 'I should have said that, allowing bulk to count, he hardly had a superior living as a critic combining instinct & scholarship. I don't think he had any originality, but

then that is true of his other work too. But I thought a few of the later poems as good as anything he had done before, tho not better than (of their kind) the earliest. I imagine he could never be what I should call quite sincere, that is why he had not style; but in the later attitude all the flimsy avoidable insincerity had gone.' *Letters to Gordon Bottomley*, 181-2, letter dated 15 March 1909.

36   Review of *Studies in Seven Arts*, by Arthur Symons, *MP*, 17 December 1906.

37   *Essays in Criticism*, VII, 4, October 1957, 404-15.

38   Letter from Thomas to Helen Noble (his future wife), 7 June 1898, quoted in R. George Thomas (ed.), *The Collected Poems of Edward Thomas* (Oxford University Press, 1978), Appendix B, 458. Thomas is attacking a poem which begins: 'Headington Hill is steep/And Margaret is old:/Her wrinkles deep, and bent her back:/How bent her back as now she climbs, behold!'

39   See note 28.

40   *Feminine Influence*, 246.

41   Review of *Studies of a Biographer*, vols. 3 and 4, by Leslie Stephen, *DC*, 12 November 1902.

42   Review of *Steps to the Temple, Delights of the Muses*, and other Poems, by Richard Crashaw, ed. A.R. Waller, *DC*, 20 August 1907.

43   Ibid.

44   Review of *A Later Pepys*, ed. A.C.C. Gaussen, *The World*, 21 June 1904.

45   *Letters to Gordon Bottomley*, 187. See note 73.

46   Review of new verse, *DC*, 4 July 1904.

47   Review of *Confessions of Lord Byron*, arranged by W.A. Lewis Bettany, *DC*, 18 July 1905. Cf. 'Mr John Foster Fraser has the common gift of self-description without the rarer one of self-revelation and style.' Review of *Life's Contrasts*, *MP*, 4 January 1909.

48   Reviewed *DC*, 29 October 1907.

49   Introduction to *W.B. Yeats: the critical heritage* (Routledge & Kegan Paul, 1977), 23.

50   Review of *Irish Literary and Musical Studies*, by Alfred Perceval Graves; *Broad Sheet Ballads: a Collection of Irish Popular Songs*, with introduction by Padraic Colum; *Irish Poems*, by Katharine Tynan; *Children of the Hills*, by Dermot O'Byrne: *The Saturday Westminster Gazette*, 21 March 1914.

51   Review of *The Dublin Book of Irish Verse*, ed. John Cooke, *MP*, 6 January 1910.

52   Review of *The Dominion of Dreams, MP*, 24 June 1909.

53   Review of new verse, *DC*, 9 August 1904. The man was Douglas Carswell, author of *The Venusiad, and Other Poems*.

54   Review of new verse, *MP*, 9 August 1909.

55   'A poem is an arrangement of words, as a picture is an arrangement of colours. The fact seems to be generally known, and if we may draw a conclusion from the number of those who attempt to write poems, the Muse is regarded as having instituted a lottery. If a hundred thousand arrangements of words are made, there is a chance that one of them will be a poem.' Review of new verse, *DC*, 4 June 1904.

56   'Oh, admirable and too rare combination of artist and citizen'.

57   Review of new verse, *MP*, 13 December 1909.

58   Reviewed *DC*, 22 June 1910.

59   Reviewed *DC*, 4 April 1913.

60   Review of *The Sailing of the Long Ships, and Other Poems, DC*, 19 November 1902

61   Review of *Drake: an English Epic*, Books IV-XII, *MP*, 5 October 1908.

62   Review of *The Clouds, B,* July 1912. 'Like "The Cliffs", the new book depicts what Mr Doughty expects to take place unless we have a strong, perpetual Conservative Government, hundreds of Dreadnoughts, Super-Dreadnoughts, Ultra-Dreadnoughts, conscription, pills to purge democracy, and so on. I have not the least idea whether Mr Doughty is a false prophet, and, if so, whether the War Office or the Admiralty is aware of his existence, but I hope that thousands of patriots, Conservatives, and Germanophobes, will buy his book when they hear that he blows the last trump of patriotism. Only thus does it seem still possible that Mr Doughty's poetry might be discovered.'

63   *Letters to Gordon Bottomley*, 118, letter dated 27 August 1906.

64   *Letters*, 135, letter dated 27 March 1907.

65   *Letters*, 233, letter dated 22 May 1914. Later in the year Thomas compared Gibson with John Masefield, to the former's disadvantage: 'Mr Masefield and Mr Gibson are, I believe, often connected. . . . Both write about "working men", and make use of words or actions which are supposed to look odd in poetry. Yet neither of them is exactly a "working man", or seems to write of "working men" except in complete detachment, however admiring. Both, perhaps in consequence, have to make up for some lack of reality in the whole by intense and often violent reality in detail. . . . Mr Gibson also admires vigorous activity, but by comparison with Mr Masefield he possesses none. They are both

spectators, to some extent connoisseurs, but Mr Gibson chiefly so. He never for a moment seems to be or to resemble the thing presented. His style, except in "Bloodybush Edge", lacks movement and even the words of movement, which Mr Masefield never leaves idle.' Review of *Philip the King, and other Poems*, by John Masefield, and *Thoroughfares* and *Borderlands*, by Wilfrid Wilson Gibson, *B*, November 1914.

66   Reviewed *DC*, 29 February 1908. The review begins: 'Any half-dozen lines in his book would prove Mr Abercrombie a poet.'

67   Reviewed *DC*, 10 January 1913.

68   Review of *The Sea is Kind*, *NW*, 4 April 1914.

69   See note 23.

70   Another review of *The Sea is Kind*, *DC*, 29 April 1914.

71   Letter to Frost, 15 December 1914. Frost told Grace Walcott Conkling: 'Anything we [Thomas and himself] may be thought to have in common we had before we met. . . . The most our congeniality could do was confirm us both in what we were. There was never a moment's thought about who may have been influencing whom. The least rivalry of that kind would have taken something from our friendship.' Letter dated 28 June 1921, *Poetry Wales*, XIII, 4, Spring 1978, 22.

72   Letter to John Freeman, 8 March 1915, in John Moore, *The Life and Letters of Edward Thomas* (Heinemann, 1939), 326.

73   On 1 May 1909 Thomas wrote to Bottomley: 'here is Ezra Pound & I think he has very great things in him & the love poems & the "Famam librosque"—in fact nearly all—are extraordinary achievements.' On 12 June he wrote: 'Oh I do humble myself over Ezra Pound. He is not & cannot ever be very good. Certainly he is not what I mesmerized myself—out of pure love of praising the new poetry!—into saying he was & I am very much ashamed & only hope I shall never meet the man. My greatest humiliation is due to regret for cheapening praise & using the same words about such a man as about, say, Sturge Moore, though of course I did indicate the chaos of the work.' *Letters to Gordon Bottomley*, 185, 187.

74   A remark made to Richard J. Stonesifer. See Stonesifer, *W.H. Davies: a critical biography* (Jonathan Cape, 1963), 239, n.39.

75   *The Nation*, 13 October 1917.

76   *The Nation*, 20 October 1917. Walter de la Mare gratefully paid tribute to the positive quality of Thomas's judgments: 'Edward Thomas must have been a critic of rhymes in his nursery. How much generous help and encouragement many living poets owe to his counsel only themselves could say. To his candour, too.

For the true cause, he believed, is better served by an uncompromising "Trespassers will be prosecuted" than by an amiable "All are welcome" '. *Westminster Gazette,* 28 April 1917, quoted in *Letters to Gordon Bottomley,* Introduction, 7.

77 Review of *The Silences of the Moon,* by Henry Law Webb, *DC,* 19 May 1911.

78 'Sunshine', *The Speaker,* 12 December 1896.

79 'The Coming of Autumn', *The Speaker,* 22 October 1898.

80 Review, without date or source, preserved in scrapbook, University College, Cardiff.

81 Eleanor Farjeon, *Edward Thomas: the last four years* (Oxford University Press, 1958), 51, letter postmarked 16 December 1913.

82 *B,* March 1907.

83 Review of *The Enchanted Woods, DC,* 28 January 1904.

84 *The Heart of England,* 133-4.

85 *Letters to Gordon Bottomley,* 251, letter dated 30 June 1915.

86 Letter to Frost, 19 May 1914.

87 'Words', Thomas's poetic celebration of the English language.

88 'A Coat', written in 1912.

89 *Letters to Gordon Bottomley,* 57, letter dated 26 June 1904.

90 The title of W.J. Keith's study of 'a curiously neglected topic' (Harvester Press, 1975).

91 *The Country,* 19.

92 *George Borrow,* 213.

93 *Richard Jefferies,* 34.

94 Review of *The Pocket Richard Jefferies,* ed. Alfred H. Hyatt, *DC,* 15 September 1905.

95 *Keats,* 36.

96 Julian Thomas says of *The Childhood of Edward Thomas*: 'it belongs to Edward's later period, when he shed all preciosity and began to write the simple prose which he finally decided was the best of all—prose, as he said to me shortly after he had finished his critical study of Walter Pater, "as near akin as possible to the talk of a Surrey peasant". He was thinking, no doubt, of George Sturt's Bettesworth.' Preface to *The Childhood of Edward Thomas,* 8.

97 *The South Country,* 13.

98 Review of *Nature Knowledge in Modern Poetry,* by Alexander Mackie, and *Notes from Nature's Garden,* by Frances A. Bardswell, *DC,* 23 April 1906.

99 Reviewed *DC,* 3 July 1902.

100 Reviewed *DC*, 25 July 1903.

101 Review of *A Shadowed Paradise*, by Mark Sale, *MP*, 26 December 1910.

102 Review of *The Charm of the Road*, England and Wales, by James John Hissey, in review of country books, *DC*, 30 May 1911.

103 Review of *In the King's Country*, by E. Kay Robinson, *WS*, 27 August 1904.

104 ' "The poetry of earth is never dead" ' it has been written. Nor is the verse, though as a rule it can hardly be said to be alive.' Review of *The Comrades: Poems Old and New*, by William Canton, *DC*, 15 October 1902.

105 Reviewed *MP*, 13 December 1909.

106 '. . . the very world, which is the world/Of all of us,—the place where in the end/We find our happiness, or not at all!' 1804 poem on the 'French Revolution'; cf. *Prelude*, 1805, X, 726-8.

107 'People have been praised for self-possession in danger. I have heard Edward doubt if he was as brave as the bravest. But who was ever so completely himself right up to the verge of destruction, so sure of his thought, so sure of his word?' Letter to Helen Thomas after Edward's death, 27 April 1917, Lawrance Thompson (ed.), *Selected Letters of Robert Frost* (Jonathan Cape, 1965), 216.

108 *New Bearings in English Poetry* (Peregrine edn., 1963), 61.

109 *Letters to Gordon Bottomley*, 147, n.1.

110 *Edward Thomas: the last four years*, 13, undated letter 1913.

111 Ibid.

112 Review of *The Duties of Women*, by Frances Power Cobbe, *DC*, 14 August 1905.

NOTES TO THE TEXT

78 *John Davidson* (1857-1909): a member of the Rhymers' Club, though antagonistic to its aestheticism. He wrote lyrics and ballads before 'the philosophic megalomania of his five *Testaments* had imprisoned and distorted his imagination'. Derek Stanford (ed.), *Three Poets of the Rhymers' Club* (Carcanet Press, 1974), Introduction, 25. *The Triumph of Mammon* is a play in the same vein as *The Testament of a Prime Minister*, *The Testament of John Davidson* etc. 'One of my saddest jobs lately has been reviewing John Davidson's drama: *Triumph of Mammon*. . . . I think his brain must be giving way. There is a lot of energy, as usual; but an unusual incoherence and much less beauty in detail. Of course I couldn't praise it yet I did not like having to say anything against this sad serious, very "clever egoist".' *Letters to Gordon Bottomley*, 137, letter dated 22 April 1907. Davidson committed suicide.

87 *J.M. Synge, Poems and Translations:* 'Have you seen Synge's poems? They are raw poetry & something more—wonderfully lean & bare & yet compelling us to clothe them in the warm & radiant life which they disdain. . . .' *Letters to Gordon Bottomley*, 190-1, letter dated 1 September 1909.

88 *W.H. Davies:* on Thomas's relationship with W.H. Davies, for whom he did 'more . . . than anyone else', see Richard J. Stonesifer, *W.H. Davies: a critical biography* (Jonathan Cape, 1963).

97 *Walter de la Mare:* Thomas's first review (*Songs of Childhood*) occurs in a fanciful survey of new verse in which the poets are characterized as 'seven quaint doves, ill-matched, pulling this way and that, and yoked to the car of Venus. . . .' Venus 'was more angry with this dove [de la Mare] than with its yoke-

279

fellows, because it had put one or two wonderful things in its book and had choked them with unsuccessful verses for children.' *DC*, 14 August 1902. Thomas's unsigned portrait of de la Mare for 'The Bookman' Gallery praises him because: 'He is connected with no party, school, fad, clique, or movement, but nourishes, to the satisfaction of those who know him, a curiosity, a discontent, and an optimism all equally boundless. In one thing, if only in one, he resembles many other poets of today—and probably most original poets of any day at their first rising: in his apparent isolation. He speaks as a solitary individual who might perhaps not write at all were it not for this solitude. He does not speak as a member of any class or body or on behalf of anything or anybody. He has written one of the truest and least rhetorical of poems on England, and a beautiful one called "The Englishman"; but this visible England of the map-makers, politicians, naturalists, and tourists could not easily be proved from his poetry to have had much to do with his composition.' *B*, December 1910.

108   *Rupert Brooke:* Thomas also refers to Brooke in a review of *Cambridge Poets, 1900-1913*: 'It is remarkable how much of England even Drayton left untouched by verses. Everything can be made new again by integration in a new place or personality. . . . But it seems likely that more will be got from the discovery than Mr Rupert Brooke gets from it in "Grantchester". The important thing is not that a thing should be small, but that it should be intense and capable of unconsciously symbolic significance.' *PD*, I, 4, December 1913. Brooke's four sonnets in *New Numbers* (poems by Gibson, Brooke, Abercrombie and Drinkwater) he calls 'brilliant variations upon what he has already done'. *NW*, 21 March 1914. Thomas told Frost that in his *ER* memoir he had not dared to say 'that those sonnets about him enlisting are probably not very personal but a nervous attempt to connect with himself the very widespread idea that self-sacrifice is the highest self indulgence. You know. And I don't dispute it. Only I doubt if he knew it or would he have troubled to drag in the fact that enlisting cleared him of "All the little emptiness of love"? Well, I daren't say so, not having enlisted or fought the keeper.' 13 June 1915. (Thomas enlisted a month later.) When Frost pressed him for his real opinion of Brooke: 'I think he succeeded in being youthful & yet intelligible & interesting (not only pathologically) more than most poets since Shelley. But thought gave him (and me) indigestion. He couldn't mix his thought or the result of it with his feeling.

He could only think about his feeling. Radically, I think he lacked power of expression. He was a rhetorician, dressing things up better than they needed. And I suspect he knew too well both what he was after & what he achieved. I think perhaps a man ought to be capable of always being surprised on being confronted with what he really is—as I am nowadays.' 19 October 1916.

112   *Georgian Poetry:* 'I was alarmed to see how chilly my notice of the Georgian Anthology appeared in the Chronicle. But I had to ask the editor to cut out the passage where I made a mistaken reference to Poetry & Drama & he cut out too much.' Thomas to Harold Monro (publisher of *Georgian Poetry, 1911-1912*), 15 January 1913, *Poetry Wales*, XIII, 4, Spring 1978, 55.

116   *Ezra Pound:* Professor R. George Thomas attributes a further unsigned review of *Personae* to Thomas, *B*, July 1909, printed in Eric Homberger (ed.), *Ezra Pound: the critical heritage* (Routledge & Kegan Paul, 1972), 54-5.

123   *The Imagists:* 'What imbeciles the Imagistes are.' *Letters to Gordon Bottomley*, 233, letter dated 22 May 1914.

131   *War Poetry:* 'The worst of the poetry being written today is that it is too deliberately, and not inevitably, English. It is for an audience: there is more in it of the shouting of rhetorician, reciter, or politician than of the talk of friends and lovers.' Opening of a review of 'Anthologies and Reprints', *PD*, II, 8, December 1914.

147   *Lafcadio Hearn* (1850-1904): a writer who, from 1891, made Japan his actual and literary home. Best known for *Glimpses of Unfamiliar Japan* (1894).

230   *Walton's book:* in an early review Thomas observes of a similar passage involving the Milk-woman: 'And we remembered that this most perfect pastoral of all time was written while hardly a stream was left long quiet by the blood and tramplings and cannonadings of war; and we caught a new hope from this revelation of the nearness of the golden age.' Review of *Izaak Walton and his friends*, by Stapleton Martin, *DC*, 30 October 1903.

260   *The Attempt*: cf. Helen Thomas's account, *As it Was* and *World Without End* (Faber & Faber, 1956), 116-17.

Bibliography

WORKS OF EDWARD THOMAS
Prose

The Woodland Life (William Blackwood, 1897).
Horae Solitariae (Duckworth, 1902).
Oxford (A. & C. Black, 1903).
Rose Acre Papers (S. C. Brown Langham, 1904).
Beautiful Wales (A. &. C. Black, 1905).
The Heart of England (J. M. Dent, 1906); references are to 1932 edn.
Richard Jefferies (Hutchinson, 1909); references are to 1978 edn.
   (Faber Paperbacks).
The South Country (J. M. Dent, 1909).
Windsor Castle (Blackie, 1910).
Rest and Unrest (Duckworth, 1910).
Feminine Influence on the Poets 'Martin Secker, 1910).
Rose Acre Papers (Duckworth, 1910); contains two essays from *Rose
   Acre Papers* (1904) and twelve from *Horae Solitariae*.
Light and Twilight (Duckworth, 1911).
Maurice Maeterlinck (Methuen, 1911).
The Tenth Muse (Martin Secker, 1911); abridgement of *Feminine
   Influence on the Poets*.
Celtic Stories (Oxford, Clarendon Press, 1911).
The Isle of Wight (Blackie, 1911).
Lafcadio Hearn (Constable, 1912).
Norse Tales (Oxford, Clarendon Press, 1912).
Algernon Charles Swinburne (Martin Secker, 1912).
George Borrow (Chapman & Hall, 1912).
The Country (B. T. Batsford, 1913).
The Icknield Way (Constable, 1913); reprinted Wildwood House,
   1981).

The Happy-Go-Lucky Morgans (Duckworth, 1913).
Walter Pater (Martin Secker, 1913).
In Pursuit of Spring (Thomas Nelson 1914; reprinted Wildwood House, 1981).
Four-and-Twenty Blackbirds (Duckworth, 1915).
The Life of the Duke of Marlborough (Chapman & Hall, 1915).
Keats (T.C. & E.C. Jack, 1916).
A Literary Pilgrim in England (Methuen, 1917; reprinted Oxford University Press, 1980).
Cloud Castle and Other Papers (Duckworth, 1922).
The Last Sheaf (Jonathan Cape, 1928).
The Childhood of Edward Thomas (Faber & Faber, 1938).
The Prose of Edward Thomas, ed. Roland Gant (Falcon Press, 1948).
Edward Thomas on the Countryside, selection of his prose and verse, ed. Roland Gant (Faber & Faber, 1977).

Editions and Anthologies

The Poems of John Dyer (T. Fisher Unwin, 1903).
The Bible in Spain, by George Borrow (J. M. Dent, 1906).
The Pocket Book of Poems and Songs for the Open Air (Grant Richards, 1907).
British Country Life in Spring and Summer, The Book of the Open Air (Hodder & Stoughton, 1907).
British Country Life in Autumn and Winter, The Book of the Open Air (Hodder & Stoughton, 1908).
Some British Birds, reprinted from *The Book of the Open Air* (Hodder & Stoughton, 1908).
British Butterflies and Other Insects, reprinted from *The Book of the Open Air* (Hodder & Stoughton, 1908).
The Temple and A Priest to the Temple, by George Herbert (J. M. Dent, 1908).

The Plays and Poems of Christopher Marlowe (J. M. Dent, 1909).
The Hills and the Vale, by Richard Jefferies (Duckworth, 1909); reprinted Oxford University Press, 1980).
Words and Places, by Isaac Taylor (J. M. Dent, 1911).
Rural Rides, by William Cobbett (J. M. Dent, 1912).
The Pocket George Borrow (Chatto & Windus, 1912).
The Zincali, by George Borrow (J. M. Dent, 1914).
This England: an anthology from her writers (Oxford University Press, 1915).
The Flowers I Love (T.C. & E.C. Jack, 1916).

Current editions of the Poems

Collected Poems [fifth impression] (Faber & Faber, 1949; Faber Paperbacks, 1979).
Selected Poems (Faber Paperbacks, 1964).
Poems and Last Poems, ed. Edna Longley (Collins Annotated Student Texts, 1973; now published by Macdonald & Evans).
The Collected Poems of Edward Thomas, ed. R. George Thomas (Oxford University Press, 1978; pbk. edn. 1981).

SELECTED BIOGRAPHY AND CRITICISM

William Cooke, *Edward Thomas: a critical biography* (Faber & Faber, 1970).
H. Coombes, *Edward Thomas* (Chatto & Windus, 1956).
Eleanor Farjeon, *Edward Thomas: the last four years* (Oxford University Press, 1958).
F. R. Leavis, *New Bearings in English Poetry* (Chatto & Windus, 1932; Peregrine, 1963).
John Moore, *The Life and Letters of Edward Thomas* (Heinemann, 1939).
Andrew Motion, *The Poetry of Edward Thomas* (Routledge & Kegan Paul, 1980).
Vernon Scannell, *Edward Thomas* (Writers and Their Work, no. 163; Longman's, 1963).
Helen Thomas, *As It Was and World Without End* (Heinemann, 1926 and 1931; Faber & Faber, 1956).
—— *Time & Again* (Carcanet New Press, 1978).
R. George Thomas (ed.), *Letters from Edward Thomas to Gordon Bottomley* (Oxford University Press, 1968).
Lawrance Thompson, *Robert Frost: the early years 1874-1915* (Jonathan Cape, 1967).
—— (ed.), *Selected Letters of Robert Frost* (Jonathan Cape, 1965).
J. P. Ward (ed.), *Poetry Wales,* XIII, 4, Spring 1978.

Selected Background Reading

Joy Grant, *Harold Monro and the Poetry Bookshop* (Routledge & Kegan Paul, 1967).
John Gross, *The Rise and Fall of the Man of Letters* (Weidenfeld & Nicolson, 1969; Pelican, 1973).
Christopher Hassall, *Edward Marsh, Patron of the Arts* (Longmans, 1959).
—— *Rupert Brooke: a biography* (Faber & Faber, 1964).

R. V. Holdsworth (ed.), *Arthur Symons: Poetry and Prose* (Carcanet Press, 1974).

Patricia Hutchins, *Ezra Pound's Kensington* (Faber & Faber, 1965).

John Press, *A Map of Modern English Verse* (Oxford University Press, 1969).

Robert H. Ross, *The Georgian Revolt* (Faber & Faber, 1967).

C. K. Stead, *The New Poetic: Yeats to Eliot* (Hutchinson, 1964; Pelican, 1967).

Richard J. Stonesifer, *W. H. Davies: a critical biography* (Jonathan Cape, 1963).

W. J. Keith, *Richard Jefferies: a critical study* (Oxford University Press, 1965).

—— *The Rural Tradition* (Harvester Press, 1975).

Raymond Williams, *The Country and the City* (Chatto & Windus, 1973).

William Cobbett, *Rural Rides* and Gilbert White, *The Natural History of Selborne* are available in Penguin English Library (1967, 1977).

Reviving interest in 'The Rural Tradition' is indicated by a number of recent reprints, including:

W. H. Hudson, *A Shepherd's Life* (Futura, 1979).

—— *Hampshire Days* (Oxford University Press, 1980).

Richard Jefferies, *Wild Life in a Southern County* (Moonraker Press, 1978).

—— *The Gamekeeper at Home* and *The Amateur Poacher* (Oxford University Press, 1978).

—— *The Hills and the Vale* (see under *Editions and Anthologies*).

—— *After London* (Oxford University Press, 1980).

—— *Nature near London* (John Clare Press, 1980).

Index